بسم الله الرحمن الرحيم

وَمَا أَرْسَلْنَاكَ إِلَّا رَحْمَةً لِّلْعَالَمِينَ

And We have not sent you, O Muhammad,
except as a mercy to the worlds

Nabiyy-i Raḥmat
Prophet of Mercy

May Allah Bless him and Give Him Peace

صلى الله عليه وسلم

Nabiyy-i Raḥmat
Prophet of Mercy

May Allah Bless him and Give Him Peace

SHAYKH ABUL ḤASAN ʿALĪ NADWĪ

translated by

DR MOHIUDDIN AHMAD

With full-colour maps

TURATH PUBLISHING
2014

First edition 1435/2014. Reprints 1438/2016, 1440/2019, 1442/2021
ISBN: 978-1-906949-24-2

Published by:
Turath Publishing
79 Mitcham Road +44 (20) 8767 3666
London SW17 9PD www.turath.co.uk

Author Shaykh Abul Ḥasan ʿAlī Nadwī
Translation Dr Mohiuddin Ahmad
Editors Shoaib Shah, Rashida Esakjee and Kolsuma Begum
Language Editor Yusuf Zanella and Muhammad Ansa
Cartography Lina Qaisy
General Editor Yahya Batha

British Library Cataloguing in Publication Data
Nadwī, Shaykh Abul Ḥasan ʿAlī
Prophet of Mercy (*Nabiyy-i Raḥmat*)
I. Title

Cover Design & typesetting ARM (www.whitethreadpress.com)
Printed by Megaprinters, Istanbul, Turkey (ahmet@mega.com.tr)

Distributors for UK and Europe
Azhar Academy Ltd.
54–56 Little Ilford Lane +44 (20) 8891 19797
Manor Park sales@azharacademy.com
London E12 5QA www.azharacademy.com

Distributors for South Africa
Darul-Ihsan Research and Education Centre
www.darulihsan.com/shop +27 (31) 577 7868
bookshop@darulihsan.com

Publishers Dedication

In memory of my dearest friend and cousin Zahra Hakim. Our time together was cut short so you could be in a better place. I pray Allah shower his blessings upon you and elevate your status in Jannah. Ameen. You will always be in my heart and prayers. Miss you always!!

Huma Batha

Contents

Publisher's Preface

ALL PRAISE IS God's alone. We praise Him, seeking His help, forgiveness and protection; and we pray also that His peace and blessings descend upon Muḥammad ﷺ, His slave and Messenger, the seal of the Prophets, the chosen one, and our leader and master, and upon his family, his Companions and those who follow them in goodness.

The biography of the Messenger of God ﷺ is the great didactic story of Islam, containing within it all the significant narratives of life, religion and society. Termed '*sīrah*', this is a historical genre of literature from which successive generations have drawn lessons that they applied to their particular environment. In the 20th century our author, Shaykh Abū 'l-Ḥasan an-Nadwī, ranks among the foremost of scholars who applied the lessons of the *sīrah* to the political, social and religious environment he saw around him in his time. He was born in in the Indian town of Rai Bareily in 1914 into a pious and scholarly family where he formed a lifelong attachment to the *sīrah* of the Prophet ﷺ. His was a childhood immersed in the sacred sciences of religion, studying the Qur'ān, ḥadīth, Islamic jurisprudence, and the history of Islam, in particular, the accounts of the life of the Messenger of God ﷺ he heard imbued him with a love that was to become the impetus for his lifelong devotion to religion. He grew to become a major figure in the Islamic world and his influence spread far beyond the boundaries of the Indian subcontinent, becoming a scholar of renown in the Arab world and even in the West.

This biography is written in contemporary style, drawing from classical works and original source materials, but it also includes details and incidental material that reveal the author's academic curiosity and fascination with history and which provide a vivid account for the reader. Of particular interest is his thorough investigation of the social, economic and moral conditions present in Makkah and Madīnah before the advent of Islam, along with descriptions of the geography and political conditions of the lands that were to become the cradle of the Islamic faith. It is my hope that this publication will be of critical importance and act as a landmark as we navigate through the difficult social, religious, and political questions that we face today.

In bringing this book to print I am immensely grateful to Dr Akram Nadwi who bought this valuable work to my attention. Gratitude is extended to Brother Yusuf Zanella and Brother Muhammad Ansa for the great work they have put in as language editors. Credit is due to our dedicated editors Ustadha Rashida Esakjee, wife of my dear friend Mufti Abdur Rahman Mangera, and Kolsuma Begum,wife of my dear friend Dr Ashik Rahman. Finally I would like to thank Moulana Shoaib Shah for translating the maps from Arabic to English and also as one of the editors. Recognition has to be given to Sister Lina Qaisy for the meticulous work she has done as the cartographer.

My gratitude would not be complete if I did not thank my late father Maulana Muhammad ibn Ahmed Batha, may Allah have Mercy on him and fill his Kabar with noor, who inculcated in me the importance of the history of the Messenger of God ﷺ.

YAHYA BATHA
London, 2012.

Foreword

The Prophetic Sīrah is a topic of great esteem. It is a topic of magnificence and will certainly stand the test of time. Allāh says, "And We raised high your name" (Qur'ān 94:4). Elsewhere, He says, "And you are surely on an excellent standard of character" (Qur'ān 68:4). After the Noble Qur'ān and the Prophetic ḥadīths, the Sīrah of the Prophet ﷺ serves as a minaret of light for humanity; its rays will never become dim and its radiant light will illuminate the Earth forever. It can be compared to an evergreen garden, whose fragrant breezes will continue to bring joy to the earth; a garden whose diverse array of flowers will always continue to captivate humankind with their inherent beauty.

These aromatic flowers are the Prophet's conduct, which brought about a colossal revolution to the world.They are essentially his perfect example of ethics, how to lead one's life, the nature of a slave's relationship with both his master and fellow humans, his sublime character, a just social and economic system and his instructions regarding the rights of one's family and others. In short, his example in every aspect of life,has been presented in light of the divine revelation. It was this noble character which led to the people of Makkah to attest to his greatness. This noble character compelled Heraclius to make the statement that the Prophet ﷺwill surely rule over his kingdom one day.

The Prophetic Sīrah transcends all bounds of time and space. Surpassing the restrictions of physical directions and realms of the ancient and modern, it is a way of life and a mercy for the whole of humanity until the end of time. In one place, Allāh says, "Say: O Mankind! I am a messenger of Allāh to all of you" and elsewhere He says, "Certainly, there is for you an excellent pattern in the Messenger of Allāh". In a third place, Allāh says, "And we have not sent you except as a messenger to the worlds." It was the responsibility of the Prophet ﷺ to present this example to everyone. In this respect, the Prophet referred to himself as a teacher and mentor. He said, "I have been sent as a teacher" whilst on another occasion, he said, "I have been sent to complete noble characteristics."

As his Sīrah was to forever remain as the perfect example for humankind, Allāh Most High ensured its complete preservation. The Noble Companions and the Mothers of the Believers committed every minute detail regarding the Prophet ﷺ to memory. This ocean of knowledge was subsequently transferred from the Companions to the coming generations and the historians; whereafter the historians compiled it as a book. Work on the Sīrah was not confined to the earlier generations, but rather continued in every age. In each era, people took direction from this fountainhead of guidance and presented it to others in light of the circumstances, requirements and temperament of the people in each respective age.

Books on the Sīrah have been written in many languages and, alongside Muslim authors, unbiased non-Muslim authors have also testified that nobody can present an example similar to that of the Prophet ﷺ, let alone better than him. His Sīrah is indeed the pinnacle of human excellence, beyond which the existence of, or even contemplating superiority in any characteristic, is an impossibility. However, certain individuals have held animosity against Islām and its followers since Islām's roots first began. They have not left any stone unturned in trying to conceal the facts, misconstrue and distort them. [They are not included in the ambit of our discussion].

Urdu is among the languages, besides Arabic, in which a considerable amount of work has been dedicated to the topic of Sīrah. In light of the significance of this topic, scholars of the Indo-Subcontinent authored many invaluable books, producing a copious list which is ever extending. *As-Sīrah an-Nabawīyyah* is Mawlānā Abū'l-Ḥasan Nadwī's highly academic and well-researched Arabic work, which was translated into Urdu—as *Nabī-i-Raḥmat*—by his nephew Mawlānā Sayyid Muḥammad al-Ḥasanī. Later on, Mawlānā reviewed the translation and made some amendments, which is mentioned in the preface to the second edition. Explaining the importance and distinguishing points of his book, Mawlānā writes, "Perhaps it was due to these reasons that I did not have the courage until now to author anything new on the topic of the Prophetic Sīrah, and I considered this colossal task to be far beyond my capacity. My respected friends tried to hearten me to write a book on the Prophetic Sīrah, which would take into account the mindset, taste and temperament of today's younger generation. Moreover, it should fully consider the needs, and the style of language and research that is prevalent in the current era; as each age has its unique style of language and expression which needs to be borne in mind." He further writes,

"Eventually, Allāh granted me unreservedness in this matter and I immersed myself in this task with full concentration and dedication. It would be correct to say that my every breath and moment was being spent dedicated to this cause. I did not just read the books of ḥadīth and Sīrah for this, but rather tried to derive full benefit from any new and old literature which contained work of benefit. I tried to ensure that the book is a fusion of both an academic perspective and that of *daʿwah* (propagation) and *tarbīyah*, without any one aspect overshadowing the other. Furthermore, I aimed to present as many animated and ebullient excerpts as possible, which will instinctively instil the reader with the zeal to emulate the prophetic example."

Haḍrat Mawlānā Abū'l-Ḥasan ʿAlī Nadwī was a verdant flower from a renowned family of scholars in Rae Bareli, Uttar Pradesh, and belonged to the Ḥasanī Sayyids [lineage of the Prophet ﷺ] of the Indo Subcontinent. Alongside being a great Islamic thinker and leader, he was an influential and outstanding author, with exemplary oratory and literary command in both Arabic and Urdu. His pen expressed his deep sympathy for humanity and served as a mouthpiece of Islamic thought. Through his speeches and writings, he presented sound Islamic thought in a contemporary perspective. He expended all his strength in awakening the Ummah and to remind it of its forgotten duties. Be it among the Arabs or non-Arabs, he spoke very candidly. At times, he would discuss the rise and decline of the Muslims in the world. On occasion, he could be heard proclaiming "Listen, O Egypt" and at times, "O Arabs, listen to me carefully."He woke the Arab world from its slumber and exposed the deception, scheming and crimes of the West. He vehemently opposed the many obscenities being perpetrated in the name of literature, declaring the eradication of high standards of character and the decadence of sublime morals to be a mockery at the expense of humanity. His cause was to invite all towards literature of pristine content, truly epitomising the values of humanity. Although he authored many outstanding books on a vast array of topics, he had been gifted with a unique competence in biographies, and hence wrote biographies of many saints. He established a standing for the scholars of the Indian Subcontinent in the hearts of the Arabs, through his work on Arabic literature and Islamic thought. His most famous work is *What the World Lost through the Decline of the Muslims* and it is this book, which earned him renowned status in the Arab world. It has been translated into English, Turkish, Urdu, and many other languages, whilst its Arabic readership is so wide that it is difficult to put a figure on the book's official and unofficial editions. Alongside these services, he was the Principal of Nadwat al-ʿUlamā' and Chairman of the All India Muslim Personal Law Board for many years. His services for Islām span over half a century.

Haḍrat Mawlānā's books take into consideration the contemporary style of logic and reasoning; with this book in particular addressing commonly recurring doubts in exceptional detail. For this reason, this book received wide acclaim in the Arab world and, within a short period of time, was incorporated into the syllabus of a number of universities. Due to its significance, there was a need to translate this book into English, allowing the English readership to also benefit from this fragrant bouquet. Shāh ʿAbdu'r-Raḥmān Nash'at had previously translated this work into English; however, English is a developing language with ever-changing styles of expression and writing. Hence, many friends felt the need to edit the existing translation or translate the book anew, a suggestion which Shāh ʿAbdu'r-Raḥmān also agreed with. In fulfilling this, brother Yahya Batha of Turath Publishing from the UK has commissioned a new edit of the book, wherein a more contemporary literary style has been adopted. Furthermore, thirty full-coloured maps relating to the Sīrah have also been added. Painstaking efforts have been made in proofreading and providing references.

The result of this collective effort is this book you have before you, remarkable on all fronts. We hope this translation will be highly appreciated by the people of knowledge and that many will benefit from it. May Allāh aptly reward all who were involved in this. May He grant us the zeal to follow the Sharīʿah and to act in accordance with the Sīrah of the Prophet ﷺ.

Salmān al-Ḥusaynī an-Nadwī

"And this is not difficult for Allāh"
May Allāh bless and send peace upon the
best of his creation, Muḥammad,
and all his family and Companions

Author's Introduction

IN THE NAME OF Allāh, the Most Benevolent, the Most Merciful. Praise be to Allāh, Lord of the Worlds and Blessings and peace be on the one, exalted amongst the prophets and the Seal of the apposite, Muḥammad, and his progeny and Companions, and on those who sincerely follow him till the Day of Judgement.

The seminary in which the writer of these lines had his first lesson was the nursery which impressed upon the author's mind the mould of the Prophet ﷺ. The age at which I was enrolled in this blessed institution was much earlier than the normal school-going age of children: this was the seminary of one's own home, permeated with an air steeped in a culture whose primal ingredient was the stamp of the Prophetic character. Every child of this household was expected to pattern his behaviour in conformity with this family tradition wherein the small collection of juvenile literature, consisting both of prose and poetry, always in circulation among the children of the family, played a significant role. Later on, the wise grooming of my elder brother, Dr. Syed ʿAbd al-ʿAlī, was to help me in going through two of the best books in Urdu on the life of the Prophet ﷺ at a comparatively young age[1]. Urdu has, thanks to the labours of the writers in the recent past, a treasure of literature on the subject second only to Arabic.

When the writer was able to grasp Arabic and appreciate its literature, I drank in with rapt attention two of the earliest works on the Prophet's life ﷺ. One of these was *As-Sīrat an-Nabawiyyah* of Ibn Hishām and the other was

1 I told this story in *Aṭ-Ṭarīq ila 'l-Madīnah,* where I expressed my appreciation of *Raḥmah li 'l-ʿĀlamīn,* a popular biography of the Prophet by Qāzī M. Sulaymān Mansūrpūrī.

Zād al-Maʿād, written by Ibn al-Qayyim. I did not simply go through them, but having almost lost myself in the study of these books, found my heart and mind enthralled by certitude and an unshakable conviction. I felt captivated by a tender feeling of affection for the Prophet ﷺ, whose life is so full of and so packed with thrilling and soul-stirring events that next to the Qur'ān, it is the most potent means for shaping one's behaviour and creating a fervour of spirit. Besides these two books I also read avidly all those Urdu and English works on the subject that fell into my hands. The result of this intensive study has been that all of my writings so far have invariably reflected a touch of the Prophet's life-story ﷺ. Whatever warmth and whatever lucidity of style in the expression of my ideas I have ever had has emanated from the fascinating charm of that paradigm of perfection, that inexhaustible source of inspiration which fires one's imagination to regions heavenly and sublime. In truth, I have never penned anything that does not in some way or the other reflect the elegance of that prophetic mould or my own thoughtful reflection on its profound wisdom.

My articles delineating different aspects of the Prophet's noble character ﷺ and his marvellous accomplishments have been brought out in the collection entitled *Kārawān-e-Madīnah*.[1]

I have penned a large number of books, but the opportunity to produce a treatise on the life of the Prophet ﷺ never arose, although I have ever felt the need of a biography written in a style intelligible to modern minds, utilising both the modern and ancient sources. Deviating not from the Qur'ān and the *ḥadīth*, such a biographical sketch has to be based on the original sources, yet it need not be merely an encyclopaedic collection amassing all the relevant as well as far-fetched reports on the subject without any critical examination. Biographies of this type have been in vogue in the past, but they unnecessarily give rise to misgivings and doubts which are, in truth, completely unfounded, nor need the Muslims trouble their minds about them. Several savants and scholars (unaffected by the sceptical disposition of the modernists and orientalist) have already pried into these questions satisfactorily. A work of this nature should also be compatible with the spiritual truths and realities which are indispensable for comprehending the true nature of revelations, prophetic guidance, miracles and the recondite facts of mute reality, and should be written by one who can put his trust in the Prophet ﷺ not as a national leader or statesman but as the Apostle of God ﷺ sent for the guidance of all mankind. Only a biography of

1 The Arabic version known as *Aṭ-Ṭarīq ila 'l-Madīnah* has been printed thrice in Madīnah, Lucknow and Damascus, while the Academy of Islamic Research and Publications, Lucknow has brought out its Urdu version.

the Prophet ﷺ so written can be placed before every unbiased educated person (whether a Muslim or a non-Muslim) without any reservation or specious reasoning. Accordingly, I have placed more reliance on the original sources in describing the events and character of the Prophet ﷺ and narrated them in a way that everything speaks for itself and allows the reader to arrive at their own conclusion. The life of the Prophet ﷺ is a living portrait, conveying the feeling of the good and the sublime, for which I had has no need to recourse to philosophies or to draw any inferences. In its charm and grace, harmony and excellence, effectiveness and appeal, the life of the Prophet ﷺ does not, in truth and reality, need the polish or refinement of any writer or the exposition of an erudite scholar. All that one need attempt is the narration of facts selected and arranged harmoniously, in a simple and unaffected style.

Also, the recital of the Prophet's life-story ﷺ requires a conjugation of intellect and emotion, both poised on an even keel. A scholarly treatment of the subject accompanied by frigid analysis and cold logical reasoning is more likely to take away the warmth of its delicate charm, the glow of whose heavenly beauty is indispensable for a correct understanding of the facts and events closely related to the sentiments of credence and belief. If the life of the Prophet ﷺ rehearsed by anybody tries to gloss over the tender susceptibilities, the attempt would undoubtedly be assiduous but wooden; it would be a tale, striking and impressive, but would fail to convey the essence and substance of prophethood. Likewise, it is equally essential that the naiveté of credulity should not be allowed to becloud the soundness of intellectual judgement, which is held as the test of validity today. Nor should it be against the accepted principles of logical reasoning or a eulogy, steeped in blind faith, acceptable only to the credulous Muslims and traditional scholars of faith living in a world of their own creations, unconnected to and without any rapport with the outer, modern world of today. An unhesitating faith with the flame of ardent love is a divine blessing, no doubt; yet, one should never forget that this is the life of the Apostle of God ﷺ who was sent as mercy for the whole universe and all the peoples of the world. His blessing can in no case be denied to any segment of humanity that has not had the opportunity of being brought up in an Islamic surrounding. Haply, it may turn out, by the mercy of the Lord, that such persons partake the blessing of Islam by catching a glimpse of the radiance emitted by the Prophet's life ﷺ. The non-Muslims have as much claim to the life of the holy Prophet ﷺ as those born in a Muslim home; or, rather they deserve it more for they stand in need of it.

The times and circumstances in which the Prophet ﷺ made his advent cannot be overlooked in recounting his story. The conditions prevailing, all over the world, in the pre-Islamic time have, therefore, to be vividly portrayed. It is but necessary to describe the universal confusion, moral degradation and spiritual restlessness and disconsolateness to which man had fallen during the sixth century, as well as the social, economic and political causes that had combined to produce that gloomy atmosphere. The authors of that global degradation—tyrannical governments, bungled religions, fallacious and extremist schools of thought, ruinous movements and deceptive calls and summons—all had joined hands in bringing the then world to almost complete destruction. The present writer still remembers the difficulties encountered in presenting a clear picture of the widespread depravation of the pre-Islamic age of the pagan past in the opening section of my book *Mādhā Khasira 'l-ʿĀlam, bi inḥiṭāṭ al-Muslimīn*[1]. I had to wade through almost the whole of Western historical literature pertaining to the period and to recreate the story by collecting bits and pieces scattered in numerous books.

This prelude to the life of the Prophet ﷺ, now described somewhat at a greater length, would help the reader to appreciate in the light of the then putrid world all around, the grand accomplishment of prophetic guidance, its greatness, the vastness of its scope, the way it sharpened the wits, solved intractable problems and harmonised seemingly irreconcilable motives and elements. What was, after all, the greatest achievement of Muḥammad's Prophethood ﷺ? It was to give hope to the despaired heart of man, to take him back to the path of righteousness, to cleanse his mind and heart of the contaminating impurity and to raise him to the sublime heights of spirituality. What a gigantic task it was!

This is correctly understood only when the reader has before him a clear picture of the perplexing and arduous nature of the task faced by the Prophet ﷺ and his companions. Often, one is unable to comprehend the turn of events and the decisions taken by the Prophet ﷺ unless he is fully aware of the social, economic and political situation then obtaining in Madīnah, its physical condition and geographical situation, the surrounding tribes and the relationship existing between them, the balance of power struck by past settlements and treaties of peace, conditions immediately preceding the *hijrah*,[2] the tribal customs and conventions and their national code of ethics and laws. Anybody trying to study the life of the Prophet ﷺ unmindful of these basic facts would be travelling in a dark tunnel wherein he can neither see to his right or left nor know where he is destined to emerge at the end of his journey.

---

1 English version since printed as *Islam and the World*, by the Academy of Islamic Research and Publications, Lucknow.

2 Lit., 'emigration', the word often transcribed as 'hegira' is applied to the emigration of the Prophet from Makkah to Madīnah. It marks the starting point of the Muslim era. The Prophet spent thirteen years of his prophethood in Madīnah.

All that has been stated about the environs of Madīnah is true for the then civilised regions around Arabia also. One can neither reckon the significance of the call of Islam nor the nature of its brave venture so long as one is unacquainted with the despotic rule as well as the splendour and vastness of the surrounding kingdoms, their culture and civilisation, their military strength and the pretension and pageantry of their rulers who were invited by the Prophet ﷺ, through his epistles, to accept Islam. Recent research has unearthed new materials about the events, life and culture of the countries around Arabia, which were either not known earlier at all or of which the historians had only a hazy picture. A biographer of the Prophet ﷺ should now take full advantage of all these new discoveries in the fields of archaeology and history and present the facts in conformity with the latest methods of comparative studies.

The writer of these lines is fully conscious of the difficulties alluded to here as well as the great fund of literature hitherto accumulated in different languages through the industry of the Prophet's biographers ﷺ. Still, one considers it an honour to enter this long and luminous list of the Prophet's biographers ﷺ by attempting a new presentation of the most lovable and admirable personality of all times and ages.

The meagre amount of leisure and the poor eyesight of the writer have, however, been the two impediments which have always prevented the undertaking this inspiring task. One was well aware of the difficult and delicate nature of biographical writings and also of the fact that to pen the life of the greatest of all prophets was certainly an arduous task. I had in fact written a large number of such life-sketches—perhaps, more than most of my contemporaries—for I had had the good fortune of penning the achievements of great reformers and revivalists of the faith ever since I learnt to take the pen in my hand. Narrations of these stories which run into a few thousand pages were no less exhilarating to me than enjoying the company of those purer souls, but one still felt diffident in driving one's pen to write the life of the Prophet ﷺ. I was conscious of the fact that very often a writer is so swayed by his own predispositions that he begins to paint the picture of his paragon of virtue in the colour of his resemblance. The portrait thus painted is more of the writer himself, for, instead of delineating the story of his ideal, in an objective and impartial manner, he unconsciously begins to view him in the light of his own experiences and inclinations.

Those who are conversant with the science of the mind and have also gained an insight into the ethical conduct of the people through personal experience and the study of the behaviour and deportment of their mates and colleagues over a length of time, will easily realise the inadequacy of diction and modes of expression in the faithful portrayal of a human character, its inner reaches as well as its spirits soaring high above the skies—it is a task so delicate and likely to inflame the passions that it is not rare for it to come in upon the writer himself. Only he can hope to succeed in this precarious job who has the capacity to touch the chords of another man's sentiments, enter into his spirit of emotions, share the tenderness as well as fervour of his passions, and echo his joys and sufferings. Such a man has to have a soft spot in his heart which can perceive how others spend their lonely nights after a bustling day, how they behave within their homes and with their friends outside, how they acquit themselves in war and peace, how they carry themselves in excitement and calm, in want and plenty, in strength and in weakness. Indeed, there are numerous heartstrings, sentiments and susceptibilities of man, still mysterious and undisclosed, for which one would not find an appropriate word in the greatest lexicon of any language. Now, in its charm and elegance, in its catholicity and comprehensiveness, and in its depiction of the most delicate and deepest feelings of human life, the biography of a prophet presents a task far more formidable than any other kind of word painting. In truth, it was only the *ḥadīth*[1] of the holy Prophet ﷺ, the like of which is to be found nowhere in the memoirs of other prophets or the greatest men whose life-story has been preserved by history, which has made it possible to penetrate into the inmost reaches of the human psyche. In the compilations containing the Prophet's acts ﷺ and sayings as well as in his earliest biographies one finds such entrancing exaltations of God and moving supplications, such impassioned entreaties and absorbing orisons, expressing such heart-felt concern for the welfare of all mankind, that one's heart begins to breathe and burn with their penetrating fervency[2]. Similarly, the utterances and speeches of the Prophet ﷺ handed down by his companions and friends ﷺ excel the most refined and eloquent pieces of literature.[3] With all this material at hand, one should have no difficulty nor need to be ingenious in recounting the life of the Prophet ﷺ, as one is wont to do in writing the lives of other great personalities. His life is the most perfect and winsome, based on unimpeachable evidence of the Divine Writ and unquestionable records of history, furnishing a vivid and detailed account of his looks and lineament, character and deportment, moral behaviour and method of Prayer, his living awareness of God and anxiety for

1 Lit., "a saying"; stands for the "prophetic tradition," a short account of some act or word of the Prophet passed on by a chain of trustworthy narrators.

2 One may read the author's article "Life of Muḥammad as reflected by his Prayers," which has since been printed as a booklet, which explains what a deep insight into the innermost feelings of the human mind and heart are reflected in the Prophet's prayers, and how effective they are in shaping one's conduct and morals.

3 See the chapter on "The Finality of Prophethood" in the author's other work *Islamic Concept of Prophethood*.

his fellow beings, the grace and elegance of his discourses, and the miraculous march of events in his momentous life. These accounts, recorded with the greatest care and restraint, present, notwithstanding the great labour undertaken by early biographers, only a glimpse of that radiant soul. God recompense them all with a goodly return, for they have left for us an undiminishing treasure in the form of the biography of the Prophet ﷺ from which every individual, group and race can partake till the end of time.

> Verily in the messenger of Allāh you have a good example for him who looks unto Allāh and the Last Day, and remembers Allāh much.[1]

For these reasons, perhaps, I never ventured to attempt writing a new biography of the Prophet ﷺ; actually, one always considered it to be beyond one's capacity. But, some of my respected friends[2] repeatedly pressed me to write a biography of the Prophet ﷺ in Arabic which should keep in view the intellectual needs and understanding of the modern generation as well as the prevalent methods of scientific study of history and interpretation and the critical attitude discernible today. Every generation writes history afresh in a language intelligible to it, for it is necessary to do so just like the continuous diagnosis of diseases and researches in medical treatment which undergo a change with the times. Yet, essential though it may be to keep these dispositions in mind, it should never be necessary to put up one's own interpretation of the past events coloured with one's own ideologies, predilections and prejudices, which differ from man to man and change with the dawn of every day; nor need the biography of the Prophet ﷺ be tainted with any ill-will or ignorance; nor yet should it be made a means to reflect the invariables of any particular social or political movement or ideology.

At last, God set the heart of the writer to the task and I devoted myself to it with rapt attention. I went through the *ḥadīth* literature and the biographical accounts of the Prophet ﷺ, old and new, in order to derive maximum benefit from all the material I could lay my hands on. Then, placing reliance on the most authentic works on the subject, I started writing the present account. The works to which I am indebted most in this task are the books of *Ṣiḥāḥ*,[3] *Sīrah Ibn Hishām*, *Zād al-Maʿād* of Ibn al-Qayyim and the *Sīrah Ibn Kathīr* (which originally formed part of his larger work entitled *Al-Bidāyah wa 'n-Nihāyah*, but

1 Qur'ān 33:21

2 One who was most insistent was Shaykh Muḥammad Sawwāf, founder-member of the Rābiṭah al-ʿĀlam al-Islāmī, Makkah and adviser to the Ministry of Education, Saudi Arabia.

3 *Ṣiḥāḥ* or *Ṣiḥāḥ Sittah* comprises the six trustworthy collections of traditions compiled by Bukhārī, Muslim, Tirmidhī, Abū Dāwūd, Nasā'ī and Ibn Mājah.

later on took the form of the biography of the Prophet ﷺ in four volumes[1]). I also tried to make the best of modern works and the sources available in European languages, some of which elucidate certain events of the Prophet's life ﷺ or shed new light on the society and kingdoms of the countries around Arabia during the early Islamic period. It has been his endeavour to present an integrated account of the intellectual, educative and missionary aspects of the Prophet's life ﷺ, rather than allow anyone of these to overshadow the others. I have also attempted to make the presentation as vivid, easy and familiar as possible, which, by itself, may win over the reader to follow the example of the great Prophet ﷺ whose life and mission are without parallel—unique as a biography of the greatest man of any nation and unmatched by the summons of any religion or movement. With full confidence in the magnetism of the Prophet's life ﷺ, the writer considers it prudent to place a true, clear and undiluted account of the Prophet's biography ﷺ before the readers. The language of truth is always simple and unadorned.

From Shawwāl, 1395 (October, 1975) to Shawwāl 1396 (October, 1976) the writer of these lines remained completely engrossed in the task save for small spells when ill or travelling abroad, and was able to submit the manuscript of the Arabic version to the press by the end of Shawwāl, 1396.

The writer expresses his pleasure in acknowledging my debt of gratitude to two friends of his who have been of great assistance to him in the writing of this book. One of them, Mawlānā Burhān ad-Dīn Sambhalī, a lecturer in *ḥadīth* in the Nadwat al-ʿUlamā', rendered me invaluable help by seeking out the relevant hadiths and verification of certain matters mentioned by the early biographers. Moḥiuddin Aḥmad is another colleague who has helped the writer in going through the western sources, encyclopaedias and historical literature. Moḥiuddin Aḥmad has also rendered this work into the English Language. May Allāh recompense them both for their sincere and arduous assistance to the author.

For quite some time the author has been used to dictating one's writings owing to my weak eyesight, and hence I had to enlist the help of some students of the Dar al-ʿUlūm in this case also. Of these, two students, Muḥammad Muʿādh of Indore and ʿAlī Aḥmad Gujrātī have been specially helpful to me, as well as Nūr ʿĀlam Amīnī Nadwī, a young teacher at the Nadwat al-ʿUlamā'. As for the maps included in this book,[2] care was taken to get them prepared as accurately as possible for they are essential for understanding the politico-geo-

1 Published by ʿĪsā al-Bābī al-Ḥalabī, Ltd. (1384/1964); (ed.) Mustafā ʿAbdul Waḥīd.

2 For this English edition, the maps have been updated to reflect the modern-day territories.

graphical situations described in this work. While Muḥammad Ḥasan Ansārī, M.A. (Geog), and Professor Muḥammad Shafīʿ, Pro-Vice-Chancellor at Aligarh (Aligarh is a town in India), as well as the colleagues of the latter have taken suggestions provided by Muḥammad Rābiʿ Nadwī who is Head of the Department of Arabic Literature in the Dār al-ʿUlūm, Nadwat al-ʿUlamā' and is also the author of a textbook on the geography of Arabia. My thanks are also due to Maḥmūd Akhtar of the Allāhabād University for recasting these maps afresh for the Urdu and English editions. Lastly, a mention may be made of his nephew, Syed Muḥammad al-Ḥasanī, who has rendered this book into Urdu with the same enthusiasm as he had translated some of the earlier Arabic works of the present writer. May Allāh bless all of them for their labours.

In the end the author seeks the mercy of God for his own self and beseeches the Lord to make this work beneficial to all those who go through it. If this work succeeds in stirring the embers of love of the Prophet ﷺ in the heart of any Muslim or creates a longing in any non-Muslim to know more about the blessed Prophet ﷺ and his teachings, the writer would deem his labour to have been amply rewarded. Yet, its true reward, as one might wish and earnestly ask for, would be its acceptance by the Lord as a means for one's salvation in the hereafter.

ABUL ḤASAN ʿALĪ
Rai Bareli
Friday, 15 December 1978

1

The Age of Ignorance

Religious Conditions

GREAT RELIGIONS of the world had spread the light of faith, morals and learning in the ages past, but every one of these had been rendered a disgrace to its name by the sixth century of the Christian era. Crafty innovators, unscrupulous dissemblers and impious priests and preachers had, with the passage of time, so completely distorted the scriptures and disfigured the teachings and commandments of their own religions that it was almost impossible to recall the original shape and content of these religions. Had the founder or the prophet of any one of them returned to earth, he would unquestionably have refused his own religion and denounced its followers as apostates and idolaters.[1]

Judaism had, by then, been reduced to an amalgam of dead rituals and sacraments without any spark of life left in it. Also, being a religion upholding racial superiority, it has never had any message for other nations or for the good of humanity in general.

It had not even remained firmly wedded to its belief in the unity of God (which had once been its distinguishing feature and had raised its adherents to a level higher than that of the followers of ancient polytheistic cults), as com-

---

1 The manner in which the scriptures of all the great religions had been deformed and mutilated, and, in most cases, given an entirely false colouring, has been treated in some detail, questioning the authorities belonging to each of them, under the heading 'Qur'ān and the Earlier Scriptures' (pp.171–183) in my earlier work entitled *Islamic Concept of Prophethood.*

menced by the Prophet Abraham ﷺ to his sons and grandson Jacob ﷺ. The Jews had, under the influence of their powerful neighbours and conquerors, adopted numerous idolatrous beliefs and practices as acknowledged by modern Jewish authorities:

The thunderings of the prophets against idolatry show, however, that deity cults were deeply rooted in the heart of the Israelites, and it does not appear to have been thoroughly suppressed until after the return from their exile from Babylon. Through mysticism and magic many polytheistic ideas and customs again found their way among the people, and the Talmud confirms the seduction of idolatrous worship.[1]

The Babylonian Gemara[2] (popular during the sixth century and often even preferred to Torah by the orthodox Jewry) typically illustrates the crudeness of intellectual and religious understanding among sixth century Jews, with its jocular and imprudent remarks about God and many an absurd and outrageous belief and idea; beliefs and ideas which lack not only sensibility but are also inconsistent with the Jewish faith in monotheism.[3]

Christianity had fallen prey, in its very infancy, to the misguided fervour of its overzealous evangelists; unwarranted interpretation of its tenets by ignorant church fathers and iconolatry of its gentile converts to Christianity. The manner in which Trinitarian doctrine came to have the first claim to the Christian dogma by the close of the fourth century has been thus described in the *New Catholic Encyclopedia*:

> It is difficult, in the second half of the 20th century to offer a clear, objective, and straightforward account of the revelation, doctrinal evolution, and theological elaboration of the mystery of the Trinity. Trinitarian discussion, Roman Catholic as well as other, presents a somewhat unsteady silhouette. Two things have happened. There is the recognition on the part of exegetes and Biblical theologians, including a constantly growing number of Roman Catholics, that one should not speak of Trinitarianism in the New Testament without serious qualification. There is also the closely parallel recognition on the part of historians of dogma and systematic theologians that when one does speak of an unqualified Trinitarianism, one has moved from the period of Christian origins to, say, the last quad-

---

1 Ludwig Blan, Ph.D., Prof. of Jewish Theological Seminary, Budapest, Hungary, in the article on 'Worship' in *Jewish Encyclopedia*, Vol.XII, pp.568–69.

2 The Talmud is the body of Jewish law and legend comprising the Mishnah (precepts of the elders codified c. 200 AD) and the Gemara is a commentary on the Mishnah (in recessions, at Jerusalem c. 400 and at Babylon c. 500).

3 For details see Dr. Rohling's Jews in the Light of Talmud. Arabic version *Al-Kanz al-Marṣūd fi Qawāʿid at-Talmūd* by Dr. Yūsuf Hins.

> rant of the 4th century. It was only then that what might be called the definitive Trinitarian dogma 'one God in three persons' became thoroughly assimilated into Christian life and thought.[1]

Tracing the origin of pagan customs, rites, festivals and religious services of the pagans in Christianity, another historian of the Christian church gives a graphic account of persistent endeavour of early Christians to subsume the idolatrous nations. Rev. James Houston Baxter, Professor of Ecclesiastical History in the University of St. Andrews writes in *The History of Christianity in the Light of Modern Knowledge*:

> If paganism had been destroyed, it was less through annihilation than through absorption. Almost all that was pagan was carried over to survive under a Christian name. Deprived of demi-gods and heroes, men easily and half consciously invested a local martyr with their attributes labelled the local statue with his name, transferring to him the cult and mythology associated with the pagan deity. Before the century was over, the martyr-cult was universal, and a beginning had been made of that imposition of a deified human being between God and man which, on the one hand, had been the consequence of Arianism, and was, on the other, the origin of so much that is typical of medieval piety and practice. Pagan festivals were adopted and renamed: by 400, Christmas Day, the ancient festival of the sun, was transformed into the birthday of Jesus.[2]

By the sixth century, the antagonism between Christians of Syria, Iraq and Egypt on the question of the human and divine natures of Christ had set them at one another's throats. The conflict had virtually turned every Christian seminary, church and home into a hostile camp, each anathematising the other and thirsting after its adversary's blood. 'Men debated with fury upon shadows or shades of belief and staked their lives on the most immaterial issues',[3] as if these differences meant a confrontation between two antagonistic religions or nations. The Christians were, thus, neither inclined nor had time to set their own house in order and smother the ever-increasing viciousness in the world for the salvation of humanity.

In Iran, from the earliest times, the Magi worshipped four elements[4] (of which fire was the chief object of devotion) in the oratories or fire-temples for

1 *The New Catholic Encyclopaedia* (1967) art., "The Holy Trinity", vol, 14, p. 295.

2 The History of Christianity in the Light of Modern Knowledge, Glasgow, 1929, Chap. Church, 312–800 AD, p. 407.

3 Alfred J. Butler, The Arab Conquest of Egypt and the last Thirty Years of the Roman Dominion, Oxford (1902) pp. 44–45.

4 These elements were light, water, earth and wind.

which they had evolved a whole mass of intricate rituals and commandments. In actual practice, the popular religion included nothing save the worship of fire and adorations of *Hvare-khshaeta* or the Shining Sun. Certain rituals performed in a place of worship were all that their religion demanded, for, after performing these rites they were free to live as they desired. There was nothing to distinguish a Magi from an unconscientious, perfidious fellow.[1]

Arthur Christensen writes in *L'Iran Sous Les Sassanides*:

> It was incumbent on the civil servants to offer prayers four times a day to the sun besides fire and water. Separate hymns were prescribed for rising and going to sleep, taking a bath, putting on the sacred cord, eating and drinking, sniffing, hair-dressing, cutting of the nails, excretion and lighting the candle, which were to be recited on each occasion with the greatest care. It was the duty of the priests to compound, purify and tend the sacred fire, which was never to be extinguished, nor was water ever allowed to touch fire. No metal was allowed to rust, for metals, too, were hallowed by their religions.[2]

All prayers were performed facing the sacred fire. The last Iranian Emperor, Yazdagird III, once took an oath, saying: 'I swear by the sun, which is the greatest of all gods'. He had ordered that those who had abjured Christianity to re-enter their original faith should publicly worship the sun in order to prove their sincerity.[3] The principle of dualism, the two rival spirits of good and evil, had been upheld by the Iranians for such a long time that it had become a mark and symbol of their national creed. They believed that *Ormuzd* creates everything good, and *Ahriman* creates all that is bad; these two are perpetually at war and the one or the other gains the upper hand alternately.[4] The Zoroastrian legends described by the historians of religion bear remarkable resemblance to the hierarchy of gods and goddesses and the fables of Hindu and Greek mythology.[5]

Buddhism, extending from India to Central Asia, had been converted into an idolatrous faith. Wherever the Buddhists went they took the idols of the Buddha with them and installed them there.[6]

Although the entire religious and cultural life of the Buddhists is over-shadowed by idolatry, the students of religion have grave doubts whether the Buddha

---

1 Arthur Christensen, *L'Iran Sous Les Sassanides,* Paris, 1936, (Urdu translation by Prof. Muḥammad Iqbāl, *Īrān ba-'Ahd Sāsāniyān)* p. 155.

2 *Ibid.*, pp. 186–7.

3 *Ibid.*

4 *Ibid.*, pp. 183–233.

5 *Ibid.*, pp. 204, 209.

6 Ishwar Topa, *Hindustānī Tamaddum*, Hyderabad (N.D.) p. 209 and Jawāhar Lāl Nehrū, *Discovery of India*, pp. 201–2.

was a nihilist or believed in the existence of God. They are surprised how this religion could at all sustain itself in the absence of any faith or conviction in the Primal Being.

In the sixth century AD, Hinduism had shot ahead of every other religion in the number of gods and goddesses. During this period the Hindus worshipped 33 million gods. The tendency to regard everything which could do harm or good as an object of personal devotion was at its height and this was the impetus to stone sculpture with novel motifs of decorative ornamentation.[1]

Describing the religious condition of India during the reign of Harsha (606–648), a little before the time when Islam made its first appearance in Arabia, a Hindu historian, C.V. Vaidya, writes in his *History of Mediaeval Hindu India*:

> Both Hinduism and Buddhism were equally idolatrous at this time. If anything, Buddhism perhaps beat the former in its intense idolatry. That religion started, indeed, with the denial of God, but ended by making Buddha' himself the Supreme God. Later developments of Buddhism added other gods like the Bodhisattvas and the idolatry of Buddhism especially in the Mahayana school was firmly established. Idolatry reached its peak in India until the word 'Buddha' became synonymous to the word 'idol' in some Eastern languages.[2]

C.V. Vaidya further says:

> No doubt idolatry was at this time rampant all over the world. From the Atlantic to the Pacific the world was immersed in idolatry; Christianity, Semitism, Hinduism and Buddhism vying, so to speak, with one another in their adoration of idols.[3]

Another historian of Hinduism expresses the same opinion about the great passion for multiplicity of deities among the Hindus in the sixth century. He writes:

> The process of deification did not stop here. Lesser gods and goddesses were added in ever growing numbers till there was a crowd of deities, many of them adopted from the more primitive peoples who were admitted to Hinduism with the gods whom they worshipped. The total number of deities is said to be 33 scores, i.e. 330 million, which, like the phrase "Thy name is legion", merely implies an innumerable host.[4]

1 See R.C. Dutta, *Ancient India*, vol. III, p. 276.

2 Like the Persian language and those languages which have borrowed words from it, they use the word 'but' to mean idol. This expression is common in poetry, literature and among people's speech in Iran and India. The word 'but' is very close in Indian pronunciation to the word 'Buddha'.

3 C.V. Vaidya, *History of Medieval Hindu India*, vol. I,Poona (1924).

4 L.S.S. O'Malley, *Popular Hinduism: The Religion of the Masses* (Cambridge, 1935) pp. 6–7.

The Arabs had been the followers of the Abrahamic religion in the olden times and had the distinction of having the first House of God in their land, but the long stretch of time from the great patriarchs and prophets of yore ﷺ and their isolation in the arid deserts of the peninsula had given rise to an abominable idolatry closely approximating the Hindu zeal for idol worship in the sixth century AD. They became progressively more idolatrous and made gods beside God, believing them to have partnership in the governance of the Universe. They believed that their deities possessed the power to do them good or harm, to give them life or death. The people sank into the worst form of idolatry, with each region and every clan, or rather every house, having a separate deity of its own.[1] Three hundred and sixty idols had been installed within the Kaʿbah and its courtyard—the house built by Abraham for the worship of the One and only God. The Arabs actually paid divine honours not merely to sculptured idols but venerated all types of stones and fetishes: angels, jinn and stars were all their deities. They believed that the angels were daughters of God and the jinn His partners in divinity,[2] and thus both enjoyed supernatural powers whose mollification was essential for their well-being.

SOCIAL AND MORAL CONDITIONS

This was the plight of great religions sent by God, from time to time, for the guidance of humanity. In the civilised countries, there were powerful governments and great centres of art, culture and learning but their religions had been garbled so completely that nothing of their original spirit and content was left in them.

Nor were there any reformers or heavenly-minded guides of humanity to be found anywhere.

BYZANTINE EMPIRE

Crushed under vexatious and burdensome taxes levied by the Byzantine Empire,[3] the allegiance to any alien ruler was considered by the populace as less oppressive than the rule of Byzantium. Insurrections had become such a common feature that in 532 AD public discontent erupted in Constantinople in the *Nika* (win

1 *Kitāb al-Aṣnām* by Ibn al-Kalabī, p. 33.

2 Bukhārī: "Kitāb al-Maghāzī".

3 The Eastern Roman or Byzantine empire, was known to the Arabs as Rum, with its capital at Constantinople, comprised Greece, Bulgaria, Turkey, Syria, Palestine, all the islands in the Mediterranean Sea, Egypt, all the coastlands in North Africa during the period. It came into existence in 395 AD and ended with the capture of Constantinople by the Turks in 1453.

or conquer) revolt that cost 30,000 lives.[1] The pastime of the chiefs and nobles was to squeeze wealth, under various pretexts, from the harassed peasantry, and squander it on their pleasure and amusement. Their craze for merriment and revelry very often sank to the depths of hideous savagery.

The authors of the *Civilisation, Past and Present* have painted a lurid picture of the contradictory passions of the Byzantine society for religious experience as well as its love of sports and recreation marked by moral corruption.

> Byzantine social life was marked by tremendous contrasts. The religious attitude was deeply ingrained in the popular mind. Asceticism and monasticism were widespread throughout the empire, and to an extraordinary degree even the most commonplace individual seemed to take a vital interest in the deepest theological discussions, while all the people were much affected by a religious mysticism in their daily life. But, in contrast, the same people were exceptionally fond of all types of amusements. The great Hippodrome, seating 80,000 wide-eyed spectators, was the scene of hotly disputed chariot races which split the entire populace into rival factions of 'Blue' and 'Green'. . . The Byzantines possessed both a love of beauty and a streak of violence and viciousness. Their sports were often bloody and sadistic, their tortures were horrible, and the lives of their aristocracy were a mixture of luxury, intrigue, and studied vice.[2]

Egypt had vast resources of corn on which Constantinople largely depended for its prosperity, but the whole machinery of the imperial government in that province was directed to wringing profits out of the ruled for the rulers. In religious matters, too, the policy of suppressing the Jacobite heresy was pursued relentlessly.[3]

In short, Egypt was like a milch cow whose masters were interested only in milking her without providing her with any fodder.

Syria, another fair dominion of the Byzantine Empire, was always treated as a hunting ground for the domineering and expansionist policy of the imperial government. Syrians were treated as slaves at the mercy of their masters, for they could never pretend to have any claim to kind or considerate behaviour from their rulers. The taxes levied were so excessive in amount and so unjust in incidence that the Syrians very often had to sell their children to clear the government dues. Unwarranted persecution, confiscation of property, enslavement and impressed labour were some of the common features of Byzantine rule.[4]

---

1 Historian's History of the World, vol. VII, p. 73

2 T. Walter Wallbank and Alastair M. Taylor, *Civilisation, Past and Present* (Scott, Foresman & Co, 1954) pp. 261–62.

3 The Arab conquest of Egypt, pp. 32, 42 and 46.

4 Kurd ʿAlī, *Khuṭaṭ al-Shām*, vol. I, p. 101.

THE PERSIAN EMPIRE

Zoroastrianism is the oldest religion of Iran. Zarathustra, the founder of Zoroastrianism, lived probably about 600–650 BC. After it had shaken off the Hellenistic influence, the Persian Empire was larger in size and greater in wealth and splendour than the Eastern Roman or Byzantine Empire. Ardashir I, the architect of the Sāsānid dynasty, laid the foundation of his kingdom by defeating Artabanus V in 224 AD. In its prime the Sāsānid Empire extended over Assyria, Khozistan, Media, Fars (Persis), Azerbaijan, Ṭabaristān (Mazandaran), Saraksh, Marjān, Marv, Balkh (Bactria), Saghd (Sagdonia), Sijistān (Saeastene), Herāt, Khurāsān, Khwarizm (Khiva), Iraq and Yemen, and, for a time, had under its control the areas lying near the delta of the river Sind; Kachh, Kathiawar, Malwa and few other districts.

Ctesiphon (Madā'in), the capital of the Sāsānids, combined a number of cities on either banks of the Tigris. During the fifth century and thereafter the Sāsānid empire was known for its magnificence and splendour, cultural refinement and the life of ease and pleasure enjoyed by its nobility.

Zoroastrianism was founded, from the earliest times, on the concept of universal struggle between the *ahuras* and the *daevas*, the forces of good and evil. In the third century Mani appeared on the scene as a reformer of Zoroastrianism. Sapor I (240–271) at first embraced the precepts uttered by the innovator, remaining faithful to them for ten years and before returning to Mazdaism. Manichaeism was based on a most thoroughgoing dualism of the two conflicting souls in man, one good and the other bad. In order, therefore, to get rid of the latter, preached Mani, one should practise strict asceticism and abstain from women. Mani spent a number of years in exile and returned to Iran after the accession of Bahrām I to the throne, but was arrested, convicted of heresy, and beheaded. His converts must have remained faithful to his teachings, for we know that Manichaeism continued to influence Iranian thought and society for a long time even after the death of Mani.[1]

Mazdak, the son of Baudad, was born at Nishapur in the fifth century. He also believed in the twin principles of light and darkness, but in order to put down the vileness emanating from darkness, he preached community of women and goods, which all men should share equally, as they do water, fire and wind. Mazdakites soon gained enough influence, thanks to the support of Emperor Kavadh, to cause a communistic upheaval in the country. People would enter into the house of a person, occupy his house and property, and he could not defend it.

1 Īrān fi ʿAhd Sāsāniyān, pp. 233–269.

In an ancient manuscript known as *Namah Tinsar* the ravages done to Iranian society by the application of the communistic version of Mazdaism have been graphically depicted thus:

> Chastity and manners were cast to the dogs. They came to the fore who had neither nobility nor character, nor acted uprightly, nor had any ancestral property; utterly indifferent to their families and the nation, they had no trade or calling; and being completely heartless they were ever willing to get into mischief, to mince the truth, vilify and malign others; for this was the only profession they knew for achieving wealth and fame.[1]

Arthur Christensen concludes:

> The result was that the peasants rose in revolt in many places, bandits started breaking into the houses of nobles to pray upon their property and to abduct their womenfolk. Gangsters took over the possession of landed estates and gradually the agricultural holdings became depopulated since the new owners knew nothing about the cultivation of land.[2]

Ancient Iran had always had a strange proclivity to subscribe to the extremist calls and radical movements, since it has ever been under the influence of irreconcilable political and religious concepts. It has often been swinging, as if by action and reaction, between Epicureanism and strict celibacy; and, at other times, either yielded passively to despotic feudalism and kingship and preposterous priesthood, or drifted to the other extreme of unruly and licentious communism; but has always missed that moderate poise and even temper which is so vital for a healthy and decent society.

Towards the end of the Sāsānid Empire, during the sixth century, all civil and military power was concentrated in the hands of the Emperors who were alienated from the people by an impassable barrier. They regarded themselves as the descendants of celestial gods; Khosrau Parwīz or Chosroes II had lavished upon himself this grandiose title: 'The immortal soul among the gods and peerless god among human beings; glorious is he whose name; dawning with the sunrise and light of the dark-eyed night.'[3]

The entire wealth of the country and its resources belonged to the Emperor. The kings, grandees and nobles were obsessed with amassing wealth and treasure, costly gems and curios. They were interested only in raising their own standard

1 Namah Tinsar, Tab'e Maynwī, p. 13 (Quoted from *Īrān fi 'Ahd Sāsāniyān*, p. 477).
2 *Īrān fi 'Ahd-Sāsāniyān*, p. 477
3 Ibid., p. 604.

of living and luxuriating in mirth and merriment to an extent that it is difficult to imagine their craze for amusement and festivity. He can alone visualise their dizzy rounds of riotous living who has studied the history, literature and poetry of ancient Iran and is also well informed about the splendour of Ctesiphon, *Īwān-i-Kisr*[1] and *Bahār-i-Kisrā,*[2] the tiara of the emperors, the awe-striking court ceremonials, the number of queens and concubines, slaves, cooks and bearers, pet birds and beasts owned by the emperors and their trainers and all.[3] The life of ease and comfort led by the kings and nobles of Persia can be judged from the way Yazdagird III fled from Ctesiphon after its capture by the Arabs; he had with him, during his flight, one thousand cooks, one thousand singers and musicians, and one thousand trainers of leopards and a thousand attendants of eagles besides innumerable leeches and hangers-on, but the Emperor still felt miserable for not having enough of them to enliven his drooping spirits.[4]

The common people were, on the other hand, extremely poor and in great distress. The uncertainty of the tariff on which each man had to pay various taxes gave a pretext to the collectors of taxes for exorbitant exactions. Impressed labour, burdensome levies and conscription in the army as footmen, without the inducement of pay or any other reward, had compelled a large number of peasants to give up their fields and take refuge in the service of temples or monasteries.[5] In their bloody wars with the Byzantines, which seemed to be without end and without any interest or profit to the common man, the Persian kings had been plying their subjects as cannon fodder.[6]

INDIA

The remarkable achievements of ancient India in the fields of mathematics, astronomy, medicine and philosophy had earned her lasting fame, but the historians are agreed that the era of her social, moral and religious degradation commenced from the opening decades of the sixth century.[7] For shameless and revolting acts of sexual wantonness were consecrated by religion, even the temples had degenerated into cesspools of corruption. Women had lost honour and

1 White palace of Chosroes. For details see *Īrān fi ʿAhd Sāsāniyān.*

2 Carpet of Silk, sixty cubits in length and as many in breadth; a paradise or garden was depicted on it, the flowers, fruits and shrubs were imitated by the figures of golden embroidery and the colours of the precious stones; and the ample square was enriched by a variegated and verdant border.

3 Shāhīn Mikarios, *Tārīkh Īrān,* (1898), p. 98.

4 *Īrān fi ʿAhd Sāsāniyān*, pp. 681 and 685.

5 Shahīn Mikario n: *Tārīkh Īrān,* p.98.

6 *Īrān fi ʿAhd Sāsāniyān.*

7 R.C. Dutt, *Ancient India,* vol.III.

respect in society and so had no values attached to her chastity. It was not rare for a man losing in a game of chance to wager his wife.[1]

The honour of the family, especially in higher classes claiming a noble descent, demanded that the widow should burn herself alive on the funeral pyre of her dead husband.

The custom, upheld by society as the supreme act of fealty on the part of a widow to her late husband,[2] was so deep-rooted that it could only be completely suppressed after the establishment of British rule in India.

India left behind her neighbours, or, rather every other country of the world, in evolving an inflexible and callously inhuman stratification of its society based on social inequality. This system, which excluded the original inhabitants of the country as exteriors or outcastes, was formulated to ensure the superiority of conquering Aryans and was invested with an aura of divine origin by the Brahmins. It canalised every aspect of the people's daily life according to heredity and the occupation of different classes and was backed by religious and social laws set forth by the religious teachers and legislators. Its comprehensive code of life was applicable to the entire society, dividing it into four distinct classes:

1. The *Brahmins* or priests enjoying the monopoly of performing religious rites;
2. The *Kshatriyas* or nobles and warriors supposed to govern the country;
3. The *Vaisyas* or merchants, peasants and artisans; and
4. The *Sudras* or the non-Aryan serfs meant to serve the first three castes.

The Sudras or the *dasas* meaning slaves (forming a majority in the population), believed to have been born from the feet of Brahma, formed the most degraded class which had sunk socially to the lowest level. Nothing was more honourable for a Sudra, according to the *Manu Shasira,* than to serve the Brahmins and other higher castes.

The social laws accorded the Brahmin class distinctive privileges and an honoured place in society, 'A Brahmin who remembers the *Rig Veda*', says the *Manu Shastra*, 'is absolutely sinless, even if he debases all the three worlds.' No tax could be imposed on a Brahmin, nor could he be executed for any crime. The Sudras, on the contrary, could never acquire any property, nor retain any assets. Prohibited from sitting near a Brahmin or touch him, the Sudras were not permitted to read the sacred scriptures.[3]

---

1 Dayanand Sarswati, *Saiyarth Prakash,* p. 344. Read the beginning of the story of Mahabharata. . . .

2 Bernier, F. *Travels,* edited by Constable, 2 vols. 1914.

3 For details see the Manu Shastra, chapters 1, 2, 8 and 11

India was drying up and losing her vitality. Divided into numerous petty states, struggling for supremacy amongst them, the whole country had been given over to lawlessness, maladministration and tyranny. The country had, furthermore, severed itself from the rest of the world and retired into her shell. Her fixed beliefs and the growing rigidity of her iniquitous social structure, norms, rites and customs had made her mind rigid and static. Her parochial outlook and prejudices of blood, race and colour carried within it the seeds of destruction. Vidya Dhar Mahajan, former professor of history in the Punjab University College, writes about the state of affairs in India on the eve of the Muslim conquest:

> The people of India were living in isolation from the rest of the world. They were so contented with themselves that they did not bother about what was happening outside their frontiers. Their ignorance of the developments outside their country put them in a very weak position. It also created a sense of stagnation among them. There was decay on all sides. There was not much life in the literature of the period. Architecture, painting and fine arts were also adversely affected. Indian society had become static and the caste system had become very rigid. There was no remarriage of widows and restrictions with regard to food and drink became very inflexible. The untouchables were forced to live outside the towns.[1]

ARABIA

The ideas of virtue and morals were unknown to the ancient Bedouin. Extremely fond of wine and gambling, he was hardhearted enough to bury alive his own daughter. Pillage of caravans and cold-blooded murder for paltry gains were the typical methods to still the demands of the nomad. Bedouin women enjoyed no social status and could be bartered away like other exchangeable goods or cattle or be inherited by the deceased's heir. Certain foods were reserved for men which could not be taken by women. A man could have as many wives as he liked and could dispose of his children if he had not enough means to provide for their sustenance.[2]

The Bedouin was bound by unbreakable bonds of fidelity to family, blood relations and, finally, to the tribe. Fights and forays were his sport and murder a trifling affair. A minor incident sometimes gave rise to a sanguine and long drawn war between two powerful tribes. Oftentimes these wars were prolonged to as many as forty years in which thousands of tribesmen came to a violent end.[3]

---

1 Vidya Dhar Mahajan: *Muslim Rule in India*, Delhi, 1970, p. 33.

2 See the Qur'ān, the books of *ḥadīth* and the poetical collection on *Ashʿār ʿArab* such as the *Ḥamāsah, Sabʿah Muʿallaqāt*, etc.

3 Details can be seen in the poetical collections of pre-Islamic era and the books on *Akhbār-e-ʿArab*.

EUROPE

At the beginning of the Dark Ages the torch of knowledge flickered dimly and all the literary and artistic achievements of the classical past seemed destined to be lost forever under the young and vigorous Germanic races which had risen to political power in the northern and western parts of Europe.[1] The new rulers found neither pleasure nor honour in the philosophy, literature and arts of the nations outside their frontiers and appeared to be as filthy as their minds were filled with superstition. Their monks and clergymen, passing their lives in a long routine of futile and atrocious self-torture, and quailing before the ghastly phantoms of their delirious brains,[2] were abhorrent to the company of human beings. They still debated the point as to whether a woman had the soul of a human being or of a beast, or whether she was blessed with a finite or infinite spirit. She could neither acquire nor inherit any property nor had the right to sell or transfer the same.

Robert Briffault writes in the *Making of Humanity*:

> From the fifth to the tenth century Europe lay sunk in a night of barbarism which grew darker and darker. It was a barbarism far more awful and horrible than that of the primitive savage, for it was the decomposing body of what had once been a great civilisation. The features and impress of the civilisation were all but completely effaced. Where its development had been fullest, e.g. in Italy and Gaul, all was ruin, squalor and dissolution.[3]

THE ERA OF DARKNESS AND DEPRESSION

The sixth century in which the Prophet of Islam ﷺ was born was, to be brief, the darkest era of history. It was the most depressing period in which crestfallen humanity had abandoned all hopes of its revival and renaissance. This is the conclusion drawn by noted historian, H.G. Wells, who recapitulates the condition of the world at the time when Sāsānid and Byzantine Empires had worn themselves out to a death-like weariness:

> Science and Political Philosophy seemed dead now in both these warring and decaying Empires. The last philosophers of Athens, until their suppression, preserved the texts of the great literature of the past with an infinite reverence and want of understanding. But there remained no class of men in the world, no free gentlemen with bold and independent habits of thought, to carry on the tradition of frank statement

---

1 Frank Thilly, History of Philosophy, New York, 1945, pp. 155–58.

2 Leckey, W.E.H., *History of European Morals,* (London,1930), part II, p. 46.

3 Robert Briffault, *The Making of Humanity,* p. 164.

> and enquiry embodied in these writings. The social and political chaos accounts largely for the disappearance of this class, but there was also another reason why the human intelligence was sterile and feverish during this age. In both Persia and Byzantium it was an age of intolerance. Both Empires were religious empires in a new way, in a way that greatly hampered the free activities of the human mind.[1]

The same writer, after describing the events leading to the onslaught of the Sāsānids on Byzantium and the eventual victory of the latter, throws light on the depth of social and moral degradation to which both these great nations had fallen, in these words:

> A Prophetic amateur of history surveying the world in the opening of the seventh century might have concluded very reasonably that it was only a question of a few centuries before the whole of Europe and Asia fell under Mongolian domination. There were no signs of order or union in Western Europe, and the Byzantine and Persian Empires were manifestly bent upon a mutual destruction. India also was divided and wasted.[2]

WORLDWIDE CHAOS

To be brief, the entire human race seemed to have taken the steepest and shortest route to self-destruction. Man had forgotten his Master, and had thus become oblivious of his own self, his future and his destiny. He had lost the sense of distinction between vice and virtue, good and bad. It was as though something had slipped his mind and heart, but he did not know what it was. He had neither any interest nor time to apply his mind to the questions of life, faith and the hereafter. He had his hands too full to spare even a moment for what constituted the nourishment of his inner self and the spirit, ultimate redemption or deliverance from sin, service to humanity and restoration of his own moral health. This was the time when not a single man could be found in a whole country who seemed to be anxious about his faith, who worshipped the One and only Lord of the world without associating partners with Him or who appeared to be sincerely worried about the darkening future of humanity. This was the prevailing situation of the world, so graphically depicted by God in the Qur'ān:

> Corruption does appear on land and sea because of (the evil) which men's hands have earned, that He may make them taste a part of that which they have done, in order that they may return.[3]

---

1 H.G. Wells, *A Short History of the World* (London, 1924), p. 140.

2 H.G. Wells, *A Short History of the World* (London, 1924), p. 144.

3 Qur'ān 30:41.

2

Selection of Arabia

For the Advent of Prophet Muḥammad ﷺ

IT WAS THE WILL OF God that the glorious sun of humanity's guidance, which was to illuminate the world without end, should rise from the orb of Arabia. For it was the darkest corner of this terrestrial globe and needed the most radiant daystar to dispel the gloom setting on it.

God had chosen the Arabs as the standard-bearers of Islam for propagating its message to the four corners of the world because these guileless people were simple-hearted; nothing was inscribed on the tablets of their mind and heart, nothing so deeply engraved as to present any difficulty in sweeping the slate clean of every impression. The Romans and the Iranians and the Indians, instinctively thrilled by the glory of their ancient arts and literatures, philosophies, cultures and civilisations were all crushed by the heavy burden of the past, that is, a conditioned reflex of superiority had become indelibly etched in their minds. The imprints in the memory of the Arabs were lightly impressed merely because of their rawness and ignorance or rather their nomadic life, and thus these were liable to be obliterated easily and replaced by new inscriptions. They were, in modern phraseology, suffering from simple ignorance which could readily be remedied while other civilised nations, whose minds were filled with vivid pictures of the past, were haunted by an obsessive irrationality that could never be dismissed from their thoughts.

The Arabs, simple-minded and straightforward, possessed an iron will. If they failed to entertain a belief, they had no hesitation in taking up the sword to fight against it; but if they were convinced of the truth of an idea, they stayed with it through fire and water and were ever prepared to lay down their lives for it.

It was this psyche of the Arab mind which had found expression through Suhayl ibn ʿAmr ﵁ while the armistice of Ḥudaybiyyah was being written. The document began with the words: "This is what Muḥammad, the Apostle of God has agreed." Suhayl promptly raised the objection, "By God, if I witnessed that you were God's Apostle I would not have excluded you from the House of God and fought you." Again, it was the same Arab turn of mind which is reflected in the summons of ʿIkrimah ibn Abī Jahl ﵁. Pressed hard by the assailing charge of the Byzantine forces he cried out, "What fools you are! I have wielded the sword against the Apostle of God. Will I turn my back upon you?" Thereafter he called out to his comrades, "Is there anyone to take the pledge of death at my hands?" Several persons immediately offered themselves and fought valiantly until they were all maimed and came to a heroic end.[1]

The Arabs were frank and unassuming, practical and sober, industrious, venturesome and plainspoken. They were neither double dealers nor did they like to be caught in a trap. Like a people with true souls, they were always out-spoken and remained firm once they had made a decision. An incident, occurring before the *hijrah* of the Prophet ﷺ, on the occasion of the second pledge of ʿAqabah, typically illustrates the character of the Arabs.

Ibn Isḥāq relates that when Aws and Khazraj pledged their loyalty to the Prophet ﷺ at ʿAqabah, ʿAbbās ibn ʿUbādah of Khazraj ﵁ said to his people, "O men of Khazraj, do you realise to what you are committing yourselves to in pledging your support to the Prophet ﷺ? It is to war against one and all. If you think that in case you lose your property and your nobles are killed you will give him up to his enemies then do so now! For, by God, it would bring you shame in this world and the next. But if you have decided that you will be true to your words, if your property is destroyed and your nobles are killed, then pledge yourselves. For, by God it will bring you profit and success both in this world and the next." The Khazraj replied: "We pledge our support even if we should lose our property and our leaders be killed. But, O Apostle of God, what will we get in return for redeeming our pledge?" "Paradise", said the Prophet ﷺ in reply. Thereupon they said, "Stretch forth your hand", and when the Prophet ﷺ did so, they took their oath.[2]

And, in truth, the Anṣār ﵃[3] lived up to their word of honour. On a subse-

1 Ṭabarī, vol. IV, p. 36.

2 *Ibn Hishām*, vol. I, p. 446.

3 Lit., "the helpers"; the name give to the Madinan followers of the Prophet used in contrast to the earliest Muslims who migrated to that city with the Prophet.

quent occasion, Saʿd ibn Muʿādh ﷺ, representing them, said to the Prophet ﷺ, 'By God, if you continue your march and go as far as Bark al-Ghimād[1] we would accompany you, and if you were to cross this sea we would plunge into it with you.'[2]

'My Lord, this ocean has interrupted my march although I wanted to go ahead and proclaim Thy name in all the lands and seas,'[3] were the despairing words uttered by ʿUqbah ibn Nāfiʿ ﷺ on reaching the shore of the Atlantic ocean. What ʿUqbah ﷺ said on finding his victorious advance blocked by the ocean speaks volumes of the seriousness, absolute trust and iron will of the Arabs in accomplishing the task they considered the truth.

The Greeks, the Byzantines and the Iranians were peoples of a different mettle. Accustomed to improving the shining hour as a godsend opportunity, they lacked the grit to fight against injustice and brutality. No ideal, no principle was attractive enough for them: no belief or call was appealing enough for them: no conviction or summons was sufficiently potent to tug at their heartstrings in such a way that they would be willing to imperil their comfort and pleasure.

Unspoiled by the nicety, polish and ostentation usually produced by the display of wealth and luxury of an advanced culture, the Arabs had not developed that fastidiousness which hardens the heart and ossifies the brain, allows no emotion to catch the flame and always acts as an inhibition when one's faith or conviction demands stirring of the blood. This is the listless apathy that is rarely erased from one's heart.

Fiercely honest and true, the Arabs had no taste for intrigue and duplicity. They were courageous, intrepid fighters accustomed to a simple and hard life filled with dangers and spent most of their time riding on horseback across the waterless desert. These were the rules of iron essential for a nation required to accomplish a great task, especially in an age when adventure and enterprise were the laws of Medes and Persians.

The common ignorance of the Arabs, exempted from the shame or reproach it involves, had helped to conserve the natural briskness and intellectual energy of these people. Being strangers to pseudo-philosophy and sophistry, ratiocination and lame and impotent quibbling, they had preserved their soundness of mind, dispatch, resolution and fervour.

The perpetual independence of Arabia from the yoke of invaders had made

---

1 Located variously by different people, some say that Bark al-Ghimād is a far off place in Yemen while others hold that it is in Abyssinia. What Saʿd ibn Muʿādh meant was that his companions would keep company of the Prophet even if he had to go to the most distant place.

2 *Zād al-Maʿād,* vol. I, pp. 342–343; *Ibn Hishām,* vol. I, p. 615.

3 Ibn Athīr, *Al-Kāmil,* vol. IV, p. 46.

the Arabs free as birds. They enjoyed the benefits of human equality and the beauty of living nature and were not acquainted with the pomp or majesty or haughty demeanour of the emperors. The servile temper of the ancient Persian had, contrarily, exalted the Sāsānid monarchs to supernatural beings. If any king took a medicine or was given phlebotomy, a proclamation was made in the capital that all and sundry should suspend their trade and business for the day.[1] If the king sneezed, nobody dared raise his voice to say grace, nor was anybody expected to say 'Amen,' when the king sent up a prayer. The day any king paid a visit to any noble or chief was regarded as an event so memorable that the elated family of the fortunate grandee instituted a new calendar from that day. It was an honour so singular that the grandee was exempted from payment of taxes for a fixed period besides enjoying other rewards, fiefs and robes of honour.[2]

We can imagine what a state audience of the king must have been like for those who were allowed to appear before him. By etiquette, all the courtiers, even the highest nobles and dignitaries, were required to stand silently with their hands folded on the navel, and their heads bowed in reverence.[3] Actually, this was the ceremonial etiquette prescribed for the State audience during the reign of Chosroes I (531–579), known as *Anushirvan* (of the Immortal Soul) and *ʿĀdil* (the Just). One can very well visualise the pompous ceremonials in vogue during the reign of Sāsānid kings, justly reputed as tyrants and despots.

Freedom of speech and expression (and not censure or criticism, in the least) was a luxury that no one in the vast kingdom of the Sāsānids ever indulged in. Christensen had related, on the authority of Ṭabarī, a story about Chosroes I, who went under the name of 'The Just' among the Sāsānid kings, which demonstrates the freedom of expression allowed by the Iranian kings, and the price paid for the imprudence of speaking the truth. Chosroes I had assembled his council and ordered the secretary for taxes to read aloud the new rates of collection.

When the secretary had announced the rates, Chosroes asked twice whether anyone had any objection to the new arrangement. Everybody remained silent but on the third time of asking, a man stood up and asked respectfully whether the king had meant to establish a tax for perpetuity on things perishable, which, as time went on, would lead to injustice. "Accursed and rash!" cried the king, "To what class do you belong?" "I am one of the secretaries", replied the man. "Then", ordered the king, "beat him to death with pen-cases." Thereupon every

1 *Īrān fi ʿAhd As-Sāsāniyān*, pp. 535–36.

2 Ibid., p. 543.

3 Exactly in the way one stands in prayer. Actually the Arabic word *'kufr'* means, etymologically, 'standing in the way Iranians pay respect to their kings' (*Lisān al-ʿArab*, vol. VII, p. 466).

secretary started beating him with his pen-case until the poor man died, and the beholders exclaimed: "O king, we find all the taxes you have levied upon us just and fair!"[1]

The horrible condition of the depressed classes in what was then India, who were condemned as untouchables by the social and religious laws promulgated by the Aryans, baffles all human understanding. Subjected to a gruesome indignity, this unfortunate class of human beings was treated pretty much the same way as pet animals except that they resembled the species of man. According to this law, a Sudra who assaulted a Brahmin or attempted to do so was to lose the limb with which the assault was made. The Sudra was forced to drink boiling oil if he made the pretentious claim of teaching somebody.[2] The penalty for killing dogs, cats, frogs, chameleons, crows and owls was the same as that for killing the Sudras.[3]

The common man in Byzantium was not subject to the same unworthy treatment that the Sāsānid Emperors meted out to their subjects, but in their pride and policy to display the titles and attributes of their omnipotence, the Caesars of Rome had all the signs of their oriental counterparts.

Victor Chopart writes about the arbitrary rule and majesty of the Roman Emperors:

> The Caesars were gods, but not by heredity, and one who rose to power would become divine in his turn, and there was no mark by which he could be recognised in advance. The transmission of the title of Augustus was governed by no regular constitutional law; it was acquired by victory over rivals, and the Senate did no more than ratify the decision of arms. This ominous fact became apparent in the first century of the Participate, which was merely a continuance of the military dictatorship.[4]

Such servitude and prostrations before kings of that time was customary. If we compare the servile submission of the common man of Byzantium and Persia with the spirit of freedom and pride as well as the temperament and social conduct of the pre-Islamic Arabs, we would see the difference between the social life and natural propensities of the Arabs and other nations of the world.

'May you be safe from frailty', and 'Wish you a happy morning', were some of the salutations very often used by the Arabs to hail their kings. So solicitous were they of preserving their dignity and pride, honour and freedom that many

---

1 *Tārikh at-Ṭabarī*, vol II, p.121–122 as quoted in *Īrān fi 'Ahd As-Sāsāniyān*, p. 511.

2 *Mani Shastra*, chapter 10.

3 R. C. Dutt, *Ancient India*, vol. III pp. 324 and 343.

4 Victor Chopart, *The Roman World* (London, 1982), p. 418.

a time they even refused to satisfy the demands of their chiefs and rulers. A story preserved by Arab historians admirably describes the rudimentary Arab virtues of courage and outspokenness. An Arab king demanded a mare known as Sikāb from its owner who belonged to the Banū Tamīm. The man flatly refused the request and instantly indicted the king in a poem of which the opening lines were:

> Sikāb is a fine mare, good as gold,
> Too precious is it to be gifted or sold.

And, in the concluding verse he said:

> To grab it from me, make no effort,
> For I am fit to balk your attempt.[1]

The traits common to all Arabs, men and women, were their overweening pride, high ambition, chivalrous bearing, magnanimous generosity and a wild, invigorating spirit of freedom. We find all these features of Arab character depicted in the affair leading to the murder of ʿAmr ibn Hind, the King of Ḥīrah. It is related that ʿAmr ibn Hind once sent an invite to ʿAmr ibn Kulthūm, the proud cavalier and noted poet of Banū Taghlīb, inviting both him and his mother, Laylā bint Muhalhil, to visit his own mother. ʿAmr came to Ḥīrah from Jazīrah with some of his friends, and Laylā came attended by a number of her women. Pavilions were erected between Ḥīrah and the Euphrates. In one of these pavilions ʿAmr bin Hind entertained ʿAmr ibn Kulthūm, while Laylā found quarters with Hind in an adjoining tent. Now, ʿAmr ibn Hind had already instructed his mother to dismiss the servants before calling for dessert, and thus cause Laylā to wait upon her. Accordingly, Hind sent off her servants at the appointed moment and asked her guest, "O Laylā, hand me that dish." Laylā felt insulted and exclaimed in shame, "Let those who want anything, fetch it for themselves." Hind insisted on her demand despite Laylā's refusal. At last Laylā cried, "O shame! Help Taghlib, help!" ʿAmr ibn Kulthūm got his blood up on hearing his mother's cry and seizing a sword hanging on the wall, smote the king dead with a single blow. At the same time, the tribesmen of Banū Taghlib ransacked the tents and made rapid strides back to Jazīrah. ʿAmr ibn Kulthūm narrated this story in an ode which is a fine illustration of the pre-Islamic ideal of chivalry. It was included in the *Sabʿah Muʿallaqāt* or the Seven Suspended Odes.[2]

---

1 *Dīwān Ḥamāsah*, Bāb-al-Ḥamāsah, pp. 67–68.

2 Ibn Qutaybah, *Kitāb ash-Shaʿr wa 'sh-Shuʿarā'*, p. 36. These odes were awarded the annual prize at the fair of ʿUkāẓ, inscribed in golden letters and suspended on the wall of the Kaʿbah.

The same Arab tradition of democracy tempered by aristocracy is to be witnessed in the meeting between the Arab envoy, Mughīra ibn Shuʿbah, and Rustam, the Sāsānid General and administrator of the empire. When Mughīra entered the splendid court of Rustam, he found the latter sitting on a throne. Mughīrah made his way directly to Rustam, as was an Arab's wont. The courtiers, however, lost no time in getting Mughīrah down from the throne of their chief. Thereupon Mughīrah said, "We had heard that you are a sagacious people but now I see that none is more blockheaded than you. We Arabs treat everybody as an equal and enslave no man save on the battlefield. I had presumed that you would also conduct yourselves similarly towards your own people. You should have told us that you have exalted some amongst you as your gods; for, we would have then known that no dialogue was possible between us and you in the ways we have done, nor come to see you, although it was you who invited us here."[1]

There was yet another reason for the advent of the last Prophet in Arabia and it was the Kaʿbah, the house of God, built by Abraham ﷺ and Ishmael ﷺ as the centre for the worship of the One God.

> Lo! the first Sanctuary appointed for mankind was that at Becca,[2] a blessed place, a guidance to the peoples.[3]

There is mention of the valley of Baca in the Old Testament. The old translators of the Bible gave this word the meaning of 'a valley of weeping', but a better understanding seems to have prevailed later on. According to later Biblical scholars, the word 'signifies rather any valley lacking water', and 'the Psalmist apparently has in mind a particular valley whose natural condition led him to adopt that name.'[4] Now, this waterless valley, which can easily be identified with the valley of Makkah, has been thus mentioned in the Book of Psalms:

> Blessed are they that dwell in thy house;
> They will still be praising thee. Selah.
> Blessed is the man whose strength is in thee;
> In whose heart are the ways of them
> Who passing through the valley of Baca make it well.[5]

---

1 Ṭabarī, vol. IV, p. 108.

2 The sacred city is known both as Becca and Makkah. The Arabic alphabets *bā* and *mīm* are etymologically interchangeable, in many cases, such as, *lāzim* and *lāzib*, and *thamīṭ* and *nabīṭ* without any change in their meanings.

3 Qur'ān 3:96.

4 *Jewish Encyclopedia*, vol. II, p. 415. Also see *Commentary on the Holy Qur'an* by ʿAbdul Majīd (Lahore, 1957), vol. I, pp. 121–2 and Qāzī Sulaymān Mansūrpūrī, *Raḥmatul-ʿĀlamīn* (Deoband, N. D.), vol. I, p. 24.

5 Ps. 84:4–6.

The birth of the Prophet Muḥammad ﷺ in the city of Makkah was really an answer to the prayer sent up by Abraham ﷺ and Ishmael ﷺ while laying the foundation of the Kaᶜbah. They had beseeched God in these words:

> Our Lord! And raise up unto them an apostle from among them, who shall recite unto them Your revelations, and shall teach them the Book and wisdom, and shall cleanse them. Verily You! You are the Mighty, the Wise.[1]

A standing norm of God Almighty is that He always answers the prayers of those who are pious and devoted and pure in heart. The Apostles of God occupy, without doubt, a higher place than the most devout and the godliest believers. All the earlier scriptures and prophecies bear witness to this fact. Even the Old Testament testifies that the supplication of Abraham ﷺ in regard to Ishmael ﷺ met the approval of the Lord. The Book of Genesis says:

> And as for Ishmael, I have heard thee: Behold, I have blessed him, and will make him fruitful, and will multiply him exceedingly; twelve princes shall he beget, and I will make him a great nation.[2]

That is why the Prophet ﷺ is reported to have said: 'I am the (answer to the) prayer of Abraham ﷺ and prophecy of Jesus ﷺ.'[3] The Old Testament still contains, notwithstanding its numerous recessions and alterations, the evidence that this prayer of Abraham ﷺ was answered by God. Mark the very clear reference in the Book of Deuteronomy to the advent of a prophet.

> The Lord, God will raise up unto thee a Prophet from the midst of thee, of thy brethren, like unto me; unto him ye shall hearken.[4]

Now, this being a prophecy by Moses ﷺ, 'thy brethren' clearly indicates that the prophet promised by God was to be raised from amongst the Ishmaelites who were the cousins of Israelites. God again reiterates His promise in the same Book:

> And the Lord said unto me, They have well spoken that which they have spoken. I will raise them up a Prophet from among their brethren, like unto you, and will put my words in his mouth; and he shall speak unto them all that I shall command him.[5]

---

1 Qur'ān 2:129.

2 Gen. 17:20.

3 *Musnad Imām Aḥmad.*

4 Dt. 18: 15.

5 Dt. 18: 17–18.

The words 'put my words in his mouth' occurring in the revelation very clearly indicate the advent of the Prophet ﷺ who was to recite and deliver to his people the divine revelation exactly as he received it. This prophecy has been substantiated by the Qur'ān also: "Nor does he speak of (his own) desire."[1]

Again, the Qur'ān says about the revelation vouchsafed to the Prophet Muḥammad ﷺ:

> Falsehood cannot come to it from before it or behind it.(It is) a revelation from the Wise, the Owner of Praise.[2]

But, quite unlike the Qur'ān, both the Bible and its followers ascribe the authorship of the 'Books' included in the Bible to the 'ancient sages' and the 'great teachers' and never to the Divine Author Himself. Modern Biblical scholars have reached the conclusion that:

> Ancient Jewish traditions attributed the authorship of the Pentateuch[3] (with the exceptions of the last eight verses describing Moses' death) to Moses himself. But the many inconsistencies and seeming contradictions contained in it attracted the attention of the Rabbis, who exercised their ingenuity in reconciling them.[4]

As for the 'Books' forming part of the New Testament, they have never been treated, either literally or in their content to be of Divine origin. These books really contain a biographical account and anecdotes of Jesus ﷺ, as narrated by later scribes, rather than a Book of revelation sent unto the Master.[5]

We now come to the geographical position of Arabia, which, being connected by land and sea routes with the continents of Asia, Africa and Europe, occupied the most suitable place as the centre of enlightenment, of radiating divine guidance and knowledge to the entire world. All the three continents had been cradles of great civilisations and powerful empires, while Arabia lay in the centre[6] through which passed the merchandise of the countries[7] far and

---

1 Qur'ān 53:3.

2 Qur'ān 41:42.

3 The first five books of the Old Testament.

4 *Jewish Encyclopaedia*, vol. IX, p. 589.

5 For detailed discussion see the chapter 'Finality of Prophethood' in *Islamic Concept of Prophethood.*

6 Dr. Ḥusayn Kamāl Uddīn, Professor Civil Engineering in the engineering College of Riyadh University informed in an interview with the correspondence of *Al-Ihrām*, Cairo, that according to his researches it could be proved that Makkah lay at the centre of the world. For devising an inexpensive instrument which could show the direction of the Kaʿbah, he had started preparing maps showing the distances of various cities in different countries from Makkah. These maps revealed that Makkah lay in the centre of the world, which is yet another reason why it was selected by God to house the Sacred Sanctuary and to radiate Divine guidance to the four corners of the world.

7 De Lacy O 'Leary, *Arabia Before Muḥammad* (London, 1927), pp. 179–88.

near, affording an opportunity to different nations and races for the exchange of thoughts and ideas.

Two great empires, Sāsānid and Byzantine, on either side of the Arabian Peninsula governed the history of the world. Both were large, rich and powerful, and both fought each other constantly; yet, Arabia jealously guarded her independence and never allowed either of the two powers to lay its hands on it, barring a few territories lying on its frontiers. Excepting a few peripheral tribes, the Arab of the desert was extremely sensitive to his regal dignity and untrammelled freedom, and he never allowed any despot to hold him bondage. Such a country, unimpeded by political and social constraints, was ideally suited to become the nucleus of a universal message preaching human equality, liberty and dignity.

For all these reasons God had selected Arabia, and the city of Makkah within it, for the advent of the Prophet ﷺ to whom divine Scripture was to be sent for the last time to pave the way for proclamation of Peace throughout the length and breadth of the world from age to age.

ARABIA'S ERA OF DEPRESSION

For their manly qualities of head and heart, the Arabs deserved, or, were rather the only people entitled to the honour of the advent of the last Prophet of God amongst them and to be made responsible for propagation of the message of Islam. But, in no part of the Peninsula was there any indication of an awakening or a vexation of spirit showing the sign of life left in the Arabs.

There were a scant few *ḥanīf*[1] who could be easily counted on one's fingers, feeling their way towards monotheism but they were no more than glow worms in a dark and chilly rainy night incapable of showing the path of righteousness to anybody or providing warmth to one being frozen to death.

This was an era of darkness and depression in the history of Arabia—a period of gloom when the country had reached the rock-bottom of putrefied decadence, leaving no hope of any reform or improvement. The shape of things in Arabia presented a task far more formidable and baffling than ever faced by any messenger of God.

Sir William Muir, a biographer of the Prophet ﷺ, who is ever willing to find fault with the Prophet ﷺ and cast aspersions upon him, has vividly depicted the state of affairs in Arabia before the birth of Muḥammad ﷺ which discredits the view held by certain European Orientalists that Arabia was fermenting with

1 Ibn Isḥāq mentions four men and Ibn Qutaybah gives the names of half a dozen other persons of the generation before Muḥammad (peace be on him), who had abandoned pagan practices to seek the ḥanafiyyah, the true religion of Abraham.

change and looking forward to a genius who could respond to it better than any other. Says Sir William Muir: "During the youth of Mahomet, this aspect of the Peninsula was strongly conservative; perhaps it was never at any period more hopeless."[1]

Reviewing the feeble stir created by Christianity and Judaism in the dark and deep ocean of Arabian paganism, Sir William Muir remarks, "In fine, viewed thus in a religious aspect, the surface of Arabia had been now and then gently rippled by the feeble efforts of Christianity; the sterner influence of Judaism had been occasionally visible in the deeper and more troubled currents; but the tide of indigenous idolatry and of Ishmaelite superstition, setting from every quarter with an unbroken and un-ebbing surge towards the Kaᶜbah, gave ample evidence that the faith and worship of Makkah held the Arab mind in a thralldom, rigorous and undisputed."[2]

Bosworth Smith is another European biographer of the Prophet ﷺ who has also reached the same conclusion:

> One of the most philosophical of historians has remarked that of all the revolutions which have had a permanent influence upon the civil history of mankind, none could so little be anticipated by human prudence as that effected by the religion of Arabia. And at first sight it must be confessed that the Science of History, if indeed there be such a science is at a loss to find the sequence of cause and effect which it is object and the test of all history, which is worthy of the name, to trace it.[3]

THE NEED FOR A NEW PROPHET

The old world was completely disarranged by the middle of the sixth century and man had fallen to such a depth of depravity that no reformer, revivalist or religious preacher could have hoped to put new life in the humanity worn to its bones. The problem was not fighting any particular heresy or reshaping a given mode of divine service, nor was the question on how to curb the social evils of any society—for there has never been any dearth of social reformers and religious preachers in any age or place. How to clear the contaminating debris of idolatry, arid fetishism, superstition and paganism, piling up from generation to generation during the past hundreds of years over the true teachings of the prophets sent by God, was, indeed a task, exceedingly toilsome and unwieldy. It was a Herculean task to make a clean sweep of this wreckage and then raise

1 Sir William Muir, *The Life of Mahomet* vol. I (London 1858) p. ccxxxviii.

2 Ibid., p. ccxxxix.

3 R. Bosworth Smith, *Mohammad and Mohammedanism* (London, 1876), p. 105.

a new edifice on the foundations of piety and godliness. In short, the question was how to remake man to think and feel differently from his predecessors as a changed man, reborn or brought back to life again.

Is he who was dead and we have raised him unto life, and set for him a light wherein he walks among men, as him whose similitude is in utter darkness whence he cannot emerge?[1]

In order to solve the problem of man once for all, it was necessary to root out paganism so completely that no trace of it was left in his heart, and to plant the sapling of monotheism so deeply that it should be difficult to conceive of a more secure foundation. It meant to create a penchant for seeking the pleasure of God and humbling oneself before Him, to bring into existence the longing to serve humanity; to generate the will to keep always to the right path and to sow the seeds of that moral courage which restrains all evil passions and desires. The whole problem, in a nutshell, was how to rescue the humanity, then too willing to commit suicide, from the misery of this world as well as of the next. This was an endeavour beginning in the form of a virtuous life, like that of an elect and godly soul, and then leading on to the paradise promised by God to those who are God fearing and just.

The advent of the holy Prophet ﷺ was thus the greatest Divine blessing on mankind; that is why it has been so elegantly clothed in words by the Writ of God.

> And remember Allāh's favour unto you: how you were enemies and He made friendship between your hearts so that you became as brothers by His grace; and (how) you were upon the brink of an abyss of fire, and He did save you from it.[2]

No task more delicate and bewildering, and no charge more onerous and gigantic, than that entrusted to Muḥammad ﷺ, the Apostle of God, was imposed on any man since the birth of man on this planet. And never has a man accomplished such a huge and lasting revolution as the Last Prophet ﷺ, for he has guided millions of men of many nationalities to the path of justice, truth and virtue by putting new life into humanity at the throes of death in the sixth century. It was the greatest marvel of human history, the greatest miracle the world has ever witnessed. The well-known French poet and litterateur, Lamartine bears witness to the grand accomplishment of the Prophet Muḥammad ﷺ in a language of incomparable elegance and facility.

Never has a man set for himself, voluntarily or involuntarily, a more sublime

1 Qur'ān 6:123.
2 Qur'ān 3:103.

aim, since this aim was superhuman; to subvert superstitions which had been interposed between man and his Creator, to render God unto man and man unto God; to restore the rational and sacred idea of divinity amidst the chaos of the material and disfigured gods of idolatry, then existing. Never has a man undertaken a work so far beyond human power with so feeble means, for he had in the conception as well as in the execution of such a great design no other instrument than himself, and no other aid, except a handful of men living in a corner of the desert.[1]

Lamartine goes on to enumerate the achievements of the Great Prophet:

> And more than that, he moved the altars, the gods, the religions, the ideas, the beliefs and the souls. On the basis of a Book, every letter of which has become Law, he created a spiritual nationality which blended together peoples of every tongue and of every race. He has left us as the indelible characteristic of this Muslim nationality, the hatred of false gods and the passion for the One and Immaterial God. This avenging patriotism against the profanation of Heaven formed the virtue of the followers of Muḥammad; the conquest of one third of the earth to his dogma was his miracle; or rather it was not the miracle of a man but of reason. The idea of the Unity of God, proclaimed amidst the exhaustion of fabulous theogonies, was in itself such a miracle that upon its utterance from his lips it destroyed all the ancient temples of idols and set on fire one third of the world.[2]1

This universal and enduring revolution whose objective was a rejuvenation of humanity or re-building of the world anew, demanded a new prophethood surpassing the apostleship that had come before—for the new Prophet had to hold aloft the banner of Divine guidance and righteousness for all times to come. God has Himself given the reason for it:

> Those who disbelieve among the people of the Scripture and the idolaters could not have left off (erring) till the clear proof came unto them. A Messenger from Allāh, reading purified pages containing correct scriptures.[3]

1 Lamartine, *Histoire de la Turquie,* vol. II (Paris. 1854), p. 276. Quoted in *Islam in the World* by Dr. Zakī ʿAlī (Lahore, 1947).

2 1. *Ibid.*, pp. 276–7

3 Qur'ān 98: 1–3

3
Arabian Peninsula

Arabia is the largest peninsula on the map of the world. The Arabs call it *Jazīrat al-ʿArab*,[1] which means the 'Island of Arabia', although it is not an island, being surrounded by water on three sides only. Lying in the south-west of Asia, the Arabian Gulf, which was known to the Greeks as the Persian Gulf, is to its east; the Indian Ocean marks the southern limits; and to its west is the Red Sea which was called *Sinus Arabicus* or the Arabian Gulf by the Greeks and Romans, and *Bahr Qulzum* by the ancient Arabs. The northern boundary is not well defined, but may be considered an imaginary line drawn due east from the head of the Gulf of ʿAqabah in the Red Sea to the mouth of the Euphrates.[2]

The Muslim geographers have divided the country into five regions: (1) Ḥijāz extends from Aylah (ʿAqabah) to Yemen and has been so named because the range of mountains running parallel to the Western coast that separates the low coastal belt of Tihāmah from Najd; (2) Tihāmah inside the inner range is a plateau extending to the foothills; (3) Yemen, south of Ḥijāz, occupies the south-west corner of Arabia; (4) Najd, the north-central plateau, extends from the mountain ranges of Ḥijāz in the west to the deserts of Baḥrayn in the east

1 The word has been commonly used since ancient times because no distinction was made in those days between a peninsula and an island, nor were there separate words to denote the two. Certain scholars have tried to prove that Arabia is an island in the modern geographical sense, as, for instance, in the *Tārīkh al-Umam al-Islamiyyah* of ʿAllāmah Khuḍarī, but it requires that one stretch the sense of the term and moves the boundaries of the Peninsula too far away from its present limits.

2 The author has relied heavily on Dr. Jawwād Alī's book, *Al-Mufassil fī Tārīkh al-ʿArab qablal Islam* (vol 1–9).

and encompasses a number of deserts and mountain ranges; (5) ʿArūḍ which is bounded by Baḥrayn to its east and Ḥijāz to its west. The area lying between Yemen and Najd was also known as Yamāmah.[1]

THE LAND AND ITS PEOPLE

Nine-tenth of Arabia is made up of barren desert, making it one of the driest and hottest regions of the world. The geological and physical features of the land along with its climatic conditions have kept its population, in the days gone by and also in the present time, to the minimum and hindered the flowering of civilised communities and empires. The nomadic life of the desert tribes, the rugged individualism of the people, and the unrestrained tribal conflict limited the settled population to the areas with sufficient rainfall, or where water surfaced to the land in the form of springs or ponds or was found near the surface of the earth. The Bedouins would dig deep wells in the ground. The way of life in Arabia was, so to say, dictated by the availability of water. Nomadic tribes continually roamed the desert in search of water. Wherever verdant land was found, the tribes would go seeking pastures without being bound to the land like the tillers of the soil. They would stay over a pasture or oasis so long as they could graze their flocks of sheep, goats and camels, before breaking up their camps to search out new pastures.

Life in the desert was hard and filled with danger. The Bedouin felt bound to the family and to the clan, on which depended his existence in the arid desert; loyalty to the tribe meant for him the same life-long alliance as others feel for the nation and state. Life was unstable and vagrant; like the desert, the Bedouin knew not ease or comfort; and understood only the language of power, of might. He knew no moral code—no legal or religious sanction—nothing save the traditional sentiment of his own tribe and the tribe's honour. In short, it was a life that always brought about hardship and trouble for him, and sowed the seeds of danger for the neighbouring sedentary populations.

The desert tribes of Arabia were continually engaged in endless strife amongst themselves, or made incursions into the settled lands around them. At the same time, the Arabs displayed a boundless loyalty to their tribes and traditions, were magnanimously hospitable, honoured the treaties, were faithful friends, and dutifully met the obligations of tribal customs. All these traits of the Arab character are amply illustrated in their forceful and elegant literature, both in prose and poetry, proverbs, fables, metaphors and simile.

1 This geographical division of the country is attributed to ʿAbdullāh ibn ʿAbbās.

The Arab was thus a born democrat, individualistic and freedom-loving, practical-minded and a realist, active and straight-thinking and would shrink from doing anything deemed vulgar or indecent. Not only was the Bedouin content with his nomadic life and the frugal demands it made upon him, he also felt satisfied with, or even proud, of his migratory existence for it fulfilled his passionate desire for freedom. The Bedouin was lukewarm to spiritual impulses, although he was absolutely loyal to the ancient traditions of his tribe. The fundamental virtues of an Arab consisted of courage, loyalty and generosity, and were derived from the concept of '*mūrūwwah*' or manliness; and he was never tired of singing its praises in odes and orations.

CULTURAL CENTRES

In places where there were sufficient periodic rains or water was available in wells or springs settlements would spring up or the nomads would gather during seasonal fairs and festivals. While such get-togethers exerted a civilising influence on the life of the Bedouin, the agricultural settlements reflected their specific characteristics depending on climatic conditions and the economic and occupational features of the sedentary population. Accordingly, Makkah had a peculiar cultural development as other settlements like Yathrib and Ḥīrah had their own distinguishing cultural features. Yemen was culturally the most developed region in the country owing to its long history and political developments in the recent past. Because of its suitable climate, Yemen had made rapid strides in cultivation of cereals, animal husbandry, quarry of minerals and construction of forts and palaces. It had commercial relations with Iraq, Syria and Africa, and imported the various commodities it needed.

ETHNIC DIVISIONS

Arab historians as well as old traditions of the land hold that the people of Arabia can be categorised into three broad divisions. The first of these were the *ʿArab Bā'idah* (extinct Arabs) who populated the country but ceased to exist well before the advent of Islam. The next were the *ʿArab ʿĀribah* (Arabian Arabs) or Banū Qaḥṭān who replaced the *ʿArab Bā'idah* and the third were the *ʿArab Mustaʿribah* (Arabised Arabs) or the progeny of Ishmael ﷺ who settled in Ḥijāz. The line of demarcation drawn according to racial division of the Arab stock makes a distinction between those descended from Qaḥṭān and ʿAdnān; the former are held to be Yemenites or southern Arabs while the latter had settled in Ḥijāz. Arab genealogists further divide the ʿAdnān into two sub-groups which they term as Rabīʿah and Muḍar. There had been a marked rivalry from the distant past between the Qaḥṭān and the ʿAdnān just as the Rabīʿah and the Muḍar had been hostile to each other. However, the historians trace the origin of the Qaḥṭān to a more distant past from which the ʿAdnān branched off at a later time[1] and they learned the Arabic vernacular from the former. It is held that the ʿAdnān were the offspring of Ishmael (Ismāʿīl) ﷺ who settled in Ḥijāz after naturalisation.

Arab genealogists give great weight to these racial classifications which also find a confirmation in the attitude of Iranians in the olden times. The Iranian General Rustam had admonished his courtiers who had derided Mughīrah ibn Shuʿbah and looked down upon him for having presented himself as the envoy of Muslims in tattered clothes. Rustam had then said to his counsellors: 'You are all fools. The Arabs give little importance to their dress and food but are vigilant about their lineage and family.'[2]

LINGUISTIC UNITY

Multiplicity of dialects and languages would not have been at all surprising in a country so immense as Arabia (actually, equal to a sub-continent), divided into north and south, not only by the trackless desert, but also by the rivalry of kindred races and clannish patriotism of a passionate, chauvinistic type, affording but little opportunity for intermixing and unification of the country's population. The tribes living in the frontier regions close to the Iranian and Byzantine empires were, quite naturally, open to influences of alien elements. Similar factors as these gave birth to numerous languages in Europe and the Indian subcontinent. In India alone, fifteen languages have been officially recognised by the Constitution of India while there are still people who have to speak in an official language other than their own mother tongue or take recourse to English to be understood by others.

But, the Arabian Peninsula has had a common language ever since the rise of Islam, despite its vastness and proliferation of tribes. Arabic has been the language of Bedouins living in the deserts as well as of the sedentary and cultured populations like the Qaḥṭān and ʿAdnān. Some local variations in the dialects of various regions arising from differences of tones and accents, wide distances and diversity of physical and geographical conditions could not be helped, yet there

---

1 Some modern experts hold the view that the ʿAdnān are really the *ʿArab ʿĀribah* and form the original stock. Others who disagree with this view, plead that the division made by earlier historians is based on the classifications made by authorities belonging to Qaḥṭān or the Yemenite stock after the advent of Islam and not prior to it.

2 *Ibn Kathīr, Al Bidāyah wa'n-Nihāyah,* vol. VIII, p. 40.

has always been a linguistic uniformity which made the Qur'ān intelligible to all. It was also helpful in the rapid diffusion of Islam to the far-flung tribes of Arabia.

ARABIA IN ANCIENT HISTORY

Archaeological excavations show the existence of human habitation in Arabia during the earliest period of Stone Age. These earliest remains pertain to Acheulean period of the Palaeolithic epoch. The people of Arabia mentioned in the Old Testament throw light on the relations between the Arabs and ancient Hebrews between 750 to 200 BC. Similarly, the Talmud also refers to the Arabs. Josephus (c. 37–100) gives some valuable historical and geographical details about the Arabs and Nabataeans.[1] There are many more Greek and Latin writings of the pre-Islamic era enumerating the tribes living in the Peninsula and giving their geographical locations and historical details, which, notwithstanding the mistakes and inconsistencies in them, are invaluable sources of information about ancient Arabia. Alexandria was also one of those important commercial centres of antiquity which had taken a keen interest in collecting data about Arabia, its people and the commodities produced in that country for commercial purposes.

The first classical writers to mention the Arabs in Greek literature were Aeschylus (525–465 BC) and Herodotus (484–425 BC). Several other writers of the classical period have left an account of Arabia and its inhabitants, of these, Claudius Ptolemaeus of Alexandria was an eminent geographer of the second century, whose *Almagest* occupied an important place in the curriculum of Arabic schools. Christian sources also contain considerable details about Arabia during the pre-Islamic and early Islamic era although these were primarily written to describe Christianity and its missionary activities in that country.

The numerous references made to the "Ereb"[2] in the Old Testament are synonymous with the nomadic tribes of Arabia since the word means desert in Semitic and the characteristics of the people described therein apply to the Bedouins. Similarly, the Arabs mentioned in the writings of the Greeks and Romans as well as in the New Testament were Bedouins who used to make plundering raids on the frontier towns of the Roman and Byzantine empires, despoiled the caravans and imposed extortionate charges on the traders and wayfarers passing through their territories.

Diodorus Siculus, a classical writer of Sicily in the second half of the first century BC, affirms that the Arabs are "self reliant and independence-loving, like to

1 Especially in the *Jewish Antiquities* ed. S. A. Naber (Leipzig, 1888).

2 Is. 21:13, 13:20, and Jer. 3:2.

live in the open desert and highly prize and value their liberty."[1] The Greek historian Herodotus (484–425 BC) also makes a similar remark about them. "They revolt against every power," he says, 'which seeks to control their freedom or demean them.'[2] The passionate attachment of the Arabs to their personal freedom was admired by almost all the Greek and Latin writers.

The acquaintance of the Arabs with the Indians and their commercial and cultural relations with India began in the days long before the advent of Islam and their conquest of India. Modern research on the subject shows that of all the Asiatic countries, India was closest to Arabia and well-acquainted with it.[3]

EARLIER REVEALED RELIGIONS OF ARABIA

Arabia had been the birthplace of several prophets of God in the bygone days. The Qur'ān says:

> And make mention (O Muḥammad) of the brother of ʿĀd when he warned his folk among the wind-curved sandhills—and verily warners came and went before and after him—saying: Serve none but Allāh. Lo! I fear for you the doom of a tremendous Day.[4]

Prophet Hūd[5] ﷺ was sent to the ʿĀd, a people, according to historians, belonging to the *ʿArab Bā'idah* who lived in a vast area to the south-west of ar-Rubʿ al-Khālī (the Empty Quarter) near Ḥaḍramawt, an area which is now a tract of white or reddish sand blown into hill banks or dunes and covering. Although this region has no habitation and is devoid of the breath of life, in ancient times it was a verdant land, flourishing with towns inhabited by a people of strength and stature. The whole area was laid to waste by a fearful and roaring wind which covered it with sand dunes.[6]

The Qur'ānic verse quoted above shows that the Prophet Hūd ﷺ was not the only messenger of God sent to the ancient Arabs of this area as many more "warners came and went before him."

Ṣāliḥ[7] ﷺ was another Arabian prophet sent to the people called Thamūd who lived in Al-Ijr situated between Tabūk and Ḥijaz. Prophet Ismāʿīl ﷺ was

1 *Bibliotheca Historica,* Book II, Chap. 1, §. 5.

2 Herodotus, *History,* Book III, Chap. 88.

3 For details see *ʿArab awr Hind ke Taʿalluqāt* by S. Sulaymān Nadwī.

4 Qur'ān 46:21.

5 Recognised by some as Heber of the Bible (Judges. iv–1).

6 For details see the chapter" The Reality" in the Qur'ān.

7 Identified by some as Salah (Genesis xi-13).

brought up in Makkah, and he died in the same city. If we extend the frontiers of the Arabian peninsula northwards to include Madyan on the borders of Syria, Prophet Shuʿayb ☙[1] would also be reckoned as an Arabian prophet. The historian Abu 'l-Fidā' says that Madyanites (or people of Madyan) were Arabs, living in Madyan near Maʿān, which is adjacent to the Sea of Lūṭ (the Dead Sea) in Syria on the frontier of Ḥijāz. The Madyanites flourished after the downfall of the people of Lūṭ.[2]

Ancient Arabia had been the cradle of many a civilised and flourishing people to whom God had sent His apostles. But all of them were either destroyed because of their evil ways or became strangers in their own homeland, or were forced to seek new homes. The prophets of God born in the lands far away had sometimes to seek refuge in Arabia from the despotic kings of their lands. Ibrāhīm ☙ (Abraham) migrated to Makkah and Moses ☙ had to flee to Madyan. Followers of other religions, too, had sought shelter in Arabia. The Jews, persecuted by the Romans, settled in Yemen and Yathrib while several Christian sects harassed by the Byzantine Emperors had migrated to Najrān.[3]

1 Identified with Jethro.
2 'Stories of the Prophets' by Shaykh 'Abd al-Wahhab an-Najjar
3 For further details see vol. 1 of *Khātam an-Nabīyyin* by Shaykh Muḥammad Abū Zahrā'.

4

Makkah Before the Prophet ﷺ

Ismāʿīl in Makkah

The Patriarch Ibrāhīm ﷺ (Abraham) came down to the valley of Makkah surrounded by mountains, naked rocks and bare and rugged crags. Nothing to sustain life was to be found there, not water, verdure or grain. He had with him his wife, Hājar (Hager), and their son Ismāʿīl ﷺ (Ishmael). Ibrāhīm ﷺ had wandered through the deserts of Arabia in order to move away from the wide-spread heathen cult of idol-worship and to establish a centre for worship of the One and Only God and where he could invite others to bow down before the Lord of the world. He wanted to lay the foundation of a lighthouse of guidance, a sanctuary of peace that should become the radiating centre of true monotheism, faith and righteousness.[1]

God blessed the sincerity of Ibrāhīm ﷺ and the dry valley of this wild country. Ibrāhīm ﷺ had left his wife and his infant son in this inhospitable territory. Here, in the midst of rugged hills, the Master of all the worlds manifested His grace by causing water to issue forth the earth, and the well of Zamzam burst forth and remains to this day. When Ismāʿīl ﷺ was a few years old, Ibrāhīm ﷺ went to visit his family in Makkah. Ibrāhīm ﷺ now made up his mind to sacrifice Ismāʿīl ﷺ for the sake of God, for the Lord had commanded him in a dream: "Offer up thy son Ismāʿīl." Obedient to the Lord as he was, Ismāʿīl ﷺ at once agreed to have his throat cut by his father. But God saved Ismāʿīl ﷺ and

1 See Sūrah al-Baqarah and Sūrah Ibrāhīm.

instituted[1] the "day of great sacrifice", in order to commemorate the event for all times, since, he was destined to help Ibrāhīm ﵇ in his mission and become the progenitor of the last Prophet ﷺ as well as of the nation charged to disseminate the message of God and to struggle for it to the end of time.

Ibrāhīm ﵇ came back to Makkah again[2] and assisted by his son. Ismāʿīl ﵇ built the House of God. While father and son occupied themselves in the work, they also beseeched God to confer His grace; cause them to live as well as die in Islam; and help their progeny to keep a watch over their patrimony of monotheism, not only by protecting their mission against every risk and peril but also by becoming its standard-bearers and preachers, braving every danger and sacrificing everything for its sake until their call reached the farthest corner of the world. They also supplicated God to raise up a prophet, amongst their offspring, who should renew and revive the summons of Ibrāhīm ﵇ and bring to completion the task initiated by him:

> And when Abraham and Ishmael were raising the foundations of the House, (Abraham prayed): Our Lord! Accept from us (this duty). Lo! You, only You, are the Hearer, the Knower.
>
> Our Lord! Make us submissive unto You and of our seed a nation submissive unto You, and show us our ways of worship, and relent toward us. Lo! You, only You, are the Relenting, the Merciful.
>
> Our Lord! And raise up in their midst a messenger from among them who shall recite unto them Your revelations, and shall instruct them in the Scripture and in wisdom and shall make them grow. Lo! You, only You, are the Mighty, the Wise.[3]

The prayer sent up by Ibrāhīm ﵇ included a plea for the House he was constructing to become a sanctuary of Peace, and that God might keep his progeny away from idol worship. Ibrāhīm ﵇ held nothing more in abomination than idolatry, nor deemed anything more fraught with danger for his progeny, for he knew the fate of earlier idolatrous nations. He was aware how the great prophets of God had earlier struggled and fought this evil throughout their lives, but not long after their departure from the world their people were again misled into fetishism by the devil's advocates disguised as promoters of faith.

Ibrāhīm ﵇ implored the Lord to bless his descendants with his own spirit

---

1 See the chapter: al-Ṣāffāt (Those who set the Ranks) of the Qur'ān.

2 Jewish legends tell how Abraham went secretly to visit Ishmael in the wilderness (cf. D. Sidersky, *Les Origines des légendes musulmanes dans le Coran et dans les vies des prophètes,* Paris, Geuthner, 1933, pp. 51–53).

3 Qur'ān 2:127–129.

of struggle against the evil of pantheism and iconolatry. He wanted his heirs to carry in their thoughts how he had to strive all his life for the sake of Truth and Faith; how he had to bid farewell to his homeland; realise why he had incurred the wrath of his idolatrous father; and appreciate the wisdom behind his making a selection of that valley, unbelievably bare with no scrap of soil, sheer from top to bottom and jagged and sharp for their habitation.

He ﷺ wanted them to understand why he had preferred that wilderness, holding no prospects of progress and civilisation, over verdant lands and flourishing towns and centres of trade, arts and commerce where one could easily meet one's wishes.

Ibrāhīm ﷺ had invoked the blessings of God on his sons ﷺ so that they might be esteemed and adored by all the nations of the world; that the people of every nation and country might become attached to his children; that they should come from every nook and corner of the world to pay homage to his posterity and thus become a means of satisfying their needs in that barren country.

And when Abraham said:

> My Lord! Make safe this territory, and preserve me and my sons from serving idols.
>
> My Lord! Lo, they have led many men astray. But whoso follows me, he verily is of me. And whoso disobeys me—still You art Forgiving, Merciful.
>
> Our Lord! Lo, I have settled some of my posterity in a barren valley near unto Your holy House, our Lord, that they may establish proper worship; so incline some hearts of men that they may yearn toward them, and provide You them with fruits in order that they may be thankful.[1]

THE QURAYSH

God answered the petitions of Ibrāhīm ﷺ and Ismāʿīl ﷺ. The descendants of Ismāʿīl ﷺ multiplied profusely, so that the barren valley overflowed with the progeny of Ibrāhīm ﷺ. Ismāʿīl ﷺ took for his wife a girl of the tribe of Jurhum,[2] a clan belonging to the *ʿArab ʿĀribah*. Among the lineal descendants of Ismāʿīl ﷺ, ʿAdnān was born whose lineage was universally recognised as the most worthy and noble among them. The Arabs being very particular about the purity of race and blood have always treasured the genealogy of ʿAdnān's progeny in the storehouse of their memory.

1 Qur'ān 14:35–37.

2 The tribe of Jurhum is supposed to be the first tribe which had settled in the valley of Makkah because of the inexhaustible spring of water existing there. There are others who hold that when Ibrāhīm left his wife and son in the valley, the tribe of Jurhum was already there.

ʿAdnān had many sons of whom Maʿadd was the most prominent. Among the sons of Maʿadd, Muḍar was more distinguished; then Fihr ibn Mālik in the lineage of Muḍar achieved eminence; and finally the descendants of Fihr ibn Mālik ibn Muḍar came to be known as Quraysh. Thus came into existence the clan of Quraysh, the nobility of Makkah, whose lineage and exalted position among the tribes of Arabia as well as whose virtues of oratory and eloquence, civility, gallantry and high mindedness were unanimously accepted by all. The recognition accorded to Quraysh without a dissenting voice throughout the Peninsula became, in due course of time, a genuine article of faith to the people of Arabia.[1]

QUṢAYY IBN KILĀB

Quṣayy ibn Kilāb was born in the direct line of Fihr but the hegemony of Makkah had, by that time, passed on from Jurhum's clansmen to the bands of the Khuzāʿites. Quṣayy ibn Kilāb recovered the administration of the Kaʿbah and the town through his organisational capacity and superior qualities of head and heart. The Quraysh strengthened the hands of Quṣayy ibn Kilāb in dislodging the Khuzāʿites from the position of leadership usurped by them. Quṣayy was now master of the town, loved and respected by all. He held the keys of the Kaʿbah and the rights to water the pilgrims from the Well of Zamzam, to feed the pilgrims,[2] to preside at assemblies and to hand out war banners. In his hands lay all the dignities of Makkah and nobody entered the Kaʿbah until he opened it for him. Such was his authority in Makkah during his lifetime that no affair of the Quraysh was decided but by him, and his decisions were followed like a religious law, which could not be violated.

After the death of Quṣayy his sons assumed his authority but ʿAbd Manāf amongst them was more illustrious. His eldest son, Hāshim ibn ʿAbd Manāf, conducted the feeding and watering of the pilgrims, and, after his death, the authority passed on to ʿAbd al-Muṭṭalib, the grandfather of the Prophet ﷺ. His people held him in the highest esteem and the popularity he gained, so they say, went beyond anything that his ancestors enjoyed.[3]

BANŪ HĀSHIM

The progeny of Hāshim now filled the stage and assumed a commanding posi-

---

1 For details see *Sīrat Ibn Hishām* and other works on the genealogy of Arabs.

2 A general feast, known as *Rifādah*, was held every year, to which all the Pilgrims, deemed to be the guests of *Al-Raḥmān*, were invited. The Quraysh contributed a specified sum for it (*al-Khuḍarī*, p. 36).

3 *Ibn Hishām*, vol. I, 'The sons of ʿAdnān.'

tion among the Quraysh like a column of light in the darkness of Arabia. The sketches of Banū Hāshim preserved by the historians and genealogists, although fewer in number, eloquently speak of the nobility of their character and the moderation of their disposition, the reverence they paid to the House of God, their sovereign contempt for the things unjust and uneven, their devotion to fair play and justice, their willingness to help the poor and the oppressed, their magnanimity of heart, their valour and horsemanship, in short, every virtue admired by the Arabs of the pagan past. Banū Hāshim, however, shared the faith of their contemporaries which had beclouded the light of their soul; but despite this failing, they possessed all this goodness as the forefathers of the great Prophet who was to inherit their ennobling qualities and to illustrate them by his own shining example for the guidance of the entire human race.

MAKKAN PAGANISM

Quraysh continued to glorify the Lord of the worlds, from whom all blessings flow, like their forefathers Ibrāhīm ﷺ and Ismāʿīl ﷺ until ʿAmr ibn Luḥayy became the chief of Khuzāʿites. He was the first to deviate from the religion of Ismāʿīl ﷺ; he set up idols in Makkah and had the people worship and venerate them. He instituted the custom of the *sā'ibah*[1] which were to be held in reverence. ʿAmr ibn Luḥayy also corrupted the divine laws of the permissible and the impermissible. It is related that once ʿAmr ibn Luḥayy went from Makkah to Syria on some business where he found the people worshipping idols. He was so impressed by the ways of the idol worshippers that he obtained a few idols from them, brought them back to Makkah and asked the people there to pay divine honours to them.[2]

It might have been so, or, perhaps, on his way to Syria ʿAmr ibn Luḥayy had happened to pass through Betra which was variously known to ancient historians and geographers as Petraea and Petra. It was the key city on the caravan route between Saba' and the Mediterranean, located on an arid plateau three thousand feet high to the south of what is today called Jordan, as mentioned by the Greek and Roman historians. The city was founded by the Nabataeans, ethnically an Arab tribe, in the early part of the sixth century BC. These people car-

1 Bulls dedicated to the idols and not used for any other purpose.

2 Ibn *Hishām,* vol. I, pp. 64–65. It is related that the Prophet once said: I saw ʿAmr ibn Luḥayy dragging his intestines in Hell as he was the first to institute the custom of dedicating beasts to the idols as Sā'ibah (*Bukhārī, Muslim, Aḥmad*). Another Tradition related by Muḥammad ibn Isḥāq says: He was the first to change the religion of Ismāʿīl, to set up idols, and to institute the custom of Sā'ibah as well as introducing innovations in the rituals of the Hajj (*Jamharah Ansāb al-ʿArab,* p.235)

ried their merchandise to Egypt, Syria, the valley of the Euphrates and to Rome. Most likely, they took the way to the valley of the Euphrates through Ḥijāz. The Nabataeans were an idolatrous people who made their deities of graven stones. Some historians hold the view that al-Lāt, the famous deity of the northern Ḥijāz during the pre-Islamic period had been originally imported from Petra and was assigned an honoured place among the local gods and goddesses.[1]

The above view finds confirmation in the *History of Syria* by Philip K. Hitti who writes about the religion of Nabataean kingdoms:

> At the head of the pantheon stood Dushara (dhu al-Shara, Dusara) a sun deity worshipped under the form of an obelisk or an unknown four-cornered black stone. Associated with Dushara was al-lāt, chief goddess of Arabia. Other Nabataean goddesses cited in the inscriptions were Manāt and al-ʿUzzā, of Qur'ānic fame. Hubal also figures in the inscriptions.[2]

It is noteworthy that the above description relates to a period when idolatry had, in different forms and shapes, engulfed Arabia and the countries around it. Jesus Christ and his disciples who later on laboured to restrain its unbridled expansion had not yet appeared on the scene. Judaism had already proved its incompetence in the task, since, being essentially a racial religion, it allowed none save the children of Israel to join his faith to the creed of monotheism preached by it.

Another writer, De Lacy O'Leary, tracing the influences responsible for introduction of idol worship in the Arabian Peninsula sums up his findings in *Arabia Before Muḥammad* in these words:

> It seems fairly safe therefore to understand that the use of images was an instance of Syro-Hellenistic culture which had come down the trade-route; it was a recent introduction in Makkah in the time of the Prophet and was probably unknown to the Arab community at large.[3]

Worship of the idols was thus the popular creed of the people in the valley of the Euphrates and the land to the east of Arabia. As the Arabs were bound, since time immemorial, by the ties of commerce with these countries, it is not unlikely that their cultural influence was responsible for grafting idol worship onto the Arabian Peninsula. In his history of ancient Iraq Georges Roux says that during the third century BC and long thereafter idol-worship was very common

1 The author happened to visit Petra on 14 August 1973, as a member of the delegation of Rābiṭah ʿĀlam-Islāmī, where he saw a large number of idols hewn in the mountains. The details can be seen in another work by the author, *Daryā'i Kābul Se Daryā'i Yarmūk Tak*.

2 Phillip K. Hitti, *History of Syria* (London, 1951), p. 384–55.

3 *Arabia before Muḥammad* (London 1927) pp. 196 97

in Mesopotamia.[1] Every city, old or new, gave shelter to several foreign gods besides the local deities.[2]

There are also reports that suggest that idol worship gradually came into vogue among the Quraysh. In olden times, as some historians relate, anyone going out on a long journey from Makkah would take a few stones from the enclosures of the sanctuary with him as a mark of grace. In due course, they started venerating the monoliths they admired most. The subsequent generations, not knowing the reason for holding such monoliths in esteem, started worshipping them like other pagan people of the surrounding countries.[3] The Quraysh, however, remained attached to some of the older traditions such as paying deference to the holy sanctuary, its circumambulation, *Ḥajj*[4] and *ᶜumrah*.[5] The gradual evolution of different religions showing substitution of means for the ends and the slow progression from suppositions to conclusions lend support to the view put forth by the historians about the beginning of idol worship among the Quraysh. The esteem and reverence in which even certain misguided Muslims sects come to hold the portraits and sepulchres of the saints and the way they sluggishly adopt this course provides incriminating evidence in support of the gradual evolution of idol worship. That is why the Islamic Sharīᶜah completely stalls all those ways and paths that lead to the undue veneration of personages, places and relics for they ultimately lead to ascribing partners to God.[6]

---

1 Georges Roux, *Ancient Iraq* (Suffolk, 1972), pp. 383–84.

2 Ibid, pp. 383–84.

3 In order to know the names of the earliest deities of Arabia and how they came to worship graven images see *Al-Asnām li 'l-Kalbī* and the second part of *Bulūgh al-Arab fī Maᶜrifat Aḥwāl al-ᶜArab* by Sayyid Maḥmūd Shukrī al-Ālūsī.

4 The pilgrimage to Makkah performed in the month of Dhū 'l Ḥijjah, the twelfth month of the Islamic year. The pilgrimage to Makkah performed in the month of Dhū 'l Ḥijjah, the twelfth month of the Islamic year.

5 The lesser pilgrimage to the holy sanctuary performed at any time other then the occasion of *Ḥajj*.

6 The Sharīᶜah as well as the authentic Sunnah of the Prophet contain innumerable injunctions showing disproval of pagan-like superstition savouring of *shirk* or plurality of deities. Some of the well-known traditions of the Prophet on the subject say: "Do not make my grave a place of mirth and festivity nor hold fair over it," "Only with the intention of paying a visit to the three Mosques is one permitted to make a journey," "Never praise me in the way Christians extol Jesus, son of Mary." There are many more similar traditions prohibiting *shirk*. And for the same reason the making of portraits of living things is forbidden. In the past, many a people had taken to idol worship through venerating the portraits or the images of their saints. Ibn Kathīr writes in reference to his exegesis of the Qur'anic verse "You shall not leave your gods. . ." (Q71:23), on the authority of Muḥammad ibn Qays, that there were a large number of persons, pious and pure in spirit in the period from Adam to Noah, who had a large number of followers. After these men of God had departed from the world, their followers had the made portraits which they thought would keep their memory alive and help them in concentration during prayers. Those who came after this

THE ELEPHANTS

It was during this period that a significant event, unparalleled in the history of Arabia, came to pass which foreshadowed something of crucial importance likely to take place in the near future. It augured well for the Arabs, in general, and indicated a unique honour for the Kaʿbah, never attained by any place of worship anywhere in the world. It afforded hope for a great future for the Kaʿbah—a future on which depended the destiny of religions or rather all of humanity since it was soon to unfold itself in the shape of an eternal message of righteousness and peace.

AN IMPLICIT BELIEF OF THE QURAYSH

Quraysh had always held the belief that the *Bayt Allāh* or the House of God had a special place of honour in the eyes of the Lord who was Himself its protector and defender. The trust placed by Quraysh in the inviolability of the Kaʿbah is amply borne out by the conversation between Abrahah and ʿAbd al-Muṭṭalib. It so happened that Abrahah seized two hundred camels belonging to ʿAbd al-Muṭṭalib, who, then, called upon him and sought permission to see Abrahah. Abrahah treated ʿAbd al-Muṭṭalib with the greatest respect and rose from his throne to make him sit by his side. Asked to tell the purpose of his visit, ʿAbd al-Muṭṭalib replied that he wanted the King to return his two hundred camels which the King had taken.

Abrahah, taken by surprise, asked ʿAbd al-Muṭṭalib, "You wish to talk about your two hundred camels taken by me, but you say nothing about the House on which your religion and the religion of your forefather depends, which I have come to destroy?" ʿAbd al-Muṭṭalib boldly replied, "I am the owner of the camels and the House has an Owner who will Himself defend it." Abrahah said again, "How can it be saved from me?" "This is a matter between you and Him", replied ʿAbd al-Muṭṭalib.[1]

Who would dare to do harm or cast a blighting glance at the House of God? Its protection was, in truth, the responsibility of God.

The episode, briefly, was that Abrahah al-Ashram, who was the viceroy of Negus, the King of Abyssinia, in Yemen built an imposing cathedral in Ṣanʿāʾ and gave it the name of al-Qullays. He intended to divert the Arab's pilgrimage to this cathedral. Being a Christian, Abrahah had found it intolerably offensive

---

generation were misled by the devil in thinking that their forefathers paid divine honours to these images that helped to bring rain to them. Thus, they gradually fell to idol worship.

1 *Ibn Hishām*, vol. I, pp. 49–50.

that the Kaʿbah should remain the great national shrine, attracting crowds of pilgrims from almost every Arabian clan. He desired that his cathedral should replace the Kaʿbah as the most sacred place of worship in Arabia.

This was, however, something inglorious for the Arabs. Veneration of the Kaʿbah was a settled disposition with the Arabs: they neither equated any other place of worship with the Kaʿbah nor would they have exchanged it with anything however precious. The perturbation caused by the declared intentions of Abrahah set them on fire. Some Kinānite dare-devils accepted the challenge and one of them defiled the cathedral by defaecating in it. Now, this caused a serious uproar. Abrahah was enraged and he swore that he would not rest until he had destroyed the Kaʿbah.

Abrahah took the road to Makkah at the head of a strong force which included a large number of elephants. The Arabs had heard astounding stories about elephants. The news made them all confused and bewildered. Some of the Arab tribes even tried to obstruct the progress of Abrahah's army, but they soon realised that it was beyond their power to measure swords with him. Now, hoping against hope, they left the matter to God; putting their trust in Him to save the sacred sanctuary.[1]

The Quraysh took to the hills and craggy gorges in order to save themselves from the excesses of Abrahah's soldiers. ʿAbd al-Muṭṭalib and a few other persons belonging to Quraysh took hold of the door of the Kaʿbah, praying and imploring God to help them ʿagainst Abrahah. On the other side, Abrahah drew up his troops to enter the town and got his elephant "Maḥmūd" ready for attack. On his way to the city, the elephant knelt down and refused to get up in spite of a severe beating. But when they turned it towards Yemen, it got up immediately and started off. God then sent upon them a flock of birds, each carrying stones in their claws. Everyone who was hit by these stones died. The Abyssinians thereupon withdrew in fright by the way they had come, continually being hit by the stones and falling dead on their way. Abrahah, too, was badly smitten, and when his soldiers tried to take him back, his limbs fell one by one, until he

1 It is just possible that Abrahah might have had a deeper objective than the avowed purpose of avenging upon the Kaʿbah a sacrilege committed by an individual. He may have intended to gain control over Makkah so that he might be able to strengthen Christianity in Arabia by opening the road on which depended the contact between Yemen and Syria. That move would have been beneficial both to the Byzantium and Abyssinia, for both were Christian kingdoms. Whatever the reason might have been, the objective of Abrahah could not have been achieved without removing the national temple of the Arabs, which was destined to become the last centre of prophethood. And, therefore, God willed it otherwise. It is also possible that the Byzantines encouraged Abrahah to conquer Makkah since this would have weakened the influence of Sāsānids who were their only serious rivals in Arabia.

met a miserable end upon reaching Ṣanʿāʾ.[1] The incident finds a reference in the Qur'ān also:

> Have you not seen how your Lord dealt with the owners of the Elephant? Did He not bring their stratagem to naught? And send against them swarms of flying creatures, that pelted them with stones of baked clay, and made them like green crops devoured (by cattle)?[2]

REPERCUSSION OF ABRAHAH'S FAILURE

When God turned back the Abyssinians from Makkah, crushed and humbled, and inflicted His punishment upon them, the Arabs, naturally, looked up to the Quraysh in great respect. They said: "Verily, these are the people of God. God defeated their enemy—and they did not even have to fight the assailants." The esteem of the people for the Kaʿbah naturally increased, strengthening their conviction in its sanctity.[3]

It was undoubtedly a miracle, a sign of the advent of a Prophet who was to cleanse the Kaʿbah of its contamination of idols. It was an indication that the honour of the Kaʿbah was to rise with the final dispensation to be brought by him. One could say that the incident foretold the advent of the great Prophet.

This great event was a landmark event for Arabs, and rightly so. They instituted a new calendar from the date of its occurrence. Accordingly, we find in their writings such references as that a certain event took place in the year of Elephant or that such and such persons were born in that year or that a certain incident came to pass so many years after the Year of Elephant. This miraculous year was 570 AD.

Five years had not elapsed since the Year of the Elephant but Allāh had swept away the Abyssinians; their rule no longer had any influence in the land of Yemen. Thus in one sweep the Arabian Peninsula was free of Christian influence and its colonisation by Abyssinia. With it approached 'the establishment of the Arabian State/nation' as summed up by Jamāl Surūr; "A national movement was established in the state of Ḥimyar to liberate Yemen from the rule of Abyssinia. Sayf Ibn Dhī Yazan sought aid from the Persian king who extended an envoy in the year 575 AD which was headed by Wahraz. Under his leadership the Abyssinians were defeated in Yemen."[4]

---

1 *Ibn Hishām*, vol.1, pp. 43–57.

2 Qur'ān 105:1–5.

3 *Ibn Hishām*, vol.1, p. 57.

4 *Qiyām ad-Dawlah al-ʿArabiyyah*, p.28, Jamāl Surūr.

5
Makkah, The Prophet's Birth Place ﷺ

The Metropolis

THOSE UNFAMILIAR WITH the conditions in Makkah at the time of the Prophet's birth ﷺ or with the social life, history, legends, literature and poetry of Arabia during pre-Islamic times might imagine Makkah to have been a hamlet with a few tents of goat's hair scattered hither and thither, surrounded by sheep, horses and camels, and half-clad women and children, within a narrow valley flanked by sharp, jagged hill-tops. They perhaps view the people as ignoble and beggarly, passing through a stage of cultural and intellectual infancy, having no aesthetic sense, polish and refinement; a people who would subsist on a diet of stale bread and half-baked mutton and wore clothes made of camel's hair.

Such a poor and miserable depiction of Makkah is inconsistent with the unmistaken landscape of the city emerging from historical records, collections of pre-Islamic poetry, habits and customs, norms and traditions of the Arabs. The people of Makkah had already been drawn into the stream of urban culture from the earlier rural, nomadic existence.

To tell the truth, such a vile and mean view of Makkah is not in keeping with the Qur'ānic description of the city, which gives it the name of "the mother of towns."

And thus we have inspired in you a Lecture in Arabic, that you may warn the

> mother-town and those around it, and may warn of a day of assembling whereof there is no doubt. A host will be in the Garden and a host of them in the Flame.[1]

At another place Makkah is designated as the "land made safe."

> By the fig and the olive, by Mount Sinai and by this land made safe.[2]

And, the Qur'ān also calls it a city.

> Nay I swear by this city, And you are a resident of this city.[3]

Makkah had, as a matter of fact, already passed from nomadic barbarism to the stage of urban civilisation by the middle of the fifth century. The city was ruled by a confederacy based on mutual co-operation, unity of purpose and a general consensus on the division of administrative and civil functions between self-governing clans, and this system had been brought into existence by Quṣayy ibn Kilāb. Prophet Muḥammad ﷺ being fifth in the line of succession to Quṣayy ibn Kilāb, means that the latter can be placed somewhere in the middle of the fifth century.

Makkah, thinly populated in the beginning, was located between the two hills called Jabl Abū Qubays (adjacent to Mount Ṣafā) and Jabl Aḥmar, known as Aʿraf during the pre-Islamic days, opposite the valley of *Quʿayqiʿān*. The population of the town increased gradually owing partly to the reverence paid to the Kaʿbah and the esteemed position of its priests and attendants, and partly because of the peace prevailing in the vicinity of the sanctuary. The tents and shacks had given place to houses made of mud and stones and the habitation had spread over the hillocks and low-lying valleys around the Kaʿbah. At the outset the people living in Makkah abstained from constructing even their housetops in a rectangular shape like the Kaʿbah since they considered it to be a sign of disrespect to the House of God, but gradually those ideas changed. Still, they kept the height of their houses lower than that of the Kaʿbah. As related by certain persons, the houses were initially made in a circular shape as a mark of respect to the Kaʿbah. The first rectangular house, reported to have been built by Ḥumayd ibn Zuhayr, was looked upon with disfavour by the Quraysh.

The chiefs and other well-to-do persons among the Quraysh usually built their houses of stones and had many rooms in them, with two doors on the opposite sides, so that the womenfolk were not inconvenienced by the presence of guests.

---

1 Qur'ān 42:7.

2 Qur'ān 95:1–3.

3 Qur'ān 90:1–2.

RECONSTRUCTION OF MAKKAH

Quṣayy ibn Kilāb had played a leading role in the reconstruction and expansion of Makkah. The Quraysh who had been dispersed over a wide area, and he brought them together in the valley of Makkah. He allocated areas for the various families to settle into and encouraged them to construct their houses in the specified localities. The successors of Quṣayy continued to consolidate the living quarters and to allocate spare lands to new families coming into Makkah. The process continued peacefully for a long time with the result that the habitations of the Quraysh and their confederate clans grew, making Makkah a flourishing city.

THE CITY STATE

Qusayy ibn Kilāb and his family had assumed a commanding position over the city and its inhabitants. They were the caretakers of the Kaʿbah, had the privilege of *Siqāyah*[1] or watering the pilgrims and arranging the annual feast, presided over the meetings of the House of Assembly *(Dār an-Nadwah)* and handed out war banners.

Quṣayy ibn Kilāb had built the House of Assembly close to the Kaʿbah with one of its doors leading to the sanctuary. It was used both as a living quarter by Qusayy and the meeting place for discussing all matters of common wealth by the Quraysh. No man or woman got married, no discussion on any important matter was held, no declaration of war was made and no sheet of cloth was cast on the 'head'[2] of any girl reaching marriageable age except in this house. Quṣayy's authority during his life and after his death was deemed sacrosanct in the vein of religious injunctions which could not be violated by anybody. The meetings of the House of Assembly could be attended only by the Quraysh and their confederate tribesmen, that is, those belonging to Hāshim, Umayyah, Makhzūm, Jumaḥ, Sahm, Taym, ʿAdī, Asad, Nawfal and Zuhrah, whatever their age, while people of other tribes above the age of forty years were allowed to participate in its meetings.

After the death of Quṣayy, the offices he had held were divided between different families. Banū Hāshim were given the right of watering the pilgrims; the standard of Quraysh called ʿUqab[3] went to Banū Umayyah; Banū Nawfal were

1 Water supplied to the pilgrims was stored in tanks especially constructed for the purpose; the water was sweetened by mixing in dates and raisins.

2 A large piece of cloth with an opening cut through it, in which the girl could put through her head, placed over her to signify her betrothal.

3 Lit. "eagle".

allocated the *Rifādah*[1]; Banū ʿAbd ad-Dār were assigned priesthood, wardenship of the Kaʿbah and the standard of war; and Banū Asad had charge of the House of Assembly. These families of the Quraysh used to entrust these responsibilities to the notable persons belonging to their families. Thus, Abū Bakr ﷺ, who came from Banū Taym, was responsible for releasing blood money, fines and gratuity; Khālid ﷺ of Banū Makhzūm held charge of the apparatus of war kept in a tent during peace-time and on the horseback during battles; ʿUmar ibn al-Khattāb ﷺ was sent as the envoy of Quraysh to other tribes with whom they intended to measure swords or where a tribe bragging of its superiority wanted the issue to be decided by a duel; Safwān ibn ʿUmayyah ﷺ of Banū Jumaḥ played at the dice[2] which was deemed essential before undertaking any important task; and, Ḥārith ibn Qays ﷺ was charged with performing all administrative business besides being the custodian of offerings to the idols kept in the Kaʿbah. The duties allocated to these persons were hereditary offices held formerly by their forefathers.

COMMERCIAL OPERATIONS

The Quraysh of Makkah used to fit out two commercial caravans: one to Syria during the summer and the other to Yemen during the winter season. The four months of *Ḥajj*, that is, Rajab, Dhū ʾl-Qaʿdah, Dhū ʾl-Ḥijjah and Muḥarram, were deemed sacred during which it was not lawful to engage in hostilities. During these months the precincts of the holy temple and the open place besides it were utilised as a trade centre where people from distant places would gather to transact business. Everything the Arabs required was easily available in this market of Makkah. The stores for the sale of various commodities were located in designated lanes and byways, as mentioned by the historians, indicating the economic and cultural growth of Makkah. The perfume vendors had their stalls in a separate lane as were the fruit-sellers, barbers, grocers, vendors of fresh dates and other wares and trades, each localised in different alleys. A number of these markets were spacious, for example the grain market was well-stocked with wheat, ghee (clarified butter), honey and the like. All these articles were brought by trading caravans. To cite an instance, wheat was brought to Makkah from Yamāmah.[3] Similarly, cloth and shoe stores had separate quarters allocated to them in the market.

---

1 A tax paid by Quraysh from their property at the time of their providing food to the pilgrim, *Al-Khuḍrī*, p. 36.

2 Dice marked "yes" and "no" on either side were thrown to decide whether any important task was to be undertaken or not. It was known as *al-aysar-wa ʾl-azlam*.

3 When Thumamah ibn Athal (the Chief of Banū Ḥanīfah) embraced Islam, he put a ban on the

Makkah also had a few meeting places where carefree young men used to come together for diversion and leisure. Those who were prosperous and accustomed to live well spent the winter in Makkah and the summer in Ṭā'if. There were even some smart young men known for their costly and trim dress, which would amount to several hundred dirhams.

Makkah was the centre of a lucrative trade, transacting business on a large scale. Its merchants sent caravans to different countries in Asia and Africa and imported almost all necessities and costly wares marketable in Arabia. They usually brought resin, ivory, gold and ebony from Africa; hide, myrrh, frankincense, spices, sandal-wood and saffron from Yemen; various oils and grains, armour, silk and wines from Egypt and Syria; cloth from Iraq; and gold, tin, precious stones and ivory from India. The wealthy merchants of Makkah sometimes presented the products of their city, of which the most valued were leather products, to the kings and nobles of other countries. When Quraysh sent ʿAbdullāh ibn Abī Rabīʿah and ʿAmr ibn al-ʿĀṣ to Abyssinia to bring back the Muslim fugitives, they sent with them leather goods of Makkah as gifts to Negus and his generals.

Women also took part in commercial undertakings and fitted out their own caravans bound for Syria and other countries. Khadījah bint Khuwaylid ﷺ and Ḥanzaliya, mother of Abū Jahl, were two merchant women of dignity and wealth. The following verse of the Qur'ān attests the freedom of women to ply a trade.

> Unto men a fortune from that which they have earned, and unto women a fortune from that which they have earned. [1]

Like other advanced nations of that age, the commercially minded citizens of Makkah had based their economy on commerce for which they sent out caravans in different directions, organised stock markets and created favourable conditions in the home market for the visiting tourists and traders. This helped to increase the fame and dignity of Makkah as a religious centre and contributed in no mean measure to the prosperity of the city. Everything required by the people of Makkah, whether a necessity or a luxury, reached their hands because of the city's commercial importance. This fact finds a reference in these verses of the Qur'ān:

> So let them worship the Lord of this House, Who has fed them against hunger, And has made them safe from fear.[2]

---

export of wheat to Makkah. The Quraysh found this so irksome that they had to make a request to the Prophet, at whose intervention, Thumāmah raised the ban. *Zād al Ma'ād*, vol 1, p.377; Muslim also relates the same in his *Ṣaḥīḥ*.

1 Qur'ān 4:32.

2 Qur'ān 106:3–5.

ECONOMIC CONDITIONS, WEIGHTS AND MEASURES

Makkah was thus the chief centre of big business in Arabia and its citizens were prosperous and wealthy. The caravan of Quraysh, involved in the battle of Badr while returning from Syria, consisted of a thousand camels and carried merchandise worth 50,000 dīnārs.[1]

Both the Byzantine and Sasanian currencies, known as dirham and dīnār were in general use in Makkah and other parts of the Peninsula. The dirham was of two kinds: one of it was an Iranian coin known to the Arabs as *baghliyyah* and *Sardā dāmiyyah,* and the other was a Byzantine coin (Greek-drachma) which was called *tabriyyah* and *Bīzanṭiyyah.* These were silver coins and therefore instead of using them as units of coinage, the Arabs reckoned their values according to their weights. The standard weight of a dirham, according to the scholars of Islamic *sharīʿah,* was equal to fifty-five grains of barley and ten dirhams were equivalent in weight to seven *mithqāls* of gold. One *mithqāl* of pure gold was, however, according to Ibn Khaldūn, equal to the weight of seventy-two grains of barley. The legal scholars unanimously agree with the weight standard of Ibn Khaldūn.

The coins in current use during the time of the Prophet ﷺ were generally silver coins. ʿAtā' states that the coins in general use during the period were not gold but silver coins.[2] The dīnār was a gold coin familiar to the Arabs as the Roman (Byzantine) coin in circulation in Syria and Ḥijāz during the pre-Islamic and early Islamic period. It was minted in Byzantium with the image and name of the Emperor impressed on it as stated by Ibn ʿAbd al-Barr in the *At-Tamhīd.* Old Arabic manuscripts mention the Latin *denarius aureus* as the Byzantine coin (synonymous with the post-Constantine *solidus*) which is stated to be the name of a coin that was still a unit of currency in the former Yugoslavia. The New Testament, too, mentions *denarius* in several places. The dīnār was considered to have the average weight of one *mithqāl,* which, as stated above, was equivalent to seventy-two grains of barley. It is generally believed that the weight standard of the dīnār was maintained from pre-Islamic days down to the 4th century of the Hijra. The *Dāʾirat al-Maʿārif al-Islāmiyyah* says that the Byzantine *denarius* weighed 425/455 grams and hence, according to the Orientalist Zambawar, the *mithqāl* of Makkah was also of 425/455 grams.[3] The ratio of weight between dirham and dīnār was 7:10 and the former weighed seven-tenth

1 Stabo once saw an Arabian caravan arriving at Petra and likened it to an army (*Arabia Before Muhammad,* p. 185).

2 Ibn Abī Shaybah, *al-Muṣannaf,* vol. 3, p. 333.

3 Vol. IX, p. 270; art. Dīnār.

of a *mithqāl*. The caliph 'Abdul Mālik b. Marwān ﷺ reduced the mithqal during his reign to 425 grams.

The par value of the dīnār, deduced from the ḥadīth, *fiqh*,[1] and historical literature, was equivalent to ten dirhams. ʿAmr ibn Shuʿayb ﷺ, as quoted in the *Sunan* of Abū Dāwūd ﷺ, relates: "Blood money during the time of the Prophet ﷺ was 800 dīnārs or 8,000 dirhams, which the Companions of the Prophet ﷺ followed, and the entire Muslim community unanimously agreed to retain it." Authentic ḥadīths fix the *niṣāb* or the amount of property upon which *zakāt*[2] is due, in terms of dirham, at 20 dīnārs. This rule upheld by a consensus of the doctors of law goes to show that during the earlier period of the Islamic era and even before it, a dīnār was deemed to have a par value of ten dirhams or other coins equivalent to them.

Imām Mālik says in the *Muwaṭṭa'* that 'the accepted rule, without any difference of opinion, is that *zakāt* is due on 20 dīnārs or 200 dirhams'.[3]

The weights and measures in general use in those days were *ṣāʿ*, *mudd*, *riṭl*, *ūqiyah* and *mithqāl* to which a few more were added later on. The Arabs also possessed knowledge of arithmetic, for it is evident that the Qur'ān relied on their ability to compute the shares of the legatees in promulgating the Islamic law of inheritance.

PROSPEROUS FAMILIES OF QURAYSH

Banū Umayyah, and Banū Makhzūm were the two prominent families of the Quraysh favoured by abundance of wealth, prosperity and comfort living. Walīd ibn al-Mughīrah, 'Abd al-ʿUzzā (Abū Lahab), Abū ʿUḥayḥah ibn Saʿīd ibn al-ʿĀs ibn Umayyah (who had a share of 30,000 dīnārs in the caravan of Abū Sufyān) and 'Abd ibn Abī Rabīʿah al-Makhzūmī had made good fortunes. 'Abdullāh ibn Jadʿān of Banū Taym was also one of the wealthiest persons of Makkah; he used to drink water in a cup of gold and maintained a public kitchen for providing food to every poor person and beggar. 'Abbās ibn 'Abd al-Muṭṭalib was another man abounding in riches who spent lavishly on the indigent and the needy and lent money at interest in Makkah. During his farewell Pilgrimage when the Apostle ﷺ abolished usurious transactions, he declared: 'The first usury I abol-

1 Dogmatic theology or the science of law covering devotional ritual, private conduct and dealing; as well as the civil and criminal law of Islam.

2 Lit. 'purification', hence a specified portion of property one is obliged to give over either privately or to the State as alms, for the sanctification of the remainder.

3 *Bulūgh al-Arab fī Maʿrifat Aḥwāl al-'Arab* by Ālūsī, *At-Tartīb al-Idāriyyah* by 'Abd al-Ḥayy al-Kattāni, *Fiqh az-Zakāt* by Yūsuf al-Qarḍāwī and *Tafsīr Mājidī* by 'Abd al-Mājid Daryabādi.

ish today is that of ʿAbbās ibn ʿAbd al-Muṭṭalib.' Makkah had also men rolling in riches whose well-furnished drawing rooms were the rendezvous of the elite of the Quraysh who rejoiced in the pleasures of wine, love and romance.

The chiefs of Quraysh usually had their sittings in front of the Kaʿbah in which prominent poets of pre-Islamic days, such as Labīd, recited their poems. It was here that ʿAbd al-Muṭṭalib used to have his gatherings and, as they say, his sons dared not take their seats around him until their father had arrived.

CULTURE AND ARTS

The Quraysh looked down upon the Industrial arts and crafts, considering it beneath their dignity to engage in handiwork. Manual occupations were regarded as tasks reserved for slaves or non-Arabs. Notwithstanding this prejudice of the Quraysh, certain crafts were a dire necessity and some would practise them. Khabbāb ibn al-Aratt is reported to have engaged in manufacturing swords. Construction activities were also indispensable but the Quraysh would employ Iranian and Byzantine workmen to do the job for them.

A few men in Makkah knew the art of reading and writing but the Arabs, as a whole, were ignorant of the way by which learning is imparted. The Qur'ān also calls them *Ummī*[1] or an unlettered people[2]:

> He it is Who has sent among the unlettered ones a messenger of their own.[3]

The people of Makkah were, however not unsophisticated. Their refined taste, polish and culture made them excel in all Arabia in the same way the townsmen of any metropolis occupy a distinctive place in their country.

The language spoken in Makkah was regarded as a model of unapproachable excellence. The Makkan dialect set the standard which the desert Bedouins as well as the Arabs of outlying areas strived to imitate. By virtue of their elegant expression and eloquence, the inhabitants of Makkah were considered to possess the finest tongue, uncorrupted by the grossness of the languages of non-Arabs. In their physical features, shapeliness and good looks, the people of Makkah were considered to be the best representatives of the Arab race. They were also endowed with the virtues of courage and magnanimity of heart, acclaimed

1 Lit. "the unlettered", also a title of the Prophet. For a detailed discussion of the subject see the article "Was Muḥammad Literate?" by Moḥyī 'd-Dīn Ahmad in *Islam and the Modern Age,* vol. VIII, No. 2 (May 1977).

2 Balādhurī lists 17 individuals who alone knew how to read and write in Makkah *(Futūḥ al-Buldān,* Leidan, pp. 471–472.

3 Qur'ān 62:2

by the Arabs as *al-futūwwaḥ* (chivalry) and *al-murū'ah* (manliness), the two oft-repeated themes of Arab poetry. These traits of their character admirably describe their recklessness which savoured both of a devil and a saint.

The matters that attracted their attention most were genealogy, legends of Arabia, poetry, astrology and planetary mansions, ominous flight of the birds and a little of medication. As expert horsemen, they possessed an intimate knowledge of the horse and preserved the memory of the purest breed; and as dwellers of the desert they were well versed in the delicate art of physiognomy. Their therapy, based partly on their own experience and partly on the traditional methods handed down to them from their forefathers, consisted of branding, phlebotomy, removal of diseased limbs and the use of certain herbs.

MILITARY PROWESS

The Quraysh were by nature or nurture, a peace-loving people, amiable in disposition; for, unlike all other peoples inside and outside the Peninsula, their prosperity depended on the development of free trade, continual movement of caravans, improvement of market facilities in their own city and maintenance of conditions peaceful enough to encourage merchants and pilgrims to bend their steps to Makkah. They were sufficiently farsighted to recognise that their mercantile business was their life: trade was the source of their livelihood as well as the means to increase their prestige as servants of the sanctuary. The Qur'ān has also referred to the fact in *Sūrah Quraysh*:

> So let them worship the Lord of this House, who hath fed them against hunger and hath made them safe from fear.[1]

In other words, they were inclined to avoid a struggle unless their tribal or religious honour was in peril. They were thus committed to the principle of peaceful coexistence; nevertheless, they possessed considerable military prowess. Their courage and intrepidity was as renowned throughout Arabia as was their skill in horsemanship. *Al-Ghaḍbah Muḍarriyyah* or "the wrath of the Muḍar," which was described as a tormenting thirst quenched by nothing save blood, was a well known adage in the Arabic language frequently used by the poets and orators of pre-Islamic Arabia.

The military prowess of Quraysh was not restricted to their own tribal reserves alone. They utilised the services of *Aḥābīsh* or the desert Arabs living around Makkah, some of whom traced their descent to Kinānah and Khuzaymah ibn Mudrikah, distant relations of Quraysh. The Khuzāʿah were also

---

1 Qur'ān 106:3–5.

confederates of the Quraysh. In addition, Makkah had always had slaves in considerable numbers who were ever willing to fight for their masters. They could thus draft, at any time, several thousand warriors under their banner. In the battle of Aḥzāb, Quraysh enlisted the strongest force ever mustered in the pre-Islamic era, numbering ten thousand combatants.

MAKKAH, THE HEART OF ARABIA

By virtue of its position as the seat of the national shrine and its flourishing commercial centre with cultured inhabitants, Makkah had secured a pre-eminent position in Arabia. It was considered a rival of Ṣanʿāʾ in Yemen, but with the Abyssinians and Iranians gaining control over Ṣanʿā, one after another, and the decline of the earlier glamour of Ḥīrah and Ghassān, Makkah had attained a place of undisputed supremacy in Arabia.

THE MORAL LIFE

A moral ideal was what the Makkans lacked most of all, or one can say, except for the binding force of some stale customs and traditional sentiments of Arab chivalry, they had no code of ethics to guide their conduct. Gambling was a favourite pastime in which they took pride, unrestrained drunkenness sent them into rapturous delight and immoderate dissipation satisfied their perverted sense of honour. Their gatherings were the scenes of drinking bouts and wanton debauchery. Without any idea of sin or crime, they never gained an aversion to wickedness, iniquity, callousness and brigandage.

The moral atmosphere of Arabia in general, and of Makkah in particular, was faithfully depicted by Jaʿfar ibn Abī Ṭālib ﷺ, a prominent member of the Quraysh, at the court of Negus when he said to him: "O King we were an unenlightened people plunged in ignorance. We worshipped idols, we ate carrion, and we committed abominations; we broke natural ties, we ill-treated our neighbours and our strong devoured the weak."[1]

RELIGIOUS LIFE

The religious practices and beliefs of the Arabs were, beyond doubt, even more despicable, particularly, by reason of the influence they exerted on the social and moral life of the people. Having lost all but little touch with the wholesome teachings of the prophets of old, they had been completely submerged in the

---

1 *Ibn Hishām*, vol.1, p. 335.

crude and materialistic form of fetishism like that prevailing in the countries surrounding them. So fond had they become of idol worship that no less than three hundred and sixty deities adorned, or rather defiled, the holy sanctuary. The greatest amongst these gods was Hubal whom Abū Sufyān ؓ had extolled at the battle of Uḥud when he cried out: "Glory be to Hubal!" The idol occupied a central place in the Kaʿbah, by the side of a well in which the offerings were stored. Sculptured in the shape of a man, it was made of a huge cornelian rock. As its right hand was missing when Quraysh discovered it, they had replaced it by a handmade of solid gold. Two idols had been placed in front of the Kaʿbah. One was called Isāf and the other Nā'ilah; the former had been installed close to the Kaʿbah and the latter by the site of Zamzam. After sometime the Quraysh shifted the first one closer the other, where they offered up sacrifices besides them. On the mounts of Ṣafā and Marwah, there were two more idols called Nahīk Mujāwid ar-Rīḥ and Muṭʿim aṭ-Ṭayr.

Every household in Makkah had an idol which they would worship. Al-ʿUzzā had been installed near ʿArafāt within a temple constructed for it. Quraysh venerated al-ʿUzzā as the chief or the noblest of all deities. The Arabs would cast lots with the help of divining arrows placed before these idols for taking a decision to commence any affair. There were also other idols. One, named al-Khalṣah, had been set up in the depression of Makkah's valley. This idol was garlanded, presented an offering of barley and wheat and bathed with milk. The Arabs used to make sacrifices and hang ostrich eggs over it. Replicas of this popular deity were sold by vendors to the villagers and pilgrims visiting Makkah.

The Arabs possessed the virtues of courage, loyalty and generosity, but during the long night of superstition and ignorance, worship of images and idols had stolen into their hearts, perhaps, more firmly than any in other nation; and they had wandered far away from the simple faith of their ancestors Ibrāhīm ؑ and Ismāʿīl ؑ which had once taught them the true meaning of religious piety, purity of morals and seemliness of conduct.

So, this was the city of Makkah, by the middle of the sixth century of the Christian era, before the birth of the Prophet ﷺ, whence we see Islam rising on a horizon shrouded in obscure darkness. In truth, the Lord has said:

> That you may warn a people whose fathers were not warned, so they are heedless.[1]

---

1 Qur'ān 36:6. Beside ḥadīth and *tafsīr*, help has also been taken in writing this section from *Kitāb al-Aṣnām l i'l-Kalabī* (d.1464 A.H.) *Sīrat Ibn Hishām* (d.213 A.H.) *Akhbār Makkah* by Imām Abū 'l-Walīd Muḥammad al-Azraqī (d.223 A.H.), *Bulūgh al-Arab fī Maʿrifat Aḥwāl al-ʿArab* by Sayyid Maḥmūd Shukrī al-Ālūsī (d.1342 A.H.), *Tārīkh Makkah* by Aḥmad Sabāʿī and *Makkah wa 'l-Madīna fī 'l-Jāhiliyya wa ʿAhd ar-Rasūl* by Ibrāhīm al-Sharīf.

6

From Birth to Prophethood

ʿAbdullāh and Āminah

Abd al-Muṭṭalib, a chieftain of the Quraysh, had ten sons, all of whom were worthy and outstanding, but ʿAbdullāh was the noblest and most prominent amongst his brothers.[1] ʿAbd al-Muṭṭalib married him to Āminah, the daughter of Wahb ibn ʿAbd Manāf, who was the leading man of Banū Zuhrah. She was the most excellent woman among the Quraysh in birth and position at that time.[2]

Muḥammad ﷺ was born after the death of his father (who fell ill while travelling back from Shām, Syria and consequently passed away in the city of his maternal family, Yathrib at the age of twenty five). Before his birth, Āminah witnessed many an omen portending a great future for her son.[3]

Birth of the Prophet ﷺ

The Prophet ﷺ was born on Monday, the 12th of Rabīʿ al-Awwal[4] in the year of the Elephant. In point of fact, it was the most auspicious day in the history of mankind.

Thus, Muḥammad ﷺ was the son of ʿAbdullāh son of ʿAbd al-Muṭṭalib, son of

1 *Ibn. Hishām,* vol. 1, p. 108.

2 Ibid., p. 110.

3 Ibid., p. 158.

4 Noted astronomer Maḥmūd Pāshā of Egypt has computed the date of birth as Monday, the 9th of Rabīʿ al-Awwal, in the year of Elephant which was, according to the Gregorian calendar, the 20th April, 571 AD.

Hāshim, son of ʿAbd Manāf, son of Quṣayy, son of Kilāb, son of Murrah, son of Kaʿb, son of Lu'ayy, son of Ghālib, son of Fihr, son of Mālik, son of al-Naḍr, son of Kinānah, son of Khuzaymah, son of Mudrikah, son of Ilyās, son of Muḍar, son of Nizār, son of Maʿadd, son of ʿAdnān.

The parentage of ʿAdnān is further traced to Ismāʿīl ibn Ibrāhīm[1] by Arab genealogists. After the birth of Muḥammad ﷺ Āminah sent to inform his grandfather. He came, looked at the baby lovingly and took him to the Kaʿbah where he praised[2] Allāh and prayed for the baby. ʿAbd al-Muṭṭalib named him Muḥammad, meaning 'He who is Praised'. The Arabs were surprised at the unfamiliar name[3] that ʿAbd al-Muṭṭalib had given to the new-born.

THE SUCKLING PERIOD

Thuwaybah, a bondswoman of the Prophet's uncle ﷺ Abū Lahab suckled him for a few days while ʿAbd al-Muṭṭalib continued to look for a wet nurse for his favourite grandson. It was customary in Makkah to place suckling babies in the care of a desert tribe, where the child would grow up in the free, chivalrous air away from the cramped, contaminating atmosphere of the city, and learn the wholesome ways of the Bedouins. Those were the days when the chaste, unaffected expression of the desert people was considered the finest model of grace and elegance of the Arabic language. Together with the milk of a Bedouin woman, the babies drank the fluent language that permeated the desert.

The people of the tribe of Banū Saʿd were known for the gracefulness of their speech. Ḥalīmah Saʿdiyyah[4], belonging to this tribe, ultimately came to take the precious baby under her wings. This was a year of famine when Banū Saʿd had been made destitute. The tribe came to Makkah to look for children to be suckled but none of their women would take the Apostle of God ﷺ because none expected a goodly return for nursing a child whose father was already dead.

1 *Ibn Hishām*, pp. 1–2 and other books of history and genealogy give the undisputed pedigree of the Prophet.

2 *Ibn Hishām*, pp. 159–60

3 *Ibn Kathīr*, vol. I, p. 210; *Ibn Hishām*, vol. I, p.158. Suhaylī's *al-Rawḍ al-Unuf* and *al-Fuṣūl* of Ibn Fawrak bear witness that only three persons in the entire history of Arabia had been called by the name of Muḥammad during the pre-Islamic period. They had been given this name since their parents had heard from the Jews and the Christians that a new Prophet was to be born in the near future and that his name would be Muḥammad. These persons whose wives were pregnant, had taken an oath that if a male child was born to their wives, they would give the child the name that they had heard—it might have been so, as related in the old traditions, or there might have been a few more persons, as related by others, but the matter needs investigation before reaching any firm conclusions.

4 Her genealogy goes back to Saʿd b. Bakr b. Hawazin—she is the daughter of Abī Dhuayb and her husband was al-Ḥārith b. ʿAbdul ʿIzza.

They said, 'An orphan! What will his mother and grandfather give in return?' At first Ḥalīmah ﷺ also declined the offer but suddenly she felt a longing for the baby. She had also failed to find a charge for herself and, therefore, before departing for her home, she returned and took the baby back with her. Before long, Ḥalīmah ﷺ found that her household was blessed with good fortune: her breasts overflowed with milk, the udders of her she-camel were full and everything seemed to bring forth happiness. The women of Ḥalīmah's tribe now let out the murmur: "Ḥalīmah, you have certainly got a blessed child,' and began to feel envious of her.

Ḥalīmah weaned the baby when he was two years old, for it was customary for the foster-children to return to their families at that age. The boy was also growing faster than other children and by the time he was two, he was a hearty child. Thus, Ḥalīmah brought the Apostle of God ﷺ back to Āminah but begged to be allowed to keep the boy for yet some time as he had brought her good fortune. Āminah agreed and allowed Ḥalīmah to take Muḥammad ﷺ back with her."[1]

Some months after his return to Banū Saᶜd two angels seized the Apostle of God ﷺ, opened up his belly and extracted a black globule from it. Then they thoroughly cleaned his heart and healed the wound after returning his heart in its place.[2]

The Apostle of God ﷺ tended the lambs with his foster-brothers in the vast wilderness of the desert—far away from the pretensions, pomp and pride of the city—where his thoughts became plain and clear like the desert air. His life was simple like the sand and he learnt to put up with the hardships and dangers of the wilderness. And, with the people of Banū Saᶜd, his ears became accustomed to the verbalism of the pure and classical language of the Bedouins. The Prophet ﷺ often used to tell his Companions: 'I am the most Arab of you all. I am of Quraysh, and I was suckled among Banū Saᶜd ibn Bakr.'[3]

---

1 The interesting story of the period, as told by Ḥalīmah, has been preserved by Ibn Hishām, pp. 162–166.

2 The detailed account of the story can be seen in the biographies of the Prophet. Imām Muslim relates the incident on the authority of Anas ibn Mālik under the heading 'Ascent of the Prophet' in his *Kitāb al-Īmān.* Shāh Walī Allāh of Delhi (d. 1176/1762) writes in *Hujjat Allāh al-Bālighah* that the angels appeared and opened the heart of the Prophet to fill it with faith and wisdom. He further says that this incident pertains to a state in between the World of Similitude and the Sensorial World, or, in that state there would neither be any harm done by the opening of the belly nor any visible effect of it would remain there. Such things happen according to the Shāh Walī Allāh, where the World of Similitude and Senses come close to one another (*Hujjat Allāh al-Bālighah,* vol. II, p. 205).

3 *Ibn Hishām,* vol I, p. 167.

DEATH OF ĀMINAH AND ʿABD AL-MUṬṬALIB

When the Apostle ﷺ was six years old his mother took him to Yathrib to pay a visit to her father. She also wanted to call on the grave of her late husband,[1] but while on her way back to Makkah, she died at a place called Abwāʾ.[2] The Apostle ﷺ must have felt lonely and grief-stricken at the death of his mother in the middle of his journey. Incidents of a like nature had come to pass ever since his birth, perhaps, by way of divine dispensation for his up-bringing in a particular way. An Abyssinian bondswoman, Umm Ayman Barakah, brought him to his grandfather in Makkah.

ʿAbd al-Muṭṭalib loved the Apostle ﷺ dearly, he was the apple of his eye and never allowed him to be away from him. He would make the Apostle ﷺ sit beside him on his couch in the shade of the Kaʿbah and caress him to show his affection.

When the Apostle ﷺ was eight years of age, ʿAbd al-Muṭṭalib also passed away.[3] The Apostle ﷺ was now left behind, alone and abandoned. He had never seen his father, and would have had no recollection of him, and the death of the adoring grandfather must have been disheartening and devastating for him.

ABŪ ṬĀLIB BECOMES THE GUARDIAN

After the death of ʿAbd al-Muṭṭalib, Abū Ṭālib took the Apostle ﷺ under his care, for he and ʿAbdullāh, the Apostle's father ﷺ, were brothers by the same mother. ʿAbd al-Muṭṭalib had also insisted that Abū Ṭālib take care of the Apostle ﷺ. Accordingly, Abū Ṭālib took the Apostle ﷺ under his protection and treated him with more care and affection than his own sons, ʿAlī, Jaʿfar and ʿAqīl[4] ﷻ.

Once, when the Apostle ﷺ was nine years old,[5] Abū Ṭālib planned to go with a merchant caravan to Syria. The Apostle ﷺ approached his uncle, and nestling close to him, insisted on accompanying him in the journey. Abū Ṭālib agreed to take him to Syria. When the caravan reached Buṣrā in Syria, it broke the journey for a short stay near the cell of a monk called Baḥīrā. Against his usual practice, he came out to welcome the merchants and made a great feast for them.

---

1 Later on the Prophet used to relate some of the incidents of his journey with his mother. After his migration to Madīnah, when the Apostle saw the house of Banū an-Najjār, he remarked that his mother had bivouacked at that place and the well there was full of husks (*Sharḥ al-Mawāhib al-Ladunniyyah,* vol I, pp. 167–8).

2 The place is near Mastūra, halfway between Makkah and Madīnah.

3 *Ibn Hishām,* vol. I, pp. 168–9.

4 *Ibn Hishām,* vol. I, p. 179.

5 As related in authentic traditions.

The caravan found favour with Baḥīrā, so they relate, because of something he had seen while in his cell. When Baḥīrā saw the Apostle of God ﷺ, he satisfied himself of the signs of apostleship he had known and advised Abū Ṭālib: 'Return to your home with this youth, and guard him from the Jews; for great dignity awaits your nephew'. Abū Ṭālib followed his advice and took the Apostle ﷺ off quickly to Makkah.[1]

---

1 The incident has been related in some detail by Ibn Hishām and other biographers of the Prophet, but the authorities doubt the correctness of the report, both on account of the weak chain of narrators as well as the circumstantial evidence cited in its support. Shiblī Nuʿmānī writes in the *Sīrat an-Nabī* that 'all the narratives of the story file under the category of intersected ḥadīth since the Companions relating it from others do not give the name of the original narrator'. The famous traditionist Tirmidhī says that one of the narrators of this happening is ʿAbd ar-Raḥmān ibn Ghazwān who has been held to be an unreliable narrator. He further classifies the ḥadīth as *ḥasan gharīb* and this as the only chain through which it is related. Dhahabī holds the view that ʿAbd ar-Raḥmān ibn Ghazwān is the narrator of the largest number of spurious Traditions and the most unreliable amongst those related by him is the story relating to the monk, Baḥīrā.It has been stated in most of the traditions on the subject that Abū Ṭālib sent the Apostle back to Makkah with Bilāl. Drawing attention to this version of the story, as related in *Tirmidhī* and other collections, Ibn al-Qayyim writes in the *Zād al-Maʿād* that Bilāl was perhaps not present on the occasion and even if he were there, Abū Ṭālib would not have sent the Apostle back even with Abū Bakr or with one of his own brothers (*Zād al-Maʿād*, vol. I, p. 18).Certain Orientalists and European biographers of the Prophet have made a mountain out of a molehill and tried to show that during this brief sojourn of the Prophet with Baḥīrā,, (about whose life, Christian denomination or leaning, we possess little or rather no information at all) the former learnt all about monotheistic belief and the teaching of Islam which he later unfolded after a spell of 30 years. It is even more amusing to see the flight of imagination of the French Orientalist Carra de Veaux, who has written a whole book called *the author of the Qur'ān* in which he has tried to prove that in a few minutes Baḥīrā dictated all 114 chapters of the Qur'ān to the Prophet. Supposing that the incident relating to the Prophet's meeting with Baḥīrā were correct, who, in his right mind would be prepared to accept that a boy whose age was only nine at that time, according to the most authentic traditions, or, twelve, at the most, was able to learn, in a meeting as brief as a single meal, all about those intricate problems, inexplicable intricacies, differences and corollaries of the abstruse creeds of the sixth century Christian heretical sects which were not adequately discussed even by the later reformers of Christianity. Such a supposition would be blatantly absurd, so far, we know, the language spoken by the monk was different, and most probably, incomprehensible to the boy. What is more, how could the monk have told about the events that were to happen in the opening decades of the seventh century (603–606CE), that is, thirty or forty years after his death, by which time his bones would have turned to dust. There are more than a few such events: the triumphant advance of the Persian armies and the retreat of the Byzantines to their capital until it seemed to be the end of the great Eastern Roman Empire; the phenomenal rise of Heraclius, his brilliant victories which carried his arms to the very centre of the Persian Empire, and his avenging the outrages of consecrated monasteries and churches. All this came to pass within a brief period of nine years as told in the Qur'ān:The Romans have been defeated in the near land, and they, after their defeat, will be victorious—within ten years. Allāh's is the command in the former and in the latter, and on that day believers will rejoice (30:2–4).Such a prophecy could never have been made by anyone save by God, praised be His name, who is the Living, the Powerful, the Mighty, the Omniscient; who makes the day to pass into the night and the night into the day and who brings forth the living from the dead and the dead from the living. When this prophecy was made there was nothing more inconceivable than its fulfilment. At the time when the pagan Quraysh were rejoicing at the defeat suffered by the believing Christian's the Qur'ān announced that after their defeat the Romans will be victorious. It even

DIVINE TUTELAGE

The Heavenly Host had made special arrangements for enlarging the mind of the holy Prophet ﷺ and taken particular care to shut out the faults and failings of the pagan past from him. From early youth, the unobtrusive young man was known for his gentle disposition and the austere purity of his life as well as his candour, honesty and integrity and the stern sense of duty. His was the straight and narrow path and none could find the slightest fault with him. The fair character and honourable bearing of the Apostle ﷺ won for him from his fellow citizens and in the flower of his youth, the title of *al-Amīn,* the Trustworthy.[1]

Evil were the ways of young men in Makkah, and no misdemeanour brought anybody into disgrace. But God helped His Apostle ﷺ to abandon the pleasures of life familiar to everybody in Makkah. On the contrary, he was kind to his kinsmen alleviated the sufferings of others and spared no expense to meet their needs, entertained guests, was ever willing to join hands with anybody in a noble and virtuous task,[2] and liked to earn his living by his labour although it meant living a life simple to the point of austerity.

When the Apostle ﷺ was fourteen or fifteen years of age, the sacrilegious war, known as the *Ḥarb al-Fijār,* broke out between Quraysh and the tribe of Qays. The Apostle ﷺ was present at these encounters and picked up the arrows that the enemy had shot and gave them back to the fighters of Quraysh. This was

---

fixed the time—within ten years they were to emerge triumphantly. The Quraysh thought the prophecy so impossible some of them even wagered on it. But, the events took a miraculous turn and the prophecy was fulfilled in such an unexpected manner in the second year of Hijrah, when the Muslims won the battle of Badr, that Gibbon, the celebrated historian of the Roman Empire, had to admit that:. . .the languid mists of the morning and evening are separated by the brightness of meridian sun: the Arcadins of the palace arose the Caesar of the camp; and the honour of Rome and Heraclius was gloriously retrieved by the exploits and trophies of six adventurous campaigns (vol. V, p. 76).This was not the solitary future event mentioned in the Qur'ān. Signal victory was promised after the truce of Ḥudaybiyyah which was considered shameful for the Muslims by friends and the foes alike (49:18). It was foretold that they would enter the religion of Allāh in troops (110:2). The victory of Islam over other faiths was predicted at a time when eyes had grown wild and hearts had reached the throats (33:11), and the assurance was given to keep the Qur'ānic text unchanged and pure forever (41:42). No man could have predicted that countless persons would ever continue to study, expound and commit the Qur'ān to their memory. In fact, the Qur'ān refers to many more astounding facts and predictions which could not have been foretold by the monk Baḥīrā. All this goes to show that only he clutches at straws whose prejudice blinds him to the truth. We would have neither mentioned this incident here nor Carra de Veaux's flight of imagination if the story told in some of the earlier biographies of the Prophet of Islam had not given rise to wild conjecture by Western writers, whose fictions of the mind cannot perhaps be adequately rewarded with anything else save the Nobel Prize in literature.

1 *Ibn Hishām,* vol. I, p. 183.

2 Khadījah, the Prophet's wife, referred to these qualities of her husband when she found him perplexed after the first revelation came to him.

his first military experience in which he learnt horsemanship and futūwa (the praised quality of chivalry).[1]

Now that the Apostle ﷺ was coming into his years of discretion he turned his attention to finding a means of livelihood. Like other young men of his age, he took to tending sheep and goats. It was not deemed a disgraceful occupation in those days; rather, it taught one watchfulness, alertness and quickened the responses; kindness and consideration to the weak, patience in leading the herd and besides, it provided an opportunity to inhale the freedom of the Arabian air and gain physical strength. More than that, it had been the custom of all the prophets of old, and this prepared him for his future prophetic office. The Prophet ﷺ afterwards used to say: 'Verily, there has been no prophet who has not tended the flocks of goats.' On being asked again whether he had also performed the work of a shepherd, the Prophet ﷺ affirmed, 'Yes, I did work.'

The Apostle ﷺ was not completely new to the job for in his childhood days he would accompany his foster-brothers who tended their flocks and herds. The reports in the *Ṣiḥāḥ* show that the Apostle ﷺ would tend the goats on the neighbouring hills and valleys for a meagre payment from the owners of the flocks.[2]

MARRIAGE WITH KHADĪJAH

The Apostle ﷺ married Khadījah ؓ when he was twenty-five years of age. Khadījah ؓ, daughter of Khuwaylid was noble and intelligent, possessed wealth and was respected for the goodness of her heart. A widow whose age was then forty years.[3] Her late husband was Abū Hālah. She carried on business and like other merchants of Makkah she would hire men to carry her merchandise outside the country on a profit-sharing basis. Khadījah ؓ had experienced the Apostle's truthfulness ﷺ, trustworthiness and honourable character and had also heard about his immense integrity during his journey. Although Khadījah ؓ had turned down several offers for her hand by some of the eminent chiefs of Quraysh she expressed her desire to marry the Apostle ﷺ. Ḥamzah ؓ, an uncle of the Apostle ﷺ, conveyed the message to him to which he readily agreed. Abū

1 *Ibn Hishām* vol. I. p. 186.

2 The Arabic term used is *qarārīt* about which Shiblī Nuʿmānī writes in the *Sīrat an-Nabī,*(vol. I), that scholars differ about the meaning of the word. Suwayd ibn Saʿīd, the teacher of Ibn Mājah, holds that a *qīrāt* (pl. *qarārīt)* is a fraction of dirham *or* dīnār. The tradition means that the Prophet would tend goats for payment and hence Bukhārī has included it under the Chapter pertaining to wages. The finding of Ibrāhīm al-Ḥarbī, on the other hand, is that the word signifies a place near al-Ajyād and Ibn al-Jawzī prefers this meaning. ʿAynī has also given many reasons to support the view and the author of *Nūr an-Nibrās* has, after a detailed discussion of the word, upheld the latter view.

3 *ıbn Hishām,* vol. I, pp. 189–90.

Ṭālib recited the wedding sermon and the Apostle ﷺ united in wedlock with Khadījah ؓ. All the children of the Prophet ﷺ (excepting Ibrāhīm who died in infancy) were born to Khadījah ؓ.[1]

RECONSTRUCTION OF THE KAʿBAH

In his thirty-fifth year, the Apostle ﷺ settled a grave quandary that threatened to plunge Quraysh into another sacrilegious war. The Quraysh wished to rebuild the Kaʿbah and to roof it, for it was made of loose stones, and its walls were a little higher than a man's height. So, the walls were demolished and the work of reconstruction taken up[2], but when it was rebuilt as far as the position of the Black Stone, the question arose as to who should place the sacred relic into its place. Every tribe claimed the honour, until such that they were ready for battle. The grounds which led to war of attrition during the days of pagan past in Arabia were often trivial, when compared to the grave issue which was made the point of honour on this occasion.

Banū ʿAbd ad-Dār brought a bowl full of blood; then they and Banū ʿAdī pledged themselves to fight unto death by thrusting their hands into the blood. The conflict appeared to be the starting point of a furious struggle that might have swallowed up all of Arabia in another of their oft-recurring wars. The impasse continued for a few days until it was agreed that the next man to enter the gate of the mosque would be made arbiter in the matter in dispute. The first man to enter was the Apostle of God ﷺ. 'This is Muḥammad', they said as soon as they saw him coming, 'He is trustworthy and we are satisfied with his decision.'

The Prophet ﷺ asked them to bring a cloth. Then he took the Black Stone and put it inside it, and asked each tribe to take hold of an end of the cloth and lift it to the required height. When the people lifted the stone in this manner, the Apostle ﷺ placed it in its position with his own hands, and building continued above it.[3] The wisdom displayed by the Apostle ﷺ on this occasion, which saved the Quraysh from measuring swords with one another, strikingly illustrates his sound judgement and the fire of his genius. The sagacity of the Prophet ﷺ foretold how he was later to save humanity from perpetual strife and bloodshed as the divine harbinger of peace. The incident foreshadowed the signs of the Apostle's prudence ﷺ, the profundity of his teachings, his consideration and

---

1 *ıbn Hishām,* vol. I, p. 190, and other biographies of the Prophet.

2 Mūsa b. ʿAqabah said: Quraysh had decided to rebuild the Kaʿbah after fearing that water from a drain pipe would enter it, so they demolished it. However a man among them pointed out that a thief could gain access to the treasures of the Kaʿbah and so they desired to strengthen its walls and raise its door so no crook could gain access. See *At-Tafḍīl fī ʿUyūn al-Athār* of Ibn Sayyīd an-Nās, vol I, p.25.

3 *Ibn Hishām,* vol. I, pp. 192–197

sweet temper, and the spirit of his friendliness and altruism; in fact, the cardinal virtues of one who was to become the 'Mercy for the Worlds'.

These were the qualities through which the Apostle ﷺ transformed a people, unruly and ferocious, continuously at war amongst themselves, into a well-knit fraternity by proving himself a Merciful Prophet ﷺ for them.

ḤILF AL-FUḌŪL

It was during this period that Quraysh came to agree upon one of the noblest covenants in which the Apostle ﷺ played a prominent part. It so happened that a man from Zabīdī[1] came to sell his merchandise in Makkah. One of the chieftains of Quraysh, al-ʿĀs ibn Wā'il, acquired the lot of it but paid nothing in return. Zabīdī approached several influential leaders of Quraysh but none agreed to pick a quarrel with ʿĀṣ ibn Wā'il. Now, Zabīdī called upon the people of Makkah exhorting every bold and fair-minded young man to come to his rescue. At last, many of them, put to shame, assembled in the house of ʿAbdullāh ibn Judʿān who entertained the people coming to his house. Then, they formed a pact, in the name of Allāh, to repress the acts of lawlessness and restore justice to the weak and the oppressed within the walls of Makkah. The covenant was called *Ḥilf al-Fuḍūl.* The parties to the pact approached ʿĀs ibn Wā'il and forced him to return the merchandise of Zabīdī.[2]

According to historians familiar with the customs of the Arabs and in particular of Makkah, the religious and cultural centre of the Arabian Peninsula, the motive for the formation of the pact was not simply the result of this one incident or the injustices committed against a few individuals. Rather it was the outcome of a deep anxiety at the anarchy and sense of suspicion that had taken hold of Makkah and its surroundings. Consequently there was a huge need for security and stability (particularly after *Ḥarb al-Fijār*), the safeguarding of rights and dignity of others as well as protecting the strangers and dignitaries who came to Makkah for trade.[3]

The Apostle ﷺ had been one of the prominent promoters of the pact and he

---

1 A town in Yemen.

2 *Ibn Hishām,* vol. I, pp. 257–59.

3 According to some, the Quraysh named the covenant the pact of *fuḍūl* because three of its prominent members all bore the name faḍl; al-Faḍl b. al-Faḍālah, al-Faḍl b. Widā'ah and al-Faḍl b. Hārith as indicated by Ibn Qutaybah. Others have named them as al-Faḍl b. Sharrā'ah, al-Faḍl b. Biḍā'ah and al-Faḍl b. Qaḍā'ah (p.113). Another opinion is that it was called the pact of *fuḍūl* because its members had taken up an allegiance of virtue (or *faḍl*). Ibn Sayyid an-Nās quotes in his book, '*ʿUyūn al-Athar fī funūn al-Maghāzī wa as-Shamāʿil wa as-Sir*' that the Apostle (peace be upon him) was twenty years of age at the time of the covenant, which took place in Dhul Qaʿdah after *Ḥarb al-Fijār*', (vol. 1, p.46).

use to always express his satisfaction with the execution of this agreement. Once he remarked: 'I had a hand in making such a pact in the house of ʿAbdullāh ibn Judʿān to which if I were invited to have a hand in it even after the advent of Islam, I would undoubtedly join again. They had agreed to restore to everyone that which was his due and to protect the weak from the arrogance of the oppressors.'

A MYSTIFYING UNREST

Muḥammad ﷺ was now approaching his fortieth year. He felt a mystifying internal unrest, yet he did not know the reason for it. He was himself not aware what the inexplicable perplexity meant to him; nor did the idea that God was about to honour him with revelation and Prophethood ever cross his mind. This was how the Prophet ﷺ felt, as has been attested by God:

> And thus have We inspired in you (Muḥammad) a Spirit of Our Command. You knew not what the Scripture was, nor what the Faith. But We have made it a light whereby We guide whom We Will of Our bondmen. And Lo! You verily do guide unto a right path.[1]

At another place, the inability of the Apostle ﷺ to know the reason for his internal unrest is evinced in these words:

> You had no hope that the Scripture would be inspired in you; but it is a mercy from your Lord, so never be a helper to the disbelievers.[2]

It pleased the Will of God, All-wise and All-knowing, that His Apostle ﷺ should remain a stranger to the arts of reading and writing. His contemporaries could thus never accuse him of fabricating the divine revelations. This, too, has been addressed by the Qur'ān to settle the matter.

> And you (O Muḥammad) were not a reader of any Scripture before it, nor did you write it with your right hand, for then might those have doubted, who follow falsehood.[3]

That is why the Qur'ān calls him an unlettered Prophet ﷺ.

> Those who follow the messenger, the Prophet who can neither read nor write, whom they will find described in the Torah and the Gospel (which are) with them.[4]

---

1 Qur'ān 42:52.
2 Qur'ān 28:86.
3 Qur'ān 29:48.
4 Qur'ān 7:157

7
The Dawn of Prophethood

Humanity's Morningtide

When the Apostle ﷺ reached his fortieth year, the world stood on the brink of an abyss of fire, or, to be more exact, one could say that the entire human race was bent upon self destruction. It was at this darkest moment in the history of mankind, when the first blush of the fragrant breath of morn announced a brightening future for humanity. The opening eyelids of prophethood rang down the curtain on the dark destiny of the unfortunate, dying world. The settled law of the Merciful God is that when the darkness of man's own doing drives him to despair, a star of hope appears again as the parent of faith, of hope and cheerfulness, to wipe away his tears.

The forces of darkness and ignorance, superstition and paganism had thrown their weight around the world and crushed the soul of man under an iron heel. It was but natural that the emptiness of life and the corrupt faith of the people around the Apostle ﷺ had made him agitated and restless, and he sought a higher aim, a glimmer of guidance from the Lord Most High. It seemed as though some celestial voice summoned him to wakeful nights in preparation for the great responsibility about to be thrust upon him. Often he was seen wandering through the countryside, far away from the bustling city of Makkah, lost in introspection and the solitude of his own soul, for this imparted in him a sense of peace and contentment. Often he betook himself to the barren desert and the wild mountains that had many caverns where no habitation was in sight and when he passed through them he clearly heard the salutation: 'Peace unto you,

O Apostle of Allāh', but when he turned to his right and left and looked behind him he saw naught but trees and stones.[1] The first signs of his prophethood were true dreams, he never dreamt a dream but the truth of it shone forth like the dawn of the morning.[2]

IN THE CAVE OF ḤIRĀ'

Very often the Apostle ﷺ preferred the solitude of the cave of Ḥirā' where he remained for as many days as the provisions with him sufficed, spending his nights in vigils and prayers, in the manner he thought resembled the way of Ibrāhīm ﷺ.[3]

It was the 17th of Ramaḍān (6th August, 610 AD) of the year following the fortieth year of the Prophet ﷺ.[4] The Apostle of God ﷺ was wide-awake and fully conscious when the angel Gabriel came to him and said, 'Read!' The Apostle ﷺ answered truthfully, 'I cannot read'. The Prophet ﷺ relates that the angel took hold of him and pressed him until he was distressed, after which he let him go and said again, 'Read!' The Prophet ﷺ replied for the second time, 'I cannot read', he took him and pressed tightly a third time in the same manner. He then let the Prophet ﷺ go and said:

> Read in the name of thy Lord who createth, Createth man from a clot. Read: and thy Lord is the Most Bounteous: Who teacheth by the pen, Teacheth man that which he knew not.[5]

Indeed this moment marked the first day of his prophethood and these were the first revelations of the Qur'ān.[6]

BACK HOME

He was lefty dizzy and frightened by the strange and unfamiliar experience, he had not heard the like of it before, for it had been a long time since the Arabs

1 *Ibn Hishām*, vol I, pp. 234–5. *Ṣaḥīḥ Muslim* relates a tradition of the Prophet who said: 'I still recognise a slab of stone in Makkah that used to salute me before the advent of Prophethood.'

2 *Al-Jāmiʿ as-Sahih* of *al-Bukhārī*, chapter on 'The Commission and the Beginning of the Revelation".

3 See the tradition related by ʿĀ'ishah, *Mishkāt al-Maṣābīḥ*, vol IV, pp. 1252–3.

4 *Ibn Kathīr*, vol I, p. 392.

5 Qur'ān 96: 1–5.

6 It is remarkable that the first revelation mentions the pen in light of the fact that it was sent to an unlettered prophet, who in turn was sent to an unlettered nation. Indeed, it is Islām's emphasis on reading and writing that has propelled Muslims on to achieve intellectual heights previously unknown, or encouraged by any other revealed religion.

were sent any prophecy. The Messenger of God came back with the verses, his heart trembling, and went to Khadījah and said: 'Wrap me up, wrap me up,' for he still felt fear for himself.

Khadījah asked the reason for the Prophet's distress ﷺ and he told her what had passed. Khadījah was intelligent and prudent and had heard a great deal about the messengers of God, prophethood and angels from her cousin Waraqah ibn Nawfal who had embraced Christianity and read the Torah and Gospels. She was herself dissatisfied with the pagan cult of the Makkans like several other enlightened persons who had broken away from the idol worshippers.

Khadījah was the wife of the Prophet ﷺ. She had spent many years with him as his closest companion and knew him intimately. Through this union, Khadījah knew best the noble character of her husband. The worthiness of his moral fibre had convinced her that the Lord's aid would in any case be there for such a man. She was certain that the good grace of God could never suffer one so high-minded, truth-loving, trustworthy and upright as her husband was, to be possessed by a jinn or a devil, and so she assured him with self-confidence: 'By no means! I swear to God that He would never shame you. You join the family ties, you speak the truth, you bear people's burdens, you help the destitute, you entertain guests and you mitigate the pains and grief suffered for the sake of truth.'[1]

THE PREDICTION OF WARAQAH IBN NAWFAL

Khadījah had tried to comfort and encourage her husband on account of what she thought to be correct or on the basis of her own knowledge and understanding. But the matter was serious and pressing. She knew no peace until she had consulted someone knowledgeable of the revealed religions, their history and scriptures, and the life of earlier prophets of God. She wished to know for sure what had befallen her husband.

Khadījah knew that Waraqah ibn Nawfal was the man who could be of help in the matter. She took the Apostle ﷺ to Waraqah and when the Prophet ﷺ told him what he had seen and heard, Waraqah cried out, 'Verily by Him in whose hand is Waraqah's soul, lo, you are the Prophet of this people. There has come unto you the greatest Nāmūs,[2] who came unto Moses before. A time will come when you will be called a liar, your people will mistreat you, cast you out and fight you.' The Apostle ﷺ was surprised to hear Waraqah's forebodings for he had always been received with courtesy and was well regarded by his fel-

1 *Mishkāt al-Maṣābīḥ*, vol. IV, p. 1253.

2 The Archangel Gabriel.

low citizens. They addressed him as the trustworthy and honest. Holding his breath in amazement, he demanded of Waraqah, 'What! Will they expel me?' 'Yes', replied Waraqah, 'for no man has ever brought the like of what you have without being opposed and fought by his people—this has always been so. If I live to see that day, I shall stand by you.'[1]

The Prophet ﷺ waited, day after day, but for a long time no revelation came. Then, it came again to the Apostle ﷺ and so the revelations of the Qur'ān began to come again in quick succession and lasted for a full twenty-three years

KHADĪJAH ACCEPTS ISLAM

Khadījah ؓ, the Apostle's wife ﷺ, was the first believer in the new faith. She had had the opportunity of being his companion and helper, his consort and defender. She stood behind him, consoling and supporting against all those who denied and scorned him. She tried to relieve his apprehensions and to encourage him by placing her trust in him.

ʿALĪ IBN ABĪ ṬĀLIB AND ZAYD IBN ḤĀRITHAH

ʿAlī ibn Abī Ṭālib ؓ was next to enter the fold of Islam. He was then a youth of ten, and had been brought up in the care of the Prophet ﷺ since early childhood. The Apostle ﷺ had taken the charge of ʿAlī ؓ from his uncle, Abū Ṭālib, and kept him as a member of his family after a grievous famine had struck the Quraysh.[2] The third accession to Islam was made with the conversion of Zayd ibn Ḥārith[3] ؓ who was a freedman of the Prophet ﷺ and whom he had adopted as his son.

ABŪ BAKR ACCEPTS ISLAM

The acceptance of the Prophet's ﷺ faith by Abū Bakr ibn Abī Quḥāfah, after Zayd ؓ, was of no mean significance. This merchant of sociable nature was known for his moderation and prudence, good character and kindliness, and enjoyed yet greater reputation for his wide knowledge of the genealogy of Quraysh, and his experience in trade. He began to preach to all those whom he relied upon and who associated with him or came to seek his company, the truth he that had attested to.[4]

---

1 *Ibn Hishām,* vol I, p. 238, *Bukhārī,* 'The Commission and the Beginning of the Revelation' on the authority of ʿĀ'ishah.

2 *Ibn Hishām,* vol. I, p. 245.

3 Ibid., p. 247.

4 Ibid., pp. 249–50.

THE FLOWER OF QURAYSH FIND FAITH

The persuasive businessman began to win over the elite of the Quraysh to place their trust in the mission of the Prophet ﷺ. Those who accepted Islam at the invitation of Abū Bakr ؓ included ʿUthmān ibn ʿAffān, Az-Zubayr ibn al-ʿAwwām, ʿAbd ar-Raḥmān ibn ʿAwf, Saʿd ibn Abī Waqqās and Ṭalḥah ibn ʿUbaydillāh ؓ. Abū Bakr ؓ brought them to the Apostle ﷺ at whose hands they accepted Islam.[1]

Slowly the mission of the Prophet ﷺ was made known to other respectable citizens of Makkah and a number of them joined their faith to Islam. Some of these elect of the Quraysh who came after the first eight were: Abū ʿUbaydāh ibn al-Jarrāh, Al-Arqam ibn Abī 'l-Arqam, ʿUthmān ibn Maẓʿūn, ʿUbaydāh ibn al-Ḥārith ibn ʿAbd al-Muṭṭalib, Saʿīd ibn Zayd, Khabbāb ibn al-Aratt, ʿAbdullāh ibn Masʿūd, ʿAmmār ibn Yāsir, Shuʿayb ibn Sinān and others ؓ.

People now began to accept Islam in large numbers; they came in bands from different tribes and families until the news spread throughout the city and it began to be talked about everywhere that Muḥammad ﷺ taught some new sort of faith.[2]

ON MOUNT ṢAFĀ

Three years had elapsed from the time the Apostle ﷺ had received the first revelation but he had remained a silent preacher. He was now commanded to announce it openly:

> So proclaim that which you art commanded, and withdraw from the idolaters[3]
>
> And warn thy tribe of near kindred, and lower thy wing (in kindness) unto those believers who follow you.[4]
>
> And say: Lo! I, even I, am a plain warner.[5]

It was an order to show himself to the peoples of the world. The Apostle ﷺ ascended the heights of mount Ṣafā and cried aloud: 'Yā Ṣabāḥāh'. The Arabs were already familiar with the call which was meant to summon them to face a surprise attack by the enemy. The alarming call made the whole of Quraysh gather quickly round the Apostle ﷺ while those who were unable to go them-

1 *Ibn Hishām*, pp. 150–51.
2 Ibid., p. 262.
3 Qur'ān 15:94
4 Qur'ān 26:214–15.
5 Qur'ān 15:89.

selves, sent others to deputise for them. Looking down at the men who waited with their eyes strained at him, the Messenger of God said to them:

> O sons of ʿAbd al-Muṭṭalib! O sons of Fihr! O sons of Kaʿb! If I tell you that horsemen were advancing to attack you from the other side of this hill, would you believe me?

The Arabs were practical-minded, possessing a keenly logical outlook that admitted of no ifs or buts. They saw the man whom they had always found, on every occasion, truthful, honest and dependable, standing on the summit, having a full view of both the sides of the hill. They had, on the other hand, the back of the hill concealed from their view. Their intelligence and understanding, their experience with the man addressing them and their own sane and sound thinking led them to one conclusion only. They unanimously replied. 'Oh Yes, we would certainly believe you.'

A COGENT ARGUMENT

The absolute truthfulness and dependability of a messenger of God constitutes the first and the most essential factor for acceptance of his mission. The question posed by the Prophet ﷺ was thus meant to obtain a confirmation of these qualities from his audience. This done, he said to them, 'Well, I am a warner to you before a severe chastisement overtakes you.'

The Prophets of God are endowed with the knowledge of minute realities which are neither perceptible nor can be explained in human parlance. The method the Prophet ﷺ used to convey to them the concept and essence of apostleship was the most incisive and effective possible. This was certainly the easiest as well as the best method to convey the accurate weight and significance of prophethood; the allegorical mode of expressing a profound reality is without parallel in the teachings of any other prophet or founder of religion. Thus in this instance, the Apostle of God ﷺ warned the Quraysh of a far greater enemy than an advancing army. His counsel was against a hidden enemy residing in the souls, of the snare of idolatry and following ones whims above the boundaries set by the Creator and Cherisher of this universe. The words of the Apostle ﷺ so struck Quraysh that they stood silent and still. Abū Lahab eventually had the audacity to exclaim: "May you perish! Is it for this, you have brought us here?"[1]

---

1 Ibn Kathīr's *Asl al-Ḥikayah*, pp. 455–56 as related on the authority of Ibn ʿAbbās and cited from the *Musnad* of Ibn Ḥanbal. Bukhārī and Muslim have also related Traditions with a similar significance from al-Aʿmash.

BEGINNING OF PERSECUTION

The Apostle of God ﷺ preached Islam openly in the streets of Makkah, yet the Quraysh remained cool and indifferent to him; they neither turned against him nor felt any danger to their religion. They did not even care to confute the Prophet ﷺ until he started speaking disparagingly of their gods, when they felt offended and decided to oppose him. Prophet Muḥammad ﷺ would have been at the mercy of the firebrands of the merchants' republic of Makkah, but Abū Ṭālib, the Prophet's uncle ﷺ, continued to treat him kindly and stood up in his defence. And, the Prophet ﷺ, equally determined to strenuously propagate his new faith, continued to call the people to Islam. Nothing could stop the Prophet ﷺ from preaching the commands of his God, and nothing could dissuade Abū Ṭālib to withdraw his protection from the nephew whom he loved more than his sons.

ABŪ ṬĀLIB'S ANXIETY

The Apostle ﷺ was now a much-discussed problem among the Quraysh. They conferred and consulted one another on how to face the danger which the Prophet ﷺ with his sweet tongue represented to them. At last, the leading men of Quraysh approached Abū Ṭālib and said to him, "O Abū Ṭālib, you are old and we hold you in high esteem. We asked you to restrain your nephew but you did nothing. By God, we cannot tolerate any longer that our fathers should be denounced, that we should be called ignoramuses and frivolous and our gods insulted. Either you must stop him or we will fight both of you, until one of us perishes."[1]

The old leader of Makkah remained deep in thought, distressed at the rift with his people and their hostility, but he was not willing to desert his nephew and give him up to his enemies. He sent for the Apostle ﷺ and said, "Son of my brother, your people came to me and threatened me with dire consequences if you continue to preach your religion. Spare my life and yours and do not impose on me a burden greater than I can bear." The Apostle ﷺ thought that his uncle was no longer willing to shield him, intending to give him up. He answered, "O my uncle, by God, if they were to place the sun in my right hand and the moon in my left, and ask me to abandon this course, I would not turn from it until God makes it victorious or I perish therein."

Tears came to the eyes of the Prophet ﷺ. Weeping, he got up to depart. But Abū Ṭālib could not look at his nephew's sorrow. Before he had reached

---

1 *Ibn Hishām*, vol. I, pp. 265–66.

the threshold, Abū Ṭālib cried out, "Come back, my nephew." And when he returned, Abū Ṭālib said, "Go where you please and say what you will. By God, I will never deliver you to your enemies."[1]

PERSECUTION BEGINS

The Apostle ﷺ continued to preach the message of God as vigorously as before. The Makkans were now despaired of forcing Abū Ṭālib to give up Prophet Muḥammad ﷺ and there was nothing that they could do to stop him. Their anger grew and grew. They started inciting the tribes against those who had accepted Islam but were without a protector. Every tribe fell on the Muslims amidst it; beating and putting them in chains, denying them food and water and forcing them to lie on the burning sand in the scorching sun of Arabia.

Bilāl was a slave who had embraced Islam. Umayyah ibn Khalaf, his master, used to bring him out at noon and throw him on his back on the burning sand. He ordered a great rock to be placed on Bilāl's chest and then he would say to him, "No, by God, you will lie here till you die or deny Muḥammad and worship Al-Lāt and Al-ʿUzzā." Bilāl endured the affliction, crying, "One. One."

Abū Bakr saw Bilāl being tortured by his master, and so brought a powerful negro slave, tougher and stronger than Bilāl, to exchange for Bilāl and set him free.[2]

ʿAmmār ibn Yāsir and his parents had accepted Islam. Banū Makhzūm used to take them out in the full glare of the sun at the hottest part of the day and then take them to task for their faith. The Prophet ﷺ would say to them whenever he passed them: "Patience, O family of Yāsir, patience. Your destination is paradise." They endured all kinds of persecutions until ʿAmmār's mother was killed by Banū Makhzūm for she refused to accept anything but Islam.[3]

Musʿab ibn ʿUmayr was the most well dressed young man of Makkah. Muṣʿab's mother, who possessed a handsome fortune, had brought him up in the lap of luxury. He would wear the costliest clothes perfumed with the best scent and always had his shoes imported from Ḥaḍramawt, then famous for manufacturing leather goods. The Apostle ﷺ is reported to have once remarked about him: "I had not seen any young man in Makkah more handsome and more well-dressed or who had been brought up in more ease and comfort than Muṣʿab ibn ʿUmayr." He came to know that the Apostle ﷺ preached a new religion in the house of Arqam. Muṣʿab ibn ʿUmayr's curiosity took him there and he

1 Ibid.

2 *Ibn Hishām*, vol I, pp. 317–18.

3 Ibid. pp. 319–20.

returned a true believer in Islam. He did not, however, declare his faith and kept on meeting the Apostle ﷺ secretly. ʿUthmān ibn Ṭalḥah once saw him performing the prayer and disclosed his secret to his mother and other tribesmen. The result was that he was seized and imprisoned, and remained in fetters until the Muslims first migrated to Abyssinia. When he returned from Abyssinia along with other refugees, he was a completely changed man. His daintiness and elegance had given place to such a rugged simplicity that his mother had to leave him alone instead of rebuking him.[1]

There were others, who, afraid of the violent temper then prevailing against Muslims in Makkah, had sought the protection of their friends who were still polytheists. One of them was ʿUthmān ibn Maẓʿūn ؓ who was under the protection of Walīd ibn al-Mughīrah, but as he felt ashamed of being shielded by anyone other than God, he renounced the protection of Walīd. Shortly thereafter, he had a heated wrangle with an idolater who struck him so hard on his face that he lost an eye. Walīd ibn al-Mughīrah was present on the occasion; he said to ʿUthmān, "By God, O son of my brother, your eye was once secured against this injury and you were well-protected". "Nay, by God," replied ʿUthmān ibn Maẓʿūn ؓ, "The eye that is still unhurt longs for what has happened to the other for God's sake. O ʿAbd ash-Shams, I am here in the vicinity and shelter of One who is exceedingly superior to you in honour and glory."[2]

When ʿUthmān ibn ʿAffān ؓ accepted Islam his uncle Ḥakam ibn Abī 'l-ʿĀs ibn Umayyah tied him securely with a rope and said, "Have you renounced the faith of your fathers for a new religion? By God, I will not release you until you abandon this new belief." ʿUthmān ؓ firmly replied, "By God, I will never renounce it." The firmness of ʿUthmān ؓ in his conviction ultimately led Ḥakam to unshackle him."[3]

Khabbāb ibn al-Aratt ؓ, a companion of the Prophet ﷺ, related his own story: "Some louts of the Quraysh came one day and seized me. Then they kindled a fire and dragged me into it, while a man kept me down by placing his foot on my chest." Khabbāb ؓ then bared his back which had white scars.[4]

ILL-TREATMENT OF THE PROPHET ﷺ BY HIS PEOPLE

The efforts of Quraysh to dissuade the Prophet's Companions ؓ from their religion failed miserably, nor did they succeed in stopping the Prophet ﷺ from

1 *Ṭabaqʿāt Ibn Saʿd*, vol. III, p. 82; *Istīʿāb*, vol. I, p. 288.

2 *Ibn Hishām*, vol. I, pp. 370–71.

3 *Ṭabaqāt Ibn Saʿd*, vol. III, p. 37.

4 *Ṭabaqāt Ibn Saʿd*, vol. III, p. 117.

preaching his religion fearlessly. The Quraysh were first annoyed and agitated, and then dismayed by the growing community of Muslims. They stirred up some louts and riff-raff against the Apostle ﷺ, who raised a hue and cry against him, calling him a liar, a sorcerer, a diviner and a poet; they insulted and abused him and started harassing him on every pretext.

The notables of Makkah assembled one day in the *Ḥijr*[1] when the Prophet ﷺ was suddenly seen coming into the holy sanctuary. As he passed them walking round the Kaʿbah, they sneered at him and made caustic remarks. They gave offence to him similarly for the second and then for the third time he passed by them. Now, the Prophet ﷺ stopped and said, "Will you listen to me, O Quraysh? By Him who holds my life in His hand I bring you a great slaughter." All of them were stupefied by these words; some even addressed him graciously to make amends for their rudeness.

The next day when they had assembled in the *Ḥijr,* the Prophet ﷺ appeared again. The Quraysh, who felt ashamed because of the occurrence the day before, fell upon him as one man. While they mobbed him thus, one of them pulled the sheet of cloth hanging round his neck which nearly choked his throat. Abū Bakr ﷺ, who was present at that moment, thrust himself in between them and the Prophet ﷺ, and with tears in his eyes he cried, "Would you kill a man simply because he says: Allāh is my Lord?" They left the Prophet ﷺ but fell upon Abū Bakr ﷺ dragging him by his hair and beard.

Another time the Apostle ﷺ had to face a far greater ordeal through the course of a whole day. Whoever he met, free or slave, cursed or vilified him or tried to hurt him in some way. He returned to his house and wrapped himself up because of the torments he had to endure that day. Then it was that God revealed to him the opening verses of 'The Enshrouded One': "O you wrapped up in thy cloak, arise and warn."[2]

THE SUFFERING OF ABŪ BAKR

One morning Abū Bakr ﷺ made bold to invite a gathering of the idolaters to the true faith in God and His Apostle ﷺ but they fell upon him furiously and beat him mercilessly. ʿUtbah ibn Rabīʿah inflicted such severe injuries to his face with a pair of shoes that one could not distinguish the eyes from the nose of his swollen face.

---

1 *Ḥijr*, also known as *Ḥijr Ismāʿīl*, is the open space between the Kaʿbah and a semicircular wall to its west, the two extremities of which are in line with the northern and southern sides of the Kaʿbah. The wall bearing the name of Ḥaṭīm was raised to mark the original length of the Kaʿbah because the Quraysh had, while reconstructing it before the advent of Islam, reduced the length owing to lack of funds.

2 *Ibn Hishām,* vol I, pp. 289–91 and *Bukhārī.*

Abū Bakr ﷺ fell unconscious and was taken to his house by Banū Taym, his kinsmen. In a precarious condition, his life hanging by a thread, he regained consciousness late in the afternoon, but the first thing he asked was whether the Prophet ﷺ was well and safe! His relations rebuked him (for his concern for the Prophet ﷺ, on whose account he had to suffer so grievously). Then, hardly raising his voice, he repeated his question to Umm Jamīl ﷺ, who had also accepted Islam. Umm Jamīl ﷺ motioned towards his mother who was standing near her, but Abū Bakr ﷺ insisted on knowing about the Prophet ﷺ, saying that there was no harm in telling him in her presence. At last, Umm Jamīl told him that the Prophet ﷺ was well but Abū Bakr ﷺ would not be satisfied until he had himself seen the Apostle ﷺ. He said, "I have taken a vow that I would not taste any food or drink anything until I have seen the Prophet ﷺ myself." The two women waited until everybody had departed and then they brought Abū Bakr ﷺ to the Prophet ﷺ who was moved to see his pitiable condition. The Prophet ﷺ prayed for his mother and invited her to accept Islam. It is reported that she readily pledged her trust in the Apostle of God ﷺ.[1]

QURAYSH IN A FIX

As the enmity of persecutors increased, so did the number of the Apostle's followers ﷺ. Quraysh were unsure as to how to stop the people taking the Prophet ﷺ and his teachings seriously; how to make them turn a blind eye to him and snub him. Makkah was a commercial centre frequented by tribes from far and near, and during the *Ḥajj,* which was near at hand, more of them were to come again. The people coming to Makkah had somehow to be kept at a distance from the Apostle ﷺ, lest they should hear his sermons and swallow his words. They went to Walīd ibn al-Mughīrah, who was old and a man of standing, to seek his advice. He said, "O people of Quraysh, the time of *Ḥajj* has come round when delegations of the Arabs will come here. They have all heard about this man (the Prophet ﷺ), so agree upon something so that you do not contradict one another and each one of you says the same thing." Different suggestions were put forward but Walīd was not satisfied. At last, he was asked to suggest some way out. He said, "The most convincing thing in my opinion would be that all of you present him as a sorcerer. You should say that he has brought a message by which be creates a rift between father and son, brother falls out from brother, husband parts company with wife and families break up under his influence."

The Quraysh came back agreeing to the stratagem suggested by Walīd. They

1 *Ibn Kathīr* vol. I, pp. 439–41.

sat on different paths, when the time of *Ḥajj* commenced, warning everyone to keep clear of Muḥammad ﷺ, repeating what they had already agreed to tell them.[1]

HEARTLESSNESS OF THE QURAYSH

The persecutors of the Apostle ﷺ were consumed by a rancour that disregarded every consideration of humanity and kinship; their torture was made bitter by the refinements of cruelty; and their demeanour was lax enough to pollute the sacred asylum held as the holiest sanctum by the Arabs.

One day while the Apostle ﷺ was praying at the Kaʿbah a company of Quraysh occupied their places in the sanctuary. ʿUtbah ibn Abī Muʿīt brought the foetus of a camel from somewhere and when the Apostle ﷺ prostrated in prayer, he laid it on his back and shoulders. The Messenger of God remained in prostration until his daughter Fāṭimah ؓ came running and threw it off him. She called down evil upon the man who had done it and the Prophet ﷺ also joined her in the imprecation.[2]

ḤAMZAH ACCEPTS ISLAM

Once Abū Jahl happened to pass by the Prophet ﷺ near Mount Ṣafā. He insulted the Apostle ﷺ and heaped all manner of indignities upon him but the Apostle of God ﷺ did not answer him back. Meanwhile, Ḥamzah ؓ had returned from the chase with his bow hanging by his shoulder. Ḥamzah ؓ was essentially a warrior, the bravest and the most courageous amongst Quraysh. A slave woman belonging to ʿAbdullāh ibn Jadʿān told him what had happened to his nephew. Ḥamzah ؓ angrily turned back to the holy Mosque where Abū Jahl was sitting with his friends. Going straight to Abū Jahl, Ḥamzah ؓ proceeded to strike his bow upon his head, saying, "Dare you insult and abuse him when I follow his religion and say what he says?" Abū Jahl kept quiet while Ḥamzah ؓ, returning to his nephew, declared himself a convert to Islam. The Quraysh were put to a great loss by the conversion of a man of unquestionable character and legendary courage.[3]

1 *Ibn Hishām*, vol. 1, p. 270.

2 *Bukhārī*, chapter titled, 'Anecdotes on What the Apostle and his Companions Endured in the Hands of the Polythesists of Makkah'.

3 *Ibn Hishām*, vol. I, pp. 291–92.

PROPOSAL OF ʿUTBAH TO THE PROPHET ﷺ

The number of the Prophet's followers ﷺ increased day by day threatening to turn the tide against Quraysh; they felt the situation highly embarrassing but were unable to do anything to stem the tide of Islam. ʿUtbah ibn Rabīʿah, the old and wise patrician of Quraysh realised that he must find a way to patch up the differences with the Apostle ﷺ. He consulted Quraysh to make some concessions to the Apostle ﷺ so that he might give up his mission. The Quraysh thought it to be a workable proposition and allowed him to negotiate with the Prophet ﷺ on their behalf.

ʿUtbah went to the Apostle ﷺ and sat by his side. He said, "O my nephew, you know the worthy position you enjoy among us. But you have created a rift in your people by ridiculing them, insulting their gods as well as their religion, declaring their forefathers heathens and denying their customs. Now, listen to me, I will make some suggestions, haply you may find one of these acceptable."

"O Abū 'l-Walīd,"[1] replied the Prophet ﷺ, "go on, I am listening." ʿUtbah continued, "My nephew, if you wish to profit from what you preach, we will collect enough that you will be the richest of us; if you desire honour, we will make you our chief and leave every decision to your choice; if you aspire to kingship, we will recognise you as our monarch; and if you are possessed of a ghost or a jinn of which you have no remedy, we will find a skilful physician for you and spend our wealth lavishly until your health is completely restored."

The Apostle ﷺ listened patiently. When ʿUtbah had finished, he asked, "Is it all that you have to say?"

"Yes," replied ʿUtbah.

"Now listen to me," said the Prophet ﷺ, "In the name of God, the Compassionate, the Merciful. . ." and he continued to recite *Sūrah* Fuṣṣilat,[2] ending the recitation at a place of prostration.[3] When ʿUtbah heard the revelation, he listened with rapt attention, putting his hands behind him and leaning on them. The recitation ended, the Prophet ﷺ prostrated and then said to ʿUtbah, "Abū 'l-Walīd, you have heard what you have heard, now it is for you to decide."

When Quraysh saw ʿUtbah returning, they said; "I swear by God, he comes with an altered expression on his face." And, when he came near they asked him what had happened.

"I have heard a discourse the like of which I have never heard before. I swear,

1 Father of Walīd.

2 Surah 41: "They are expounded".

3 Verse 37.

by God, O Quraysh, that it is neither poetry, nor spells, nor witchcraft. Take my advice and let this man be."

The Quraysh reviled ʿUtbah, and said, "You have been bewitched by his tongue."

This is my opinion," replied ʿUtbah, "Now you may do whatever you see fit."[1]

MUSLIMS MIGRATE TO ABYSSINIA

The Apostle ﷺ saw his followers stand their ground in spite of persecutions, and his heart was laden with grief. And since he could do nothing to protect them, he advised them to migrate to the country of the Christian ruler, Negus of Abyssinia, who was known to be just and kind-hearted. It was a friendly country, said the Apostle ﷺ, where the Muslims could remain until such time as God relieved them of their distress.

Thereupon a group of Muslims left Makkah for Abyssinia, a total of ten men and four women among them; this was the first migration in the history of Islam. ʿUthmān ibn Maẓʿūn ؓ was elected leader of this first group of emigrants, who included the Apostle's daughter ؓ Ruqayyiah and her husband ʿUthmān b. ʿAffān ؓ. After them Jaʿfar ibn Abī Ṭālib ؓ departed from Makkah, then a number of Muslims withdrew, one after another. Some went alone, others took their families with them. A total of eighty-three persons ؓ are reported to have fled to Abyssinia.[2]

Fleeing the persecution of Quraysh was not the sole objective but that it also provided an opportunity to spread the message of Islām, and lessen the fears of the Apostle ﷺ for his Companions. Indeed, the amalgam of both rich and poor, young and old, man and woman of these first emigrants portrays the power of Islām to overcome social divides and thereby highlights its universal and inclusive message.

QURAYSH PURSUE THE MUSLIMS

The news that the Muslims were living in peace in Abyssinia reached Makkah and the faces of Quraysh clouded over. They decided to send ʿAbdullāh ibn Abī Rabīʿah and ʿAmr ibn al-ʿĀs ibn Wā'īl ؓ as their emissaries, laden with the choicest presents of Makkah for the Negus, his nobles and chiefs, to bring the exiles back from Abyssinia. The agents of Quraysh first bribed the courtiers of

1 *Ibn Hishām*, vol. I, pp. 293–94.
2 *Ibn Hishām*, vol. I, pp. 320–21.

the Negus with their presents to espouse their cause before the king. Then they took their presents to the Negus and said:

Some foolish young men of our people have taken refuge in your majesty's country. They have abandoned their own religion but neither accepted yours, and have invented a new faith of which we know nothing, nor do you. Our nobles, who are their elders and guardians, have sent us to your majesty to get the exiles back from you, for they are nearer to them and know their faults.

The courtiers of the Negus who had his ear came out with one voice, "They are correct, surrender the refugees to them". But the Negus was enraged; he disliked to forsake those who had sought his shelter. He said, "No, by God, I will not surrender them." Thereafter he summoned the Muslims to his court where his bishops were present, and asked the Muslims, "What is that religion for which you have forsaken your people, and neither accepted my religion nor any other?"

JAʿFAR'S PORTRAYAL OF ISLAM AND IGNORANCE

Jaʿfar ibn Abī Ṭālib ﵁, the cousin of the Prophet ﷺ, then rose to answer the king's query. He said:

> O King, we were an unenlightened people plunged in ignorance. We worshipped idols, we ate carrion, and we committed abominations; we broke natural ties, we ill-treated our neighbours and our strong devoured the weak. We thus lived until God raised among us an Apostle ﷺ, of whose noble birth and lineage, truthfulness, honesty and purity we were aware. He invited us to acknowledge the Unity of God and to worship Him, and to renounce the stones and idols we and our forefathers used to venerate. He enjoined us to speak the truth, to redeem our pledges, to be kind and considerate to our kin and neighbours; he bade us refrain from every vice, bloodshed, shamelessness, untruth and deceit; and asked us not to encroach upon the property of orphans nor to vilify chaste women. He commanded us to pay divine honours to Allāh alone and associate naught with Him; he ordered us to offer prayers, spend in charity, to observe the fast [thus enumerating other injunctions of Islam]. We acknowledged his truth and believed in him; we followed him in whatever he brought from God; and we worshipped only One God, associating naught with Him. We treated as unlawful what he forbade and accepted what he made lawful for us. Hence our people were estranged; they persecuted us, tried to seduce us from our faith and forced us to take the idols back in place of our God; and they pressed us to return to the abominations we used to commit before.
>
> So when they tortured us and grinded us under their tyranny and stood between us and our religion we fled to your country, having chosen you above

> others as our refuge. We have come here, O king, to your country seeking your protection and we do hope that we shall not be dealt with unjustly.

Negus listened patiently to Jaʿfar ibn Abī Ṭālib. Then he asked Jaʿfar if he had something brought by his Prophet from God. Jaʿfar replied in the affirmative. Negus asked him to recite it, and thereupon Jaʿfar recited the opening verses of *Sūrah Maryam*.[1] Negus wept until his beard was wet; the bishops wept until their scrolls were wet with their tears.

Indeed the wise words of Jaʿfar ibn Abī Ṭālib before this King reveals the astuteness of the Apostle's Companions, which could only be derived from a heavenly source aiming to aid this religion and make it triumph above all others. To speak pertinent words of advice and truth, especially when one is in the minority, is far more challenging than any debate.[2]

DISCOMFITURE OF THE QURAYSHITE EMISSARIES

"Of a truth, this and what Jesus brought are radiations from the same Heavenly light", said the Negus. Then turning to the envoys of the Quraysh he continued, "You may go. By God, I shall never give them up to you."

Now, the shrewd poet ʿAmr ibn al-ʿĀs flung his last shot—and a deadly shot, too—for he said, "O king, they assert a dreadful thing about Jesus which is even unwholesome to repeat before you."

Negus demanded from Jaʿfar, "What do you say about Jesus?" Jaʿfar ibn Abī Tālib replied, "We say about him that which our Prophet ﷺ has taught us. He was creature of God and His Prophet, and His Spirit, and His Word, which was cast undo the blessed Virgin Maryam."

Negus took a straw from the ground and said, "By God, Jesus, son of Mary, does not exceed what you have said by the length of this straw."

Negus treated the Muslims with honour and pledged his protection to them. Both the crestfallen envoys of Quraysh had to leave Abyssinia in great shame while the Muslims lived there in peace and security.[3]

The migration of the Muslims to Negus took place in the fifth year of prophethood, Jaʿfar and a number of Companions remained there until 8 AH. He returned to the Apostle's side ﷺ for the Battle of Khaybar, thus remaining in Abyssinia for fifteen long years. In that time, the Muslims came to the aid of Negus in times of war, never forgetting his favour on them[4] and hence showing

1 Chapter 19: "Mary".

2 Quoted from the author's book, '*Rawāiʿ min Adab ad-Da ʿwah fil Qur'ān*' pp.122–123

3 *Ibn Hishām*, pp.334–38.

4 *Musnad Ibn Hanbal*, vol. I, p.203

them the good moral character of those who submit to God. Their presence in the land was one way of propagating Islām in one of the most tolerant lands of Christianity at the time. Sadly there are no records of the events that took place there over this period.

ʿUMAR EMBRACES ISLAM

Islam was then strengthened by the conversion of ʿUmar ؓ to the truth brought by the Apostle of God ﷺ. ʿUmar was one of the nobles of Quraysh, broad shouldered, tall and brave. He was feared and respected by all. The Apostle ﷺ wished that he should accept Islam; for he often prayed to God to show him the right path.

Fāṭimah bint al-Khaṭṭāb ؓ, the sister of ʿUmar ؓ, accepted Islam and shortly thereafter her husband Saʿīd ibn Zayd ؓ, too, followed suit. But both kept it a closely guarded secret since they feared the violent bent of ʿUmar's ؓ nature. They knew that ʿUmar ؓ was a zealous adherent of the religion of his forefathers and carried a bitter aversion to the new faith in his bosom. Khabbāb ibn al-Aratt ؓ secretly taught the Qur'ān to Fāṭimah bint al-Khaṭṭāb ؓ after her conversion.

ʿUmar ؓ planned one day to murder the Apostle ﷺ. He sallied forth, with a sword hanging from his neck, to find out the house near Mount Ṣafā where the Apostle ﷺ and his Companions ؓ were reported to have assembled. Nuʿaym ibn ʿAbdullāh ؓ, who belonged to ʿUmar's tribe of Banū ʿAdī, and had already acknowledged faith in the Prophet ﷺ, happened to see ʿUmar ؓ on the way, armed and fiercely excited. He asked, "ʿUmar, where are you going?"

"I seek Muḥammad," was ʿUmar's reply, "and I will slay him. He has forsaken our religion, shattered the unity of Quraysh, ridiculed them and vilified their gods. Today I will settle the affair once for all."

"Anger has blinded you," retorted Nuʿaym ؓ, "would it not be far better to put your own family in order?"

ʿUmar ؓ was taken aback. He asked, "And who are they in my family?"

Nuʿaym ؓ replied, "Your brother-in-law and cousin Saʿīd ibn Zayd and your sister Fāṭimah. They have given faith to Muḥammad and accepted his religion. Better deal first with them."

ʿUmar ؓ forthwith hurried on to the house of his sister. Khabbāb ؓ was at the time reading *Sūrah Ṭāhā*[1] to the couple from a manuscript he had with him. When they heard the footsteps of ʿUmar ؓ, Khabbāb ؓ hid himself in a small

---

1 Chapter 20.

room inside and Fāṭimah hurriedly concealed the manuscript beneath her thigh. But as ʿUmar had already heard Khabbāb reciting the scripture, he demanded on entering the house, "What was that gabble I heard?"

"Nothing," said both, "what have you heard?"

"Yes, I have heard," rejoined ʿUmar angrily. "I know that both of you have joined the sect of Muḥammad." With these words ʿUmar threw himself upon his brother-in-law. Fāṭimah rushed in to save her husband but ʿUmar struck her hard and wounded her.

All this had come off abruptly; but now both husband and wife boldly asserted: "Yes, we are Muslims. We believe in Allāh and His Apostle ﷺ. Do whatever you will."

ʿUmar saw the blood flowing from the wound he had inflicted on his sister. His anger gave place to shame coupled with admiration for her courage. Cooled down, he asked for the manuscript which he had heard Khabbāb reading. He said "Show me the manuscript. I want to know what Muḥammad has brought." ʿUmar knew the art of reading and writing.

Fāṭimah, however, replied, "I fear what you might do with it." ʿUmar promised with solemn assurances not to destroy it. Fāṭimah, too, thought that he might change his views after reading the scripture. She said to him politely but firmly, "My brother, you are unclean because of your polytheism, and only the pure can touch it." ʿUmar rose and took a bath. His sister then gave him the pages on which *Sūrah Ṭāhā* was written.

He had read only a few lines when he exclaimed in amazement, "How noble and sublime is this speech!" Thereupon Khabbāb came out of his concealment and said, "O ʿUmar, by God, I hope that Allāh would bless you with His Apostle's call ﷺ; for I heard him but last night imploring God earnestly: 'O Allāh, strengthen Islam by Abū 'l-Ḥakam[1] or ʿUmar ibn al-Khaṭṭāb.' Now, ʿUmar, have some fear of God."

ʿUmar asked Khabbāb to lead him to the Apostle ﷺ so that he might accept Islam. Khabbāb told him that the Apostle ﷺ was in a house at Ṣafā with his Companions and ʿUmar immediately took his sword and made for the Apostle ﷺ. When ʿUmar knocked at the door that Khabbāb had indicated to him, one of the Companions got up and looked through a chink in the door to make sure of the newcomer. Finding ʿUmar girt with his sword, he hurried back frightened to report, "O Apostle of Allāh, ʿUmar ibn al-Khaṭṭāb is here with his sword."

Ḥamzah intervened to say, "Let him in. If he comes with peaceful intent,

1 Abū Jahl.

it is alright; if not, we will kill him with his own sword." The Apostle ﷺ gave the word to let ʿUmar in and the companion opened the door.

As ʿUmar ؓ entered the door, the Apostle ﷺ went forth to meet him in the room. He seized his cloak and pulling it rather violently, said to ʿUmar ؓ, "Why have you come, O son of Khaṭṭāb? By God, I see that some calamity is to befall you before your final summoning."

But ʿUmar ؓ replied submissively, "O Messenger of Allāh, I have come to attest my faith in Allāh and His Apostle ﷺ and what he has brought from God."

The Apostle ﷺ raised the cry of *Allāhu Akbar* so loudly that all the Companions present in the house knew that ʿUmar, had accepted Islam.[1]

ʿUmar's ؓ conversion was a turning point in the fortunes of Islam: it made Muslims feel confident and strengthened. Ḥamzah ؓ had already accepted Islam. And now ʿUmar's conversion, the Muslims knew, was likely to set Quraysh jittering. Indeed, they were particularly embittered about ʿUmar's conversion. The Muslims were thus not mistaken in their reckoning that nobody's acceptance of Islam made such a stir nor created such a tense excitement as did that of ʿUmar ؓ.

ʿUmar ؓ proclaimed his faith publicly. As soon as Quraysh came to know about it, they drew the sword against ʿUmar but found him prepared to take the field. Ultimately whoever valued their life dared not pick quarrels with ʿUmar ؓ and they decided to keep their hands off him.[2]

BOYCOTT OF BANŪ HĀSHIM

The spread of Islam among the tribes further angered Quraysh. They came together and decided to draw up a decree ostracizing Banū Hāshim and Banū ʿAbd al-Muṭṭalib. It was decided that nobody should marry the women of these two clans nor give their women to them in marriage; neither should anyone buy from them nor sell to them. Having solemnly agreed to these points, the agreement was put into writing and the parchment was hung in the Kaʿbah in order to give it a religious sanction thereby making it mandatory for all.

IN THE SHIʿB ABĪ ṬĀLIB

Banū Hāshim and Banū ʿAbd al-Muṭṭalib joined Abū Ṭālib after the boycott was enforced and withdrew to a narrow glen or wādī known as Shiʿb Abī Ṭālib. It

1 *Ibn Hishām*. vol. I, pp. 342–46.

2 *Ibn Hishām*, vol. I, p. 349.

was the seventh year of the Prophet's mission ﷺ. Abū Lahab ibn ʿAbd al-Muṭṭalib, however, decided to side with Quraysh, leaving his kith and kin who were under the ban. Weeks and months passed and the people of Hāshim lived in misery and hunger. The ban was so rigorously enforced that the Prophet's clan ﷺ was reduced to eating acacia leaves, and the cries of hungry children echoed all over the valley.

The caravans passed peacefully through the streets of Makkah but Quraysh told the merchants not to buy or sell anything to the two forsaken clans with the result that they pegged the prices so high that it was well nigh impossible for the beleaguered people to purchase even the bare necessities.

The decree of proscription lasted three years. Banū Hāshim and Banū ʿAbd al-Muṭṭalib lived in exile and endured the hardships of the blockade. But not all the people of Quraysh were utterly depraved. Those among them who were well-natured and kind-hearted occasionally supplied food to the exiles secretly. However, the Apostle ﷺ never ceased preaching the message he had brought to his own people, and even to others, whenever he found the opportunity. Banū Hāshim on their part endured every trouble with exemplary patience and fortitude.

ANNULMENT OF THE DECREE

The pitiable condition of the exiles gave rise to a feeling of indignation against the ban among the gracious and genial sons of the desert. Hishām ibn ʿAmr ibn Rabīʿah took the initiative to end the boycott. He was amiable and kind-hearted as well as highly esteemed by Quraysh. He contacted some other considerate and well-disposed persons and put them to shame for allowing the tyranny to linger on. At last, Hishām supported by four other persons agreed to stand together till the decree of the boycott was cancelled. On the morrow, when the Quraysh had assembled in the sanctuary, Zuhayr whose mother ʿĀtikah was daughter of ʿAbd al-Muṭṭalib, cried out to the people, "O you people of Makkah, shall we eat and drink while Banū Hāshim die of hunger, unable even to buy or sell? By God I will not take rest until this cruel and unjust decree is torn to pieces."

Abū Jahl tried to intervene but found everybody against him. Muṭʿim ibn ʿAdī then went up to tear the document to pieces but he found that with the exception of the words "In Thy name, O Allāh" the rest of the document had already been eaten up by white ants. (The Apostle ﷺ had already told his uncle, Abū Ṭālib, that God had given white ants power over the document.)

The blighted document was, however, taken out and thrown away and thus ended the boycott and what was written on it.[1]

---

1 *Ibn Hishām*, vol. I, pp. 350–51.

DEATH OF ABŪ ṬĀLIB AND KHADĪJAH

Soon after the end of the boycott, in the tenth year of his mission, the Prophet ﷺ lost Abū Ṭālib, his uncle, and his loving wife, Khadījah ﷺ. Both were his protectors—tried and true helpers devotedly attached to him. Their deaths meant a great misfortune to the Apostle ﷺ who was to face many a trouble in succession soon thereafter.

SPARKLING SYMPHONY OF THE QUR'ĀN

Aṭ-Ṭufayl ibn ʿAmr ad-Dawsī ﷺ was a prominent poet honoured by the Arabs. When he came to Makkah, some of Quraysh warned him against meeting the Apostle ﷺ. They told him, as usual, that Muḥammad ﷺ had created dissensions among the Quraysh and so he had to be careful lest he should also fall under the Prophet's spell ﷺ. Aṭ-Ṭufayl relates: "By God, they were so insistent that I decided not to listen or speak to him. I went so far as to stuff cotton in my ears before going to the holy mosque. Suddenly, my eyes met the Apostle ﷺ who was offering prayer near me. I stood by his side and thus God caused me to hear something of his speech. It was beautiful and noble. I thought, my mother curse me, I am a poet and a connoisseur; no good or evil in a speech can elude me. Why should anything prevent me from listening to this speech? If it is good I shall accept it; if bad, I shall reject it."

He met the Apostle ﷺ at his house where he invited him to accept Islam and recited the Qur'ān to him. Aṭ-Ṭufayl ﷺ accepted Islam and went back to his tribe determined to preach the faith of God. He refused to do anything with his household members until they had also acknowledged God and His Apostle ﷺ. All of them became Muslims and Islam spread thereafter in the tribe of Daws.[1]

Abū Bakr ﷺ used to pray within his house. Not being satisfied with it, he selected a place in the courtyard of his house where he started offering prayers and reciting the Qur'ān. Abū Bakr ﷺ was tender-hearted and when he recited the Qur'ān, shedding tears all the while, youths, slaves and women used to gather round him listening to his recitation. Now, the chiefs of Quraysh took alarm at Abū Bakr's recitation of the Qur'ān and sent for Ibn ad-Dughunnah who had pledged protection to Abū Bakr ﷺ.

When Ibn ad-Dughunnah came, they said to him, "We accepted your pledge of protection to Abū Bakr ﷺ on the condition that he prays inside his house, but he has started praying and reciting in the open. We fear he might seduce our women and children. Now if he agrees to offer his prayers secretly within his

1 *Ibn Hishām,* vol. I, pp. 382–84.

house, it is well and good, otherwise he should renounce your protection. We neither want to make you break your word nor can we allow him to do it openly."

Ibn ad-Dughunnah informed Abu Bakr ﷺ of what he had been told by Quraysh, but he replied, "I renounce your guarantee; I prefer the protection and guarantee of my Lord."[1]

JOURNEY TO ṬĀ'IF

The death of Abū Ṭālib signalled the beginning of a difficult time for the Apostle ﷺ. None of the Quraysh dared touch the Apostle ﷺ during the lifetime of Abū Ṭālib but now that restraint was gone. Once, dust was thrown on his head. Quraysh insulted and mocked the Apostle ﷺ and made caustic remarks about Islam. When the pagans persisted with their scoffs and scorn and contumacious behaviour, the Apostle ﷺ thought of going to Ṭā'if to seek the help of Thaqīf. The Prophet ﷺ intended to invite them to Islam for he hoped that they would receive his message with sympathy. This was a reasonable expectation as he had spent his childhood with Banū Saᶜd,[2] who were settled near Ṭā'if.

Ṭā'if was a beautiful city, second only to Makkah in its population and prosperity, and held an important position in the Peninsula as alluded to in this verse of the Qur'ān.

> And they say: If only this Qur'ān had been revealed to some great man of the two towns (Makkah and Ṭā'if).[3]

Ṭā'if is located seventy five kilometres South-East of Makkah,[4] on the foothills of Mount of Ghazwān which stands at six hundred feet. The city derives its name from the walls which use to surround it; its ancient name was *Wajj*. Ṭā'if was also a religious centre; the temple of al-Lāt in that city was visited by pilgrims from every part of the country and thus it vied with Makkah which housed Hubal, the chief deity of Arabia. Ṭā'if was, as it still is, the summer resort of the Makkan aristocracy. An Umayyad poet, ᶜUmar ibn Rabīᶜah said about his beloved:

Winter in Makkah, living in clover,
In Ṭā'if she spends the summer.

---

1 *Bukhārī* in the section on. *Hijrah,*on the authority of ᶜĀ'ishah

2 Authorities hold the view that the Prophet undertook the journey to Ṭā'if towards the end of Shawwāl in the tenth year of Apostleship (*Khātim an-Nabiyyīn*, vol. I. p. 580, by Shaykh Muḥammad Abū Zahrah and *Tabaqāt* Ibn Saᶜd, vol I, p.221).

3 Qur'ān 43:3.

4 *Tārīkh Al-ᶜArab Qabl al-Islām*, vol. IV, p.142

The inhabitants of Ṭā'if were endowed with large cultivations and vineyards, and were wealthy and prosperous. They had become conceited and boastful answering to the following description of the Qur'ānic verses:

> And We sent not unto any township a warner, but its pampered ones declared: Lo! we are disbelievers in that which ye bring unto us.
>
> And they say: We are more (than you) in wealth and children. We are not the punished![1]

In Ṭā'if, the Apostle ﷺ (accompanied by his freed slave, Zayd ibn Hārithah ؓ) first met the chiefs and leaders of Thaqīf, whom he invited to accept Islam. They were, however, rude and discourteous in their behaviour toward the Apostle ﷺ. Not content with their insolent replies, they stirred up some rabble of the town to harass the Apostle ﷺ. These riff-raff followed the Prophet ﷺ, abusing and shouting and pelting him with stones until he was compelled to take refuge in an orchard. The Apostle ﷺ had thus to endure even more troubles in Ṭā'if than he had faced in Makkah. These louts standing on either side of the path hurled stones at him until his feet were injured and smeared with blood. Their oppression weighed so heavily upon the Apostle ﷺ that in a state of constriction a prayer came to his lips, complaining of his helplessness and pitiable condition and seeking the succour of God.

"O Allāh", said the Prophet ﷺ, "to You I complain of my weakness, my lack of resources and humiliation before the people. You art the Most Merciful, the Lord of the weak and my Master. To whom wilt You confide me? To one estranged, bearing ill will, or an enemy given power over me? If You art not wroth with me, I care not, for Thy favour is abundant for me. I seek refuge in the light of Thy countenance by which all darkness is dispelled and every affair of this world and the next is set right, lest Thy anger should descend upon me or Thy displeasure light upon me. I need only Thy pleasure and satisfaction for only You enabled me to do good and evade evil. There is no power and no might save in You."

The Lord then sent the angel of the mountains who sought the Prophet's permission ﷺ to join together the two hills between which Ṭā'if was located but the Messenger of God replied, "No, I hope God will bring forth from their loins people who will worship God alone, associating nothing with Him."[2]

Moved to compassion by the distress of the Apostle ﷺ, ʿUtbah ibn Rabīʿah

---

1 Qur'ān 55:34–35.

2 *Muslim, Kitāb al-Jihād.* It was narrated that after the death of the Messenger of Allāh (peace be upon him), many of the Arab tribes became apostates apart from Quraysh and Thaqīf, who remained steadfast and contributed greatly to the success of the Islamic conquests beyond the Arabian Peninsula, *Al-Bidayah wa An-Nihayah*, vol. VI, p.304.

and Shaybah ibn Rabīʿah sent for ʿAddās ﷺ, one of their young Christian slaves, and told him to take a bunch of grapes on a platter to the Apostle ﷺ. ʿAddās took the platter to the Apostle ﷺ. He observed the kind demeanour of the Apostle ﷺ and talked to him and instantly gave witness to his faith in Allāh and His Apostle ﷺ.[1]

The Apostle ﷺ thus returned to Makkah where the Quraysh were as bitterly opposed to him as ever, deriding and annoying and assailing him day after day.

THE ASCENSION

It was during this period that the Prophet ﷺ found himself transported at night to the Kaʿbah and from there to the place of the Solomon's Temple in Jerusalem, where Masjid al-Aqṣā now stands; and was then borne to the celestial regions where he witnessed the seven heavens, met the prophets of yore and beheld the remarkable sign of divine majesty[2] about which the Qur'ān says:

> The eye turned not aside nor yet was overbold, verily, he saw one of the greater revelations of his Lord.[3]

The occurrence of the event at that time was meant to confer dignity upon the Apostle ﷺ. It signified a noble hospitality from God in order to console and alleviate the feelings of distress that the persecution of the pagans at Ṭā'if had caused him. On the morrow of the Ascension the Apostle ﷺ told the people about his nocturnal journey, but Quraysh mocked and shook their heads saying that it was inconceivable and beyond the bounds of reason. When Abū Bakr saw Quraysh accusing the Apostle ﷺ of falsehood he said, "What makes you wonder about it? If he has said this, it must be true. By God, he tells me that revelation descends on him from the Heaven in a trice during the day or night and I avouch him. This is even more unimaginable and difficult than what seems to astound you."[4]

THE REAL SIGNIFICANCE OF THE ASCENSION

The ascension did not break through the mundane only to reveal the hidden phe-

---

1 *Ibn Hishām,* vol I, pp. 419–22, *Ibn Kathīr,* voL II, pp. 149–53, *Zād al-Maʿād,* vol. I, p. 302.

2 There is some disagreement about the exact timing of the events, although the majority hold the view that it took place on the 27th of Rajāb, a few months before the *Hijrah* and after the trials of Ṭā'if, *Khātam an-Nabiyyīn* by Muhammād Abū Zuhrah, vol. I, p.596.

3 Qur'ān 53:17–18.To understand the significance of Ascension, see Shāh Walī Allāh's '*Ḥujjat Allāh al-Bālighah*'.

4 *Ibn Kathīr,* vol. II, p. 96 and *Ibn Hishām,* vol. I, p. 399.

nomena of the kingdom of God in the Heavens and the earth to the Prophet of Islam; rather, this prophetic journey was of tremendous importance and alluded to a number of other significant and profound realities of far-reaching concern to humanity. The two *Sūrahs* of *Isrā'* and *An-Najm* revealed in connection with this heavenly journey indicate that Prophet Muḥammad ﷺ was charged with the office of prophethood for both the Houses of God, those in Jerusalem and Makkah, and was sent as the leader of the east and the west or the entire human race to the end of time. As the inheritor of all the prophets of old, he represented the fulfilment and consummation of mankind's religious development. His nightly journey from Makkah to Jerusalem expresses, in a figurative way, that his personality unified Bayt al-Ḥarām[1] and Masjid al-Aqṣā.[2] That all the prophets arranged themselves behind him in the Masjid al-Aqṣā shows that the doctrine of Islam, preached by him, was final, universal and all-comprehensive—meant for every class and section of human society throughout the ages.

The event is, at the same time, indicative of the comprehensiveness of the Holy Prophet's apostleship ﷺ, the place accorded to his followers in the great task of humanity's guidance and the distinctive character of his message.

Truly speaking, the ascension of the Apostle ﷺ represents a line of demarcation between the regional, limited and variable rules of divine guidance entrusted to the prophets of old and the global, comprehensive and abiding principles of faith vouchsafed to the universal leader of human race. Had the Apostle ﷺ been a sectional or regional guide, a national leader, the saviour of any particular race or the restorer of glory to a particular people, there would have been no need to honour him with ascension to the heavens nor would he have been required to perceive the hidden phenomena of the Heavens and the earth. Neither would it have been necessary to create the new link between the celestial and the earthly planes of the Divine Kingdom; in that case the confines of his own land, his surroundings, environs and the times would have been sufficient; and there would have then been no need for him to divert his attention to any other land or country. Neither his ascension to the most sublime regions of the Heaven and to the "Lote Tree of the Farthest Limit"[3] nor the nocturnal Journey to far away Jerusalem then in the grip of the powerful Christian Empire of Byzantium would have been necessary at all.

The ascension of the Apostle ﷺ was a divine proclamation that he tran-

---

1 The Ka'bah at Makkah.

2 The Dome of the Rock at Jerusalem.

3 The Qur'ānic expression *Sidrat al-muntahā* (cf. Qur'ān 53:14) alludes to the shady lote-tree of Paradise. According to some of the earliest commentators of the Qur'ān, the divine writs are first sent to the lote-tree from where the angels bring them to earth.

scended the category of national or political leaders whose endeavours are limited to their own country and nation. For they serve the nations and races to which they belong and are a product of their time, they serve the need of a particular juncture. The Apostle of Islam ﷺ on the contrary, belonged to the luminous line of the messengers of God who communicate the inspired message of Heaven to the earth. They are the links between God and His creatures. Their messages transcend the limitations of time and space, race and colour and country and nation, for they are meant for the exaltation of man regardless of his colour, race or country.

OBLIGATORY PRAYERS

On this occasion, God made fifty prayers a day obligatory upon the Apostle ﷺ and his followers. The Apostle ﷺ constantly implored God to alleviate the burden of prayers until the Lord limited these to only five daily prayers. The Lord was pleased to decree that whoever properly performs these five prayers every day would be recompensed as if he had performed all the fifty daily prayers enjoined initially.[1]

TRIBES INVITED TO ISLAM

Thereafter the Apostle ﷺ started contacting the members of different tribes who came to Makkah for pilgrimage. He would explain to them the doctrines of Islam and ask them to support him in his mission. He often told the tribesmen, "O ye people, I have been sent to you as the messenger of God to call you to worship Him, to call on you to associate nothing with Him and to renounce everything you have elevated as His equal. Believe in God and His Apostle and protect me until I have made clear that which God has sent to me."

Whenever the Apostle ﷺ contacted any tribe and finished his invitation to them, Abū Lahab usually stood up to say, "O ye people, the fellow wants you to cast off your obedience to al-Lāt and al-ʿUzzā and your allies, the jinn, and to exchange your gods for the wickedness and innovation he has brought. Don't take orders from him nor pay him any heed."[2]

THE RISKY PATH TO ISLAM

The way leading to Allāh and Islam was fraught with grave danger and anyone

1 Bukhārī, Kitāb aṣ-Ṣalāt.

2 *Ibn Hishām,* vol. I, pp. 422–23.

who wanted to walk the path had to be prepared for hardship. Makkah had become so unsafe and unprotected for the Muslims that acceptance of Islam meant taking one's life in one's hand.

The story of Abū Dharr Ghifārī's ﷺ conversion to Islam, recorded in the words of ʿAbdullah ibn ʿAbbās ﷺ, indicates how perilous it had become even to call upon the Apostle ﷺ in those days.

> When Abū Dharr heard of the advent of the Prophet ﷺ, he said unto his brother: 'Proceed to that valley and enlighten me about the man who claims to be a prophet and to receive communications from Heaven. Listen to some of his sayings and then return unto me.'—So the brother went forth, reached the Prophet ﷺ and heard some of his sayings. Thereafter he returned to Abū Dharr and said unto him: 'I found that he enjoins the highest principles of morality, and that his speech is not poetry.' But [Abū Dharr] said: You have not been able to satisfy me.
>
> Thereupon he took some provision, together with an old waterskin full of water, and proceeded to Makkah. He went to the mosque (Kaʿbah) and began to look for the Prophet ﷺ for he knew him not, and was loath to ask about him; and thus he spent part of the night. Thereupon ʿAlī saw him and knew him to be a stranger; and when [Abū Dharr] met ʿAlī, he went with him [to his house]. And until daybreak neither of the two asked any questions of the other. Then [Abū Dharr] betook himself with his waterskin and his provisions to the mosque and passed that day until evening without finding the Prophet ﷺ, although he saw him in the mosque. Then he returned to his resting place. And ʿAlī passed him and said: 'Is it not time that a man should know his abode?' And he made him rise and took him to his house, neither of the two asking any questions of the other. And on the third day ʿAlī did likewise, and [Abū Dharr] stayed with him. Thereafter [ʿAlī] said: 'Will you not tell me what has brought you here?' [Abū Dharr] answered: 'I will do so if you promise me that you will guide me aright' And [ʿAlī] agreed to this. Thereupon [Abū Dharr] told him [all]. [ʿAlī] said: 'Behold, it is true, and he is [indeed] an Apostle of God! Tomorrow morning, then, follow me. If I see any danger for you, I shall stop as if to pass water; but if I go on, then follow me and enter the place which I enter'. [Abū Dharr] did so, and followed the other until he entered the Prophet's house ﷺ; and [Abū Dharr] went in with him. Then he listened to some of the Prophet's sayings ﷺ and embraced Islam on the spot. Thereupon the Prophet ﷺ said unto him: 'Return unto your people and inform them [about me] and await my bidding'. [Abū Dharr] said: 'By Him in Whose hand is my soul, indeed, I shall loudly proclaim this [truth] among them!'"
>
> "Then he left and went to the mosque and called out at the top of his voice: 'I bear witness that there is no deity but God, and that Muḥammad is the Apostle of God;' Thereupon the people [of Makkah] fell upon him and beat him and threw

him to the ground. And there came ʿAbbās, who knelt down to see to him and said to the people: 'Woe unto you! Know you not that he belongs to [the tribe of] Ghifār, and that your merchants' road to Syria [passes] through their country?' And so he rescued him from them. On the morrow [Abū Dharr] did the same again, and they fell upon him and beat him, and [again] ʿAbbās rescued him."[1]

THE BEGINNING OF ISLĀM AMONG THE ANṢĀR

The Apostle ﷺ met some of the Anṣār belonging to Khazraj at ʿAqabah,[2] when he went to preach Islam to the tribes during the time of pilgrimage. He told them about Islam and called on them to serve God alone, and then recited some of the Qur'ān to them. These people lived in Yathrib side by side with the Jews who often told them that an Apostle of God ﷺ was soon to come, and so they said to one another: "By God, this is the same Prophet of whom the Jews informed us! Lo! Let no one proceed you in accepting his message." Thereupon they accepted his teachings and embraced Islam. They also said to the Apostle ﷺ, "When we left our people discord and conflict and enmity divided them more than any other. Perhaps God will unite them through you. We shall inform them to accept this religion of yours which we have accepted, and if God unites them through you, then no man shall be more honoured than you."[3]

These men returned to their homes after accepting Islam, where they told others about the Apostle ﷺ and invited them to accept the new faith. Islam quickly spread in Madīnah until there was no home of the Anṣār wherein the Apostle ﷺ was not mentioned.[4]

FIRST PLEDGE OF ʿAQABAH

During the pilgrimage, the following year twelve men belonging to the Anṣār met the Apostle ﷺ at ʿAqabah. They pledged themselves to the Apostle ﷺ undertaking neither to commit theft nor fornication, nor to kill their children, to obey him in what was right, and to associate nothing with God. When these people left for Madīnah, the Apostle ﷺ sent Muṣʿab ibn ʿUmayr ؓ with them to teach

1 *Bukhārī,* "Abū Dharr's conversion to Islam".

2 ʿAqabah means a deep valley. In the hills at Minā a culvert facing Makkah is known by that name. The place being near Jamrat-al-Kubrā, is also known as Jamrat al-ʿAqabah. Now a mosque stands there to mark the place where the Prophet met the Anṣār. Here pilgrims returning from ʿArafāt spend the three nights of *ʿĪd al-Aḍḥā*. Even in pre-Islamic times this was the custom of the heathen Arabs who had preserved the ancient ceremonies of the pilgrimage.

3 *Ibn Hishām,* vol. I, pp. 428–29.

4 *Ibn Hishām,* vol. I, pp. 428–29.

the Qur'ān to the people there as well as to expound Islam and instruct them about religion; wherefore ʿUmayr came to be called "The Reader" in Madīnah. He lodged with Asʿad ibn Zurārah ﷺ and also led the prayers.[1]

THE REASON FOR ANṢĀR'S ACCEPTANCE OF ISLAM

It was a critical juncture when God afforded the opportunity of helping and defending Islam to Aws and Khazraj,[2] the two influential tribes of Yathrib. For there was nothing more precious at the moment than to own and accept Islām, they were really fortunate in getting the most well-timed chance to take precedence of all other tribes of Ḥijāz in welcoming and defending the religion of God. They overshadowed their compatriots, since all the tribes of Arabia, in general, and Quraysh, in particular, had proved themselves ungrateful as well as incompetent to take advantage of the greatest favour bestowed on them. "Allāh guides who He wills unto a right path."[3]

Diverse causes and circumstances, proceeding from the Will of Almighty God, had opened the door for the Aws and the Khazraj to accept Islam. These tribes were not like the Makkan Quraysh: the Aws and the Khazraj were kind-hearted and sweet tempered, immune from the traits of intemperance, obstinacy and vanity of the Quraysh, and hence they were responsive, and open to reason. These were the characteristics inherited from their progenitors, the Yemenites, about whom the Apostle ﷺ had remarked after meeting one of their deputations: "The people of Yemen have come to you. They have the most tender manners and gentlest hearts." Both these tribes of Yathrib were originally Yemenites, for their forefathers had come from there. Commending the merits of these people God has said in the Qur'ān:

Those who entered the city and the faith before them love those who flee unto them for refuge, and find in their breasts no need for that which has been given them, but prefer [the fugitives] above themselves though poverty become their lot.[4]

Another reason was that continuous internecine warfare had already exhausted both the tribes. Wearied and distracted by the famous battle of Buʿāth,[5]

1 Ibid., p. 434.

2 The tribes of Aws and Khazraj branched off from the tribe of Azd, belonging to Qaḥṭān. The forefather of these tribes, Thaʿlabah ibn ʿAmr, had migrated from Yemen to Ḥijāz after the destruction of Ma'ārib Dam (120 BCE) and settled in Madīnah.

3 Qur'ān 2:213.

4 Qur'ān 59:9.

5 Fought in about 615 CE, about five years before the *Hijrah*.

fought a short time before, both tribes were desirous of peace and harmony and wanted to avoid a renewal of warfare. Such was their anxiety for peace that the first Muslims of Madīnah had said to the Prophet ﷺ, "When we left our people, discord and conflict and enmity divided them more than any other. Perhaps God will unite them through you . . . and if God unites them behind you, then no man will be more honoured than you." ʿĀ'ishah once said that the battle of Buʿāth was really a divine ministration in disguise which served as a prelude to the Apostle's migration ﷺ to Madīnah.

Yet another reason was that Quraysh, like the rest of the Arab tribes, had long ago lost touch with prophethood and the prophets and had hardly any recollection of their teachings. Plunged deep in ignorance and idolatry and being complete strangers to the art of reading and writing, they had become over-zealous heathens; actually, they had but little contact even with the Jews and Christians, the followers of the prophets and their scriptures (although these had since been distorted). This was a plain fact to which the Qur'ān makes a reference in these words:

> That you may warn a people whose fathers were not warned, so they are heedless.[1]

But the Aws and the Khazraj were neighbours of the Jews of Yathrib whom they heard talking about the prophets and reciting their scriptures. The Jews often warned them that a prophet was to come in the later times with whom they would ally themselves and kill the heathens just as the people of ʿĀd and Iram were massacred.[2]

> And when there comes to them a Scripture from Allāh, confirming that in their possession—though before that they were asking for signal triumph over those who disbelieved—and when there comes to them that which they know (to be the Truth) they disbelieve therein. The curse of Allāh is on disbelievers.[3]

The Aws and the Khazraj as well as other Arab tribes settled in Madīnah were heathens like the idolatrous Quraysh and the rest of the Arabs but unlike them they had become accustomed to the idea of revelation in the form of a scripture of supernatural origin, prophecy, apostleship, inspiration, requital and the hereafter through their uninterrupted contact with the Jews of the city with whom they had business transactions, made war and peace and lived side by side. They had, thus, become familiar with the teachings of the prophets of old and the purpose for which God sends them from time to time. This was of great

1 Qur'ān 36:6.
2 *Tafsīr Ibn Kathīr*, vol. I, p. 217.
3 Qur'ān 2:89.

advantage to them, for when they learnt about the Apostle ﷺ on the occasion *Hajj* at Makkah, they seized the opportunity immediately as if they were already prepared for it.

STRATEGIC IMPORTANCE OF MADĪNAH

Apart from the great honour to be bestowed on the people of Madīnah and such other reasons as might be known to the All-Knowing Lord, one of the considerations in the selection of the town as the future centre of Islam was that it was, from a geographical and defensive point of view, impregnable like a fortified city. No other town of the Peninsula enjoyed the same advantage. Lying on a lava plain, surrounded on all sides by chains of high mountains, the Western side of the city was protected by the lava and extremely uneven hilly terrain known as Ḥarrat al-Wabrah[1] while Ḥarrah Wāqim surrounds it on the eastern side. Madīnah lies unprotected and vulnerable to military advances only in the north (where, in 5 AH, the Apostle ﷺ ordered to dig trenches on the occasion of the battle of clans). Thickly clustered plantations of date-palm groves encompassed the town on the remaining sides. An army taking this route would have had to maintain communication through deep valleys and gorges. It would have thus been difficult to attack Madīnah in full force from these sides, while the defender could have easily beaten off the invaders using small outlying pickets.

Ibn Isḥāq writes: "Only one side of Madīnah was, exposed, and the rest of the sides were strongly protected by buildings and date-palm groves through which an enemy could not get access."

The Apostle ﷺ had perhaps covertly referred to this very aspect of Madīnah when he said before his emigration: "I have been shown the goal of your migration—a land of palm-trees lying between two tracts strewn with black, rugged stones." All those who resolved upon emigration emigrated thereupon to Madīnah.[2]

The two Arab tribes of Madīnah, Aws and Khazraj, were well known for their passionate, chauvinistic spirit of the clan, self-respect, boldness and valour while riding was one of the manly skills in which they excelled. Freedom of the desert was in their blood: neither had they ever submitted to any authority nor paid tax

1 Ḥarrah or al-Lābah is a terrain full of volcanic igneous rocks of dark green colour and uneven shape which are produced by the matter flowing from a volcano. Such an uneven hilly terrain is absolutely useless as a fighting ground or for communication either for infantry of cavalry. Majd ad-Dīn Fīrōzābādī (d. 823 AH) writes in the *al-Maghānim al-Maṭābah fī Maʿālim Ṭābah* that a number of ḥarra's, some nearer the town and some at a distance, surround Madīnah from all sides and protect it from attack or at least make the advance difficult for an invading army (see pp. 108–114 and *Bukhārī*, "Emigration of the Prophet").

2 *Bukhārī*, "Emigration of the Apostle".

to a sovereign. The heroic character of these tribes was plainly set forth when the Chief of Aws, Saʿd ibn Muʿādh said to the Apostle ﷺ during the battle of Trenches: "When we and these people were polytheists and idolaters, not serving God nor knowing Him, they never hoped to eat a single date except as guests or by purchase."[1]

"The two clans of Yathrib," writes Ibn Khaldūn, "dominated the Jews and were distinguished because of their prestige and eminence. The tribe of Muḍar living near them was related to them."[2] Ibn ʿAbd Rabbihī, another Arab historian, writes in the *Al-ʿIqd al-Farīd*: "The Anṣār descended from the tribe of Azd. Known as the Aws and the Khazraj, they were lineal descendants of the two sons of Ḥārithah ibn ʿAmr ibn ʿĀmir. Being more proud and dignified than others, they had never paid tribute to any regime or suzerain."[3]

They were related, on the maternal side, to the Banū ʿAdī ibn an-Najjār who had given one of their daughters, Salmā bint ʿAmr, to Hāshim in marriage. To Hāshim she bore ʿAbd al-Muṭṭalib. Hāshim, however, left the boy with his mother in Yathrib where he was brought up and was taken to Makkah by his uncle after he had grown up into a youth. These blood relationships, which were the adhesive elements in tribal organisation, cannot be ignored since kinship played an important role in the social life of the Arabs. On reaching Madīnah the Apostle ﷺ stayed with Abū Ayyūb al-Anṣārī ؓ who belonged to Banū ʿAdī ibn an-Najjār.

The Aws and the Khazraj traced back their derivation from Qaḥṭān while the emigrants (Mūhājirīn) and other Muslims hailing from Makkah or other places near it claimed their descent from ʿAdnān. Thus, after the Apostle ﷺ migrated to Madīnah and the Anṣār pledged their support to him, both the ʿAdnān and Qaḥṭān rallied round the flag of Islām as one man. The ʿAdnān and Qaḥṭān had been at odds with one another during the pre-Islamic times but they were banded together in Madīnah and thus the pagan passions of blood and clan, of vanity and pride and of vainglorious self-conceit were stamped out by the wholesome influence of Islām.

For all these causes and considerations as well as its strategic location, Madīnah was the fittest place for the emigration of the Apostle ﷺ and his Companions; it was eminently suited to be made the radiating centre of Islam until it gained enough strength to prevail over the Peninsula and charge the whole country with a new spirit of virtue and godliness.

---

1 *Ibn Hishām,* vol. II, p. 223.

2 *Tārīkh Ibn Khaldūn*, vol. II, p. 289.

3 *Al-ʿIqd al-Farīd,* vol. III, p. 334.

EXPANSION OF ISLAM IN MADĪNAH

The teachings of Islam were so dazzling that the people of Aws and Khazraj, awakened to interest, quickly attested their faith in Islam. Saʿd ibn Muʿādh ﷺ was first to embrace Islam, then Usayd ibn Ḥuḍayr ﷺ, the leader of Banū ʿAbd al-Ashhal, a clan of Aws, recognised the truth of the Apostle's faith ﷺ. The wise and courteous bearing of Muṣʿab ibn ʿUmayr ﷺ and the way he presented Islam to them convinced them of the truth of Islam. Then the remaining clansmen of Banū ʿAbd al-Ashhal were led to accept the faith and, shortly afterwards there was not a house of the Anṣār in which some of the men and women had not given their faith to Islam.[1]

SECOND PLEDGE OF ʿAQABAH

In the following year, at the time of *Ḥajj,* Muṣʿab ibn ʿUmayr ﷺ, went back to Makkah with a number of people from Madīnah, both Anṣār Muslims and polytheists. After the Anṣār had performed that pilgrimage, the Apostle ﷺ met them at the previous year's meeting place late in the night. This time their number was seventy-three, including two women. The Apostle of God ﷺ came accompanied by his uncle, ʿAbbās ibn ʿAbd al-Muṭṭalib, who had still not embraced Islam.

The Apostle ﷺ talked to them, read some of the Qur'ān and invited them to accept Islam. Then he said, "I Invite your allegiance on this condition that you would protect me in the same way as you would your women and children." They gave allegiance to the Apostle ﷺ but demanded that he would not leave them nor return to his own people. The Prophet ﷺ then said in reply, "I am of you and you are of me. I will war against them that make war upon you and have peace with those that keep peace with you".

Thereafter the Apostle ﷺ selected twelve of them, nine from Khazraj and three from Aws, as their leaders.[2]

PERMISSION TO MIGRATE TO MADĪNAH

Thanks to the allegiance and support offered by the Anṣār, the Muslims found a new rock of refuge. The Apostle ﷺ commanded the Muslims in Makkah to migrate and join their brothers in faith, the Anṣār, in Madīnah. He told his Companions, "God has provided to you some brethren and homes where you will live in safety." So the Muslims betook themselves in groups from Makkah to

1 *Ibn Hishām*, vol. I, pp. 436–98.

2 Ibid., pp. 441–42.

Yathrib, but the Apostle himself remained in Makkah awaiting the command of God to leave the city.

It was not an easy emigration. The Quraysh at once decided to take stringent measures against the emigrants. The pagan Quraysh did everything they could to stop the emigration. They created obstacles in the way of emigrants to prevent their departure, but the Muslims were equally determined not to retrace their steps. Bent on leaving Makkah at all costs, some like Abū Salamah ﷺ had to depart alone leaving their wives and children while others like Ṣuhayb ﷺ had to give up their lifelong earnings before leaving Makkah. Umm Salamah ﷺ relates:

> When Abū Salamah had made up his mind to set out for Madīnah he saddled his camel and mounted me on it with my son Salamah. Then taking hold of the camel's halter he went ahead. When some of the men belonging to Banū al-Mughīrah saw him, they came near us saying, 'It is alright so far as you are concerned, but how can we allow your wife to go with you.' They snatched the camel's halter from his hand and took me with them. At this Banū ʿAbd al-Asad, the clansmen of Abū Salamah, got angry. They said: 'By God, you have torn her from our brother, but we will not let our son go with her.' A scuffle started between them for the child, Salamah until his arm was dislocated, and Banū ʿAbd al-Asad took him away leaving me with Banū 'l-Mughīrah while my husband went away to Madīnah. Thus, all the three of us, myself, my husband and my son were separated. I would go out every morning to Abṭaḥ weeping till nightfall. A whole year passed in this manner when one of my cousins of al-Mughīrah had pity on me and said to Banū 'l-Mughīrah: 'Why don't you let this poor woman go? You have separated her from her husband and son.' So they said to me: 'You can go to your husband if you like.' Then Banū ʿAbd al-Asad restored my son to me. I saddled my camel and taking my son with me, set out for Madīnah in search of my husband accompanied by not a blessed soul. When I arrived at Tanʿīm I happened to meet ʿUthmān ibn Ṭalḥah[1] ﷺ of Banū ʿAbd ad-Dār who asked me where I intended to go. I replied that I was going to my husband in Madīnah. He asked if I had anybody with me to which I said in reply, 'None save this child and God.' He said, 'By God, it will not be easy for you to reach your destination'. He took hold of the camel's rope and went ahead leading it. By God, I have never met a man more noble than he. Whenever we had to make a halt, he would kneel the camel and withdraw. After I had got down, he would unload the camel, tie it to a tree and go away to take rest under a tree. In the evening he would saddle the camel and load it, and then withdrew asking me to ride.

---

1 ʿUthmān ibn Ṭalḥah embraced Islam after the conquest of Makkah when the Apostle handed over the keys of the Kaʿbah to him (*Al-Iṣābah fī Tamyīzi 'ṣ-Ṣaḥābah*, p. 217).

> He came back after I had mounted and taking the halter in his hand, he went ahead to the next destination. Thus he escorted me until I reached Madīnah. When he saw Qubā, the habitation of Banū ʿAmr ibn ʿAwf, he said, 'Your husband is in this village. Now go to him with the blessing of God.' Thus he bade me farewell and went off on his way back to Makkah.

She ﷺ also used to say that no family in Islām suffered the troubles that the family of Abū Salamah ﷺ underwent.[1]

When Ṣuhayb ﷺ tried to leave for Madīnah the disbelieving Quraysh said to him "You came to us as a destitute beggar and have grown rich among us, and now you want to go away safely with your life and wealth. By God, It shall never be so!" Ṣuhayb asked, "Would you allow me to go if I give my property to you?" When they replied in the affirmative, Ṣuhayb said, "I give you the whole of it."

When the Apostle ﷺ was told of it, he exclaimed, "Ṣuhayb, has made a profit! Ṣuhayb has made a profit!"[2]

The emigrants to Madīnah during this period were: ʿUmar, Ṭalḥah, Ḥamzah, Zayd ibn Ḥārithah, ʿAbd ar-Raḥmān ibn ʿAwf, az-Zubayr ibn al-ʿAwwām, Abū Hudhayfah, ʿUthmān ibn ʿAffān and several other Companions ﷺ of the Prophet ﷺ. Thereafter the emigrants trickled away one by one. Only those were left in Makkah—besides the Apostle ﷺ, Abū Bakr and ʿAlī ﷺ —who were detained because of some restraint or those who had fallen victim to trials of the Quraysh.[3]

UNSUCCESSFUL CONSPIRACY AGAINST THE APOSTLE ﷺ

The emigration of the Muslims to Madīnah gravely frightened the Makkans. They soon realised that the Apostle ﷺ had already established a base with a large number of adherents in a foreign territory beyond their reach and if he were also to join them there, they would be rendered helpless, deprived of all authority over him. They held a council in Dār an-Nadwah[4] where all the chiefs of Quraysh assembled to deliberate how to solve the problem.

They debated the various suggestions and ultimately decided unanimously that each clan should volunteer a young, courageous and blue-blooded warrior so that all of them fall upon Muḥammad ﷺ jointly to kill him. Thus, the responsibility or shedding his blood would lie equally on all the clans, without a single

1 *Ibn Kathīr,* vol. II, pp. 215–17.
2 Ibid. p. 223.
3 *Ibn Hishām.* vol. I. pp. 470–79.
4 The house of Quṣayy ibn Kilāb where they would decide every important affair.

clan bearing the responsibility for it; and ʿAbd Manāf would dare not take up a hatchet against all the people. Determined to slay the Apostle ﷺ, the pagans dispersed to execute their plot.

But the Apostle ﷺ was warned of their conspiracy by the All-Knowing God. He asked ʿAlī ؓ to lie on his bed and to wrap himself in his mantle. He also told ʿAlī ؓ that no harm would come to him.

The murderous band stood outside the Apostle's house ﷺ with drawn scimitars in their hands, in readiness to attack the Prophet ﷺ. The Apostle of God ﷺ came out and took a handful of dust. God instantly took away their sight and the Apostle ﷺ went through their ranks, sprinkling the dust, over their heads and reciting *Sūrah Yāsīn*—"And We have set a bar before them and a bar behind them, and (thus) have covered them so that they see not."[1] He went through them but nobody was able to see him.

Then, there came a man who asked them, "What are you waiting for here?" When they replied that they were waiting for Muḥammad (peace be upon him), he said, "May God confound you! He has gone away." They peeped through the chink of the door and saw ʿAlī sleeping on the bed wrapped in the Apostle's mantle ﷺ. They had taken him for the Prophet ﷺ and so had waited till morning when ʿAlī got up from the bed. All of them were now brought to shame.[2]

PROPHET'S MIGRATION TO MADĪNAH

The Apostle ﷺ came to Abū Bakr ؓ and told him that God had given him permission to emigrate from Makkah. Abū Bakr ؓ exclaimed, "Together, O Apostle of God?" for he was anxious to keep company with him. The Apostle ﷺ answered: "Yes, you will accompany me." Then Abū Bakr presented two dromedaries he had been keeping in readiness for the purpose. Abū Bakr then hired ʿAbdullāh ibn Urayqiṭ ؓ to act as a guide.

THE STRANGE INCONSISTENCY

The unbelieving Quraysh of Makkah were bitterly set against the Apostle ﷺ. Yet they were absolutely convinced of his truthfulness and trustworthiness, nobility and magnanimity. If anybody in Makkah feared the loss or misappropriation of his property, he would usually deposit it with the Apostle ﷺ. The Apostle ﷺ had thus a number of things committed to his care. He therefore charged ʿAlī

1 Qur'ān 36:9.
2 *Ibn Hishām*, vol. I, pp. 480–83.

ﷺ to return these to their owners before leaving Makkah. In fact, such square dealing at this critical moment is a remarkable commentary on the nobility of the Prophet ﷺ as well as the callousness of his persecutors thus clarified by God.

> We know well how their talk grieves you. Though in truth they deny not you [Muḥammad] but evil-doers flout the revelations of Allāh."[1]

THE MORAL OF THE EMIGRATION

The emigration of the Prophet ﷺ exemplifies the principle of sacrifice, in that everything, however much one may covet it, ought to be sacrificed for the sake of one's faith or ideal. Worldly estate and effects or any other thing that a man is disposed to value can never take the place of his faith nor can the faith be bartered away for all the world.

Makkah was the birthplace of the Apostle ﷺ. As the homeland of the Apostle of God ﷺ and his Companions, they would have had a particular love for it. Then, it had also the House of God, that they loved and adored like the light of one's eye, yet none of this stood in the way of bidding farewell to their hearths and homes, families and kin for the simple fact that the pagans of Makkah would not allow them the freedom of conscience and liberty to practise their faith.

The Prophet ﷺ loved Makkah but he also loved his faith: one was a natural affection and the other an insatiate thirst of the soul. We find the two most tender feelings of human nature articulately expressed by the Apostle ﷺ while leaving Makkah.

> What a fine city you are and how ardently I love you. Had my people not exiled me, I would have never settled anywhere save in your city.[2]

In truth and reality, the Apostle ﷺ had to leave his homeland in pursuance of the divine command.

> O my bondmen who believe! Lo! My earth is spacious. Therefore serve Me alone.[3]

TOWARDS THE CAVE ON MOUNT THAWR

The Apostle ﷺ and Abū Bakr ﷺ secretly made for the cave on Mount Thawr. Abū Bakr ﷺ instructed his son ʿAbdullāh ﷺ to find out what the Makkans were

1 Qur'ān 6:33.
2 Tirmidhī: Faḍl Makkah.
3 Qur'ān 29:56.

saying concerning them and then relay them to him. And he asked ʿĀmir ibn Fuhayrah ؓ, his slave, to feed his flock by the day and bring their milk to them in the evening. Asmā' ؓ, his daughter, would bring food for them at night.

THE MIRACLE OF LOVE

The flame of love is the light of Heaven that illuminates the soul. It has been, ever since the creation of this world, the most ardent passion of the human heart, advising, directing and guiding man along the right path in moments of danger. It is like the worried expression of one mad about something, for the innermost instinct of such a man is never remiss and is able to perceive even the slightest danger to his avidly desired object. Such were the feelings of Abū Bakr ؓ about the Apostle of God ﷺ during this journey. It is related that when the Apostle ﷺ set out for the cave on Mount Thawr, Abū Bakr ؓ sometimes went ahead of the Apostle ﷺ and then behind him, until the Apostle ﷺ marked his uneasiness and asked, "Abū Bakr, what's the matter? Often you go behind me and sometimes you go ahead!" Abū Bakr replied, "O Apostle of God, when I think of those in pursuit I go behind you but then I apprehend an ambush and I go on before you."[1]

When the two arrived at the cave on Mount Thawr, Abū Bakr ؓ asked the Apostle ﷺ to wait until he had searched and cleaned up the cave. So, he went in and searched it and came out after cleaning it up. Then he remembered that he had not properly searched one crevice. He again asked the Apostle ﷺ to wait a while and went in to see it for the second time. He let the Apostle ﷺ go into the cave only after he had fully satisfied himself that it did not harbour wild beasts or reptiles.

THE CELESTIAL ASSISTANT

After the two companions had entered the cave, a spider spun its web across the mouth of the cave on a bush at the entrance, concealing the Apostle ﷺ from those who might look into it. Then came two doves, who fluttered over the cave for some time, and then sat down to lay eggs there.[2] Allāh's are the hosts of the heavens and the earth.[3]

1 Ibn Kathīr, *Al-Bidayah*, vol.III, p.180

2 Ibn Kathīr, vol.II, pp.240–241

3 Qur'ān 48:7

THE MOST CRITICAL MOMENT OF HUMAN HISTORY

The most critical moment of the world's history, when the fate of mankind hung by a thread, drew near as Quraysh horsemen on the look-out for the two fugitives galloping over the desert came to the cave where the two hunkered down. The world held its breath in suspense: did a dark and disastrous future lie ahead of humanity or was it to take the most favourable turn? The pursuers who stood debating among themselves on the mouth of the cave had only to look down in the cave, but the web on the mouth of the cave convinced them that nobody could possibly be inside it.[1]

One may think it fantastic or miraculous but it was how God helped His Apostle ﷺ.

> Then Allāh caused the peace of His reassurance to descend upon him and supported him with hosts you cannot see.[2]

LO! ALLĀH IS WITH US

Peering, Abū Bakr ؓ looked over his head. He saw the blood-thirsty warriors of Quraysh standing at the mouth of the cave. He said to his companion with a trembling heart, "O Apostle of God, if any one of them steps forward they will see us." "What misgivings have you," replied the Apostle ﷺ, "about the two with whom the third is Allāh?"[3] It was as a reminder of this event that the revelation came down from God:

> When they two were in the cave, when he said unto his comrade: Grieve not, Lo! Allāh is with us.[4]

SURĀQAH TRACKS THE APOSTLE ﷺ

The Quraysh offered a reward of one hundred camels to anyone who brought back the Apostle ﷺ. The Prophet ﷺ and Abū Bakr ؓ spent three nights in the cave and then guided by ʿĀmir ibn Fuhayrah ؓ went along the road by the seacoast. Surāqah ibn Mālik ibn Juʿsham heard of the price that the Quraysh had set on the head of the Apostle and hurried after him. The reward of a hundred camels spurred him on and he tracked their footsteps along the shore. He set his

---

1 Ibn Kathīr, vol.II, p.239

2 Qur'ān 9:40.

3 Bukhārī: "Kitāb at-Tafsīr."

4 Qur'ān 9:40.

mare go in a canter until the fugitives were within sight. But, lo, his mare stumbled abruptly, and he was thrown off. He resumed the chase until he could see three men up ahead. Suddenly, his mare stumbled for the third time, its forelegs sinking up to the knees in the ground, throwing him off again. He also saw dust rising from the ground like a sandstorm.

Surāqah was now convinced that the Apostle ﷺ was protected against him and he would not in any case triumph over him. He called out saying that he was Surāqah ibn Juʿsham and that no harm would come to them from him. The Apostle ﷺ asked Abū Bakr, Ask him what he wants from us. Surāqah answered, "Write for me a warrant of security." Thereupon the Apostle ﷺ ordered ʿĀmir ibn Fuhayrah ﷺ to write the warrant which he wrote on a piece of tanned leather or bone. Surāqah preserved the writing for long as a keepsake.[1]

A PREDICTION

The Apostle of God had been driven out of his homeland, the enemy on the look-out for him was after his blood, but his mind's eye was calling up the day when his followers would be trampling the realms of Caesars and Chosroes. In those adverse circumstances, the darkest hour of his life, he made a prediction of the bright times ahead. To Surāqah he said, "Surāqah, how would you feel when you put on Chosroes' bracelets?"[2]

God had indeed promised succour and victory and prosperity to His Apostle ﷺ and the triumphant ascendancy of His Religion of Truth.

> He it is who has sent His messenger with the guidance and the Religion of Truth, that He may cause it to prevail over all religions, however much the disbelievers may be averse."[3]

Those who cannot see beyond the material agency of cause and effect would shrug their shoulders at this prediction. The Quraysh discarded the forebodings of the Apostle as incredulous and inconceivable, but the foresight of the Apostle ﷺ opened far into the future:

> Lo! Allāh fails not to keep the tryst."[4]

And the events took shape exactly the way the Apostle ﷺ had foretold to

1 Ibn Hishām, vol. I, pp. 489–90; Bukhārī, "Hijrat an-Nabī.

2 This does indeed come to pass during the Caliphate of ʿUmar ibn al-Khaṭṭāb, see *Itmām al-Wafā'*, Turath.

3 Qur'ān 9:33.

4 Qur'ān 13:31.

Surāqah. When Persia was conquered and the tiara, robe and bracelets of Chosroes were brought to ʿUmar, he sent for Surāqah and asked him to put on the royal dress.[1]

Surāqah took the warrant of security for he was by then convinced of the victory of the Prophet ﷺ. He offered some provisions and utensils, but the Apostle ﷺ accepted nothing from him. He simply said to Surāqah, "Keep secret our whereabouts."

THE BLESSED HOST

Abū Bakr ؓ and Apostle ﷺ passed by the tent of Umm Maʿbad, a woman of Khuzāʿah, who had an ewe but its udder had dried up owing to drought. God's Messenger ﷺ wiped its udder with his hand and mentioning the name of God most High, he prayed that Umm Maʿbad might find blessing in her ewe. Milk began to flow from it. He first gave Umm Maʿbad ؓ and others a drink until all of them were fully sated. He himself drank last of all. He milked it a second time, and when the vessel was full he left it with her. When Abū Maʿbad came back and his wife ؓ told him about the prodigious happening and the angelic stranger, he replied, "By God, he appears to be the same man of Quraysh whom they are prowling after."[2]

They continued their Journey with the guide until they reached Qubā' in the vicinity of Madīnah. This was Monday, the 12th day of Rabīʿ al-Awwal.[3] A new era was indeed beginning, because it was from the start of this year that the Islamic calendar of *Hijrah* takes its origin.

1 *Al-Istīʿāb fī Maʿrifati 'l-Aṣḥāb*, vol. II, p. 597. See also *Itmām al-wafā'*, al-Khuḍarī, published by Turath.

2 *Zād al-Maʿād*, Vol. II, p.309.

3 24th September, 622 AD.

8

Yathrib before Islam

Difference between Makkan and Madīnan Societies

Yathrib had been marked by Providence to shelter the Messenger of God ﷺ after his emigration and to bring forth not only the first Islamic society but also to serve as a radiant centre for the universal call of Islam. The great honour accorded to the city makes it necessary to know its distinctive features—its physical, social and cultural conditions, the Arab tribes living there and their mutual relations, the economic and political machinations of the Jews and their fighting strength as well as the way life was sustained by its fertile land. Various religions, cultures and communities flourished in the city side by side; it contrasted starkly with Makkah which was dominated by one faith and one cultural pattern. The details given here, albeit brief, depict the state of affairs in Madīnah when the Apostle ﷺ made his entrance in that city.

Jews

The preferred view of historians concerning the Jewish settlements in Arabia, at large, and those in Madīnah, in particular, is that they date from the first century AD. Dr. Israel Wellphenson writes:

> After Palestine and Jerusalem were laid waste in 70 AD and the Jews dispersed to different parts of the world, a number of them made their way to Arabia, according to the Jewish historian Josephus, who was himself present at the siege of Jerusalem

and had led the Jewish units on several occasions. Arab sources also corroborate his statement.[1]

Three Jewish tribes, Qaynuqāʿ, an-Naḍīr and Qurayẓah, had settled in Madīnah. In total, over two thousand adults belonged to these tribes: Qaynuqāʾ were estimated to have seven hundred combatants, an-Naḍīr too had almost the same number while Qurayẓah were reported to have between seven and nine hundred men of fighting age.[2] These tribes were not on good terms with one another and would come to blows very often. Dr. Israel Wellphenson says:

> Banū Qaynuqāʾ were set against the rest of the Jews because they had sided with Banū Khazraj in the battle of Buʿāth in which Banū ʾn-Naḍīr and Banū Qurayẓah had inflicted a crushing defeat and massacred Banū Qaynuqāʾ even though the latter had paid bloodwit for their prisoners of war. The bitterness between the Jewish tribes continued to persist after the battle of Buʿāth. When Banū Qaynuqāʾ subsequently fell out with the Anṣār, no other Jewish tribe came to their aid against the Anṣār.[3]

The Qurʾān also makes a reference to the mutual discord between the Jews:

> And when We made with you a covenant (saying): Shed not the blood of your people nor turn (a party of) your people out of your dwellings. Then you ratified (Our covenant) and you were witness (thereto).
>
> Yet you it is who slay each other and drive out a party of your people from their homes, supporting one another against them by sin and transgression—and if they come to you as captives you would ransom them, whereas their expulsion was itself unlawful for you.[4]

The Jews of Madīnah had their dwellings in their own separate localities in different parts of the city. When Banū ʾn-Naḍīr and Banū Qurayẓah forced Banū Qaynuqāʾ to vacate their settlement on the outskirts of the town, they took up

1 Dr. Israel Wellphenson, *Tārīkh al-Yahūd fī Bilād al-ʾArab fī ʾl-Jāhiliyyah wa Ṣadr al-Islām*, p. 9.

2 These figures are based on the number of Jews of different tribes given by the biographers like Ibn Hishām in connection to the exile of Banū ʾn-Naḍīr and the massacre of Banū Qurayẓah, etc. Banū Qaynuqāʿ, an-Naḍīr and Qurayẓah were the chief tribes consisting of several clans as, for example, Banū hadal was a clan allied to Banū Qurayẓah. A number of persons belonging to this clan who accepted Islam became eminent Companions. Banū Zanbāʿ was another branch of Banū Qurayẓah. A few of the Jewish clans, such as, Banū ʿAwf, Banū ʾn-Najjār, Banū Sāʿidah, Banū Thaʿlabah, Banū Jafnah, Banū ʾl-Ḥārith etc., have been mentioned in the treaty made by the Apostle with the Jews. After mentioning those tribes the treaty says: "The chiefs and friends of the Jews are themselves." Samhūdī says in *Wafāʾ al-Wafāʾ* that the Jews were divided into more than twenty clans (p. 116).

3 *Tārīkh al-Yahūd fī Bilād al-ʿArab fī ʾl-Jāhiliyyah wa Ṣadr al-Islām*, p. 129.

4 Qurʾān 2:84–5.

their quarters in a section of the city. Banū 'n-Naḍīr had their habitation in the higher parts, some four or five kilometres from the city, towards the valley of Bathān, having some of the richest groves and agricultural lands of Madīnah. The third Jewish tribe, Banū Qurayẓah, occupied a district known as Mahzur a few kilometres to the south of the city.[1]

The Jews of Madīnah lived in compact settlements where they erected fortifications and citadels. They were, however, not independent but lived as confederate clans of the stronger Arab tribes which guaranteed them immunity from raids by the nomads. Predatory incursions by the nomadic tribes being a perpetual menace, the Jewish tribes had always to seek protection of one or another chieftain of the powerful Arab tribes.[2]

RELIGIOUS AFFAIRS OF THE JEWS

The Jews considered themselves to be blessed with a divine religion and law. They had their own seminaries, known as *midrā*[3] which imparted instruction in their religious and secular sciences, law, history and the Talmudic lore. Similarly, for offering prayers and performing other religious rites they had synagogues wherein they also consulted each other regarding their affairs. They observed the laws taken from Pentateuch as well as many more rigid and uncompromising customary rules imposed by their priests and rabbis, and celebrated Jewish feasts and fasts, as, for example, they would observe on the tenth day of the month of Tishri, the fast of Atonement.[4]

The Jews had however lost the spirit of their religion, and nothing distinguished them from their polytheist neighbours apart from the tenets of *tawhid*, or monotheism, and some of its divine laws. However, when they refused to accept Islam with its absolute monotheism even their prestige of being a monotheistic faith was lost.

Moreover, the Jews of Madīnah had lost the moral teachings of their faith and dabbled in the art of magic, soothsaying, and dispensing poison to meet their personal desires and passions. Indeed, their leaders and scholars continued such wicked practices even though they were fully aware it was in defiance of God's will. The Qur'ān alludes to this:

---

1 Dr. Muḥammad Sayyid aṭ-Ṭanṭāwī, *Banū Isrāʿīl fi 'l-Qur'ān wa 's-Sunnah,* p.77.

2 Dr. Jawwād ʿAlī, *Tarīkh al-ʿArab qabl al-Islām* (Baghdad), vol. VII, p. 23.

3 Banū Isrāʿīl fi 'l-Qur'ān wa 's-Sunnah, pp. 80–81.

4 Dāʿiratul Maʿārif al-Yahūdiyyah

> And they followed [instead] what the devils had recited during the reign of Solomon.[1]

This was the religious state of the Jews in Madīnah right up to the messengership of Muḥammad ﷺ. The renowned Jewish orientalist (well known for his censure of the teachings of Islām), Margoliouth states about the Jews of Madīnah:

> These Jews were highly skilled in magic, and preferred its dark arts to fighting openly in the battlefield.[2]

The incident during the battle of Khaybar reveals how the Jews attempted to take the life of the Apostle ﷺ through poisoning him, though their attempt failed.[3]

As for their distorting words through mockery and ill meaning, the Qur'ān reveals:

> You who believe, do not say: Rāʿinā (attend to us) and say: Unẓurnā (look at us) and listen, and the disbelievers will have a humiliating punishment.[4]

The Jews would use the term *rāʿinā* behind the messenger's back ﷺ as an insult to indicate that they were not listening to him, and to mock him with a reference to its root meaning *ar-raʿan*, ignorant and dumb.[5] Thus in this verse God tells the believers to use words with clear meaning and not to refer to ambiguous terms with hidden and underlying connotations. The Qur'ān addresses yet another incident in which the Jews would greet the Apostle ﷺ with *as-sām*[6] *alayka* (death be upon you as opposed to peace, *as-salām*):

And they come to you, they greet you with the words with which Allah has not greeted you.[7]

FINANCES

The financial relationship of the Madinan Jews with other tribes was mainly limited to lending money on interest on security of personal property. In an agricultural region like Madīnah, there was ample scope for money lending businesses since farmers would very often needed capital for purposes of cultivation.[8]

1 Qur'ān 2:102
2 D.S. Margoliouth's *Muhammad and the Rise of Islam*, p. 189.
3 Bukhārī
4 Qur'ān 2:104
5 *Rūḥ al-Ma'ānī*, al-Baghdādī, vol.I, pp.348–349.
6 *Majma' Biḥār al-Anwār*, vol.III, p.155
7 Qur'ān 58:8. See also *Rūḥ al-Ma'ānī* and *Tafsīr ibn Kathīr*.
8 Ibid.

The system of lending money was not limited merely to pledging personal property as security for repayment of the loan, for the creditors very often forced the borrowers to pledge even their women and children. An incident related to the murder of Kaʿb ibn Ashraf, narrated by Bukhārī, bears testimony to the prevailing practice:

> Muḥammad ibn Maslamah said to Kaʿb: Now we hope that you will lend us a camel-load or two (of food). Kaʿb answered, I will do so, (but) you shall pledge something with me. [The Muslims] said: What do you want? Kaʿb answered, Pledge your women with me. They said, How can we pledge our women with you, the most beautiful of the Arabs? Kaʿb said, Then pledge your sons with me. [The Muslims] replied, How can we pledge our sons with you? (Later) they would be abused (on this account), and people would say: He has been pledged for a camel-load or two (of food)! This would disgrace us! We shall, however, pledge our armour with you.[1]

Such transactions produced, naturally enough, hatred and disgust between the mortgagees and the mortgagors, particularly since the Arabs were famously thin-skinned where the honour of their women was concerned.

The concentration of capital in the hands of Jews had given them power to exercise economic pressure on the social economy of the city. The markets were at their mercy. They rigged the market through hoarding, creating artificial scarcity and causing price inflation. The Jews faced public opprobrium from the people of Madīnah owing to these malpractices, usuriousness and profiteering, which went against the grain of the common Arab.[2]

With their predilection for avarice and acquisitiveness the Jews inevitably adopted an expansionist attitude as pointed out by De Lacy O' Leary:

> In the seventh century there was a strong feeling between these Bedouin[3] and the Jewish colonists because the latter, by extending their agricultural area, were encroaching upon the land which Bedouin regarded as their own pastures.[4]

The Jews misguided by overweening cupidity and selfishness in their social dealings with the Arab tribes, the Aws and the Khazraj, spent lavishly, though judiciously, in creating a rift between the two tribes. On a number of occasions in the past they had pitted one tribe against the other so that both had been worn

1 Bukhārī: Kitāb al-Maghāzī, see Qatl Kaʿb ibn Ashraf.

2 Dr. Muḥammad Sayyid aṭ-Ṭanṭāwī, *Banū Isrāʾīl fi 'l-Qur'ān wa 's-Sunnah*, p. 79.

3 De Lacy O'Leary is referring to the Aws and the Khazraj and other Arab tribes living in and around Madīnah.

4 Arabia Before Mohammad, p. 174.

out and economically ruined. The primary objective the Jews had set before themselves was to maintain their economic hold over Madīnah.

For many centuries the Jews had been waiting for a redeemer. This belief of the Jews in the coming of a prophet, about which they used to talk with the Arabs, had prepared the Aws and the Khazraj to give their faith readily to the Apostle ﷺ.[1]

RELIGIOUS AND CULTURAL CONDITIONS

The Jews of Arabia spoke Arabic although their dialect was interspersed with Hebrew for they had not completely given up their religious language, which they used for educational and religious purposes. In regard to the missionary activities of the Jews, Dr. Israel Wellphenson says:

> There is less uncertainty about the opportunities offered to the Jews in consolidating their religious supremacy in Arabia. Had they so wished, they could have used their influence to their best advantage, but as it is too well known to every student of the history of the Jews, they have never made any effort to invite other nations to embrace their faith; rather, for certain reasons, they have been forbidden to preach their religion to others.[2]

Be that as it may, many of the Aws and the Khazraj and certain other Arab tribals had been Judaised owing to their close social connections with the Jews, or to ties of blood. Thus, there were Jews in Arabia who were of Israelite descent, with an addition of Arab proselytes. An example was the well-known poet and influential Jewish merchant Kaʿb ibn Ashraf (often called an-Naḍrī) belonging to the tribe of Ṭayy. His father had married into the tribe of Banū 'n-Naḍīr but he grew up to be a zealous Jew. Ibn Hishām writes about him: Kaʿb ibn Ashraf who was one of the Ṭayy of the sub-section of Banū Nabhān whose mother was from the Banū 'n-Naḍīr.[3]

Among the pagan Arabs it was a custom for someone whose son died in infancy to swear an oath to God to entrust his next son to a Jew in order to bring him up in his own religion if he survived. A Tradition referring to this custom is found in the *Sunan Abī Dāwūd.*

Ibn ʿAbbās said: "Any woman whose children died would make a vow that if her next child remained alive, she would make him a Jew. Accordingly, when

---

1 Dr. Muḥammad Sayyid aṭ-Ṭanṭāwī, *Banū Isrāʾīl fī 'l-Qur'ān wa 's-Sunnah* pp. 73–101.

2 Dr. Israel Wellphenson; *Tārīkh al-Yahūd fī Bilād al-'Arab fī 'l-Jāhiliyyah wa Ṣadr al-Islām,* p. 72.

3 *Ibn Hishām,* vol. I, p. 514.

Banū 'n-Naḍīr were exiled they had the sons of Anṣār with them; they said, 'We would not forsake our sons'; thereupon the revelation came: There is no compulsion in religion."[1]

THE AWS AND THE KHAZRAJ

The two great Arab tribes of Madīnah, the Aws and the Khazraj, traced a common descent from the Yemeni tribe of Azd, from whence successive waves of emigrants inundated the northern regions from time to time. These emigrations were brought about by any number of reasons, including unstable political conditions in Yemen, Abyssinian aggression and disruption of the irrigation system supporting agriculture after the destruction of Ma'ārib dam. However, both the Aws and the Khazraj came to Madīnah after the Jews. The Aws settled down in ʿAwālī, an area in the south-east of Madīnah while Khazraj occupied the lands in the central and northern parts of the city. The northern part of the city being low-lying, nothing intervened between the habitation of Khazraj and Ḥarrat al-Wabrah in the west.[2]

The Khazraj consisted of four clans: Mālik, ʿAdī, Māzin and Dīnār, all collaterals to Banū Najjār, and also known as Taym al-Lāt. Banū Najjār took up residence in the central part of the city where now stands the Prophet's mosque. The Aws having settled in the fertile, cultivable lands were the neighbours of more influential and powerful Jewish tribes. The lands occupied by Khazraj were comparatively less fertile and they had only Banū Qaynuqā' as their neighbours.[3]

It is rather difficult to reckon the numerical strength of the Aws and the Khazraj with any amount of certainty, but an estimate can be formed from the various battles in which they took part after the Apostle's emigration ﷺ to Madīnah. The combatants drafted from these two tribes on the occasion of the conquest of Makkah numbered four thousand.[4]

When the Apostle ﷺ emigrated to Madīnah, the Arabs were in the ascendancy and in a position of dominance. The Jews had become disunited and forced to take a subordinate position by seeking alliances either with the Aws or the Khazraj. Their mutual relationships were even worse for they were more tyrannical to their co-religionists in times of warfare than were the Arabs. It was due to the deeply ingrained enmity between Banū Qaynuqā', Banū 'n-Naḍīr and

1 *Sunan Abī Dāwūd, Kitāb al-Jihād,* vol. II.

2 *Makkah wa 'l-Madīnah fī'l-Jāhiliyyah wa ʿAhd Ar-Rasūl,* p. 311. [Aḥmad Ibrāhīm ash-Sharīf]

3 *Makkah wa 'l-Madīnah fī'l-Jāhiliyyah wa ʿAhd Ar-Rasūl,* p. 311. [Aḥmad Ibrāhīm ash-Sharīf]

4 *Al-Imtāʿ,* Taqī ad-Din Abī Muḥammad al-Maqrīzī vol. I, p. 364.

Banū Qurayẓah, that Banū Qaynuqā' were forced to abandon their cultivated lands and take up the profession of artisans.[1]

The Aws and the Khazraj, too, often came to the scratch. The first of these encounters was the battle of Samīr while the last one, the battle of Buʿāth, was fought five years before the *hijrah*.[2] The Jews always tried to sow dissension between Aws and Khazraj and made them run afoul of one another so as to divert their attention from them. The Arab tribes were conscious of their nefarious activities: "the fox" was the popular nickname they had given to the Jews.

An incident related by Ibn Hishām, on the authority of Ibn Isḥāq, sheds light upon the character of the Jews. Shaʿth ibn Qays was a Jew, old and bitter towards the Muslims. He passed by a place where a number of the Apostle's Companions ﷺ from the Aws and the Khazraj were talking together. He was filled with rage to see their amity and unity; so he asked a Jewish youth friendly with the Anṣār to join them and mention the battle of Buʿāth and the preceding battles, and to recite some of the poems concerning those events in order to stir up their tribal sentiments.

The cunning device of Shaʿth did not fail. The two tribes had been at daggers in the past. Their passions were aroused and they started bragging and quarrelling until they were about to unsheathe their swords when the Apostle ﷺ came with some of the Muhājirūn. He pacified them and appealed to their bonds of harmony brought about by Islam. Then the Anṣār realised that the enemy had duped them. The Aws and the Khazraj wept and embraced one another as if nothing had happened.[3]

PHYSICAL AND GEOGRAPHICAL CONDITIONS

At the time the Apostle ﷺ migrated to Yathrib the city was divided into distinct sections inhabited by Arabs and Jews, with a separate district allocated to each clan. Each division consisted of residential quarters and the soil used for agricultural purposes while in another part they had their strongholds or fortress-like structures.[4] The Jews had fifty-nine such strongholds in Madīnah.[5] Dr. Israel Wellphenson writes:

> The fortresses were of great importance in Yathrib for the people belonging to a

---

1 Makkah wa 'l-Madīnah, p. 322.

2 *Makkah wa 'l-Madīnah*, p. 322–323. *Fatḥ al-Bārī*, vol. 7, VII, p. 85. See *Ibn Kathīr* for a detailed account of the battle of Buʿāth.

3 *Ibn Hishām*, vol. I, pp.555–56.

4 *Tārīkh al-Yahūd fī Bilād al-'Arab fī 'l-Jāhiliyyah wa Ṣadr al-Islām*, Dr Israel Wellphenson p. 116.

5 As-Samhūdī, *Wafā' al-Wafā' fī Akhbār Dār al-Muṣṭafā*, vol. I, p. 116.

clan took shelter in them during raids by the enemy. They afforded protection to the women and children who retreated to them in times of fights and forays while the men went out to engage the enemy. These safeholds were also utilised as store-houses for storage of food-grains and fruits for the enemy could easily pillage them in open places. Goods and arms were, also, kept in the fortress and caravans carrying merchandise used to halt near them for the markets were usually held along the doors of these fortresses. The strongholds also housed the synagogues and educational institutions known as midrās.[1] The costly goods that were stored in the fortresses show that the religious scriptures, were also kept in them. Jewish leaders and chieftains used to assemble in these fortresses for consultations or taking decisions on important issues which were sealed by taking an oath on the scripture."[2]

Defining the word *aṭam*, as these fortresses were called, Dr. Wellphenson writes: "The term connotes in Hebrew, to shut out or to obstruct. When it is used in connexion with a wall it denotes such windows as are shut down from outside but can be opened from inside. The word is also expressive of a defensive wall or a rampart and therefore we can presume that *utum* was the name given by the Jews to their fortresses. They had shutters which could be shut from the outer side and opened from the inner side."

Yathrib was, thus, a cluster of such strongholds or fortified suburbs which had taken the shape of a town because of their proximity. The Qur'ān also hints to this peculiar feature of the city in these words:

That which Allāh gives as spoils unto His messenger from the people of the townships.[3]

Again, another reference to Madīnah signifies the same peculiarity.

They will not fight against you in a body save in fortified villages or from behind walls.[4]

Lava plains occupy a place of special importance in the physical geography of Madīnah. These plains, formed by the matter flowing from a volcano which cools into rocks of burnt basalt of dark brown and black colour and of irregular shape and size, stretch out far and wide, and cannot be traversed on foot or even on horseback or by camel. Two of these lava plains are more extensive; one is

1 An abbreviation of *Bel ha-Midras* signifying house of study or the place: where students of the law gathered to listen to Midrash. Used in contradiction to the *Bel ha-Sefer*, i.e. the primary, school attended by children under the age of thirteen to learn the scripture, it goes without saying that the Jews of Madīnah had higher institutions of learning (*Jewish Encyclopedia*, vol. II, art, *Bel ha-Midras*).

2 *Tārīkh al-Yahūd fī Bilād al-'Arab fī 'l-Jāhiliyyah wa Ṣadr al-Islām*, pp.116–117

3 Qur'ān 59:7.

4 Qur'ān 59:14.

to the east and is known as Ḥarrat al-Wāqim, while the other lies in the west and is called Ḥarrat al-Wabarah. Majduddīn Fīrōzābādī writes in *Al-Maghānim al-Maṭābah fī Maʿālim aṭ-Ṭābah* that there are, several lava plains surrounding Madīnah. The two lava plains of the east and the west have virtually made the city a fortified stronghold that could be attacked only from the north (where trenches were dug on the occasion of the battle of trenches).

On the southern side the oases, thickets and clumped date-palm groves as well as intertied houses of the densely populated area defended the city against enemy incursions.[1] The strategic location of Madīnah was one of the factors responsible for its selection as the new home of the emigrants.

Ḥarrat al-Wāqim, to the east of the city, dotted with numerous green oases, was more populous than Ḥarrat al-Wabarah. When the Apostle ﷺ emigrated to Yathrib, the more influential Jewish tribes such as Banū 'n-Naḍīr and Banū Qurayẓah were living in Ḥarrat al-Wāqim along with some of the important clans of Aws such as Banū ʿAbd al-Ashhal, Banū Zufar, Banū Ḥārithah and Banū MuʿĀwiyah. The eastern lava plain went was known as Wāqim, named after a locality in the district occupied by Banū ʿAbd al-Ashhal.[2]

RELIGIOUS AND SOCIAL CONDITIONS

By and large, the inhabitants of Madīnah followed the Quraysh whom they held to be the guardians of the Holy sanctuary and the matrix of their religious creed as well as social ethics. Like other Arabs, the population of Madīnah was pagan and principally devoted to the same idols as worshipped by the inhabitants of Ḥijāz, and of Makkah in particular, in addition to a few regional or tribal deities considered to be the personal or private gods of the particular clans. Thus, Manāt was the oldest and the most popular deity of the inhabitants of Madīnah: Aws and Khazraj rendered honour to it as the co-partner of God. The idol was set up on the seashore, between Makkah and Madīnah, at Mushallal near Qadīd. Al-Lāt was the favourite god of the people of Ṭā'if, while the Quraysh revered Al-ʿUzzā as their national deity. It was so because the people of every place had a particular patron god to which they were emotionally attached. If anyone in Madīnah had a wooden replica of an idol he typically consider it to be Manāt, the idol that ʿAmr ibn Jamūḥ ﵁, the chief of Banū Salamah in Madīnah kept in his house before his conversion to Islam.[3]

1 *Al-Maghānim al-Maṭābah fī Maʿālim aṭ-Ṭābah,* pp. 108–114.

2 Dr. Muḥammad Husayn Haikal. *Manzil al-Waḥy.* p. 557.

3 Maḥmūd Shukrī al-Ālūsī, *Bulūgh al-Arab fī Maʿrifat Aḥwāl al-ʿArab,* vol. I, p. 346 and vol. II, p. 208.

Aḥmad ibn Ḥanbal ﷺ relates a tradition from ʿUrwah ﷺ, on the authority of ʿĀ'ishah ﷺ, which says: "The Anṣār would cry *labbayk*[1] to Manāt and to worship it near Mushallal before accepting Islam. Anyone who performed pilgrimage in the name of Manāt did not consider it lawful to go round the mounts of Ṣafā and Marwah.[2] When the people once enquired of the Apostle ﷺ: O Messenger of Allāh, we felt some hesitation during the pagan past in going round Ṣafā and Marwah, God sent down the revelation:[3] 'Lo! Ṣafā and Marwah are amongst the signs of Allāh'

However, we are not aware of any other idol in Madīnah as glamorised as Lāt, Manāt, ʿUzzā and Hubal or venerated like them, nor were idols set up in Madīnah which people from other tribes would visit. Madīnah does not appear to be bristling with idols, unlike Makkah, where idols were set up in every house and vendors would offer them for sale to the pilgrims. Makkah was, all in all, the prototype and symbol of idolatry in Arabia whereas Madīnah simply trailed behind it.

In Madīnah the people had two days on which they engaged in games. When the Apostle ﷺ came to Madīnah, he said to them, "God has substituted something better for you, the day of sacrifice and the day of the breaking fast."[4] Certain commentators of the traditions hold the view that the two festivals celebrated by the people of Madīnah were Nowrūz and Mahrajān which had perhaps been adopted from the Persians.[5]

The Aws and the Khazraj came of a lineage whose nobility was acknowledged even by the Quraysh. The Anṣār were descendants of Banū Qaḥṭān belonging to the southern stock of *ʿArab ʿĀribah,* with whom Quraysh had marital affinity. Hāshim ibn ʿAbd Manāf had married Salmā bint ʿAmr ibn Zayd of Banū ʿAdī ibn an-Najjār, which was a clan of the Khazraj. Nevertheless, the Quraysh considered their own ancestry to be nobler than that of the Arab clans of Madīnah. On the day of Badr when ʿUtbah ibn Rabīʿah, Shaybah ibn Rabīʿah and Walīd ibn Rabīʿah came ahead of their ranks and challenged the Muslims to single combat, some youths of the Anṣār stepped forth to fight them. The warriors of Quraysh, however, asked who they were and on coming to know that they belonged to the Anṣār, replied, "We have nothing to do with you." Then one of them called out, "Muḥammad ﷺ, send forth some of our own rank and blood to face us." Thereupon the Apostle ﷺ ordered, "Advance, O ʿUbaydah ibn al-Ḥārith! Advance, O

---

1 Lit. "At Thy Service."

2 A few more traditions have been related by other Companions on this connection.

3 Qur'ān 2:158.

4 *Bulūgh al-Arab.*

5 *Bukhārī* and *Muslim.*

Ḥamzah! Advance, O ʿAlī!" When the three were in place and told their names, Quraysh said, "Yes, these are noble and our peers".[1]

The self-conceited Quraysh would look down upon farming, the occupation taken up by the Anṣār owing to the physical features of their city. We find an echo of the same conceit in what Abū Jahl said when he was slain by two youth of the Anṣār who were sons of ʿAfrā'. Abū Jahl said to ʿAbdullāh ibn Masʿūd ﷺ, although he was nearing his end, "Would that somebody other than a farmer had slain me!"[2]

ECONOMIC CULTURAL CONDITIONS

Madīnah was a veritable oasis. The soil warranted a systematic cultivation and hence its population was given over to farming and gardening. The main produce of the city consisted of grapes and dates, of which there were numerous groves,[3] trellised and untrellised. Two or more palm-trees occasionally grew out of a single root.[4]

Cereals and vegetables of different varieties were cultivated in the farms but the date was the chief item on the menu of the people specially in times of drought, for the fruit could be stored for sale or exchanged with other necessities. The date-palm was the queen of Arabian trees, the source of the prosperity of people of Madīnah, providing them with solid food and fodder for the camels. Its stems, bark and leaves were also utilised in the construction of houses and the manufacture of other goods of daily use.[5]

Countless varieties of dates[6] were grown in Madīnah where the people had developed methods to improve the quality and produce of the dates through experience and experimentation. Of these, one was the distinction made

---

1 *Ibn Hishām*, vol. I, p. 625.

2 Muḥammad ibn Ṭāhir Fatnī writes in *Majmaʿ al-Biḥār* that the Arabs did not consider cultivation to be an occupation befitting a man of noble descent. Abū Jahl meant that if anybody other than the sons of ʿAfrā', who was a farmer, had killed him he would not have felt ashamed (vol. I, p. 68).

3 The date-palm groves of Madīnah grew into thick clusters spreading out extensively. A tradition mentions that Abū Ṭalḥah was one of the Anṣār who possessed a grove so thickly clustered that if a small bird got into his grove, it found it difficult to come out of it. Once, when he was offering prayers his eyes happened to meet a sparrow which was fluttering to get out. He was so fascinated that his thoughts turned away from the prayer for a moment. He felt so oppressed by his momentary inattentiveness to the prayers that he gave away that grove called Bīrḥā' in the way of God. Related by Imām Mālik in his *Muwaṭṭa*.

4 See Qur'ān 13:4.

5 See *Bukhārī*: *Kitāb al-ʿIlm* and its commentaries by Ibn Ḥajar and ʿAynī.

6 Arab authors list an enormous vocabulary for dates which is an indication of the importance it held for the Arab, in general, and for the people of Madīnah in particular. *Adab al-Kātib* by Ibn Qutaybah, *Fiqh al-Lughah* by Thaʿālibī and *al-Mukhaṣṣaṣ* by Ibn Sīdah should be seen in this connection. There are also treatises written on dates by other authors.

between the male pollen and female pistils of date-palms and the fertilisation (or breeding or cultivation) of ovules which was known as *ta'bīr*.[1]

Madīnah was a leading agricultural centre, it also had a flourishing mercantile business but not of the same scale as in Makkah. The barren, rocky valley of Makkah allowed no other occupation save to set out with trade caravans regularly during the summer and winter sessions to earn their livelihood.

Certain industrial pursuits were restricted to the Jews of Madīnah. They had probably brought these crafts to Madīnah from Yemen as, for instance, Banū Qaynuqā' practised the trade of goldsmithing. Wealthier than other tribes inhabiting Madīnah, the houses of the Jews were flush with money and abounding in gold and silver.[2]

The soil of Madīnah is extremely fertile because of the volcanic matter from the surrounding lava plains. The town stands in the lower part of the valley where water-courses running from the higher altitudes irrigate the agricultural lands and date-plantations. A verdant wādī well, then known by the name of ʿAqīq, supplied with water and abounding in gardens and vineyards was the pleasure spot of Madīnah's population. There were many wells scattered about the terrain; almost every garden had one by which it was irrigated, for subterranean water was found in plenty.

The vineyards and date-plantations, enclosed by garden walls, were known as *Ḥā'iṭ*.[3] The wells had sweet and plentiful supplies of water which was conducted to the orchards by means of canals or through lift irrigation.[4]

Barley was the main cereal produced in Madīnah while wheat occupied a secondary place, but vegetables were grown in abundance. Transactions of different types[5] like *muzāraʿah, mu'ājarah, muzābanah*,[6] *muḥāqalah*,[7] *mukhābarah*,[8] *mudāwamah*,[9] etc., were in vogue, some of which were retained by Islam while others were reformed or forbidden altogether.

---

1 The device used was to incise ovules for injecting pollen.

2 *Tārīkh al-Yahūd fī Bilād al-'Arab fī 'l-Jāhiliyyah wa Ṣadr al-Islām*, p. 128.

3 *Bukhārī: Kitāb al-Maghāzī*—Kaʿb ibn Mālik says that after he had endured much harshness from the people, he walked off and climbed over the wall of Abū Qatadah's orchard (*Ḥā'iṭ*), who was his paternal uncle.

4 See the tradition related by Abū Hurayrah in which he makes a mention of channels and spades for digging them (*Muslim*).

5 See the chapter dealing with cultivation and farmers in the *Ṣiḥāḥ*.

6 The sale of fruit on the palm-trees for a specified measure of dates.

7 The sale of a harvest before it was reaped for a specified measure of the same grain.

8 Renting land for a third or a quarter of the produce on the condition that the seed was provided by the owner of the land. It was called *muzāraʿah* if the seed was provided by the cultivator but certain lexicographers consider the two to be synonyms (See *Sharḥ Ṣaḥīḥ Muslim* by an-Nawawī).

9 Selling of harvest two or three years ahead.

The coins in circulation in Makkah and Madīnah were the same as already discussed in the section dealing with Makkah. However, as the inhabitants of Madīnah had to transact their business in grains and fruits, they had more of their dealings with volumetric measures.[1] These measures were *mudd, ṣāᶜ, faraq, ᶜaraq* and *wasaq*. The measures of weight prevalent in Madīnah were dirham, *thiqāf, dāniq, qīrāṭ, nawāt, riṭl, qinṭār* and *ūqiyah*.[2]

Madīnah had fertile soil but it was not self-sufficient in food grains and had to import some of the food it required. Flour,[3] refined butter and honey were brought from Syria. Tirmidhī relates on the authority of Qatādah ibn Nuᶜmān that the staple diet of the people of Madīnah consisted of dates and barley but those who were rich would purchase flour from the Syrian merchants[4] for their own consumption while other members of the family had to make do with dates and barley.[5] This report brings to light the culinary habits as well as the disparity in the standards of living of the well-to-do and the poorer sections of the people in Madīnah existing before the emigration of the Apostle ﷺ.

In Madīnah the Jews constituted the affluent class while the Arab tribesman, like other guileless Bedouins were not given to trouble their heads about the future or to feather their nests for rainy days. In addition to it, generosity was in their blood; this manifested itself in their sparing no expense in entertaining their guests. Naturally enough, they were very often forced to borrow money on interest from the Jews by pledging their personal property.

The livestock raised by the people consisted, for the most part, of camels, cows and ewes. The camels were also employed for irrigating the agricultural lands and such camels were known as *al-Ibil an-Nawāḍiḥ*. Madīnah had several pastures, of which the two, *Zaghābah* and *Ghābah*, were more well-known. The people in Madīnah would graze their flocks in these pastures and also obtained firewood from them.[6] They reared horses for military operations as well, though not on the same scale as did the inhabitants of Makkah. Banū Sulaym were renowned for their horsemanship although they used to import their horses from other regions.

Madīnah had a number of markets, the most important among these being

---

1 For this reason the Prophet said, "the measures of weight are with the people of Makkah, while the measures of volume are known by the people of Madīnah", related by *Abū Dawūd* and *an-Nisā'ī*.

2 For details see the books on tradition and *At-Tarātib al-Idāriyyah* by ᶜAbd al-Ḥayy al-Kattānī, vol. I. pp. 413–15.

3 The word used in Arabic is *darmak* which stands for fine, soft powder of wheat meal.

4 Known as *ṣafīq*, they were Nabataean merchants as stated by Muḥammad Ṭāhir Patnī. (*Majmaᶜ al-Biḥār*, vol. Ill, p. 140).

5 See *Tirmidhī*: commentary on 4:107 of the Qur'ān.

6 *Muᶜjamᶜ al-Buldān*, Yāqūt al-Ḥamawī and *Wafaᶜ al-Wafā* by al-Samhūdī.

the one run by Banū Qaynuqā' which was stocked with silver and gold ornaments, cloth and other handiworks, cotton and silk fabrics. Colourful carpets and curtains with decorative designs[1] were normally available in this market. Perfumes of different types and musk were also sold. Similarly, there were shopkeepers who sold ambergris and quicksilver.[2] Numerous forms of business transactions had come into practice, some of which were upheld by Islam while others were forbidden. The dealings that had come into vogue were known as *najash* (raising the price in an auction with no intention to buy or praising a commodity which belongs to an accomplice with the intention of exploiting another customer into buying it for a higher price) *al-Iḥtikār* (creating a Monopoly), *talaqqī 'r-rukbān* (purchasing the lot of one product from a merchant at wholesale price then selling it in the town for a high price creating a monopoly of that product), *bayᶜ al-muṣarrāt* (asking someone to cancel a transaction—when he has the choice of cancelation—tempting him with a cheaper deal), *bayᶜ bi 'n-nasī'ah* (purchasing on credit when the time of repayment is not known), *bayᶜ al-ḥāḍir li 'l-bādī* (purchasing the lot of one product from a merchant at wholesale price then selling it in the town for a high price creating a monopoly of that product), *bayᶜ al-mujāzafah* (randomly selling without weighing), *bayᶜ al-muzābanah* (purchasing fruits still on the tree with plucked fruits by estimation of weight. Estimating the weight of the fruits on the tree) and *mukhāḍarah* (purchasing fruits or grain before they have ripened fully).[3] Certain persons belonging to the Aws and the Khazraj also had their hands in lending money at interest but they were comparatively fewer in number than the Jews.The social and cultural life of the common people in Madīnah was, thanks to their refined taste, fairly well advanced. Double storied houses were common in Madīnah[4] and some of these had attached kitchen gardens. The people were used to drinking sweet water that often had to be conducted from a distance. Cushions[5] were used for sitting and the household utensils included bowls and drinking vessels made of stone and glass. Lamps were manufactured in various designs.[6] Bags and

---

1 In a tradition related by ᶜĀ'ishah, recorded in *Bukhārī* and *Muslim*, the word used for the curtain is *qirām*, which, according to Muḥammad Ṭāhir Patnī, was fine multi-coloured wool fabric or a cloth with decorative designs hung as a screen in the bridal chamber (*Majmaᶜ Biḥār al-Anwār*, Hyderabad, vol. IV, p. 258).

2 *At-Tarātīb al-Idāriyyah, by* ᶜAllamāh ᶜAbdul Ḥayy al-Kattāni vol I. p. 97.

3 For details see the chapters dealing with business transaction in the books on traditions and *Fiqh* which explain the legality or otherwise of the different forms of these transactions. Also see *Majmaᶜ Bihār al-Anwār.*

4 See the traditions relating to arrival of the Prophet in Madīnah and his stay in the ground floor of Abū Ayyūb Anṣārī's house.

5 *At-Tarātīb al-Idāriyyah*. vol I. p. 97.

6 Ibid., p. 104.

small baskets were used for carrying articles of daily use and corn from the fields. The dwellings of those who were well off, particularly the Jews, were well-stocked with many more types of household furniture. The jewellery worn by the womenfolk included bracelets, armlets, anklets, wristlets, earrings circlets, rings, golden or gem necklaces.[1]

Spinning and weaving were popular domestic pursuits in which the women spent their time in Madīnah. Sewing and dyeing of clothes, house building, brick-laying and stone crafts were some of the manual arts already known to the people of the city before the Apostle ﷺ emigrated there.

YATHRIB'S ADVANCED AND COMPOSITE SOCIETY

The *hijrah* of the Apostle ﷺ and his Companions from Makkah to Madīnah was, in no ways, an emigration from a town to any hinterland known by the name of Yathrib but from one city to another. The new home of the emigrants was, at the same time, dissimilar in many respects from the town they had left; it was comparatively smaller from the former but the society there was more complex in comparison to the social life of Makkah. The Apostle ﷺ was, therefore, expected to come across problems of a different nature. The town was peopled by men subscribing to different religions with dissimilar social codes and customs and having divergent cultural patterns. The task now presented to him was how to overcome the difficulties arising out of a heterogeneous community and how to unite them on one creed and faith. It was a difficult assignment which could be accomplished only by a prophet, commissioned and blessed by God with wisdom, foresight, firmness of purpose and capacity to unite them under one set of beliefs thus ushering the dying humanity into a new brave world. And, above all, the saviour had to have a loveable personality. How very correctly has God set forth the service rendered by that benefactor of the human race, "He is, Who has supported you with His Help and with the believers. He has united their hearts (If you had spent all that is in the earth you could not have attuned their hearts, but Allāh has attuned them. Lo! He is Mighty, Wise."[2]

1 Relating the event of *Ifk*, contained in the *Kitāb al-Maghāzī* of *Bukhārī*, ʿĀ'ishah has used the word *jizʿ* for the necklace lost by her. The word stands for precious stones of white and black colour found at Ẓifār in Yemen.

2 Qur'ān 8:63.

9
In Madīnah

How Madīnah received the Messenger of God ﷺ

The news about the Apostle's ﷺ departure from Makkah spread fast. The Anṣār, eagerly expecting his arrival went out after morning prayers to the outskirts of the city and awaited him until there was no more shade and the sun became unbearable. Then, it being the hot season, they returned to their homes, sad and disappointed.

At last, one day the Apostle ﷺ arrived. The Anṣār had already returned to their houses but a Jew who happened to see him, cried aloud announcing his arrival. Everybody rushed out to greet the Apostle ﷺ whom they found sitting beneath a tree with Abū Bakr ﷺ who was of a like age. Many of them had never seen the Apostle ﷺ and did not know which of the two was the Prophet. They crowded round both, but, now, Abū Bakr ﷺ realised their difficulty. He rose, stood behind the Apostle ﷺ shielding him with a piece of cloth from the sun, and thus dispelled the doubts of the people.[1]

More or less five hundred Anṣār rushed ahead to pay their respects to the Apostle of God ﷺ; they requested him to enter the city, saying, "Ride on! The two of you are safe and we shall obey you!"

The Apostle ﷺ went on, accompanied by his companion and the welcoming crowd. The inhabitants of Madīnah stood in front of their doors, the women

1 *Ibn Hishām*, vol. I, p. 492.

lined up on the roofs asking one another about the Prophet. Anas ﷺ says that he never came across such a happy event similar to that day.[1]

The people thronged in the way and in their doors and windows and on the roofs of the houses. The slaves and youths cried excitedly, "*Allāhu Akbar*, The Prophet of God has come! *Allāhu Akbar*, The Prophet of God has come![2]

Barā' ibn ʿĀzib ﷺ was a youth then. He says, "Never did I see the people of Madīnah show joy so great as the joy on the arrival of the Apostle of God ﷺ. Even the slave-girls cried: The Apostle of God ﷺ has arrived!"[3]

The faithful greeted the arrival of the Apostle with the joyful cries of *Allāhu Akbar*. No other welcome wore that festive glance to gladden their hearts.

Madīnah appeared to be jubilant and celebrating. The maidens of the Aws and Khazraj felt elated and sang in chorus.[4]

On the hillside where caravans are bid goodbye,
The full moon rises this day.
All the while God is praised.
We had better give our thanks.
Blessed one, O you, sent to us,
You have brought binding commands.[5]

---

1 *Ibn Kathīr*, vol. II, p. 269. Aḥmad ibn Ḥanbal on the authority of Anas ibn Mālik.

2 *Bukhārī*: "The Migration of the Prophet", on the authority of Abū Bakr.

3 Ibid

4 *Ibn Kathīr*, vol. II, p. 269. On the authority of ʿĀ'ishah.

5 Ibn al-Qayyim has raised the issue about these verses wherein he says that the hillside, "*Thaniyyāt al-Wadāʿ*," mentioned in these verses is not on the (north-south) road leading from Makkah to Madīnah, but on the road one takes for Syria from Madīnah. He, therefore, holds the view that these verses were recited on the occasion of the Apostle's triumphant return from Tabūk. Bukhārī also mentions the place in question in connection with the expedition of Tabūk. On the other hand, almost all the biographers, including the earliest ones, relate that the verses were recited on the Prophet's first coming to Madīnah. The writer has enquired about it from the inhabitants of Madīnah who told him that one coming from Makkah can also take the road going towards Syria. It is just possible that in view of the conditions in which the Prophet had to emigrate to Madīnah, he might have preferred the other route. It is also to be noted that *Thaniyyat al-Wadāʿ* was not the name given to a single spot in Madīnah. On the way to Makkah, there is a similar elevation which slopes down to the Wādī ʿAqīq, surrounded by low plains on all sides. It was a pleasure resort of Madīnah in olden times where people used to assemble in the evening during the summer season. It is also probable that the verses allude to this place, for, at this place also the caravans going to Makkah were given a send off (*Āthār al-Madīnah al-Munawwarah*, 3rd edition, p. 160).The verses in question furnish intrinsic evidence that they were sung at a time when the Prophet first came to Madīnah. The vigour and spirit of the verses, particularly the last one, clearly indicate that these were recited when the people of Madīnah first found the Prophet among them. Even if the verses were recited on the return of the Prophet from the expedition of Tabūk, as some of the authentic traditions relate, it merely means that the verses were recited again on that occasion, since, a popular song like this is very often repeated on joyous occasions.

Anas ibn Mālik ﵁ had not come of age when the Apostle ﷺ came to Madīnah. He was present on the occasion and he says, "I never saw a day more graceful and radiant than the day when the Apostle ﷺ came to us."[1]

THE MOSQUE OR QUBĀ'

The Apostle ﷺ stayed for four days in Qubā' where he laid the foundation of a mosque. He left Qubā' on Friday. The time for Friday prayers found him among the clan of Banū Sālim ibn ʿAwf where he performed the prayer in their mosque. This was the first Friday prayer offered by the Apostle of God ﷺ in Madīnah.[2]

IN THE HOUSE OF ABŪ AYYŪB ANṢĀRĪ

As the Apostle ﷺ rode through the streets of the city, people approached him in groups with the request that he stay with them. They said, "Live with us and enjoy our wealth, honour and protection." Sometimes they took hold of his camel's halter, but he said to one and all: "Let her go her way. She is guided by Allāh." This happened more than once.

While the Apostle ﷺ was going through the locality of Banū 'n-Najjār, the slave-girls of the clan recited these verses to greet him:

> Daughters of Banū 'n-Najjār we are,
> What fortune! Muḥammad is our neighbour![3]

On reaching the house of Banū Mālik ibn an-Najjār ﵁, the Apostle's ﷺ camel knelt by herself at the place where now stands the gate of the Prophet's mosque ﷺ. The place was then used for drying the dates and belonged to two orphan boys who were related to the Apostle ﷺ on his mother's side.

The Apostle ﷺ alighted from his camel. Abū Ayyūb Khālid ibn Zayd ﵁, who belonged to the clan of an-Najjār, hastily unloaded the camel and took the luggage to his house. Thus, the Prophet ﷺ stayed with Abū Ayyūb ﵁, who paid him the greatest respect and did all he could to entertain the honoured guest. Abū Ayyūb ﵁ was loath even to live in the upper storey. He asked the Apostle ﷺ to occupy the upper portion and came down with his family to live on the ground floor. The Apostle ﷺ, however, said to him, "O Abū Ayyūb, it would be more convenient for me as well as those who come to see me if I stay in the lower portion."

Abū Ayyūb al-Anṣārī ﵁ was not a man of means, but he was overjoyed by

---

1 *Sunan ad-Dāramī*, On the authority of Anas

2 *Ibn Hishām*, vol. I p. 494.

3 Related by al-Bayhaqī on the authority of Anas, *Ibn Kathīr*, vol. II, p.274

having the Apostle ﷺ as his guest. He was beside himself with happiness at the great honour bestowed on him by God. The loving regard he paid to the Apostle ﷺ was an indication of his genuine gratitude to God and the Apostle ﷺ. "We used to prepare the evening meal for the Apostle of God ﷺ," says Abū Ayyūb, "and send it to him. We would take only what was left over. I and Umm Ayyūb took it from the side the Apostle ﷺ had taken in order to partake in the blessing. The Apostle ﷺ was on the ground floor, while we occupied the upper portion. Once we broke a jar of water. I and Umm Ayyūb mopped up the water with the only robe we had in the fear that it would drop on the Apostle causing him inconvenience."[1]

CONSTRUCTION OF THE PROPHET'S MOSQUE AND QUARTERS

The Apostle ﷺ sent for the two boys who owned the date-store and asked them to name the price of the yard. They answered, "No, but we shall make you a gift of it, O Apostle of God! ﷺ" The Apostle ﷺ, however, refused their offer, said its price to them and built a mosque there.[2]

The Apostle set himself to carrying the unburnt bricks for the construction of the building along with other Muslims. He is reported to have recited as he worked.

> O God! The true reward is the reward of the Hereafter. Have mercy, O God, on the Anṣār and Mūhājirīn.[3]

Overjoyed to see the Messenger of God ﷺ invoking blessings on them, the Muslims, too, sang and thanked God.

The Prophet ﷺ lived in the house of Abū Ayyūb al-Anṣāri for seven months.[4] In the meantime the construction of the mosque and apartments for the Apostle's family ﷺ were completed and he moved to live in his house. Muslims of Makkah continued to emigrate to Madīnah, with the exception of those who were forcibly detained or had fallen victim to persecution. On the other

---

1 *Ibn Isḥāq* on the authority of Abū Ayyūb al-Anṣārī, *Ibn Kathīr*, vol. II, p. 277.

2 *Bukhārī*: "Arrival of the Prophet and his Companions in Madīnah."

3 *Ibn Kathīr*, vol. II, p. 251.

4 *Ibn Kathīr* vol.II, p.279. The narration is also found with al-Wāqadī on the authority of Abū Saʿd as well as Ibn Hajr in *al-Fatḥ*. Ibn Isḥāq relates, 'The Messenger of God ﷺ first resided in Madīnah at the commencement of Rabīʿ al-Awwal, and right up to the month of Safar the following year his masjid and quarters were being built. Thus making his residence with Abū Ayyub more than ten months'.

hand, not one house of Anṣār was left in which the people had not sworn allegiance to God and His apostle ﷺ.[1]

The Apostle's arrival ﷺ in the city heralded a new era, and it was only natural that the city should discard its old name, Yathrib[2] (connoting baseness, lowness or something reprehensible)[3] for a better one assigned to it by its messenger.[4]

BONDS OF BROTHERHOOD BETWEEN THE ANṢĀR AND MUHĀJIRŪN (EMIGRANTS)

The Apostle ﷺ established bonds of brotherhood between the Mūhājirīn and the Anṣār, placing them under an obligation to mutual welfare, benevolence and assistance. Each Anṣār took a Muhājir as his brother, going so far as to give his Muhājir brother half of whatever he possessed by way of dwellings, assets, land and groves. Such was the enthusiasm of the Anṣār to share everything with their brothers in faith that they divided everything into two parts to draw lots for allocating their shares. More often than not they tried to give the Mūhājirūn the fairer portion of their property.

An Anṣārī would say to his emigrant brother, "Behold, I shall divide my possessions into two halves. And I have two wives. See whichever of the two pleases you more, and tell me her name. I shall divorce her and you wed her." The Muhājir would answer, "God bless your family and your possessions. Just tell me, where is the market?"

The Anṣār were magnanimous and self-denying and the Mūhājirīn patient, self-reliant.[5] Indeed this bond of brotherhood between the Anṣār and Mūhājirīn is the foundation and exemplar of the unique global Muslim brotherhood. The Apostle's message ﷺ was the introduction of the revival of a nation, to be set free into a new world based on a sound *aqīdah* (belief) and upright goals, a nation delivered from a wretched world into a place of new bonds of faith, of spiritual brotherhood and a common striving; a vanguard reviving new life into the world and humanity itself. This is the reason God refers to this handful of humanity and its small city, "And if you do not become allies of one another, there will be oppression on the earth and a great mischief and corruption."[6]

1 *Ibn Hishām*. vol. I, pp. 499–500.

2 See Qu'rān 33:13 for reference to Madīnah with its ancient name.

3 *Lisān al-Arab*.

4 *Musnad*, Imām Aḥmad, vol.I, p. 221

5 *Bukhārī*, see the conversation between ʿAbd ar-Raḥmān ibn ʿAwf and Saʿd ibn Rabīʿ in the section dealing with the "Brotherhood established by the Prophet between the Mūhājirūn and Anṣār."

6 Qur'ān 8: 73.

COVENANT BETWEEN THE MUSLIMS AND THE JEWS

Shortly thereafter the Apostle ﷺ had a document written which bound the Mūhājirīn and the Anṣār to a friendly agreement. The covenant[1] made the Jews a party to the agreement which guaranteed them the freedom of their faith as well the title of their property, and set forth their rights and obligations.[2]

THE CALL TO PRAYER

After the Apostle ﷺ had settled down and Islam was planted deep in the soil of Madīnah, the mode of calling the faithful to prayer engaged the attention of the Prophet. He disliked the customs of the Jews and Christians like kindling fire or the use of bell and horn to summon the people. At first the Muslims would come by themselves for prayer at the appointed time without any announcement or call. While different proposals were being considered, God guided the Muslims to the method of giving the call to prayer. A number of Companions had a vision of the call in their dreams that the Apostle ﷺ approved of, and prescribed as the official form for summoning the Muslims for prayers. Bilāl ibn Rabāh al-Ḥabashī ؓ was charged by the Apostle ﷺ to give the call to prayer and thus he came to be known as the *mu'adhdhin* of the Prophet and the leader of all those who would call the faithful to prayer to the end of time.

HYPOCRISY REARS ITS HEAD IN MADĪNAH

There was no room for insincerity and double dealing in Makkah.[3] Islam was helpless, harried and harassed there. None had the power to turn the tide in Makkah, nor was there any worldly advantage in accepting Islam. Giving one's faith to Islam meant that one was prepared to defy all of Makkah and to risk one's life. Only those venturesome in spirit, possessing the courage of convictions would dare play with the fire of hostility raging in hearts of Islam's enemies. Only a man of mettle chances his life and property, future and prosperity. In Makkah there were not two powers equally poised; the heathens were strong and tyrannical, and the Muslims weak and oppressed. This was the situation in Makkah, which has been expressed cogently in the eloquence of the Qur'ān.

---

1 The political wisdom of the oldest written constitution in the world has been discussed extensively, see: *Ibn Hishām*, vol.I, pp.501–504; *Kitāb al-Amwāl*, Abī ʿUbayd; *Al-Bidāyah*, vol. III, pp.224–226;, and *Majmu' al-Wathā'īq as-Siyāsiya*, Muhammad Hamidullah.

2 *Ibn Hishām*, vol. I p. 501.

3 Most of the exegetes of the Qur'ān agree that the verses making mention of hypocrisy and hypocrites were revealed in Madīnah. A verse of the Qur'ān in chapter "Repentance" (9:101) specifically refers to the hypocrites among the inhabitants of Madīnah.

And remember, when you were few and reckoned feeble in the land, and were in fear lest men should extirpate you.[1]

When Islam found a new haven in Madīnah and the Apostle ﷺ and his Companions were blessed with peace and stability, Islam began to prosper. It brought into existence a new society, a new brotherhood of men united by the consciousness of a common outlook on life and common aspirations as expressed by the Islamic principles. The dazzling spectacle of an idealistic commonwealth meant a complete break with the past. The change was so radical as to induce the faint-hearted to sail under false colours. This was quite logical or rather based on the natural instincts of those who could not go hand-in-hand with the world-shattering movement. Also, pharisaism shows its face only where two contending powers or principles are pitted against each other. For the irresolute and the spineless are always wavering, swinging from one extreme to another. They are always in two minds, never able to take a final decision. Often they hang together with one of the two contenders, profess loyalty to it and try to go along with it, but their self-solicitude and egotistical inducements do not permit them to throw in their lot with it. The fear that the other party might recover its strength someday never escapes them, nor can they break the habits that tie them to their old ways, not even for the call of God's Apostle ﷺ. This is a delicate state of inconstancy or infirmity of purpose portrayed vividly in the Qur'ān:

> And among men is he who worships Allāh as upon an edge so that if good befalls him he is content therewith, but if a trial befalls him, he falls away utterly. He loses both the world and the Hereafter. That is the sheer loss.[2]

The distinctive trait of this group is delineated in another verse which says:

> Swaying between this (and that), (belonging) neither to these nor to those.[3]

The leader of the hypocrites, drawn from the ranks of the Aws and the Khazraj as well as the Jews of Madīnah, was ʿAbdullāh ibn Ubayy ibn Salūl. Exhausted by the battle of Buʿāth between the Aws and the Khazraj about five years before the arrival of the Apostle of God ﷺ in Madīnah, both these tribes had agreed to recognise ʿAbdullāh ibn Ubayy as their leader. By the time Islam came to gain adherents in Madīnah, preparations were being made to formally crown him as the king of the city. When he saw that the people were being won over by Islam, speedily and in large numbers, he became so annoyed that his resentment ever continued to prey on his mind.

1 Qur'ān 8:26.
2 Qur'ān 22:11.
3 Qur'ān 4:143.

Ibn Hishām writes: "When the Apostle came to Madīnah the leader there was ʿAbdullāh ibn Ubayy ibn Salūl al-ʿAwfī, none of his own people contested his authority and the Aws and the Khazraj had never rallied behind one man before or after him until Islam came . . . ʿAbdullāh ibn Ubayy's people had made a sort of jewelled diadem to crown him with and make him their king when God sent His Apostle ﷺ to them. So when his people forsook him in favour of Islam he was filled with enmity, realising that the Apostle ﷺ had deprived him of his kingship. However, when he saw that his people were determined to go over to Islam he went too, but unwillingly, retaining his enmity and dissimulating."[1]

All those who had a suppressed desire concealed in their hearts or were eager for a name or power or authority felt cut to the heart at the success of a religion that welded the Mūhājirūn and the Anṣār as two bodies with one soul and inspired them with the love for the Prophet ﷺ, a love more intense even than that felt for one's own father, son or wife. Hate and ill will against the Apostle ﷺ filled their hearts and they started hatching plots against the Muslims. This was how a coalition of the two-faced malcontents came into existence within the Islamic society. For they masqueraded as a part and parcel of the Muslim community, but were in reality no better than the snake in the grass, the Muslims had to be even more wary of them than the declared enemies of God.

This is why the Qur'ān repeatedly exposes their false-heartedness and warns against their concealed designs. Their surreptitious intrigues continued to undermine the stability of the Islamic society and hence the works on the life of the Prophet ﷺ cannot do otherwise than describe their activities.

BEGINNING OF JEWISH ANIMOSITY

After maintaining an attitude of indifference and neutrality at the start, the Jews gradually began to display hatred and rancour against Islam. In the beginning they steered a middle course between the Muslims and the pagans and the Arab tribes of Makkah and Madīnah; or, were rather inclined towards the Muslims. The Jews of Madīnah had, in the beginning, felt closer to the Muslims owing to the striking resemblance between such fundamental teachings of Islam as prophecy and prophethood, belief in the Hereafter, Unity of Godhead, etc., and their own faith, notwithstanding the differences in details as well as the fact that undue veneration of certain prophets and adoption of pagan customs through their age-long association with the heathens had clouded their pristine faith in monotheism.[2]

1 *Ibn Hishām*, vol. I pp. 277–8 (Trans. A Guillaume).

2 See the chapter "The age of Ignorance."

It was thus reasonably expected that if they did not side with the Muslims, they would at least remain non-partisan. At any rate, Islam testified to the divine origin of their scriptures and called upon the Muslims to have faith in all the Hebrew prophets. This was a fundamental dogma of faith in Islam, thus expressed by the Qur'ān:

> Each believes in Allāh and His angels and His scriptures and His messengers. We make no distinction between any of His messengers.[1]

Would that the Jews had understood the conciliatory tenor of Islam. Had it been so, the history of Islam or rather the world's history would have been entirely different. Then Islam would not have faced the impediments it had to encounter in the dissemination of its message, especially in its initial stages, resulting from the strife between the early Muslims, armed only with the strength of their faith, and the powerful and influential, educated and wealthy Jews of the time. The attitude of the Jews could be attributed to two causes. One of these was their tendency for obstinacy while the other lay in their errant beliefs, as described in the Qur'ān and illustrated with references to their past doings. For instance, the constant wrangling with their own prophets, opposition to their teachings and even putting them to death, refusing to take the right path, bearing ill will and malice to those who commended the path of virtue, speaking slightly of God, excessive longing for wealth, driving hard usurious bargains despite its interdiction, grabbing the property of others, making interpolations in the Torah to suit their convenience, the insatiate thirst for worldly life and what it stands for and the national and racial jingoism which had become their characteristic hallmarks.

Had there been a political leader in the place of the Apostle of God ﷺ, he would have tactfully met the Jews halfway, especially in view of their importance in the tangle that was Madīnan politics. Even if it were not possible to placate the Jews, a national leader would have at least avoided setting them at odds against him by concealing his ultimate objective. But, as a messenger of God, the Prophet ﷺ was obliged to preach the message sent by God, proclaim the truth, interdict what was forbidden and countenance no vestiges of evil and peccancy. He had been saddled with the responsibility to deliver the message of God to the whole world, to all races and nations including the Jews and Christians, and to invite them to accept Islam regardless of the cost or consequences it involved. This was really the path taken by all the prophets of old, in clear contradistinction to the ways of politicians and national leaders.

But, this grated against Medina's Jews, leading them to become hostile to

1 Qur'ān 2:285.

Islam and the Muslims. They gave up their earlier policy of steering the middle course and decided to oppose Islam in every way possible, openly as well as through intrigues. Israel Wellphenson, quoted here, has been frank and straightforward in his analysis of the reasons for ill will between Jews and Muslims.

> If the teachings of the Prophet had been restricted only to the denunciation of idolatry and the Jews had not been called upon to acknowledge his prophethood, there would have been no conflict between the Jews and the Muslims. The Jews might have then commended and acclaimed the Prophet's doctrine of monotheism and backed him or even supported him with men and material until he had succeeded in destroying the idols and effacing the polytheistic creed rampant in Arabia. But this depended on the condition that he left the Jews and their religion well enough alone, and did not demand the acceptance of the new prophethood. For the bent of Jewish temperament cannot take kindly to anything that tries to seduce it from its faith, they can never acknowledge any prophet save one belonging to Banū Isrā'īl.[1]

The Jews were further shocked and agitated when some of their learned rabbis like ʿAbdullāh ibn Salām ﷺ, whom they held in esteem, embraced Islam. The Jews could never conceive that a man of his standing and erudition would accept the new faith. However, this only served to make the Jews still more annoyed and envious of Islam.[2]

The animosity of the Jews against Islam did not rest at defiance against Islam; rather they went beyond the pale by openly preferring the pagans over Muslims even though the Muslims shared their faith in monotheism. It would be logical as well as reasonable to expect that if the Jews were called upon to pronounce a verdict on the Prophet's faith *vis-a-vis* the idolatrous creed of the Quraysh, they would speak well of Islam and the soundness of its belief in one God against the multiplicity of deities taken for granted by the pagans of Makkah. But their animus against Islam had so maddened them that they were willing even to deny that patent truth. Once, when some of the rabbis went to Makkah, the Quraysh asked them whether their idolatrous religion or that of the Prophet ﷺ was better, the answer these rabbis gave was: "Your religion is better than his and you

1 *Tārīkh al-Yahūd fī Bilād al-ʿArab fī 'l-Jāhiliyyah wa Ṣadr al-Islām*, p. 123.

2 The number of Jews who accepted Islam and had the honour of enjoying the Apostle's company was 39. Some of them belong to the category of eminent Companions, as can be seen from their biographical details. Contained in the books on the lives of the Companions, such as, *Al-Iṣābah*, *Al-Istīʿāb*, *Usd al-Ghābah*, etc. Also see *Ahl-e-Kitāb Ṣaḥābah wa Tābiʿūn* by Mujīb Ullāh Nadwī from which the number of Jewish converts to Islam, quoted above, has been taken.

are more rightly-guided than they."[1] The comment of Dr. Israel Wellphenson on the reply given by the Jews is worth repeating here.

> But, surely, the thing for which they deserved to be reproached and which would be painful to all those who believe in the Unity of God, whether they be Jews or Muslims, was the conversation between the Jews and pagan Quraysh wherein they had given preference to the religion of the Quraysh over what had been brought by the Prophet of Islam.[2]

The same writer further goes on to say:

> Deception, mendacity and similar means for entrapping the enemy have been sanctioned by the nations for achieving a military objective in times of warfare, yet, the Jews ought not to have committed the grievous mistake of declaring roundly that adoration of idols was preferable to the Islamic faith in the Unity of God, not even if they feared to miss the mark by doing so. For Banī Isrā'īl had, in the name of their forefathers, held aloft the banner of God's Unity for ages amidst the heathen nations of old, had all along braved innumerable trials and tribulations, and gone through fire and blood for its sake. It was their bounden duty to sacrifice their lives and whatever they held dear to humble the idolaters and polytheists.[3]

In fact, the matter was sufficiently serious to warrant a reference in the Qur'ān:

> Have you not seen those unto whom a portion of the Scripture has been given, how they believe in idols and false deities, and how they say of those (idolaters) who disbelieve: These are more rightly guided than those who believe?[4]

CHANGE OF THE QIBLAH

The Apostle ﷺ as well as the Muslims had been facing towards Jerusalem while worshipping, or, as they phrased it, took Jerusalem as their *qiblah*.[5] The practice was followed for one year and four months after emigration to Madīnah. The Apostle desired that the Kaʿbah be made the *qiblah* for prayers as did the other Arab converts to Islam, since they had been holding the sanctuary at Makkah in a reverential regard since immemorial times. To them the house of worship

---

1 *Ibn Hishām,* vol. II p. 214. It was on this occasions that verse 4:51 of the Qur'ān was sent down by God.

2 *Tārīkh al-Yahūd fī Bilād al-ʿArab fī 'l-Jāhiliyyah wa Ṣadr al-Islām*, p. 142.

3 *Tārīkh al-Yahūd fī Bilād al-ʿArab fī 'l-Jāhiliyyah wa Ṣadr al-Islām*, p.142.

4 Qur'ān 4:51.

5 Lit., anything opposite. The direction in which all Muslims must pray, whether in their private or in their public devotions, namely, towards the Kaʿbah.

built by Ibrāhīm and Ismāʿīl was the holy of the holies, incomparable in sanctity to any other sanctum or shrine. They were put to a severe test by being asked to face Jerusalem instead of the Kaʿbah, and they stood this trial by dutifully obeying the divine command. Such was their devotion to the Apostle that they always replied: "We hear, and we obey,"[1] and "We believe therein: the whole is from our Lord,"[2] whether they found anything to their liking or not. Thus, after the faith of the earliest Muslims had been brought to the test and they had stood it successfully, the *qiblah* for the prayer was changed to Kaʿbah. Says God in the Qur'ān:

> Thus We have appointed you a middle nation, that you may be witnesses against mankind and that the messenger may be a witness against you. We appointed the qiblah which you formerly observed only that We might know him who follows the messenger, from him who turns on his heels. In truth it was a hard (test) save for those whom Allāh guided.[3]

The Muslims promptly changed their direction in prayer in compliance with the divine command towards the Kaʿbah which was henceforth selected as the *qiblah* for all the believers, living in any part of the world, for all times to come.

JEWS GIVE OFFENCE TO MUSLIMS

It preyed upon the minds of the Jews that Islam had gained a footing in Madīnah and was making rapid strides day after day. They were intelligent enough to realise that if the popularity of Islam continued unabated for some time more, they would lose their allies as well as influence and this would limit their ability to stand up against their potential enemies. They decided to put up a front against the Muslims and launched a campaign to slight, vilify and ridicule the Muslims who, however, were not permitted to return the "compliments" paid to them: they were commanded to be long-suffering and forbearing.

"Withhold your hands, establish worship"[4] was the code of behaviour enjoined upon them so that they might learn to disdain the world and its pleasures, become self-denying, be prepared to make sacrifices for a higher cause and have the experience of obeying the commands of God.

1 Qur'ān 24:51.
2 Qur'ān 3:7.
3 Qur'ān 2:143.
4 Qur'ān 4:77.

PERMISSION TO FIGHT

Gradually the Muslims were invested with power and became strong enough to take up arms against their enemies. They were then allowed to resist aggression and to fight against the mischief-loving people. But it was only permission rather than obligation to clash with the enemies.[1]

> Sanction is given unto those who fight because they have been wronged; and Allāh is indeed able to give them victory.[2]

EXPEDITION OF ABWĀʾ AND ʿABDULLĀH IBN JAḤSH

In pursuance of God's command, the Apostle ﷺ started sending raiding parties to fall suddenly on the hostile tribes. These raids were not meant to launch out against the enemy but simply to frighten the tribes inimical to Islam with a show of force.

We shall mention here one of the earliest raids, led by ʿAbdullāh ibn Jaḥsh ﷺ, for it gave occasion to a revelation sent down by God which shows that Islam does not countenance the least excess or highhandedness even by its own followers. Islam is always fair and impartial in bringing its verdict on every affair, without any regard to persons or parties.

The Apostle sent ʿAbdullāh ibn Jaḥsh ﷺ on an expedition with eight emigrants during the month of Rajab, 2 AH. He gave him a letter with the instruction that he was not to read it until he had journeyed for two days, and then act according to the directions contained in it but not to force his Companions to follow his orders.

ʿAbdullāh ibn Jaḥsh ﷺ read the letter after he had travelled for two days. The instruction contained in it was, "When you have read this letter, proceed to the oasis of Nakhlah between Makkah and Ṭā'if. Pitch your tents there to find out the movements of Quraysh and send the information to us". Having gone through the letter, ʿAbdullāh ibn Jaḥsh ﷺ said, "We hear, and we obey;" and then he said to his companions: "The Apostle of God ﷺ has ordered me to lie in wait at the oasis on the road between Makkah and Ṭā'if and watch the movements of Quraysh so as to bring him news of them, but he has also asked me not to compel anyone of you to follow me. If anyone wishes martyrdom, he may come with me, and whoever wishes may go back, for I have to abide by the instructions

1 See *Zād al-Maʿād,* vol. I, p. 314.

2 Qur'ān 22:39.

of the Apostle." Then he went ahead, and so did all of his comrades, not one of them falling out.

The party moved on to the oasis where they camped. After a short while a caravan of Quraysh passed by them. ʿAmr ibn al-Ḥaḍramī was also with the caravan. When Quraysh saw the party camping so near them, they got frightened but when they saw Ukāshah, whose head was shaved, their suspicions were lulled for they took the party to be pilgrims. They said: "We have nothing to fear from them, they are pilgrims."[1] That was the last day of Rajab.[2] The raiding party, on the other hand, took counsel among themselves and decided that if they left Quraysh alone that night, they would get into the sacred area and obstruct their entry there. But if they fought them, they would be fighting during the sacred month. At first they felt hesitant as well as dismayed but ultimately made up their mind to kill as many of Quraysh as possible and plunder as much of their goods as feasible. Wāqid ibn ʿAbdillāh at-Tamīmī ﷺ shot the first arrow killing ʿAmr ibn al-Ḥaḍramī while his companions captured two men of Quraysh. ʿAbdullāh ibn Jaḥsh and his companions ﷺ returned to Madīnah with the captives.

When ʿAbdullāh ibn Jaḥsh and his companions ﷺ came back to the Apostle ﷺ, he said, "I did not ask you to fight in the sacred month, nor to seize the caravan and take captives." The Apostle ﷺ also refused to accept the spoils brought by the party.

The campaigners were worried and fearfully apprehensive of being doomed. They were also reproached by other Muslims. On the other hand, Quraysh laid the charge, saying, "Lo! Muḥammad has allowed war and bloodshed in the sacred months!" It was on this occasion that God sent down the revelation to the Apostle:

> They question you (O Muḥammad) with regard to warfare in the sacred month. Say: Warfare therein is a great (transgression), but to turn (men) from the way of Allāh, and to disbelieve in Him and in the inviolable place of worship, and to

---

1 Arabs preferred to perform *ʿumrah* during the month of Rajab.

2 Rajab was first of the four months held to be sacred, in which it was not lawful to fight. The remaining three months were Dhū 'l-Qaʿda, Dhū 'l-Ḥijjah and Muḥarram. Arabs observed this custom during the pre-Islamic and in the initial period of Islamic era, and this also finds a mention in the Qur'ān (9:36). But the consensus of the scholars is that the interdiction in this regard has been abrogated by later revelations which say, "Slay the idolaters wherever you find them" (9:5) and "Wage war on all the idolaters, they are waging war on all of you" (9: 36).Saʿīd ibn al-Musayyib was asked if the Muslims were permitted to fight the disbelievers during the sacred months. He replied, "Yes. This was so during the wars waged by the earlier Muslims for there is not one instance in the history when the battles were suspended during the month of Rajab or for three months of Dhū 'l-Qaʿdah. Dhū 'l-Ḥijjah and Muḥarram, or when Muslim forces left the battlefield for their cantonments during these months."

> expel the people thence, is a greater (sin) with Allāh; for persecution is worse than killing.[1]

God has given a fair deal to His friends as well as foes," writes Ibn al-Qayyim in *Zād al-Maʿād,* "for He has not commended the sin of fighting in the sacred month, committed by His pious and devout servants.

God has held it to be a serious act of transgression but He also reminds that the idolaters have been guilty of even greater sins through their acts of persecution in the sacred city of Makkah, and thus they deserve still more condemnation and punishment. Since, however, the believing servants of God had been guilty of indiscretion or they had made a mistake, God has lent them a hope that they might be forgiven on account of their faith in the Unity of God, submission to Him, migration with the Apostle and their strivings in His way."[2]

The expedition of Abwā', also known as that of Buwāṭ, was the first drive that the Apostle ﷺ led in person but there was no fighting. Thereafter several raiding parties were sent out by the Apostle ﷺ.

FAST MADE OBLIGATORY

When the Muslims had taken the prayer as a mark and symbol of their faith and it had a hold on their minds as the light of their lives, the readiness to follow divine commands entered into their hearts and souls. Then it was, in the second year of the *hijrah,* that God commanded them to observe the fasts also.[3]

> O you who believe! Fasting is prescribed for you, even as it was prescribed for those before you, that you may ward off (evil).[4]

In another verse it is said:

> The month of Ramadan in which was revealed the Qur'ān, counsel for mankind and clear proofs of the guidance, and the Criterion (of right and wrong). And whosoever of you is present, let him fast the month.[5]

---

1 Qur'ān 2:217. *Ibn Hishām,* vol. I, pp. 601–2.

2 *Zād al-Maʿād,* vol. I, p. 341.

3 *Ibn Hishām,* vol. I pp. 591–606. Also see the chapter dealing with "Fasts" in the *Four Pillars of Islam* by the author.

4 Qur'ān 2:183.

5 Qur'ān 2:185.

10
The Decisive Battle of Badr

IN THE SECOND YEAR of the *hijrah,* during the month of Ramadan, the Muslims came up against the infidels in the decisive battle of Badr which was to prove the turning point not only in the destiny of Islam but of the entire human race.

All the subsequent conquests that the Muslims won, along with the empires they founded come from the triumphant success achieved by a handful of followers of Islam at that crucial moment of battle. God has identified it as the Day of Discrimination:

> If you believe in Allāh and that which We revealed unto Our slave on the Day of Discrimination, the day when two armies met.[1]

The circumstances that led to this battle were that the Apostle ﷺ received the news of a great caravan with a large amount of money and merchandise heading back to Makkah from Syria, led by Abū Sufyān ؓ. A state of hostility already existed between the Muslims and Quraysh, for they were doing all that was in their power to play mischief with Muslims, to impede their progress and to crush their rising power. They spared none of their financial and physical resources to achieve this and their armed detachments very often advanced deep inside the boundaries of Madīnah and its pastures to ambush the Muslims.

Abū Sufyān ؓ, was a bitter enemy of Islam then and so the Apostle ﷺ prepared the Muslims to intercept the caravan. Since it was a commercial caravan

1 Qur'ān 8:41.

and the Apostle ﷺ merely wanted to surprise it, and so elaborate arrangements required for giving fight to an army were not considered necessary.

Informed of the Prophet's ﷺ plans to intercept him, Abū Sufyān ؓ sent a courier to Makkah with an urgent request for reinforcements. Thereupon the Quraysh hastily assembled an armed force. All the notable chiefs of Makkah accompanied the force to which was enlisted every man available from the neighbouring tribes—and this army went forth to the aid of their caravan. Quraysh were so flared up that hardly a man remained behind in Makkah.

FAITHFULNESS OF THE ANṢĀR

News came to the Apostle ﷺ that a strong Makkan army was on its way to engage him in battle. The Apostle ﷺ summoned his followers and asked for their counsel. He wanted to appraise the reaction of the Anṣār, for their original pact with him entailed their defence of him in Madīnah and did not put them under an obligation to take part in a military expedition outside their territory. The Mūhājirīn responded first and assured him of their help and loyalty. The Apostle ﷺ then repeated his question and the Mūhājirīn gave the same reply but the Apostle ﷺ put the same question again for the third time. Now the Anṣār realised that the question was meant for them. Saʿd ibn Muʿādh ؓ immediately got up to say in reply, "O Apostle of God, it seems as if you mean us and you want to have our answer. Perhaps you think, O Apostle of God, that the Anṣār have undertaken to help you on their own territory alone. I want to say on behalf of the Anṣār that you may lead us where you like, align with whom you may desire or break relations with whom you may think fit; you may take whatever you desire from our property and give us as much as you want. For, whatever you take from our property would be dearer to us than what you would leave with us. We will follow whatever you would command us. By God, if you march to Bark Ghumdān,[1] we will accompany you and by God if you plunge into the sea, we will also plunge in with you."

Then Miqdād ؓ got up and said, "O Apostle of God, we will not say as the Children of Israel said to Moses ؑ: "Go you and your Lord and fight, we will sit here.[2] We will fight with you on your left and on your right, ahead of you and behind you."

1 A place in Yemen. Others say that it is the farthest point of *Hijr Suhaylī*: (the commentator of Ibn Hishām) says that according to certain exegetes it was a city in Abyssinia. It thus meant far off place. Ibn Hishām cites it as Bark al-Ghumād by (*Zād al-Maʿād*, vol. I, p. 342).

2 Qur'ān 5:24.

The Apostle ﷺ was delighted to hear the replies given by his Companions. He said, "Go ahead and glad tidings unto you."[1]

ENTHUSIASM OF THE YOUNGSTERS

When the detachments went out from Madīnah, a boy of sixteen, whose name was ʿUmayr ibn Abī Waqqās ؓ also accompanied the warriors stealthily because he feared that if the Apostle ﷺ saw him, he would turn him back as a minor. When his elder brother, Saʿd ibn Abī Waqqās saw ʿUmayr ؓ avoiding the gaze of the Apostle, he asked him the reason for it. ʿUmayr replied, "I am afraid that the Apostle of God ﷺ would turn me back as a minor but I want to take part in the battle. God may perhaps honour me with martyrdom." When the Prophet ﷺ saw ʿUmayr he asked him to go back but he started crying and was allowed to stay on. ʿUmayr ؓ was killed in the battle and thus his heart's desire was fulfilled.[2]

STRENGTH OF THE CONTENDING PARTIES

The Apostle ﷺ rallied forth to the battlefield with three hundred and thirteen poorly equipped combatants. The Muslims had seventy camels and two horses on which men rode by turns;[3] there was nothing to distinguish soldier from captain, even the eminent Companions like Abū Bakr and ʿUmar ؓ or the Prophet ﷺ himself bore no marks of distinction.

The standard of the army was given to Muṣʿab ibn ʿUmayr ؓ, the flag of the Mūhājirīn was with ʿAlī ؓ and that of the Anṣār with Saʿd ibn Muʿādh ؓ.

On coming to know of the approaching Muslim army, Abū Sufyān turned his caravan towards the coast. He also sent word to the Qurayshi army when he was at a safe distance from the Muslims, to go back home as it was of no purpose for them to proceed since the caravan was safe. The Makkans too wanted to return home but Abū Jahl insisted on going ahead to punish the raiders. His force was a thousand strong with all the veterans and noted warriors of Makkah, and all were well armed. He did not want to lose the opportunity to give battle to the Muslims.[4] On coming to know the names of the Makkan chiefs accompanying Abū Jahl, the Apostle ﷺ remarked: "Makkah has brought pieces of its heart to you!"

---

1 *Zād al-Maʿād*, vol. I, pp. 342–43, *Ibn Hishām*, vol. I, p. 614. *Bukhārī* and Muslim have also related the conversation with a little variation.

2 *Usd al-Ghābah*, vol. IV, p. 148.

3 *Zād al-Maʿād*, vol. I, p. 342.

4 *Zād al-Maʿād*, vol. I, p. 343 and *Ibn Hishām*, vol. I pp. 618–19.

THE DEMOCRATIC WAY

The Quraysh army halted at a valley near Badr while the Muslims pitched their tents on the farther side of the enemy. Ḥubāb ibn al-Mundhir ﷺ, however, called upon the Apostle ﷺ to enquire: "O Apostle of God, is this a position which God has ordered you to occupy, so that we cannot position ourselves elsewhere, or is it a matter of opinion and military tactics?" "No", replied the Apostle ﷺ, "it is a matter of opinion and military tactics and everything can be done to ambush the enemy." Ḥubāb ﷺ then said, "O Apostle of God, it is not the position we should occupy." He suggested another place nearest to the water which was more suitable for giving battle to the enemy. The Apostle ﷺ agreed and ordered his men to move on there.[1]

The Apostle ﷺ and some of his Companions were first to occupy the new camping ground in the night. A cistern was built and filled with water from which the enemy was also allowed to replenish its drinking-vessels.[2]

God sent down rain during the night which caused the infidels great inconvenience by hindering their movement. But it revived the vanishing spirits of the Muslims by making the weather pleasant and turned the soft sand of the wadi into a compact surface.

This was a sign of victory as God has disclosed in this verse of the Qur'ān:

> And [God] sent down water from the sky upon you, that thereby He might purify you, and remove from you the fear of Satan, and make strong your hearts and firm (your) feet thereby.[3]

THE APOSTLE ﷺ AS A GENERAL

We find, on this occasion, the Apostle ﷺ exhibiting marvellous qualities of a military tactician and strategist which chime with his eternal and universal guidance to mankind, providing yet another indication that the inspiration he drew was from the supernatural agency.[4] His battle formations, his responses to sudden and surprise attacks by the superior forces and the deployment of his troops to win the battle against the enemy superior in numbers need to be studied to appreciate the prodigious military genius of the Apostle ﷺ.

---

1 *Ibn Hishām,* vol. I, p. 620.

2 Ibid., p. 622.

3 Qur'ān 8:11.

4 A detailed account of the defensive measures taken by the Apostle of God at Badr can be found in the *Ḥadīth ad-Difāʿ* by Maj. General Muḥammad Akbar Khān, a Pakistani general, and *Ar-Rasūl al-Qāʾid* by Maḥmūd Sheeth Khattab, a former Commander-in-chief of the Iraqi Armed Forces.

PREPARATION FOR THE FIGHTING

A booth of palm-branches was erected for the Apostle ﷺ on an elevation overlooking the battlefield. Thereafter, the Apostle ﷺ traversed the plain and pointed out the spots where the enemy chiefs were to fall dead to his Companions. As it was found later on, his prediction proved entirely correct for not a single Quraysh chief was found slain at a place different from that indicated by the Apostle of God ﷺ.

When the two armies came face to face, the Apostle ﷺ said, "O God, here come Quraysh in their vanity and pride. They contend with You calling Your Apostle a liar."

This was the night of Friday, the seventeenth of Ramaḍān. With the first flush of morning, the entire force of Quraysh streamed out into the valley and ranged itself in the battlefield while the Muslims arrayed themselves before them in the foreground.[1]

AN ENTREATMENT TO BESEECH THE LORD

The Apostle ﷺ set the ranks of his force in order and returned to the booth with Abū Bakr. Putting his head on the dust, he supplicated and beseeched God for divine succour. He knew full well that if victory in the battle was to go by numbers and strength, prowess and the weapons of the two forces, the result was a foregone conclusion. He had no illusions for he fully realised that the Muslims were weak and few, and the enemy strong and numerous. He clearly saw the balance inclining in the favour of Quraysh, and now he sought to counterpoise it with a heavier weight. Lamenting, he entreated the Lord of the heavens and the earth, who shapes all ends and the means, to come to the assistance of Muslims in their hour of difficulty.

He appealed to God: "O God! If You were to exterminate this small group of Muslims, You will be worshipped on earth no more!" In a state of extreme exaltation, his hands raised in prayer and on bended knees, he sent up the prayer: "O God! Fulfil what You have promised me! Help us, O God!" So lost was he in the prayer that the mantle on his shoulder fell on the ground. Abū Bakr ﷺ, who was distressed to see the Apostle of God ﷺ in tears, consoled and comforted him.[2]

---

1 *Zād al-Maʿād,* Vol. I, pp. 343–344

2 See *Zād al-Maʿād,* and other biographies of the Apostle ﷺ. Muslim relates (in *Kitāb al-Jihād wa 's-Siyar)* on the authority of ʿUmar ibn al-Khaṭṭāb that "On the day of Badr when the Apostle ﷺ camped with his three hundred and nineteen Companions, he turned towards the *qiblah* and, raising his hands, started imploring God: 'O God! Grant me the help which You did promise me. O God! Grant me the

THE TRUE POSITION AND STATION OF THE MUSLIMS

The prayer of the Apostle ﷺ, although brief, speaks volumes of his pure-hearted Companions, his unflinching confidence in the succour of God in the hour of crisis, his feelings of humbleness and meekness before God, and the serenity of his own heart. At the same time, the Apostle's ﷺ prayer sets forth, in terms as clear as crystal, the true position and station of his followers amidst the nations of the world. It brings out the worth, utility as well as the indispensability of the people charged with the responsibility of taking his mission ahead. It is, in fact, a plain and clear annunciation that the responsibility placed on these people is to surrender to the Will of God, to bend down their necks before Him with a contrite heart, and to summon the people to yield obedience to Him.

And the Apostle's ﷺ prayer was answered by God with a resounding victory which was beyond the bounds of reason and probability. It was but a demonstration of the truth of his affirmation concerning the true character of his followers.

The Apostle ﷺ then came back to his men and delivered a short speech stressing the merits of fighting in the way of God. In the meantime ʿUtbah ibn Rabīʿah and his brother and son, Shaybah and Walīd, stepped forward in the fashion of the Arabs. Three of the Anṣār came forward to give them battle, but the Quraysh asked, "Who are you?"

"We are Anṣār", they answered.

"You are of noble blood," said the Quraysh, "but send our peers, the men of our own tribe."

The Apostle ﷺ now said, "Step forth, ʿUbaydah ibn al-Ḥārith, Ḥamzah and ʿAlī! Advance! All three of you are to oppose them."

The Quraysh then said, "Yes. You are noble and our peers."

Now ʿUbaydah ؓ being the eldest, challenged ʿUtbah ibn Rabīʿah, Ḥamzah ؓ faced Shaybah and ʿAlī ؓ went against Walīd ibn ʿUtbah. With swift dispatch Ḥamzah and ʿAlī ؓ slew their opponents, but ʿUbaydah and ʿUtbah ؓ still struggled with one another. Ḥamzah and ʿAlī ؓ then made for ʿUtbah and did away with him. They bore away and brought ʿUbaydah back to their ranks for he had been badly injured. Later on ʿUbaydah ؓ died of excessive loss of blood.[1]

THE GENERAL ATTACK

The Quraysh were now filled with a renewed fury. With a cry of rage, they

help which You did promise me. O God! If this small group of Muslims is exterminated today You will be worshipped on earth no more!'"

1 *Ibn Hishām*, vol. I, p. 625.

charged and assailed the Muslim champions whereupon the Apostle ﷺ cried, "Rise to Paradise the breadth of which is equal to the heavens and the earth!"

THE FIRST MARTYR

ʿUmayr ibn al-Ḥumām ؓ heard the Prophet's ﷺ call and asked, "Is that paradise equal to the heavens and the earth, O Apostle of God?" "Yes", replied the Apostle. "Fine. Fine." he said, and when the Apostle ﷺ asked what had made him say that, he replied, "Nothing, O Apostle of God, but I hope that I might be amongst its inhabitants." The Prophet ﷺ told him that he would be among them. ʿUmayr ؓ then took some dates out of his quiver and began to eat them, but suddenly he said, "If I live till my dates last, it would mean delaying it for long." So he threw away the dates in his hand and ran to the battlefield and fought with the enemy until he was dead. He was the first martyr on the day of Badr.[1]

The Muslims fought the Makkans like a firm, united and disciplined army with the name of God on their lips. Up to that moment the Apostle ﷺ had remained quiet and collected, but now he charged into the ranks of the enemy. None was now braver than he, none dared engage the enemy so closely.[2] God now sent down the hosts of heaven to the succour of the Muslims. The enemy seemed to be giving way to the Muslims and was driven back by the fierce charge of the invisible warriors.

> When your Lord inspired the angels, (saying): I am with you. So make those who believe stand firm. I will throw fear into the hearts of those who disbelieve. Then smite the necks and smite of them each finger.[3]

THE DESIRE OF TWO BROTHERS

Full of enthusiasm, everybody seemed bent upon outdoing others in deeds of valour and to be honoured with martyrdom. Even close friends and full brothers vied with one another to excel. ʿAbd ar-Raḥmān ibn ʿAwf said: "I was fighting in my rank on the day of Badr, when, lo! I saw on my right and left two very young boys. And I did not feel quite happy to see them at my side.[4] Suddenly one of them asked me in a low voice, so that his companion should not hear: O my uncle! Show me Abū Jahl! I said: O my brother's son! What have you to do

---

1 *Zād al-Maʿād*, vol. I, p. 345; and *Ibn Hishām*, vol. II, p. 215.

2 *Ibn Kathīr*, vol. II, p. 425.

3 Qur'ān 8:12.

4 ʿAbd ar-Raḥmān expected grown men with him who could be expected to assist him in the fight.

with him? He answered: I have vowed before God that I shall kill him when I see him, or shall be killed by him! And the other boy spoke to me likewise in a low voice, so that his companion should not hear. I pointed him out to them, and they threw themselves upon him like two hawks, and struck him down. And they were the sons of ʿAfrā'.”[1]

When Abū Jahl was killed, the Apostle of God ﷺ remarked, “This is Abū Jahl, the Pharaoh of this nation.”

THE GREAT VICTORY

The day of Badr drew toward its close with the Muslims flushed with success and the infidels trampled in the dust. On this occasion the Apostle ﷺ paid homage to God, saying: “Praise be to Allāh who fulfilled His promise, and helped His servant, and alone routed all the hordes.”

That was exactly what had happened, for the Qur'ān also says:

> Allāh had already given you the victory at Badr, when you were contemptible, So observe your duty to Allāh in order that you may be thankful.[2]

The Apostle ﷺ ordered that the dead among the infidels should be thrown into a pit. As the Muslims threw them, the Apostle ﷺ went there and said standing over the pit: “O people of the pit, did you find that what your Lord said is true? For I have found that what my God promised me is true.”[3] On the day of Badr, seventy infidels were slain and an equal number taken captive. Casualties among the Muslims were fourteen, six belonging to the Mūhājirīn and eight to the Anṣār.[4]

EFFECTS OF THE VICTORY OF BADR

The Prophet ﷺ returned to Madīnah at the head of a victorious army. The enemies of Islam were appalled and disheartened by the victory at Badr. The Apostle's ﷺ prestige rose in Madīnah and his influence gained a hold upon the surrounding districts. Many who had been hesitant so long in Madīnah accepted the faith of the Apostle ﷺ.

ʿAbdullāh ibn Rawāḥah was one of the two persons sent by the Apostle ﷺ

---

1 *Bukhārī* and *Muslim*: the incident quoted here has been taken from *Bukhārī*: "*Kitāb al-Maghāzī*", see "*Gazwah Badr*", *Ibn Kathīr,* vol. II, p. 444.

2 Qur'ān 3: 123

3 *Bukhārī,* on the authority of Barā' ibn ʿĀzib.

4 *Ibn Kathīr,* vol. II, p. 463.

to Madīnah in advance, before he returned to the city. He gave the good news to the people, saying. "Rejoice, O Anṣār, for the Apostle of God is safe and infidels have been killed and captured". He enumerated the names of the Quraysh nobles and chiefs killed in the battle to every man he met. Children accompanied him singing songs of joy. Some took the news to be true while others were confounded. Then the Apostle ﷺ returned to Madīnah, followed by the prisoners of war with the Apostle's ﷺ slave Shaqrān keeping an eye on them.[1] When the Apostle ﷺ reached Rūḥā, the Muslims met him and congratulated him and his Companions on the victory God had given him.

The defeat suffered by the polytheists plunged Makkah into gloom. There was not a house in the city which did not go into mourning. The Makkans stood aghast and agitated. Abū Sufyān swore not to have a bath until he had fought with the Apostle ﷺ. The suppressed Muslims of Makkah on the other had breathed a sigh of relief and felt elated.

TIES OF BLOOD OR FAITH

One of the captives was Abū ʿAzīz ibn ʿUmayr ibn Hāshim, a full brother of Muṣʿab ibn ʿUmayr. The two brothers were the standard bearers of the rival armies.

Muṣʿab ibn ʿUmayr passed by his brother when an Anṣārī youth was tying up the hands of Abū ʿAzīz ibn ʿUmayr, Muṣʿab called out, "Bind him fast, for his mother is sufficiently rich. Perhaps she would pay a princely ransom."

Turning to Muṣʿab in amazement, Abū ʿAzīz ibn ʿUmayr said, "Brother, is it you who gives this counsel?" "You are not my brother," replied ʿUmayr, "he who is tying up your hands is my brother."

TREATMENT OF THE CAPTIVES

The Apostle ﷺ ordered his followers to treat the prisoners generously. He said, "Deal kindly with them." Abū ʿAzīz ibn ʿUmayr relates that he was lodged with an Anṣār family after being brought from Badr. They gave him bread for the morning and evening meals but themselves took only dates as ordered by the Messenger of God ﷺ. If anybody had a morsel of bread, he gave it to Abū ʿAzīz although he felt ashamed and refused it, but they returned it untouched and insisted on his taking it.[2]

---

1 *Ibn Kathīr*, vol. II, pp. 470–73.

2 *Ibn Kathīr*, vol. II, p. 475.

RANSOM OF THE PRISONERS

The Apostle ﷺ accepted ransom for the prisoner according to their means. The Quraysh kinsmen of the captives paid sums of money for their relatives, while those who could not pay any ransom were set free without any payment. The Apostle's ﷺ uncle ʿAbbās ibn ʿAbd al-Muṭṭalib, his cousin, ʿAqīl ibn Abī Ṭālib,[1] his son-in-law, Abū 'l-ʿĀṣ ibn ar-Rabīʿ, who was married to his daughter Zaynab, were among the prisoners of war but none was shown any favour. All were treated like other captives.

There were some prisoners who were unable to pay any ransom, but as they were literate, they were allowed to earn their freedom by teaching the art of reading and writing to the children of Anṣār,[2]—ten children being taught by every prisoner.[3] Zayd ibn Thābit ﷺ was one of those who had been taught by the captives of Badr. The importance attached to edification and enlightenment by the Prophet of Islam ﷺ as exemplified by his decision on this occasion needs no further explanation.

OTHER EXPEDITIONS

The ironclad oath of Abū Sufyān, as mentioned earlier, bound him to refrain from even splashing water over his head until he had wreaked his vengeance on the Muslims. He came to Madīnah with two hundred raiders to acquit himself of his oath, and called upon Sallām ibn Mishkam, the chief of the Jewish tribe of Banū 'n-Naḍīr, who entertained him with food and drink and also gave the information he desired about Madīnah. Thereupon Abū Sufyān succeeded in getting away after killing two of the Anṣār.

The Apostle ﷺ received warning of the raiders and went out in pursuit of them. Abū Sufyān eluded the Apostle ﷺ but was obliged to throw away a good deal of his provisions consisting of food grains, especially parched corn or *as-sawīq*, and hence the expedition goes by its name.[4]

The Jews of Madīnah who first broke their covenant with the Apostle ﷺ were Banū Qaynuqāʿ. They contended with the Muslims and spoke slightingly of the Prophet ﷺ. Ultimately, the Apostle ﷺ besieged them—the siege lasting for fifteen nights—until Banū Qaynuqāʿ surrendered unconditionally. The siege was

1 *Ibn Hishām*, vol. II, p. 3
2 Musnad Aḥmad ibn Ḥanbal, vol. I, p. 247.
3 *Ṭabaqāt Ibn Saʿd*, vol.II, p. 14.
4 *Ibn Hishām*, vol. II, pp. 144–45.

raised on the recommendation of ʿAbdullāh ibn Ubayy, the leader of the hypocrites.[1]

Banū Qaynuqā' conducted a market in Madīnah and practised crafts such as goldsmithing.[2] They were forced to leave the city although the numbers who could bear arms among them was seven hundred.

The Apostle ﷺ granted Banū Qaynuqā' a general amnesty on the condition they leave Madīnah and go wherever they wished. Although they anticipated death as a penalty for their treachery and betrayal, they were given leave to exit the city in security without any harassment from the Muslims. They departed Madīnah carrying what they could of their possessions and headed for Syria.

KAʿB IBN ASHRAF MEETS HIS DOOM

Kaʿb ibn Ashraf was a prominent leader of the Jews. An implacable enemy of Islam, he always did his utmost to give the Prophet trouble. He was also a poet of considerable standing, availing of his talents to compose and recite derogatory verses against the honour of Muslim women—an act intolerable enough to try one's patience. Immediately after the battle of Badr he went all the way to Makkah to cry out vengeance with his inflammatory verses and stirred up Quraysh to even the score of their defeat at Badr. Nevertheless, he returned to Madīnah where, in his dogged conceit, he continued his mischievous propaganda against Islam. When the Apostle ﷺ heard about his return to Madīnah, he said to his Companions, "Kaʿb ibn Ashraf has offended God and His Apostle. Who will rid me of him?" A few persons[3] belonging to the Anṣār immediately offered their services and killed that enemy of God.[4]

1 Ibid., pp.47–49.

2 *Zād al-Maʿād*, vol. I, p. 348.

3 Muḥammad ibn Maslamah accompanied by four of his friends.

4 *Zād al-Maʿād*, vol. II, p. 348.

11

The Battle of Uḥud

Revenge: A Binding Obligation

The news of disaster at Badr in which a number of Quraysh nobles had fallen in the fray and the survivors had returned pell-mell to Makkah was received with a dismay that completely bewildered the Quraysh. It had proved an unimaginable catastrophe for them. All those whose fathers, sons or brothers had been killed at Badr met Abū Sufyān and others who had merchandise in the caravan brought back safely to Makkah. It was agreed to set aside the profits of the caravan for the conduct of a new war against the Muslims. The poets, as usual, began inciting the people with their songs of vengeance. To the pagan Arabs, blood was called for in order to vindicate their honour.

A well-equipped army set out from Makkah to fight the Apostle in the middle of Shawwāl, 3 AH. Quraysh had mustered an army of three thousand soldiers consisting of their own warriors and such of tribes as would obey them. Their women went with them riding the dromedaries to stir their valour and prevent them from taking flight[1]. The nobles of Quraysh also took their wives with them. The army advanced by easy stages and camped at the gates of Madīnah. The Apostle's ﷺ plan was to remain in the city, leaving the invading army alone, and fight only when it decided to enter the city. He was not for going out of the city to face the enemy in the battlefield. ʿAbdullāh ibn Ubayy too, agreed with the Apostle ﷺ, but some of the Muslims who had somehow missed the opportunity of engaging the enemy at Badr were more enthusiastic. They said, "O Apostle

1 *Ibn Hishām,* vol. II, pp. 60–62.

of Allāh, go forth and smite our foes, otherwise they would think that we fear to leave the city and face them." While they kept on urging the Prophet ﷺ in this way, he went into his house and put on his coat of mail. The young men who had been keen on meeting the enemy outside the city, repented of their imprudent zeal when they saw the Apostle ﷺ putting on the armour. Realising their mistake, they begged the Prophet ﷺ to follow his first counsel for they were mistaken in persuading him against his will. "If you wish to remain inside the city," they said, "We will not oppose you."

But the Apostle of God ﷺ replied, "It befits not a prophet, once he has put on armour, to lay it off until he has fought."[1] The Apostle ﷺ marched out with an army of one thousand strong. But he had not gone far when ʿAbdullāh ibn Ubayy withdrew with a third of the army's strength. ʿAbdullāh said to his comrades, "He disregarded my advice but accepted theirs."[2]

THE PROPHET TAKES THE POSITION

The Prophet ﷺ marched into the gorge of mount Uḥud, about three kilometres north of Madīnah, and took up his position with the mount at his back. He also instructed his men, "Let none of you fight until I give you the word."

The Apostle ﷺ then drew up his troops for battle, which numbered 700 men in all. On an adjoining mount he established 50 archers under ʿAbdullāh ibn Jubayr and instructed them to keep the enemy cavalry away, for, he said, in no case should they be allowed to come on the Muslims from the rear whether the Muslims won the day or lost it.[3] "Abandon not your position," he commanded them sternly, "even if the birds snatch up these men."[4]

The Apostle ﷺ put on two coats of mail on the day of Uḥud and gave the standard to Muṣʿab ibn ʿUmayr.

ENTHUSIASM OF THE YOUNGSTERS

The Apostle ﷺ had sent back two boys, Samurah ibn Jundub and Rāfiʿ ibn Khadīj as they were but fifteen years of age. The Prophet ﷺ later allowed Rāfiʿ to join the troops on the recommendation of his father who said that Rāfiʿ was a good archer. When Samurah was asked to go back, he pleaded that the Prophet

1 Ibid., p. 63.

2 To get a clear picture of the disposition of troops, see *The Battlefield of the Prophet Muḥammad,* by Dr. Muhammad Hamidullah, pp. 24–25.

3 *Ibn Hishām,* vol. II, p. 66.

4 *Zād al-Maʿād* vol. I, p. 349 and *Bukhārī*: *Kitāb al-Maghāzī*: on the "Battle of Uḥud."

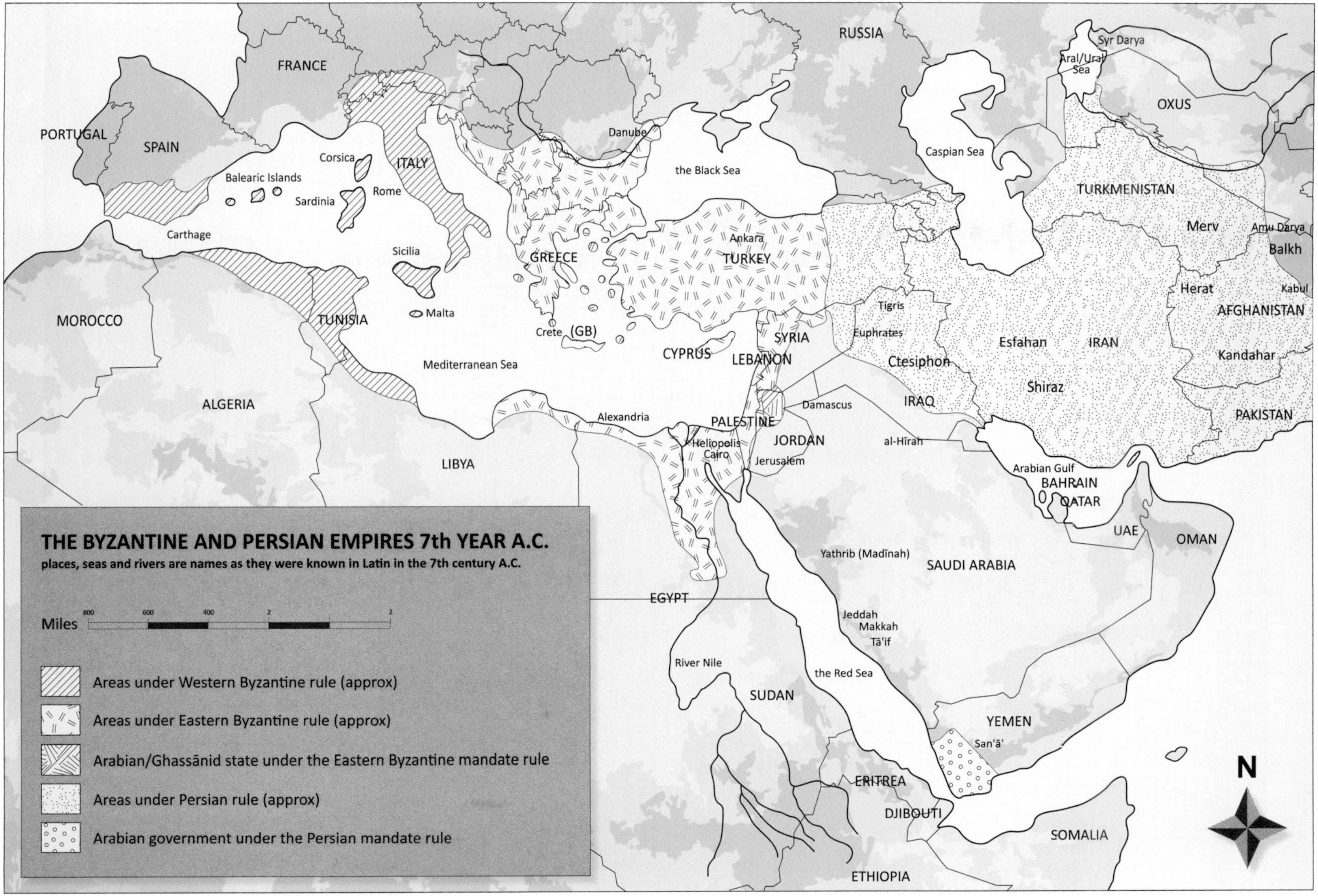
THE BYZANTINE AND PERSIAN EMPIRES 7th YEAR A.C.
places, seas and rivers are names as they were known in Latin in the 7th century A.C.
Miles
800
600
400
2
2
Areas under Western Byzantine rule (approx)
Areas under Eastern Byzantine rule (approx)
Arabian/Ghassānid state under the Eastern Byzantine mandate rule
Areas under Persian rule (approx)
Arabian government under the Persian mandate rule
N
PORTUGAL
SPAIN
FRANCE
Balearic Islands
Corsica
Sardinia
ITALY
Rome
Carthage
Sicilia
Malta
MOROCCO
TUNISIA
ALGERIA
LIBYA
Mediterranean Sea
Danube
GREECE
Crete
(GB)
the Black Sea
RUSSIA
Ankara
TURKEY
CYPRUS
SYRIA
LEBANON
PALESTINE
Heliopolis
Cairo
Alexandria
Jerusalem
JORDAN
Damascus
EGYPT
River Nile
SUDAN
Caspian Sea
Aral/Ural Sea
Syr Darya
OXUS
TURKMENISTAN
Merv
Amu Darya
Balkh
Herat
Kabul
AFGHANISTAN
Kandahar
PAKISTAN
Tigris
Euphrates
Ctesiphon
IRAQ
Esfahan
IRAN
Shiraz
al-Hīrah
Arabian Gulf
BAHRAIN
QATAR
UAE
OMAN
Yathrib (Madīnah)
SAUDI ARABIA
Jeddah
Makkah
Tā'if
the Red Sea
YEMEN
San'ā'
ERITREA
DJIBOUTI
SOMALIA
ETHIOPIA

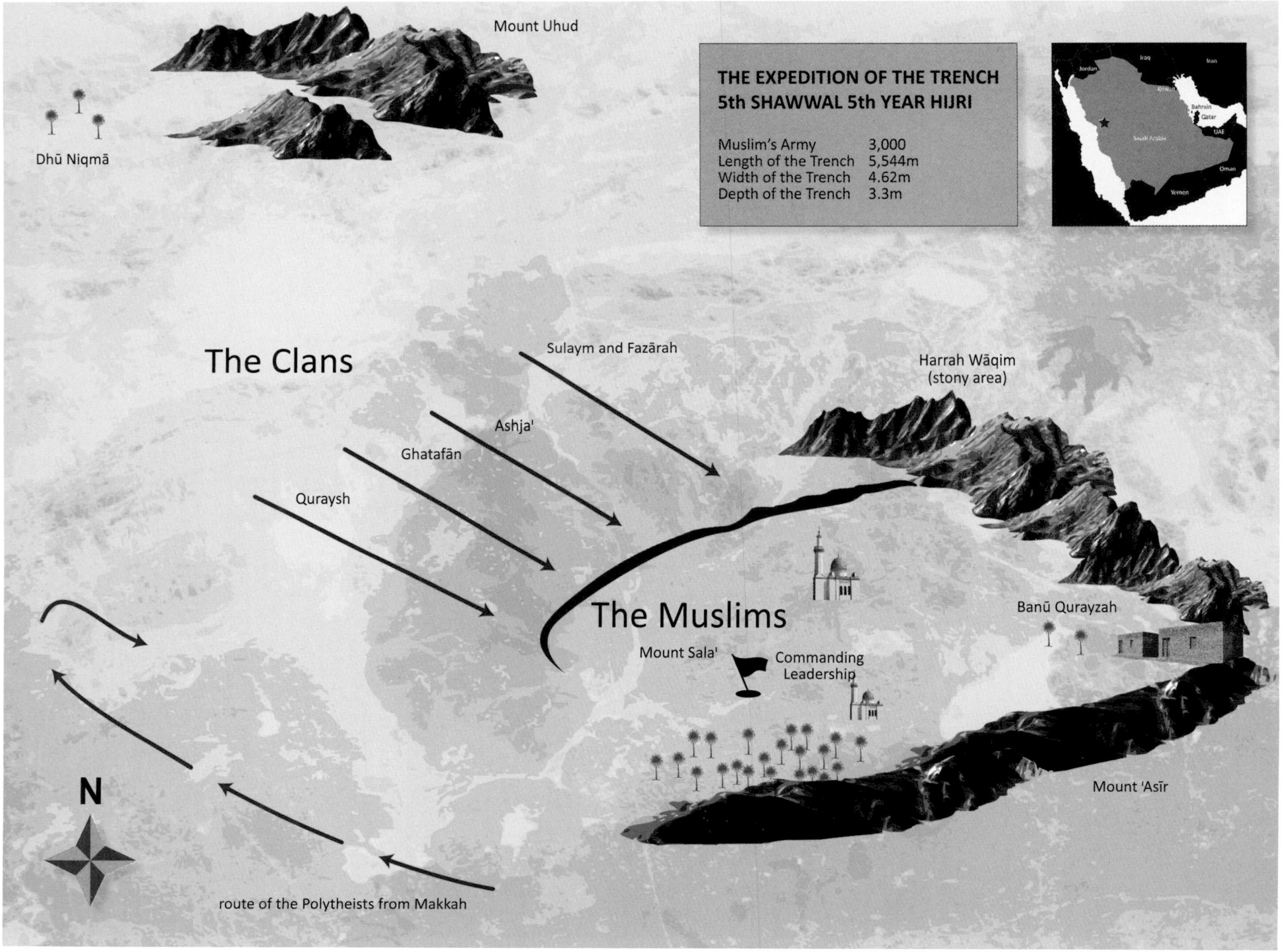
THE EXPEDITION OF THE TRENCH
5th SHAWWAL 5th YEAR HIJRI
Muslim's Army 3,000
Length of the Trench 5,544m
Width of the Trench 4.62m
Depth of the Trench 3.3m
Mount Uhud
Dhū Niqmā
The Clans
Sulaym and Fazārah
Ashja'
Ghatafān
Quraysh
Harrah Wāqim
(stony area)
The Muslims
Mount Sala'
Commanding
Leadership
Banū Qurayzah
Mount 'Asīr
N
route of the Polytheists from Makkah
Iraq
Iran
Jordan
Bahrain
Qatar
UAE
Oman
Yemen

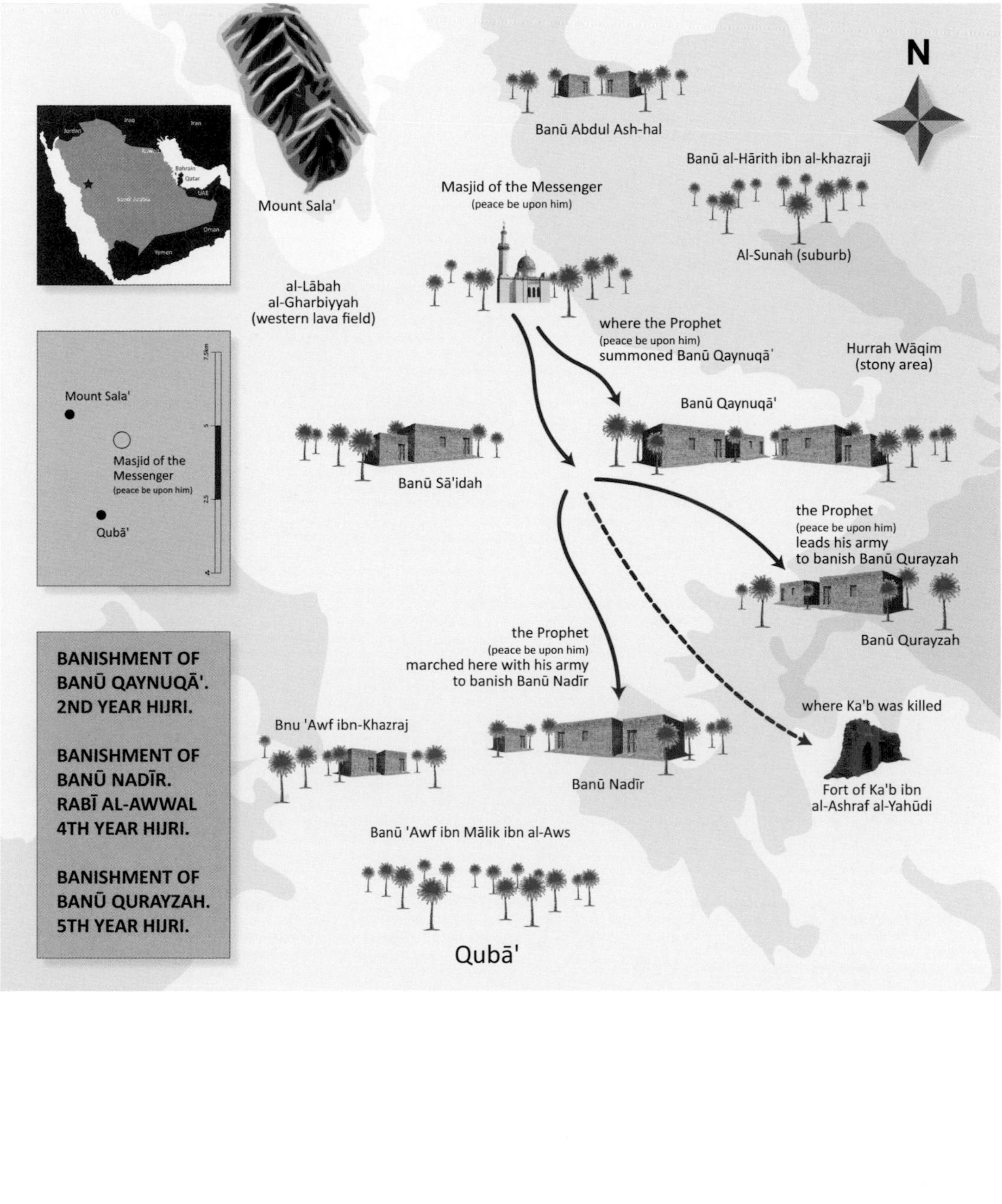
N
Banū Abdul Ash-hal
Banū al-Hārith ibn al-khazraji
Mount Sala'
Masjid of the Messenger (peace be upon him)
Al-Sunah (suburb)
al-Lābah al-Gharbiyyah (western lava field)
where the Prophet (peace be upon him) summoned Banū Qaynuqā'
Hurrah Wāqim (stony area)
Banū Qaynuqā'
Banū Sā'idah
the Prophet (peace be upon him) leads his army to banish Banū Qurayzah
Banū Qurayzah
the Prophet (peace be upon him) marched here with his army to banish Banū Nadīr
where Ka'b was killed
Bnu 'Awf ibn-Khazraj
Banū Nadīr
Fort of Ka'b ibn al-Ashraf al-Yahūdi
Banū 'Awf ibn Mālik ibn al-Aws
Qubā'
Mount Sala'
Masjid of the Messenger (peace be upon him)
Qubā'
BANISHMENT OF BANŪ QAYNUQĀ'. 2ND YEAR HIJRI.
BANISHMENT OF BANŪ NADĪR. RABĪ AL-AWWAL 4TH YEAR HIJRI.
BANISHMENT OF BANŪ QURAYZAH. 5TH YEAR HIJRI.

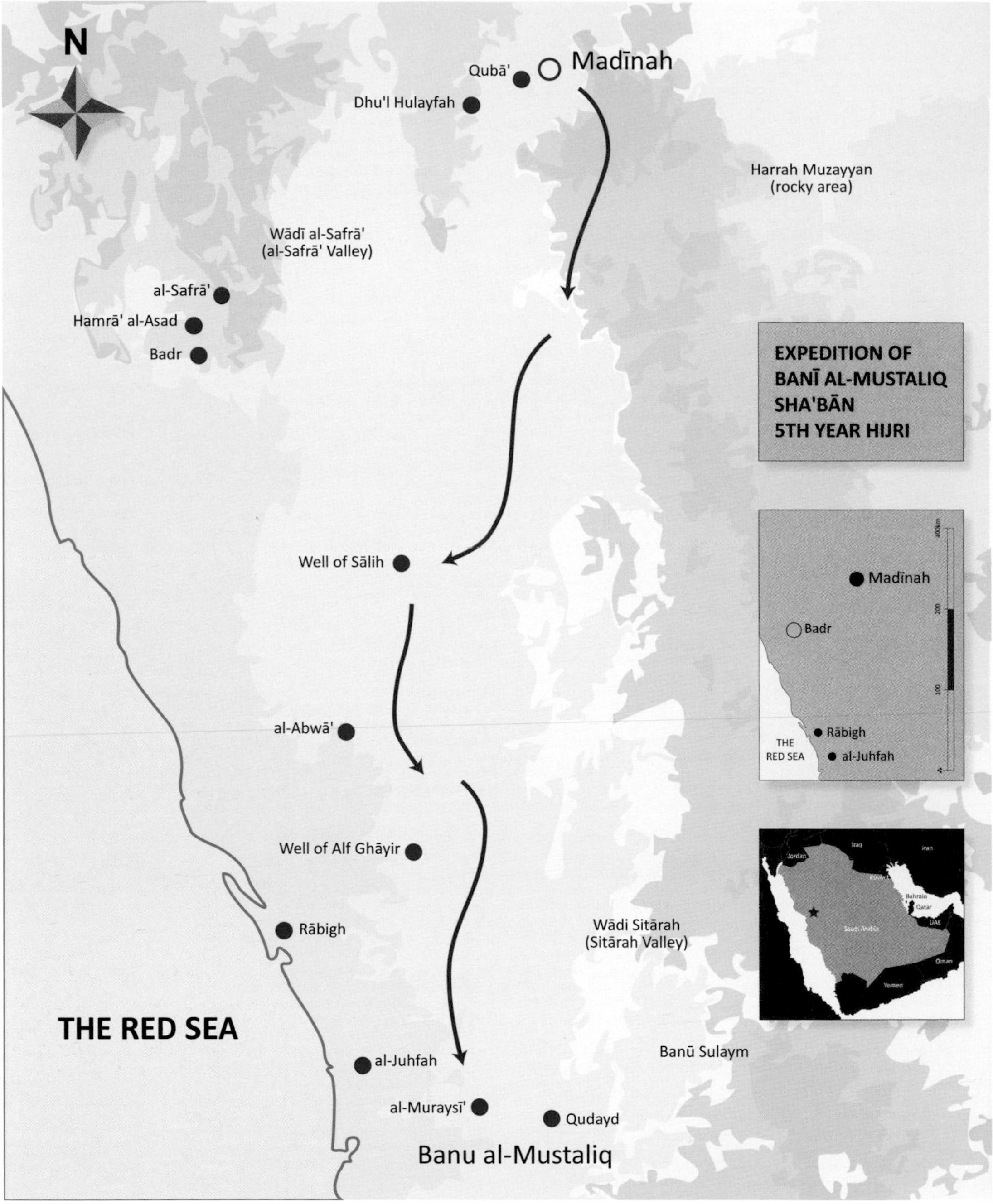
N
Qubā'
Madīnah
Dhu'l Hulayfah
Harrah Muzayyan
(rocky area)
Wādī al-Safrā'
(al-Safrā' Valley)
al-Safrā'
Hamrā' al-Asad
Badr
EXPEDITION OF
BANĪ AL-MUSTALIQ
SHA'BĀN
5TH YEAR HIJRI
Well of Sālih
Madīnah
Badr
al-Abwā'
Rābigh
THE
RED SEA
al-Juhfah
Well of Alf Ghāyir
Rābigh
Wādi Sitārah
(Sitārah Valley)
THE RED SEA
Banū Sulaym
al-Juhfah
al-Muraysī'
Qudayd
Banu al-Mustaliq

ﷺ had allowed Rāfiᶜ although he could throw Rāfiᶜ in wrestling. Thereupon the two lads had a wrestling bout in which Samurah defeated Rāfiᶜ ؓ, and he was also allowed to go to battle.[1]

THE FIRST PHASE OF ACTION

The battle began and each side hurled itself against the other, while a group of women, headed by the blood-thirsty Hind, rattling tambourines with singing urged the Quraysh troops to deeds of valour. A general engagement ensued and the battle grew hot. Abū Dujānah ؓ fought with the Apostle's ﷺ sword, killing everybody who came up against him, and advanced deep into the enemy's rank.[2]

MARTYRDOM OF ḤAMZAH AND MUṢᶜAB IBN ᶜUMAYR

Ḥamzah ؓ fought gallantly and killed a number of notable Quraysh leaders. Nobody was able to stand his dashing charge. But Waḥshī, the slave of Jubayr ibn Muṭᶜim, was watching the movements of Ḥamzah, for he had been promised freedom by his master on the condition that he killed Ḥamzah. Jubayr's uncle Tu'ayma had been killed by Ḥamzah ؓ at Badr, while Hind had also urged Jubayr to use Waḥshī to assassinate Ḥamzah ؓ. At last Waḥshī got his chance and took Ḥamzah ؓ unaware. An expert javelin thrower as he was, he launched his javelin at Ḥamzah ؓ, piercing the lower part of his body. Ḥamzah ؓ staggered, then he collapsed and dropped in the battlefield as a martyr.[3]

Muṣᶜab ibn ᶜUmayr ؓ entrenched himself in the defence of the Prophet ﷺ, exhibited singular courage in the thick of the battle and kept the attacking infidels at bay. He fell, at last, nobly discharging the duty he owed to Allāh and His Messenger ﷺ.[4]

VICTORY OF THE MUSLIMS

Allāh fulfilled the promise He had made to the Muslims. The history of Badr was repeated once again. A number of Quraysh nobles fell in succession and their troops took to their heels. The Muslims found Hind and her companions abandoning their songs and running away tucking up their garments.[5]

---

1 *Ibn Hishām*, vol. II, p. 66.

2 Ibid., pp. 67–68.

3 *Ibn Hishām*, vol.II pp. 70–72. Waḥshī himself later narrated the event as related in *Ṣaḥīḥ Bukhārī*: "Battle of Uḥud."

4 *Ibn Hishām*, vol. II, p. 73.

5 Ibid., p. 77.

THE TABLE TURNS ON THE MUSLIMS

The Quraysh had suffered an obvious rout. The ignominious retreat of the enemy troops and the women accompanying them, taking to their heels made the archers certain of their victory. Uttering shouts of glee, they deserted their post to despoil the enemy camp of the booty won. ʿAbdullāh ibn Jubayr ﷺ, the leader of the archers, reminded his men of the command given by the Apostle, ﷺ but none was prepared to listen him. So certain were they of their victory that the return of the enemy running away for its life seemed inconceivable to them. Then the situation changed. No longer parried by the flying charge of arrows, the Makkan cavalry found its way to the unprotected rear of the Muslim army.[1]

The standard bearers of Quraysh had been killed. Their standard was lying in the dust and nobody dared come near it. Suddenly, Quraysh came smashing through the Muslim rear and someone called out: "Ha, Muḥammad has been killed!" The Muslim troops, bounding after the fugitives, turned back to face the enemy in the rear. The decamping Quraysh soldiers were emboldened and returned to resume their attack on the Muslims. The situation now became critical for the Muslims—the enemy was bent upon taking full advantage of the opportunity afforded to it.

The surprise and confusion overtaking the Muslims was as sudden as the two-pronged attack by the Makkans was violent. Qurayshi troops led by ʿAbdullāh ibn Qumiyah and ʿUtbah ibn Abī Waqqās, made a bold charge and reached well nigh the Apostle ﷺ. The Muslim troops began to waver, several were honoured with martyrdom, and the Apostle ﷺ was hit by a stone. He fell on his side, one of his front teeth was smashed, his face was scoured, and his lip was injured. The Apostle ﷺ wiped the blood running down his face, saying the while, "How can a people prosper who have stained their prophet's face with blood while he summons them to their Lord?"[2]

The majority of the Muslim soldiers had been scattered and nobody knew where the Prophet ﷺ was. ʿAlī took hold of the Apostle's ﷺ hand while Ṭalḥah ibn ʿUbaydillāh ﷺ lifted him up until the Prophet ﷺ got on his feet. Mālik ibn Sinān ﷺ was so carried away that he even licked the blood flowing from the Apostle's ﷺ face.

The Muslims had actually neither fled away nor had they been discomfited. Their flanks had folded up and so they had to make good their retreat in order to gather their strength to face the suddenly altered situation. It was, no doubt,

1 *Zād al-Maʿād,* vol.I, p. 350.

2 *Ibn Hishām,* vol. II, pp. 78–80.

a day of trial and adversity for the Muslims in which they lost a number of their gallant warriors and virtuous comrades of the Apostle ﷺ, but all this had come to pass because of the mistake of the archers who had exposed the Muslim flank. They had disobeyed the Apostle ﷺ by abandoning the post on which the Apostle ﷺ had stationed them.

> Allāh verily made good His promise unto you when you routed them by His leave, until (the moment) when your courage failed you, and you disagreed about the order and you disobeyed after He had shown you that for which you long. Some of you desired the world, and some of you desired the Hereafter. Therefore He made you flee from them, that He might try you. Yet now He has forgiven you. Allāh is a Lord of Kindness to believers.[1]

THE LOVING COMPANIONS

The battle of Uḥud also gave occasion to the reflection of worthiness and ardent affection of the Companions for the Prophet ﷺ. Two rings from the metal chain strap of the helmet put on by the Apostle ﷺ had been driven into his cheek. Abū ʿUbaydah ibn al-Jarrāh ؓ pulled out one of the rings and one of his front teeth dropped out; he pulled out another ring and another tooth dropped out. Abū Dujānah ؓ leaned over the Apostle ﷺ to shield him from arrows until many were stuck in his back. Saʿd ibn Abī Waqqās ؓ stood by the Apostle ﷺ shooting arrows in his defence, while the Apostle ﷺ handed him the arrows one by one, saying, "Shoot, may my father and my mother be your ransom."[2]

Qatādah ibn an-Nuʿmān ؓ received a blow on his face which made one of his eyes come out of its socket. The Prophet ﷺ restored it to its place with his own hand and it was so completely healed that its eyesight became better than that of the other one.[3]

The blood-thirsty infidels surged toward the Apostle ﷺ. They were ready to die a hundred times to kill the Apostle ﷺ, but God had willed it otherwise. Ten of his Companions laid down their lives, one by one, defending him. Ṭalḥah ibn ʿUbaydillāh ؓ protected the Apostle ﷺ from the arrows shot by the enemy with his hands, until his fingers bled profusely and his hands were paralysed. The Apostle ﷺ wanted to climb up a rock on the mountain. He tried to get onto it but could not do so owing to weakness caused by the injuries. Ṭalḥah ibn ʿUbaydillāh ؓ squatted beneath him and helped him to clamber up the rock.

1 Qur'ān 3:152.

2 *Ibn Hishām*, vol. II, pp. 80–82; *Bukhārī*.

3 *Ibn Hishām*, vol. II p. 82.

The Apostle ﷺ performed the noon-prayer on the rock while sitting, because of the wounds he had received.[1]

When the Muslims had been taken by surprise and dispersed by the enemy horsemen, prodding them on the one side and the foot-soldiers on the other, Anas ibn an-Naḍr ؓ[2] continued to fight valiantly; advancing far into the enemy ranks. Saʿd ibn Muʿādh ؓ happened to pass by him and he asked, "Where do you intend to go?" Anas ibn an-Naḍr ؓ replied, "Saʿd, I inhale fragrance of paradise beyond the hill of Uḥud."[3]

Anas ibn an-Naḍr ؓ came by a few Anṣār and Mūhājirīn ؓ who were sitting gloomily. He asked them, "What makes you sit there?"

"Alas! The Prophet of God has gone to glory", they replied.

"Then what's the use of surviving him?" answered Anas ibn an-Naḍr "Come, let us die for what the Prophet ﷺ gave his life." Anas then advanced, dead set upon the enemy, and died fighting like a hero. His nephew, Anas ibn Mālik ؓ, later on counted seventy wounds his uncle had received that day. In fact it was difficult to recognise the corpse of Anas ibn an-Naḍr ؓ, his sister ؓ was able to identify him by a special mark on the tip of a finger.[4]

Ziyād ibn as-Sakan and five others of the Anṣār ؓ were holding off the enemy bearing down upon the Apostle ﷺ. The friends of Ziyād fought and died, man by man, and Ziyād fell disabled with numerous wounds ؓ. The Apostle ﷺ asked certain persons to bring Ziyād near him and made his foot a support for Ziyād's head. Ziyād ؓ died in that condition keeping his cheeks on the Prophet's ﷺ foot.[5]

ʿAmr ibn al-Jamūh ؓ was lame of leg. He had four sons ؓ, all of them were young and sturdy, and each was anxious to take part in the battle. On the day of Uḥud ʿAmr ibn al-Jamūh expressed his desire to go to the battlefield, but his sons asked him to remain at home, saying that God had excused him. He called upon the Apostle ﷺ and told him that his sons wanted to prevent him from taking part in the *jihād*.[6] "Yet, by God, I wish to be slain so that I may stroll lamely in the paradise," said ʿAmr ibn al-Jamūh ؓ. The Apostle ﷺ replied, "God has not made *jihād* incumbent on you," and to his sons he said, "What is the harm if

---

1 Ibid., p. 67; *Zād al-Maʿād*, vol. I, p. 350.

2 Uncle of Anas ibn Mālik, the personal attendant of the Prophet ﷺ.

3 *Zād al-Maʿād*, vol. I, p. 350.

4 *Ibn Hishām*, vol.II, p. 8.3

5 Ibid., p. 81.

6 Lit. An effort or striving: fighting in the way of God. It may include offensive attacks, but solely for a cause just and right.

you allow him to go? It may be that God intends martyrdom for him" ʿAmr ibn al-Jamūh went with the army and was killed in the battle.[1]

Zayd ibn Thābit relates that on the day of Uḥud the Apostle asked him to seek out Saʿd ibn ar-Rabīʿ and ask Saʿd, after conveying his greetings to him, how he felt at the moment. Zayd searched for Saʿd ibn ar-Rabīʿ and found him lying wounded among the slain, breathing his last. Zayd counted seventy cuts of swords and arrows and javelins on his body. Zayd conveyed the message of the Apostle to Saʿd ibn ar-Rabīʿ to which he replied, "Convey my greetings to the Prophet and tell him that I am inhaling the fragrance of the Garden." "And tell my people," continued Saʿd ibn ar-Rabīʿ, "you would have no excuse with God if the enemy lays its hand on the Apostle of God while you still live and breathe." Saʿd had hardly finished his message when he gave up his life.[2]

Before departing for the battle of Uḥud, ʿAbdullāh ibn Jaḥsh had thus implored God, "Upon Your Word, O God, tomorrow I shall fight the enemy. They ought to slay me, rip up my belly and cut off my nose and ears. Then thou should ask me: For what reason did it happen? And I would give the reply: For You, My Lord."[3]

MUSLIMS REGAIN CONFIDENCE

A new life was put into the Muslims when they found that the Apostle was still alive. Many of them pulled round him and took him up towards the glen. Ubayy ibn Khalaf caught up with the Apostle's party and said, "Muḥammad, if you escape, I will be doomed." The Apostle, however, asked his Companions to let him be. But when Ubayy insisted on coming near the Apostle he took the lance from one of his Companions. Then, turning to face him, the Apostle thrust it in the neck of Ubayy ibn Khalaf who fell head over heels from his horse.[4]

On reaching the mouth of the glen, ʿAlī brought water in his shield and Fāṭimah washed the blood from the Apostle's face. As, however, his wounds were still bleeding, Fāṭimah burnt a piece of mat and dressed the wounds of the Apostle with its ash and then the bleeding stopped.[5]

1 *Zād al-Maʿād*, vol.I, p. 353.

2 Ibid.

3 Ibid.

4 *Ibn Hishām*, vol, II, p. 84.

5 Ibid., p. 85; *Bukhārī* and *Muslim*: "Battle of Uḥud."

ʿĀ'ishah and Umm Sulaym brought drinking water on their backs in leather bags for the wounded[1] while Umm Salīṭ drew water for them.[2]

Hind ibn ʿUtbah and the women with her, mutilated the dead bodies of Muslims and cut off their ears and noses. Hind cut out Ḥamzah's liver and chewed it, but as she could not swallow it, she threw it away.[3]

Before ordering his army to retire Abū Sufyān ascended a hillock and shouted, "Victory in wars goes by turns: one wins today and the other tomorrow—Glory be to Hubal." The Apostle ﷺ told ʿUmar to get up and say in reply, "God is the Highest and Most Majestic; None exists besides him. Our dead are in paradise and yours in hell."[4] Abū Sufyān came back with reply "We have the idol ʿUzzā while you have none." 'The Prophet ﷺ said: "Answer him." They asked what to say and he (the Prophet ﷺ) said: "Say: 'God is our Guardian but you have none.'"[5]

Before Abū Sufyān departed, he called out, "We shall meet again at Badr next year." Thereupon the Apostle ﷺ asked a companion to say, "Yes, it is an appointment between us."[6]

The people searched for their dead and gave them a burial. The Prophet was visibly moved by the death of Ḥamzah, his uncle as well as foster-brother, who had always been a source of strength to him.

THE EXEMPLARY ENDURANCE

Ṣafiyyah bint ʿAbd al-Muṭṭalib was the full-sister of Ḥamzah. When she stepped forward to see her brother, the Prophet ﷺ asked her son, Zubayr ibn al-ʿAwwām to send her back so that she might not see her brother's dead body which had been mutilated. Accordingly Zubayr said to her, "Mother, the Prophet ﷺ wants you to go back." She replied, "Why? I know that my brother has been mutilated but it was for the sake of God. I hope for a goodly return to him and shall be patient, if God wills." She went to see her brother and prayed for him. Then the Apostle ﷺ ordered that he should be buried at Uḥud, where his grave still is.[7]

1 *Bukhārī*: "Battle of Uḥud."
2 *Bukhārī*, "Umm Salīṭ."
3 *Ibn Hishām*, vol.II, p. 91.
4 Ibid., p. 93.
5 *Ibn Hishām*,vol. II, p. 94.
6 *Bukhārī*, "Battle of Uḥud."
7 *Ibn Hishām*, vol.II, p. 97.

BURIAL OF MUṢʿAB IBN ʿUMAYR

The standard bearer of the Prophet ﷺ on the day of Uḥud was Muṣʿab ibn ʿUmayr. Before his conversion to Islam he was one of the best dressed young men among the Quraysh, brought up in the lap of luxury. Only a piece of coarse cloth could be found as a shroud for his burial when he was slain in the battle of Uḥud. The cloth was so small that when his head was covered, his feet were exposed and when his feet were covered his head was exposed; so the Apostle ﷺ said, "Cover his head and put some rushes over his feet".[1]

The Apostle ﷺ instructed that the martyrs be shrouded in pairs and that the corpse of that martyr who had learnt more of the Qur'ān be lowered first into the grave. While the martyrs were being buried, he said, "I shall be a witness unto them on the Day of Resurrection." He also ordered to bury them in the condition in which they had fallen.[2]

THE PROPHET'S ﷺ INFLUENCE ON THE WOMENFOLK

On their way back to their homes certain Muslims passed by a woman whose husband, brother and father had been killed at Uḥud. When she was told of their death she asked, "Tell me first about the Apostle ﷺ?" The people replied, "Thank God, the Apostle ﷺ is safe." But she was not satisfied and asked whether she could herself see the Apostle ﷺ. When the people brought her to the Apostle ﷺ she said, "Now that you are safe, every adversity is gone".[3]

DEVOTION AND FAITH

The Makkan army had departed from Uḥud but they had not gone far before they were heard complaining against one another and accusing their leaders for withdrawing without pressing home their advantage. On the other hand, the Prophet ﷺ decided the very next day, which was a Sunday, to set out in pursuit of the retreating enemy. It was at a time when most of the Muslims were tired

1 *Bukhārī,* "Battle of Uḥud."

2 *Bukhārī,* "Battle of Uḥud." There is no difference of opinion in regard to burying the martyrs, without washing them, so that they present themselves before God in the condition they were slain. As for the burial service, Imām Mālik, Imām Shāfiʿī and Imām Aḥmad do not consider it necessary while Imām Abū Ḥanifah (and others like Imām Awzāʿī Sufyān Thawrī, Isḥāq ibn Rāḥawayh) say that the burial service should be performed. Imām Aḥmad also relates a tradition about the offering of burial service over the martyrs. Bukhārī has also related a tradition on the authority of ʿUqbah ibn ʿAmr that once the Prophet went to Uḥud and recited the burial service for the martyrs.

3 *Ibn Hishām,* vol.II, p. 99.

and wounded, but the Apostle ﷺ sent a crier to announce that everybody who had been present in the Battle of Uḥud should get ready to pursue the enemy. None demurred, none protested; every Muslim who had fought at Uḥud the day before followed the Apostle ﷺ on his way out of Madīnah in spite of his fatigue and wounds. The Prophet ﷺ camped with his followers at Hamra' al-Asad, about 13 kilometres from Madīnah, where he remained from Monday to Wednesday. The Prophet ﷺ returned when there was no more possibility of the enemy's return.[1] The dutiful compliance of the Companions to the Prophet's ﷺ command at this difficult hour exhibits their love for him felt all too deeply which has been made immortal by God through the exquisite expression of the Qur'ān:

> As for those who heard the call of Allāh and His Messenger after the harm befell them (in the fight); for such of them as do right and ward off (evil), there is great reward.
>
> Those unto whom men said: Lo! The people have gathered against you, therefore fear them. (The threat of danger) but increased the faith of them and they cried; Allāh is sufficient for us! Most Excellent is He Whom we trust!
>
> So they returned with grace and favour from Allāh, and no harm touched them. They followed the good pleasure of Allāh and Allāh is of infinite bounty.
>
> It is only the devil who would make (men) fear his partisans. Fear them not; Fear Me, if you are true believers."[2]

Seventy were martyred on that day, the majority being from among the Anṣār—may Allāh be pleased with them all, while the Makkans lost twelve altogether.[3]

A LESSON FOR THE MUSLIMS

Indeed the events of Uḥud were a great trial for the Muslims. It demonstrated that faith should not be placed in groups or numbers or the certainty of victory. No one is safe from trials and loss, which is a means for the Almighty to test people's faith. Thus God says:

> And remember) when you ran away (dreadfully) without even casting a side glance at anyone, and the Messenger was in your rear calling you back. There did Allah give you one distress after another by way of requital to teach you not to

---

1 *Ibn Kathīr,* vol.III, p. 97.

2 Qur'ān 3:172–75.

3 Ibn Hisām, vol.III, pp.101–102

> grieve for that which had escaped you, nor for that which had befallen you. And Allah is Well-Aware of all that you do.[1]

Uḥud was also a pre-warning and preparation for the death of the Apostle ﷺ. It came to caution the Muslims against turning their backs on Islām after the inevitable demise of the Apostle ﷺ:

> Muhammad is no more than a Messenger, and indeed (many) Messengers have passed away before him. If he dies or is killed, will you then turn back on your heels (as disbelievers)? And he who turns back on his heels, not the least harm will he do to Allah, and Allah will give reward to those who are grateful.[2]

APPLE OF THE EYE

In the third year after *hijra,* the tribes of ʿAḍal and Qārah sent an embassy to the Prophet asking for missionaries who could teach them the rudiments of faith. The Apostle sent them six of his Companions who included ʿĀṣim ibn Thābit, Khubayb ibn ʿAdī and Zayd ibn Dathinah رضي الله عنهم. When this party reached ar-Rajīʿ, a place between ʿAsfān and Makkah, the two tribes treacherously fell on them. The Muslims took out their swords to fight them. Three of the Muslims replied that they could not accept any undertaking given by the pagans; so they fought and were killed. The remaining three, Zayd, Khubayb and ʿAbdullāh ibn Ṭāriq رضي الله عنهم surrendered. The last one also broke loose on the way but was killed by the polytheists while they sold the remaining two to the Quraysh. Ḥujayr ibn Abī Ahāb bought Khubayb رضي الله عنه to even the score of his father Ahāb, and Zayd رضي الله عنه was purchased by Ṣafwān ibn Umayyah to have his revenge for Umayyah ibn Khalaf.

When Zayd رضي الله عنه was taken out for execution, a number of Qurayshites including Abū Sufyān gathered to witness the barbaric spectacle. Abū Sufyān asked Zayd رضي الله عنه, "Verily, for God's sake, O Zayd, don't you wish that Muḥammad had now been in your place and you with your family?" "By God," replied Zayd, "I don't wish Muḥammad ﷺ to be hurt even by a thorn when I should be in sweet repose with my family." Thereupon Abū Sufyān remarked: "I have never seen any man so much adored as Muḥammad is loved by his Companions." Zayd رضي الله عنه was killed thereafter.[3]

Then they brought Khubayb رضي الله عنه to crucify him. He asked his executioners to allow him to offer two *rakʿās* of prayer. Having performed the prayers in complete repose, Khubayb رضي الله عنه said to them, "Were it not that you would think that I

---

1 Qur'ān 2: 153.

2 Qur'ān 2: 144.

3 Ibn Hishām, vol.II, p. 169–76, Bukhārī, "Kitāb al-Maghāzī."

only delayed out of fear of death I would have prolonged my prayer." Then he recited these verses:

> When I am killed as a Muslim, I do not care on which side I fall in the path of God;
> It's all for God who will bless the limbs taken apart.

Khubayb ﷺ was struck dead with the song of love on his lips.[1]

BI'R MAᶜŪNAH

Another act of treachery took place shortly thereafter. A tribal chief, ᶜĀmir ibn Mālik, expressed the desire to have the doctrines of Islam explained to his people. The Apostle deputed 70 persons, some of whom were his eminent Companions ﷺ, but when they reached the place called Bi'r Maᶜūnah, the tribesmen of Banū Sulaym, ᶜUṣayyah, Riᶜl and Dhakwān ambushed the party. The Muslims fought bravely and all were killed except one. Kaᶜb ibn Zayd ﷺ returned to tell the story. He later died in the Battle of the Trenches.[2]

DYING DECLARATION OF A MARTYR

One of the Muslims who was killed treacherously on this occasion was Ḥarām ibn Milḥān ﷺ. The words he uttered at the time of his death brought about the conversion of his killer Jabbār ibn Salmā ﷺ to Islam. Jabbār would later relate that what led him to accept Islam was his attack of a man with his spear, and when he saw the point of his spear coming out of his chest, he also heard him crying, "By the Lord of Kaᶜbah, I have succeeded!" Jabbār further says that he wondered what sort of success it was. Had he not killed the man? Jabbār enquired of another who told him that the man had meant martyrdom and thus he was convinced that his victim had really been successful.[3]

EXPULSION OF BANŪ 'N-NAḌĪR

The Apostle ﷺ approached Banū 'n-Naḍīr to demand a contribution to be paid as blood-money to the Banū ᶜĀmir since two men had been killed inadvertently by the lone survivor of Bi'r Maᶜūnah. Banū 'n-Naḍīr, being one of the two influ-

---

1 Ibid., p. 174; *Ibn Kathīr*, vol.III, pp. 123–25.

2 Bukhārī, Muslim and Ibn Hishām, vol.II, p. 186.

3 *Ibn Hishām*, vol.II, p. 187.

ential tribes of the Jews settled in Madīnah were in alliance with Banū ʿĀmir and were thus liable to pay the blood writ. They feigned willingness to accept the demand with pleasure, but kept themselves busy in plotting against the Prophet ﷺ. While the Apostle ﷺ was asked to make himself comfortable by the side of a wall of one of their houses, they took counsel with one another, saying; "Never would you get such a golden chance. If some one of us drops a rock on him from the top of the house, we shall all get rid of him." Abū Bakr, ʿAlī and ʿUmar and a few more Companions ﷺ were with the Apostle on this occasion.

God informed the Prophet ﷺ of the treacherous plan of the Jews. He went back to Madīnah and ordered to make preparation for war against the Banū 'n-Naḍīr. Thus, the Apostle ﷺ came upon them in Rabīʿ al-Awwal, 4 AH. The siege of Banū 'n-Naḍīr lasted for six nights whilst God cast terror in the hearts of the Jews. They told the Prophet ﷺ that if he agreed to spare their lives they would quit the city with their belongings except their arms. The offer was accepted and Banū 'n-Naḍīr departed from Madīnah after destroying their houses and loading all that they could on their camels.[1]

The *Surah al-Ḥashr* ("Exile") in the Qur'ān calls attention to the punishment of Banū 'n-Naḍīr.

> He it is Who has caused those of the People of the Scripture who disbelieved to go forth from their homes into the first exile. You deemed not that they would go forth, while they deemed that their strongholds would protect them from Allāh. But Allāh reached them from a place whereof they reckoned not and cast terror in their hearts, so that they ruined their houses with their own hands and the hands of the believers. So learn a lesson. O you who have eyes![2]

Many of these exiles settled in Khaybar, the Jewish centre in the north of Ḥijāz, others went away to the far off lands of Syria, and the Muslims got rid of an enemy without having to meet them in an open fight. The lands and groves left by the Jews were divided up among the first Makkan emigrants.

THE RAID OF DHĀT AR-RIQĀʿ

In the fourth year of the *hijrah,* the Apostle of God ﷺ decided to make a raid into Najd. With six of his Companions of whom Abū Mūsā al-Ashʿarī ﷺ was one, he made for an oasis in that area. The party had to cover the distance mostly on foot, as only one camel was at their service. The incursion was called Dhāt

1 Ibid., pp. 190–91.
2 Qur'ān 59:2.

ar-Riqāᶜ as the Companions taking part in the expedition had to bandage their injured feet and toes.[1]

The Apostle's ﷺ party approached the enemy, but there was no fighting for each feared the other. The Apostle ﷺ led the prayer of fear in this expedition.[2]

WHO NOW CAN SAVE YOU?

While the Prophet was on his way back to Madīnah, he happened to lie down to take rest under the shade of a thicket of acacia trees after hanging his sword on a branch.

Jābir ؓ related that he was taking a nap along with his friends when they heard the Apostle ﷺ calling them. There was a Bedouin sitting by the side of the Apostle ﷺ and when they went to him, he said, "I was sleeping when this man came and took hold of my sword. As I woke up I saw him with the sword drawn over my head, and he was asking me, 'Who now can save you from me?' I replied, 'Allāh'. Now he is sitting before you." The Apostle ﷺ did not, however, punish the Bedouin.[3]

EXPEDITIONS WITHOUT FIGHTING

The same year, in Shaᶜbān, the Prophet ﷺ went forth to Badr to keep his appointment with Abū Sufyān at Uḥud. He remained at Badr for eight days with a large force awaiting arrival of the Makkan army. Abū Sufyān did come out of Makkah to vindicate his call, but he did not venture to advance more than a few miles into the desert. He persuaded his men to return since it was a season of drought in which his people were in a bad shape. There was thus no fighting and the Muslims retuned with their prestige and morale higher than before.

The Apostle ﷺ undertook another expedition to Dūmat al-Jandal a few months later, but the Muslims returned to Madīnah without any fighting.[4]

---

1 Bukhārī, "Expedition of Dhāt ar-Riqāᶜ.

2 *Ibn Hishām*, vol.II, p. 204.

3 Bukhārī, "Expedition of Dhāt ar-Riqāᶜ.

4 *Ibn Hishām*, vol.II, pp. 209–213

12

The Battle of Trenches

THE BATTLE OF TRENCHES, or of Clans[1] as it is sometimes called, took place in the month of Shawwāl, 5 AH. The battle was accompanied with great difficulties and overcome with comparable courage. It forged and tested the fortitude and patience of the Muslims that was to prove of immense benefit to them not only in winning over the Arabian Peninsula to their faith but also in taking its message to the distant lands. It was a decisive conflict between Islam and non-Islam, between light and darkness, whereby the Muslims were put to the most severe trial, worse than anything they had faced before.

> When they came upon you from above you and from below you, and when eyes grew wild and hearts reached to the throats, and you were imagining vain thoughts concerning Allāh. There the believers were sorely tried, and shaken with mighty shock."[2]

The Jews were the real instigators of hostilities leading to the Battle of Trenches. Certain persons belonging to Banū 'n-Naḍīr and Banū Wā'il, who made no secret of their desire to see the Muslims uprooted, called upon the Quraysh at Makkah and invited them to extirpate the Muslims altogether. At first the Quraysh did not show much interest in the venture for they had already twice measured swords with the Muslims, but the Jews painted a rosy picture of the affair and promised support of all the Jewish settlements in Arabia for getting rid of the Muslims once and for all. The Quraysh ultimately agreed to their sug-

1 *Ibn Hishām*, vol. 11, p. 214.

2 Qur'ān 33:10–11.

gestion. The Jewish deputation then went to the great desert tribe of Ghaṭafān and urged them to join in the expedition for the destruction of Yathrib. They called upon all the clans of Ghaṭafān, assiduously inviting them to join Quraysh in their combined drive against Islam.[1]

An alliance was thus formed between the Quraysh, the Jews and Ghaṭafān to wage a total war against the Muslims. An important clause of the agreement made for the venture was that Ghaṭafān would muster six thousand soldiers for the military operations while the Jews would give them a whole year's harvest of Khaybar to compensate for the expenses they would incur. The Quraysh, on their part, agreed to contribute four thousand combatants. An army ten thousand strong was thus mobilised and Abū Sufyān assumed command of the combined force.[2]

WISDOM: A LOST PROPERTY OF THE MUSLIMS

When the Prophet ﷺ heard news of their design to wipe the Muslims out of existence he conferred with his Companions ﷺ how to meet the threat. It was decided to fight a defensive war, resisting the attack of the enemy on the city, instead of facing the coalition in a pitched battle outside Madīnah. The Apostle ﷺ assembled a force of three thousand men-at-arms for the defence of the city.

It was the Persian Companion, Salmān al-Fārasī ﷺ who advised the Muslims to dig a trench on the side of Madīnah that lay open to cavalry attack. This device was well known to the Iranians.[3] Salmān ﷺ is reported to have said: "O Apostle of God, when we feared a charge by the cavalry we would dig trenches to keep the invaders at bay." The Apostle ﷺ agreed to his suggestion and decided to have a trench dug in the open ground lying to the north of Madīnah. The city was exposed only on that side and was well protected to the west, south and east by dense plantations, rock-strewn volcanic plains and granite hills, presenting a considerable obstacle to the progress of a mounted army.[4]

The Apostle ﷺ marked the planned ditch and assigned forty cubits of digging to every batch of ten men.[5] The length of the trench was about five thousand cubits, its depth varied between seven to ten cubits and the width was around nine cubits or a little more.[6]

---

1 *Ibn Hishām,* vol. II, pp. 214–15.

2 Ibid., pp. 219–20.

3 *Khandaq,* as the trench is called, is the Arabised form of the Persian *Khandak* and *Kandah.*

4 The trench lay in the north of the city, its eastern end began at *ḥarrat al-Wāqim* and extended up to the valley of *Baṭḥān* where the basalt plain of the west begins (ʿAbd al-Quddūs Anṣārī, *Āthār al-Madīnah*).

5 *Ibn Kathīr,* vol. III, p. 192 (a cubit measures somewhere between 43–56 cm; 17–22 in).

6 *Ghazwah Aḥzāb* by Aḥmad Ba-Shum'īl.

ENTHUSIASM AND THE CO-OPERATIVE SPIRIT

The Apostle ﷺ himself helped the parties digging the portions of trench allotted to them. Although the winter season that had set in was extremely harsh[1] and the impoverished Muslims had but little provisions to satisfy their pangs of hunger, the work proceeded smoothly owing to the enthusiasm and perseverance of the volunteers.

Abū Ṭalḥah ؓ relates that once when he was exhausted by hunger, he complained to the Apostle ﷺ and showed his belly to which he had tied a slab of stone to allay the hunger pangs. The Apostle of God ﷺ then showed him his own belly to which he had tied two slabs of rock.[2] But, everybody was happy and cheerful in spite of these privations. The Apostle's ﷺ Companions sang songs of pride[3] and chanted praise to God to keep themselves busy in their task without a word of complaint on their lips.

Anas ؓ relates that once the Apostle ﷺ came to the place where they were digging the trench. He saw the Anṣār and the Mūhājirīn ؓ working hard to complete their work despite the biting cold of morning for they had neither slaves nor servants to dig the trench for them. Seeing how they were labouring with their empty stomachs, the Prophet ﷺ said: "O Allāh, life is truly the life of the Hereafter; so pardon the Anṣār and the Mūhājirīn."

Overjoyed to hear the Apostle ﷺ invoking forgiveness for them, the people present there said in reply:

> It is we who have pledged to Muḥammad,
> To fight in *Jihād* till the spark of life is imbued.[4]

Anas ؓ further says that if one of them happened to procure a handful of barley, he would grind and mix it with a little fat to be shared by all even if its smell and taste were disagreeable.

MIRACLE PREDICTING A BRIGHT FUTURE

A large rock was causing great difficulty in digging the trench for it could not be broken by the pick. When the Apostle ﷺ was informed he dropped down into the trench and gave such a blow with the pick that one-third of the rock was

1 *Ibn Hishām*, vol. II, p. 216.

2 *Mishkāt al-Maṣābīḥ*, vol. II, p. 418. It was a custom among the Arabs when they felt unbearable pangs of hunger to tie a slab of rock to their bellies in order to calm the sensation so that they were able to do their work.

3 Called *rajz*.

4 Bukhārī, Kitāb al-Maghāzī, "Ghazwat al-Khandaq."

hewn asunder. Thereupon the Prophet ﷺ said, "Glory be to God, the keys of Syria have been given to me." With the second blow of the pick, the Prophet ﷺ broke-off another third of the rock and said, "Glory be to God, the keys of Persia have been given to me. By God, I see the white castle of Madā'in (Ctesiphon)." In the third attempt, the remaining portion of the rock was broken to pieces. The Apostle ﷺ then said, "Glory be to God, I have been given the keys of Yemen. By God, I can now see the gate of Ṣanʿā."[1]

At the time when this prediction was made, no prophecy could be more remote from the way things were. The Muslims were then emaciated by a meagre diet and bleak weather and the army advancing against the not too well-fortified city was threatening to deal a death blow to its defenders.

SOME MORE MIRACLES

The Companions of the Prophet witnessed a number of miracles while digging the trench. Whenever any party felt a difficulty owing to the existence of any rock which could not be broken or removed by them, the Apostle ﷺ called for some water and put a little of his saliva into it; then he prayed as God willed him to pray, and ordered to have the water sprinkled on the rock which pulverised like a heap of sand.[2]

Very often, so they say, a little food sufficed for a large number of persons or even the entire army of three thousand workers. Jābir ibn ʿAbdillāh ؓ says: "When we were digging at the trench a huge pile of rock appeared as an obstruction. The people went to the Apostle ﷺ and told him that pieces of rock had obstructed their work. Saying, "I shall go down", he stood up while he had a stone tied on his belly, for we had been three days without tasting any food. The Prophet ﷺ then took the pick and struck it and it became a mound of sand pouring down. I then took leave of the Prophet ﷺ and went to my house. I asked my wife if she had anything, for I had seen the Prophet ﷺ very hungry. "Yes", said she, "I have a little barely, and we put the meat in a pot for cooking. When the meat was being cooked and the flour had been kneaded, I went to the Apostle ﷺ and told him secretly that I had a little food for him, so that he might come over with one or two more persons. The Apostle ﷺ asked me how much food I had and I told him all I had, enough for the guests. The Prophet ﷺ replied, "It is good and sufficient." Then he asked me to go back and tell my wife not to take off the pot nor bake the dough until he had arrived. The Apostle ﷺ invited all the people, Anṣār and Mūhājirīn, who came with him. I went back to my wife

1 *Ibn Kathīr,* vol. III, p. 194.
2 *Ibn Hishām,* vol. II, pp. 217–18.

and told her if she knew that the Apostle ﷺ had invited all the people, Mūhājirīn and Anṣār, and everybody present there was coming with him. She asked, "Did the Prophet ﷺ ask you about the food available?" I replied in the affirmative. Then the Apostle ﷺ came and told the people to enter the house.

He took pieces of the loaves and placing meat on it, gave it to the people by turn, and kept the oven and the pot covered with a cloth. In this way he gave loaves and meat to all his Companions, until everyone had his fill. Then he asked me and my wife to take the food and give it to others for we were also without food for a few days."[1]

In another version of the incident related by Jābir ؓ, he went to the Apostle ﷺ and told him in a whisper that he had slaughtered a ewe and had a little barley which had been ground and so he might come with a few persons to partake in the food. But the Apostle ﷺ said aloud, "You who are working at the trench, Jābir has prepared a banquet."

THE FIERY ORDEAL

The Muslims had hardly finished work on the trench when Quraysh arrived and camped outside Madīnah. They had ten thousand well-equipped warriors with them. Ghaṭafān had come with confederate tribes and made their camp with Quraysh. The Apostle assembled his three thousand men to face them, the trench intervening between the camps of the two armies. Banū Qurayẓah, the Jewish tribe of Madīnah, had made a treaty with the Apostle ﷺ for the defence of the city. However, Ḥuyayy ibn Akhtab who was the chief of Banū 'n-Naḍīr, deported earlier from the city, coaxed Banū Qurayẓah into breaking the pledge made by them.

The Muslims were placed in a desperate position; an air of insecurity and fear enveloped the city. The faint-hearted hypocrites now showed their pale feathers, sowing seeds of discontent among the rank and file. The Prophet ﷺ immediately realised the dangerous plight of the Muslims in general, and that of the Anṣār, in particular, who had always had to bear the major brunt of war with the infidels. The Apostle ﷺ, therefore, proposed that it might be worthwhile to make peace with Banū Ghaṭafān by giving them one-third of Madīnah's date harvest. The Apostle ﷺ did not want the Anṣār to have any more trouble for his sake. But Saʿd ibn Muʿādh and Saʿd ibn ʿUbādah ؓ, the two chiefs of Aws and Khazraj, did not agree to the suggestion. They said, "O Messenger of God, when we and Ghaṭafān were polytheists and idolaters, neither serving God nor knowing Him,

1 Bukhārī, "Bāb al-Khandaq."

they got none of our dates except as guests or by purchase. Shall we give them our property after God has honoured us with Islam and your guidance? No, by Allāh, we shall not give them anything but the sword until God decides between us." "As you please," replied the Prophet ﷺ and he gave up the idea.[1]

THE ACTUAL FIGHT

The army of the Prophet ﷺ pitched its tents behind the trench and kept watch day and night. Beyond the trench, the allied forces laid a siege of the city but the stalemate continued for a few days without any actual fighting between the two armies. The enemy cavalry rode ahead and, on coming nearer, suddenly saw a wide ditch. The unexpected find filled them with consternation.

"A novel device, a deceptive ploy" they exclaimed in amazement. They asked one another how the ditch could be traversed and decided to go round the trench to find where it was most narrow. Some beat their horses so that they jumped over the moat and carried their riders into the territory of Madīnah. One of these was the well-known warrior, ʿAmr ibn Abū Wudd, who was considered a match for a thousand horsemen. After crossing the ditch, he stopped and challenged anyone to fight him.

ʿAlī immediately sprang forward and said to him, "ʿAmr, you declared to God that if a man of Quraysh offered you two alternatives you would accept one of them."

"Yes, I did", replied ʿAmr.

"Then," said ʿAlī, "I invite you to Allāh and His Apostle ﷺ and to Islam."

ʿAmr replied, "It's of no use to me."

"Then I call on you to face me", rejoined ʿAlī.

"Why?", said ʿAmr, "O son of my brother, by God, I do not want to kill you."

"However," retorted ʿAlī, "I do want to kill you."

ʿAmr was flushed with anger. He dismounted his horse and hamstrung it and slapped its face, then he made for ʿAlī ؓ. ʿAmr fought, joined with ʿAlī, made thrusts and parried, but ultimately ʿAlī cut off ʿAmr's head with a sweeping slash of his scimitar. Two of his comrades who had stormed the trench with him, Nawfil Ibn Mughayrah being one of them darted back on their horses.

THE ARDENT ZEAL OF MUSLIM WOMEN

ʿĀ'ishah ؓ was then in the citadel of Banū Ḥārithah with other Muslim women ؓ, that was before the command of ḥijāb (veiling) came down. She says that

1 *Ibn Kathīr,* vol. III, pp. 202–3.

Saᶜd ibn Muᶜādh passed that way. He was putting on a coat of mail so small that his hands were fully exposed. He was reciting some verses when his mother told him to hurry up lest he should be late. ᶜĀ'ishah ﷺ said to his mother, "Umm Saᶜd, by God, I wish that his coat of mail were longer." The fear expressed by ᶜĀ'ishah ultimately proved to be well justified for Saᶜd was hit by an arrow on his arm and died of excessive bleeding during the subsequent battle with Banū Qurayẓah.[1]

DIVINE SUCCOUR

The siege continued for a month or so. The Muslims were hungry and weary while the besieging army was fully provided with arms and provisions. The hypocrites showed their true colours and many of them asked for the permission of the Prophet ﷺ to return to Madīnah on the pretext that they had come in a hurry leaving the doors of their houses unlocked. They simply wanted to pull out from the battle-front.

The Apostle ﷺ and his Companions passed their days in a nervous strain, harassed by the enemy in front and worried by the menace of the Jews in the rear. Then, suddenly one day Nuᶜaym ibn Masᶜūd ﷺ who belonged to Ghaṭafān came to the Apostle ﷺ and told him that he had secretly embraced Islam, but his own people did not know of it. He also offered to do whatever he was bidden. The Prophet ﷺ replied, "You are the only man there, so remain with them and try to help us, for war is but an artifice and deception."

After taking leave of the Prophet ﷺ, Nuᶜaym ibn Masᶜūd ﷺ went off to Banū Qurayẓah with whom he talked in a way that they began to wonder whether they had taken a correct decision in abandoning the Muslims, their next-door neighbours, for the sake of the distant tribes like Quraysh and Ghaṭafān. He advised them that it would be wise of them to demand some notable members of Quraysh and Ghaṭafān chiefs as hostages before joining their fight, so that they got a fair deal from their new allies. Banū Qurayẓah expressed their gratefulness to Nuᶜaym for his excellent advice.

Nuᶜaym then went to the leaders of Quraysh and after assuring them of his sincerity, told them that Banū Qurayẓah were unhappy about taking sides with them. They were thinking of demanding some of their nobles as hostages, by way of security, on the pretext that the promise made to them by the allies not be broken. He also said that Banū Qurayẓah had actually sent word to Muḥammad ﷺ that they would hand over to him a few chiefs of the two tribes to prove their sincerity to him, so that he might cut off their heads. Nuᶜaym told the same story

1 *Ibn Kathīr*, vol. III, p. 207.

to Ghaṭafān as well. The seeds of distrust thus sowed by Nuᶜaym between Banū Qurayẓah, on the one hand, and Quraysh and the Ghaṭafān, on the other, made each cautious as well as suspicious of the other party. Abū Sufyān decided upon a general attack. When he tried to move the Jews to participate in the attack, they demanded hostages from Quraysh and Ghaṭafān before pulling together with them. The stratagem of Nuᶜaym ibn Masᶜūd رضي الله عنه proved a complete success. Quraysh and Ghaṭafān were convinced that the news brought by Nuᶜaym was entirely correct, and they promptly turned down the demand of the Jews. Banū Qurayẓah, on their part, became dead sure that their allies were not sincere to them. The discouragement suffered by the allied forces smashed their unity and exhausted their patience.

Then, on a cold and cloudy night, a violent hurricane from the desert uprooted the tents of the nomads and overturned their cooking pots. The severe weather, sent by God, disheartened the enemy. Calling his men, Abū Sufyān said to them, "O Quraysh, it is no longer a fit place to camp here. Our horses have died, Banū Qurayẓah have not kept faith with us and we have heard dreadful tidings of them. You can see the havoc caused by the gale. We have neither a cooking pot at its place, nor a fire to light, nor a standing tent, nor yet a shelter to rely on. Get you gone, for I have decided to go." Abū Sufyān then got up abruptly and going to his camel which was hobbled, mounted it and beat it, and he did not even free it from its hobble until it had stood up.

When Ghaṭafān learned that Quraysh had departed, they also vanished in the darkness of the desert.

Hudhayfah ibn al-Yamān, who had been sent by the Apostle ﷺ to spy the movement of the enemy, returned with news of the enemy's departure when the Prophet ﷺ was offering prayers. He told the Apostle ﷺ what he had seen[1]. No trace of the enemy was left by daybreak when the Apostle ﷺ and the Muslims left their camp, not to the trench, but to their houses in Madīnah, where they laid aside their arms.[2] This was a miracle worked by the mercy of God, as the Qur'ān says:

> O you who believe! Remember Allāh's favour unto you when there came against you hosts, and We sent against them a great wind and hosts you could not see. And Allāh is ever Seer of what you do.[3]
>
> And Allāh repulsed the disbelievers in their wrath. They gained no good. Allāh averted their attack from the believers. Allāh is Strong Mighty.[4]

---

1 Muslim, "Ghazwatul Aḥzāb."

2 *Ibn Kathīr*, vol. III, pp. 214–21.

3 Qur'ān 33:9.

4 Qur'ān 33:25.

And then the billowy clouds that had covered the heavens disappeared without any rainstorm or thunderbolt—leaving the sky of Madīnah clear as ever. The Apostle ﷺ said to his Companions, "The Quraysh shall not attack you again after this year but you will attack them."[1]

Seven Muslims ﷺ gave their lives in the Battle of Trenches while four of the infidels where killed by the Muslims.

1 *Ibn Kathīr*, vol.III, p. 221.

13

Action against Banū Qurayẓah

Banū Qurayẓah's Breach of Faith

Not long after his arrival in Madīnah, the Prophet ﷺ made a covenant between Anṣār and Mūhājirīn to which the Jews were also a party and were guaranteed protection of life and property as well as the freedom of professing their faith. The covenant, which was put down in writing, accepted certain rights of the Jews and also put them under certain obligations. Some of the important clauses of this covenant were as follows:

> Those among the Jews who side with us shall be liable to equality and help. They shall not be wronged nor shall their enemies be given any help. No polytheist of Madīnah shall afford protection to the property or life of any Quraysh [of Madīnah], nor shall he intervene against a believer on their behalf. The Jews shall bear the expenses of war, so long as the war lasts, like the believers. The Jews shall be considered as one community along with the believers they shall have the freedom of their religion and the believers shall be free to profess their faith. They shall have full freedom to deal with their allies and slaves and to settle their affairs. (The covenant gives the names of various Jewish tribes of Madīnah such as Banū ʿAwf, Banū Sāʿidah, Banū Jusham, Banū al-Aws and Banū Thaʿlabah who were made party to the covenant).

The pact also made both the parties liable to help one another in the event of war, and, subject to the limits of divine injunctions, to promote mutual co-operation, goodwill and cordial relations between the confederates. One of its clauses stated that if an enemy attacked Yathrib, both the Jews and the Muslims should join hands in its defence.[1]

But in spite of this clear agreement, Banū Qurayẓah were won over by Ḥuyayy ibn Akhtab an-Naḍrī to go back on their words in order to help Quraysh. As a matter of fact, when Ḥuyayy ibn Akhtab came to Banū Qurayẓah to win them over to the allies against the Muslims, their chief Kaᶜb ibn Asad replied, "I have always found Muḥammad truthful and trustworthy." However, Kaᶜb ibn Asad broke his word and absolved himself of every responsibility devolving upon him by the covenant.

When the Apostle ﷺ heard of the betrayal of Banū Qurayẓah, he sent a few persons including Saᶜd ibn Muᶜādh and Saᶜd ibn ᶜUbadah ﷺ, the two chiefs of Aws and Khazraj, to see if the report was correct. What they found out was that the situation was even worse than they had heard. Banū Qurayẓah spoke disparagingly of the Apostle ﷺ and said, "Who is the apostle of God? We have no pact or pledge with Muḥammad."[2]

Banū Qurayẓah then started making preparations for an armed conflict with the Muslims. They threatened to stab them in the back and actually placed the Apostle ﷺ and his followers between the hammer and the anvil.[3] In truth the situation would not have been so hazardous had the Jews declared their intention from the outset to fall out with the Muslims. The Qur'ān has vividly depicted the plight of the Muslims then:

> When they came upon you from above you and from below you. . .[4]

It was but natural that the Muslims felt upset by the perfidy of the Jews. How great a blow it was to the Muslims can be judged from the prayer sent up fervently by Saᶜd ibn Muᶜādh ﷺ. As the chief of Aws he had been in partnership with these Jews for many years and was, thus, their ally and sympathiser. When he was shot by an arrow which severed the vein of his arm, and he lost the hope of surviving for long, he supplicated to God, saying, "O Allāh, do not let me die until I have set my eyes on the destruction of Banū Qurayẓah."

---

1 *Ibn Hishām*, vol. II, pp. 503–4.

2 Ibid., pp. 220–23.

3 Concerning the action of the Jews on this occasion, W. Montgomery Watt writes in the *Cambridge History of Islam*: "The remaining large Jewish group in Madīnah, the clan of Qurayẓah had been overtly correct in its behaviour during the siege, but had almost certainly been in contact with the enemy, and would have attacked Muḥammad in the rear had there been an opportunity" (vol. I, p. 49).

4 Qur'ān 33:10.

BANŪ QURAYẒAH ASSAILED

The Prophet ﷺ as well as the Muslims laid their arms aside on their return from the Battle of Trenches. An account of what happened thereafter, as related by the traditions, is that Gabriel came to the Prophet ﷺ and asked, "O Apostle of God, have you put aside your arms?" When the Apostle ﷺ replied that he had, Gabriel said, "But the angels have not put away their arms." "Allāh commands you", continued Gabriel, "to march on Banū Qurayẓah. I am also to go there to make them tremble." Thereupon the Prophet ﷺ announced that everyone who listened and followed him ought to perform the *ʿaṣr* prayer at Banū Qurayẓah.[1]

The Prophet ﷺ besieged the district inhabited by the Jewish clan of Banū Qurayẓah. The beleaguered Jews defied the siege for twenty five days; Allāh cast terror into their hearts[2] after which they gave in and offered to surrender.

REPENTANCE OF ABŪ LUBĀBAH

In the meantime the Jews asked the Apostle ﷺ to send them Abū Lubābah ؓ of Banū ʿAmr ibn ʿAwf (who were allies of Aws) so that they might consult him. The Apostle ﷺ accepted their request. When Abū Lubābah went to the Jews, all of them stood up to receive him. Abū Lubābah was moved by the plight of the women and children who started wailing and dissolving into tears in his presence. The Jews asked Abū Lubābah whether they should surrender to the judgement of the Apostle ﷺ. "Yes," replied Abū Lubābah, but he also pointed with his hand to his throat.

Abū Lubābah ؓ says that before he left the place it he realised that he had not been faithful to the Apostle of God ﷺ. He hastened back but instead of presenting himself to the Prophet ﷺ he tied himself to one of the pillars in the Prophet's mosque. He declared his intention not to leave the place until God had forgiven him. He also resolved not to go back to Banū Qurayẓah nor to set his eyes again on the place where he had betrayed Allāh and His Apostle ﷺ.

The repentance of Abū Lubābah ؓ wiped away his guilt, with the revelation descending from God:

> And others have acknowledged their faults. They mixed a righteous action with another that was evil. It may be that Allāh will relent toward them. Lo! Allāh is Relenting, Merciful.[3]

---

1 *Ibn Hishām,* vol. II, pp. 233–34. For a detailed version see *Bukhārī, "Kitāb al-Jihād wa 's-Siyar."*

2 *Ibn Hishām,* vol. II, p. 235.

3 Qur'ān 9:102.

Several people rushed forward to set Abū Lubābah free but he refused, saying, "No. By God, not until the Apostle of Allāh frees me with his own hands." The Apostle removed the rope with which Abū Lubābah had tied himself when he came out to perform the morning prayer. Abū Lubābah had remained bound to the pillar of date-palm trunk in the Prophet's mosque for about twenty days. At the time for prayers his wife would set him free and he again bound himself after the prayer was over.[1]

TRUTH IN ACTION

Banū Qurayẓah submitted to the Apostle's judgement but the people of Aws who had long been friendly with the Jews had a soft corner in their hearts for them. They said to the Apostle, "O Messenger of Allāh, they are our allies against Khazraj and you know well what they have done jointly with Banū Qaynuqāʿ, the allies of our brothers." The Apostle listened to them patiently and then asked, "Would you agree to place the decision in the hands of an arbitrator from amongst you." They agreed and the role was entrusted to their chief, Saʿd ibn Muʿādh.

When Saʿd arrived, his clansmen begged him to be lenient to Banū Qurayẓah, for, they insisted, the Apostle had made him arbiter so that he might be considerate to his allies. When they persisted in their demand, Saʿd ibn Muʿādh replied, "Fate has brought this opportunity to Saʿd, let him not be ashamed of aught in fulfilling the commandment of God." Then Saʿd gave his decision: "I judge that the men should be killed, the property divided, and the women and children taken as captives." The Prophet, on hearing the award of Saʿd, remarked: "You have awarded them God's decision."[2]

DECISION CONSISTENT WITH THE LAW OF MOSES

Saʿd ibn Muʿādh's verdict was nothing more than what is laid down by the Israelite law of war. The fifth Book of Moses, Deuteronomy, containing the sacred law of the Jews on the subject runs:

> When thou comest nigh unto a city to fight against it, then proclaim peace unto it. And it shall be, if it make thee answer of peace and open unto thee, then it shall be, that all the people that are found therein shall be tributaries unto thee, and they

1 *Ibn Hishām*, vol. 11, pp. 236–38.

2 Ibid., pp. 239–40. The words of the Prophet quoted in *Muslim* are: "You have awarded them God's decision" or the Prophet said, "the King's decision." (*Muslim, Kitāb al-jihād wa 's-siyar*).

> shall serve thee. And if it will make no peace with thee, but, will make war against thee, then thou shalt besiege it; and when the Lord thy God hath delivered it into thine hands, thou shalt smite every male thereof with the edge of the sword; but the women, and the little ones, and the cattle and all that is in the city, even all the spoil thereof, shalt thou take unto thyself; and thou shalt eat the spoil of thine enemies, which the Lord thy God hath given thee.

Jews had adhered to this practice since the ancient times. We read in the Book of Numbers that:

> And they warred against the Midianites, as the Lord commanded Moses; and they slew all the males. And they slew the kings of Midian, beside the rest of them that were slain; namely, Evi and Rekem, and Zur, and Hur, and Reba, five kings of Midian; Balaam also the son of Beor they slew with the sword. And the children of Israel took all the women of Midian captives, and their little ones, and took the spoil of all their cattle; and all their flocks, and all their goods. And they burnt all their cities wherein they dwelt, and all their goodly castles, with fire.[1]

This law not only enjoyed the approval of Moses ﷺ but was also enforced by him.

> And Moses, and Eleazar the priest, and all the princes of the congregation, went forth to meet them without the camp. And Moses was wroth with the officers of the host, with the captains over thousands, and captains over hundreds, which came from the battle. And Moses said unto them: Have ye saved all the women alive?[2]

The sentence that Saʿd ibn Muʿādh ﷺ had pronounced was soon carried out, and ensured that Madīnah would henceforth be safe from them. The Muslims could now be confident that none would act the traitor.

Sallām ibn Abū 'l-Ḥuqayq was one of the Jews who had played a leading role in inciting the desert clans to make a united bid to uproot Islam. The Khazraj killed him at his house in Khaybar. Aws had already done away with Kaʿb ibn al-Ashraf who had done his utmost to incite Quraysh against the Muslims and to slander the Apostle of God ﷺ. The assassination of these two implacable enemies of Islam removed the source of danger ever willing to foment new trouble for the nascent community in Madīnah.[3]

The pact that the Apostle ﷺ entered into with Banū Qurayẓah and other Jews of Madīnah was a defensive alliance along with an arrangement that provided

1 Num. 31:7–10.

2 Num. 31:13–15.

3 *Ibn Hishām*, vol. III, p. 273.

the basis for establishing a confederate administration of the city which gave considerable autonomy to the members and was consistent with the needs and wishes of the Jewish tribes of Arabia. But Banū Qurayẓah had broken their word without any justification whatsoever. Therefore, an exemplary punishment was called for, if only to warn other double-dealing people against running with the hare and hunting with the hounds.

Commenting upon the imperative need of a deterrent punishment of the traitors on this occasion, R. V. C. Bodley writes in *The Messenger: The Life of Muḥammad*:

> Mohammad stood alone in Arabia, a country equivalent in area to one-third of the United States, populated by about five million people. His own dominion was not much larger than Central Park; his means of enforcing his wishes, three thousand badly armed soldiers. Had he been weak, had he allowed treachery to go unpunished, Islam would never have survived. This massacre of the Hebrews was drastic but not original in religious history. From a Moslem point of view, it was justified. From now on, the Arab tribes, as well as the Jewish, thought twice about defying this man who evidently intended to have his own way.[1]

Another advantage gained by the destruction of this last but influential warren of treachery was that the bastion of hypocrisy built by ʿAbdullāh ibn Ubayy automatically became weak and impotent. The lukewarm among the Muslims at Madīnah, who masqueraded as believers but concealed evil designs against the Muslims, were shocked and dejected and were ultimately driven to despair. With the stalking-horse destroyed before their eyes they gave up the habit of spreading cynicism among Muslims. A Jewish scholar, Dr. Israel Wellphenson, reached this very same inference, concluding that the punishment dealt out to Banū Qurayẓah helped to frighten and discourage the hypocrites. He says:

> In so far as the hypocrites were concerned, their clamours declined after the expedition against Banū Qurayẓah. Thereafter they said or did nothing against the decisions of the Apostle and his companions, as was expected earlier.[2]

BENEVOLENCE AND LARGESSE

The Apostle ﷺ sent some cavalrymen on an expedition to Najd who captured Thumāmah ibn Athal, the chieftain of Banū Ḥanīfah. When they returned to Madīnah they tied him to a stump in the Prophet's Mosque ﷺ. God's Messenger ﷺ came out to him and asked, "What do you imagine will happen to you,

1 p. 217.

2 *Tārīkh al-Yahūd fī Bilād al-ʿArab fi 'l-Jāhiliyyah wa Ṣadr al-Islām*, p. 155.

Thumāmah?" He replied, "If you kill me, Muḥammad, you will kill one whose blood will be avenged. If you show me favour, you will show it to one who is grateful. And if you want property, you will be given as much as you wish." The Apostle ﷺ left him and when he passed next time by him he asked him the same question. Thumāmah repeated his earlier reply and the Apostle ﷺ left him again. When the Prophet ﷺ passed by him for the third time, he ordered Thumāmah to be set free.

Thumāmah ﷺ went away to a grove of palms and returned to the Prophet ﷺ after taking a bath. He accepted Islam and said to the Apostle ﷺ, "I swear to God, Muḥammad that there was no face on the face of the earth that I detested more than yours, but now your face is the dearest of all to me. And I swear to God that there was no religion more hateful to me than yours in the entire world, but it is now the dearest of all to me. What happened to me is that your cavalry seized me when I was going to perform ʿUmrah." The Apostle ﷺ congratulated him and bade him perform the *ʿumrah*.

When Thumāmah ﷺ came to Makkah, someone asked him if he had turned a disbeliever. He replied, "No, by God, I have adopted faith at the hands of the Messenger of God ﷺ. I swear to God that not a grain of corn will reach you from al-Yamāmah until God's Messenger accords permission to it."

Al-Yamāmah was the chief market of food-grains in Arabia from where the Makkans used to import their requirements. When Thumāmah ﷺ went back to al-Yamāmah he prevented the caravans that carried wheat to Makkah. The people of Makkah were so hard pressed by the ban imposed by Thumāmah ﷺ that they wrote to the Apostle ﷺ requesting him to get the ban lifted. The kind-hearted Apostle ﷺ asked Thumāmah ﷺ to allow the supplies of food grains to Makkah.[1]

EXPEDITION OF BANŪ AL-MUṢṬALAQ AND THE AFFAIR OF IFK

After some time the Apostle ﷺ led an expedition against Banū Liḥyān and went up to the hills of Dhū Qaraḍ in pursuit of some raiders, but there was no fighting. In Shaʿbān, 6 AH, the Apostle ﷺ was informed that Banū al-Muṣṭalaq were gathering to attack him. The Apostle ﷺ went out with a force to face the enemy. A large party of the hypocrites, still sceptical and reticent, accompanied the Apostle ﷺ with their leader ʿAbdullāh ibn Ubayy ibn Salūl. The hypocrites had

1 *Zād al-Maʿād*, vol. I, p. 377; *Ṣaḥiḥ Muslim*, "Kitāb al-jihād wa 's-siyar."

never gone out before with the Apostle ﷺ in such large numbers on any previous expedition.[1]

The failure of the Quraysh in the battle of Trenches, even when they had mustered all the warriors of their confederate clans for the destruction of Islam, had made the hypocrites bitter and resentful, burning with the jaundice of their souls. The Muslims were gaining victory after victory. The star of their fortune was in the ascendant and this had set the Quraysh, the Jews and their fellow travellers among the pagans and hypocrites on tenterhooks. They knew that the Muslims could not be humbled in "open" combat by their enemies and the only way to checkmate them was through sowing dissension in their ranks and pitting them against one another. They also knew that the means at their disposal to undermine the confidence of the Muslims in Islam and its Apostle ﷺ and to create a rift between them was to disparage the holy Prophet ﷺ and arouse pre-Islamic sentiments of tribal pride. With this end in view the hypocrites started a furtive campaign of casting aspersions upon the honour of the Prophet ﷺ. An entirely new type of society, had, however, been brought into existence at Madīnah, whose members loved and respected every other man and went by the common ideal. These pretenders had therefore realised that nothing could weaken the foundations of this ideological fraternity more effectively than a slanderous campaign aimed at creating misgivings about the leader of that order and his family. Undoubtedly, this was a well-devised conspiracy of the hypocrites which was vigorously pursued during the expedition of Banū al-Muṣṭalaq, when, for the first time, as stated earlier, a large number of them accompanied the Apostle ﷺ.

The Apostle ﷺ met the enemy at a watering place of Banū al-Muṣṭalaq, in the direction of Qudayd towards the shore known as al-Muraysīᶜ,[2] where the battle brought Banū al-Muṣṭalaq to defeat and flight.

While the Prophet ﷺ was still at this place, a hired servant of Banū Ghifār, belonging to the Mūhājirīn, got into a row with another man belonging to the tribe of Jahīnah, which was an ally of the Khazraj. The man of Jahīnah called out, "O ye Anṣār!" and the hired servant shouted, "O ye Mūhājirīn." ᶜAbdullāh ibn Ubayy ibn Salūl at once flared up and said to his friends who happened to be present with him, "Did they dare it? They set themselves against us in our own country and tried to outnumber us. By God, it is just the same as the ancient saying: Feed the dog and it will bite you. I swear by God that when we return to Madīnah those who, are worthy and noble will drive out the unworthy

1 Ibn Saᶜd, *Kitāb al-Ṭabaqāt al-Kabīrah,* vol. II, part I, p. 45.

2 The expedition is therefore also called as the "Expedition of Muraysīᶜ." See *Ṭabaqāt Ibn Saᶜd.*

wretches." Then, admonishing his men, ʿAbdullāh continued, "You have yourselves wrought it. You allowed them to settle in your country and shared your property with them. By God, had you held back and not been so generous, they certainly would have gone elsewhere."

The Apostle ﷺ came to know about the incident and he at once gave orders to break the camp and set off, although he was not accustomed to travel at that disagreeable hour. The Apostle ﷺ did not want to give the people time for vain disputation and the promptings of the devil. The Apostle ﷺ continued to move all that day, and through the night till dawn and during the following day till the sun became gruelling. He made a halt when the people had become so tired that they fell asleep as soon as their backs touched the ground.

ʿAbdullāh ؓ was the worthy son of the unworthy ʿAbdullāh ibn Ubayy. He rushed to Madīnah ahead of the troops and awaited his father's arrival. When ʿAbdullāh ibn Ubayy came, his son knelt his camel obstructing the passage of his father whom he told that he would not allow him to enter Madīnah until he had acknowledged that he was the unworthy wretch while the Apostle ﷺ was worthy and noble. In the meanwhile the Apostle ﷺ also came up. He said to ʿAbdullāh "No, let us deal kindly with him while he is with us."[1]

The Apostle ﷺ would cast lots whenever he intended to go on an expedition to decide which one of his wives would accompany him. In the expedition of Banū al-Muṣṭaliq the lot had fallen on ʿĀ'ishah ؓ and she had accordingly accompanied the Prophet ﷺ. At one of the halts on the way back to Madīnah, the Apostle ﷺ spent a part of the night before he ordered to break the camp. ʿĀ'ishah ؓ had gone to relieve the needs of nature, and when she returned she discovered that she had dropped her necklace. She went back to search for it but by the time she returned the army had moved off. The camel drivers, who had the charge of Aisha's transport, saddled her litter thinking that she would be in it as usual. Now ʿĀ'ishah ؓ was small and very light, so none would notice if she was in the litter or not. When ʿĀ'ishah ؓ came back she found no trace of the army. She wrapped herself in her smock and lay down in the hope that as soon as they would discover the mistake someone would come to fetch her. Ṣafwān ibn al-Muʿaṭṭal as-Salamī ؓ had earlier fallen behind the army for a purpose. He happened to pass by ʿĀ'ishah ؓ. He saw her. "*Innā li 'Llāh*", he called out, "The Apostle's wife!" Then he brought his camel near her and turned back a few paces. After ʿĀ'ishah ؓ had mounted, Ṣafwān took hold of the halter and went ahead quickly in search of the army. Ṣafwān overtook the army when it had again halted. Nobody took any notice of the incident, for such mishaps were not

---

1 *Ṭabaqāt Ibn Saʿd*,vol. II, p. 46.

unusual in the caravans trekking the vast emptiness of the Arabian wilderness. To the wayfaring Arabs it was just a familiar happening and their code of honour, even in the days of pagan past, never tolerated the disgrace of their daughters. The Arabs, both as pagans as well as after embracing Islam, were chivalrous enough to lay down their lives defending the honour of their women rather than to countenance any disgrace.

A poet of pre-Islamic days expresses the Arab sentiment of chastity and virtue in a couplet that gives a fine picture of Arab womanhood.[1]

If my glance meets the eyes of a neighbouring maiden,
I cast low my gaze till her abode takes her in.[2]

The companion beheld the Apostle ﷺ with the same esteem and reverence that one would have for one's father, while the wives of the Apostle ﷺ were all "mothers of the faithful" to every Muslim. In fact, never have any people loved anyone more than the Prophet ﷺ was loved by his companions. Ṣafwān ibn al-Muʿaṭṭal ؓ was, as they say, a man of sterling qualities, noble, true of soul and God fearing, who had the reputation of being least interested in women.

In short, nobody paid any attention to the incident and the matter would have been forgotten had not ʿAbdullāh ibn Ubayy walked into the picture. On coming back to Madīnah. ʿAbdullāh ibn Ubayy went to work to capitalise on the incident. He had found out, as he would have thought, something by which he could slander the Apostle ﷺ and his household and thus weaken the sentiments of love and admiration the Muslims held for the Prophet ﷺ. His treacherous disposition was not slow to realise that his shameless attack on the Apostle's ﷺ honour would create enough misgivings to destroy the mutual trust among the Muslims as well. The crafty conspirator also took in a few injudicious Muslims, who were used to rambling on without confirming the veracity of the matter they talked about.[3]

---

1 An illustration of Arab conduct towards women is provided by the incident relating to the emigration of Umm Salmah. When she was not allowed to emigrate to Madīnah with her husband, she used to go every morning and sit in the valley weeping till nightfall. So it continued until a year or so had passed when her clan took pity on her and allowed her to join her husband. She saddled her camel and set forth for Madīnah. ʿUthmān ibn Ṭalḥah met her on the way and on coming to know her plight decided to escort her to Madīnah. He took hold of her camel's halter and went with her to Madīnah. Umm Salmah says that she never met an Arab more noble than ʿUthmān. When she had to halt, ʿUthmān would kneel her camel and then withdraw. After she had alighted, he unloaded the camel and tied it to a tree. This ʿUthmān did all the way to Madīnah (*Ibn Kathīr*, vol. II, pp. 215–17). This was the conduct of ʿUthmān when he had not accepted Islam. Ṣafwān ibn al-Muʿaṭṭal as-Salamī was a righteous man of upright character who had already accepted Islam and had had the benefit of the Prophet's ﷺ guidance.

2 *Dīwān al-Ḥamāsah*.

3 "When you rumoured with your tongues after hearing such matters, and uttered with your mouths

ʿĀ'ishah ﷺ had no idea of her vilification. As it normally happens in such cases, she came to know of it very late, and when she did realise it, she was bewildered. Plunged into sorrow, her anguish brought her to tears and she kept on sobbing with overflowing eyes.

The scandal was even more distressing to the Apostle of God ﷺ. When he had made sure who was at the bottom of this intrigue, he came to the mosque and ascending the pulpit he said, "O you believers, who would allow me to say something about the man, who, I have come to know, has caused trouble to my family. What I know of my family is naught but good and what they say concerning the man—I have heard only good of him. Whenever he enters my house, he enters with me."

The people of Aws were filled with indignation at the unhappiness of the Prophet ﷺ. They said, "Whether he belongs to Aws or Khazraj, we are prepared to behead the man, who has given tongue to this calumny." ʿAbdullāh ibn Ubayy belonged to the Khazraj, and hence his tribesmen took the remark as an affront to their tribal honour. Feelings ran high, and the two tribes were about to engage one another, but the presence of the Apostle ﷺ calmed them down and the matter ended there.

ʿĀ'ishah ﷺ was convinced of her innocence. She was distressed, but was also confident and composed like one who knows that truth ultimately prevails. She knew in her heart of hearts that God would ultimately protect her honour and bring shame to the lying slanderers but it had never crossed her mind that God would send down a revelation concerning her that would be read in the mosques and in prayers to the end of time. She had not to wait for long when the verses attesting her innocence were sent down by God.

"Lo! they who spread the slander are a gang among you. Deem it not a bad thing for you. No, it is good for you. Unto every man among them (will be paid) that which he hath earned of the sin, and for him among them who had the greater share therein, his will be an awful doom. Why did not the believers, men and women, when you heard it, think good of their own folk, and say: It is a manifest lie?[1]

And thus ended the foul menace which was forgotten completely by the Muslims of Madīnah who devoted themselves again to the great task on which depended not only their own success, but the salvation of all mankind.[2]

---

about which you had no knowledge, and you considered it light; and that, in the sight of Allah, is very great," Qur'ān 24:15.

1 Qur'ān 24:11–12.

2 *Ibn Hishām*, vol. II, pp. 289–302, and *Bukhārī*.

14
The Truce of Ḥūdaybiyyah

Vision of the Prophet ﷺ

The Apostle ﷺ had a vision that he had entered Makkah and circumambulated the Sacred House of God. It was a true dream from on high as proved later with the conquest of Makkah, although the period, month or year of the pilgrimage had not been indicated in the vision.[1] The Companions of the Prophet ﷺ were overjoyed when the Prophet ﷺ told them about the vision. Everybody esteemed and revered Makkah and the Holy Sanctuary there. The opportunity of paying a visit had been denied to them for a long time but nobody had cause to think of the Holy City. They had been pining to make the pilgrimage to Makkah all those years and were looking forward to the day when their hearts' desire would be fulfilled. The Mūhājirīn were especially consumed by longing since Makkah was their birthplace. They had grown up to manhood in that city but had been forced to abandon it. As soon as the Apostle informed the companions of the vision, all of them started making preparations for the journey while their enthusiasm at the prospect of realising the ambition of their life convinced them that they were going to call upon the House of God that very year. Almost all of them promptly agreed to accompany the Apostle ﷺ for there was hardly one who wanted to be left behind.

1 See the Commentary on *Surah Fatḥ*, verse 27, in *Ibn Kathīr*.

TRIP TO MAKKAH

It was the month of *Dhū 'l-Qaʿdah,* in the sixth year of *hijrah,* when the Apostle ﷺ set out for Makkah with the intention of performing *ʿUmrah* or the lesser pilgrimage. The Apostle ﷺ had no intention of performing the *ḥajj,* however. Making a detour through the gullies of the hills he came near Makkah and encamped at al-Ḥūdaybiyyah. He had with him fourteen hundred Companions in the garb of pilgrims, along with the sacrificial animals, so that everybody would know that he was going not for war but to pay a visit to the Kaʿbah.[1]

The Apostle ﷺ sent ahead a man of Khuzāʿah to find out the reaction of Quraysh. When the Apostle ﷺ reached ʿAsfān,[2] the informer came back to report to him that the tribesmen of Kaʿb ibn Lu'ayy had assembled a strong force of nomad warriors to check his advance to Makkah. The Prophet ﷺ, however, continued to drive ahead but when he reached the place where the valley of Makkah slopes down, his dromedary, called Qaṣwā', knelt down and would not get up. The men around the Apostle ﷺ started talking rapidly, "Qaṣwā' won't get up, Qaṣwā' won't get up!" But the Apostle ﷺ said, "Qaṣwā' has not refused for such is not her nature. The one who restrained the elephants[3] is keeping her back. I swear by Him Who holds my life that if they propose anything to me which reckons with the regard due to Allāh and ask me to show kindness, I will certainly accede to their request." The Apostle ﷺ then rebuked the camel which at once sprang up on her legs, but changed her direction and started off towards Ḥudaybiyyah. She came to a halt in an expanse at the end of which there was a ditch that contained but little water. Certain persons complained to the Apostle ﷺ that they were thirsty. He took out an arrow from his quiver and asked them to throw it in the ditch. Thereupon water gushed forth and everyone drank to their satisfaction.[4]

IRRITATION OF THE QURAYSH

The Quraysh vacillated when they learned that the Apostle ﷺ had pitched his camp so near Makkah. But as the Prophet ﷺ had no intention of fighting the Quraysh, he thought it fit to send one of his companions to remove their disquiet. He sent for ʿUmar ؓ to order him to go to Makkah, but ʿUmar ؓ said, "O Apostle of God, there is none of Banū ʿAdī ibn Kaʿb in Makkah who would protect

1 *Zād al-Maʿād,* vol. I. p. 380, *Ibn Hishām,* vol. II. p. 308.

2 A village between Makkah and Madīnah.

3 The reference is to the elephants Abrahah had brought for an attack on Makkah.

4 *Zād al-Maʿād,* vol. I, p. 381.

me in case the Quraysh decide to lay hands on me." ʿUmar also suggested that ʿUthmān ؓ be sent as his entire clan was there and he could very well deliver the message. ʿUthmān ؓ was then summoned by the Apostle ﷺ and sent him to the Quraysh to tell them that he had not come to war but merely to perform the *ʿumrah*. The Prophet ﷺ also asked ʿUthmān ؓ to invite the Quraysh to Islam and to bring cheer to the believing men and women still in Makkah with the glad tidings that God was about to make their religion victorious when they no longer would need to conceal their faith.[1]

LOVE PUT TO TRIAL

ʿUthmān ؓ went to Makkah and delivered the message of the Apostle ﷺ to Abū Sufyān and other leaders of the Quraysh. After the Makkans had heard the message that ʿUthmān had brought them they said, "If you want to go round the Holy Sanctuary you may do so." ʿUthmān, however, replied, "I won't do so until the Apostle ﷺ has gone round the Kaʿbah."[2] After his return from Makkah certain Muslims said to him, "Abū ʿAbdullāh, you have been fortunate enough to fulfil your heart's desire by circumambulating the Kaʿbah." "Don't be unfair to me," replied ʿUthmān, "I declare by Him Who holds my life that if I were detained there for a whole year and the Prophet ﷺ were to remain in Ḥudaybiyyah, I would not have circumambulated the Kaʿbah until the Prophet ﷺ had done so. Truly, the Quraysh did invite me to circumambulate the House of God, but I declined."[3]

THE PLEDGE OF RIḌWĀN

The Apostle ﷺ was misinformed that ʿUthmān ؓ had been killed. He summoned the people to take an oath to avenge ʿUthmān's death. Everybody gathered round the Apostle ﷺ impatiently. Standing under the shade of a tree, the Apostle ﷺ took the oath one by one from the fourteen hundred standing round him. Not one failed to take the oath and at last the Apostle ﷺ struck one of his hands on the other, saying, "This is the pledge on behalf of ʿUthmān."[4] Thus was the pledge of Riḍwān taken under an acacia which finds mention in the Qur'ān:

> Allāh was well pleased with the believers when they swore allegiance unto you

---

1 Ibid.

2 *Ibn Hishām*, vol. II, p. 315.

3 *Zād al-Maʿād*, vol. I, p. 382.

4 Ibid.

> beneath the tree, and He knew what was in their hearts, and He sent down the peace of reassurance on them, and has rewarded them with a near victory.[1]

PARLEYS, CONCILIATION AND ACCORD

The deadlock still lingered on when Budayl ibn Warqā' of the tribe of Khuzāʿah suddenly appeared with a few of his clansmen to straighten out the impasse. He asked the Apostle ﷺ, "What have you come for?"

"We have come to perform the *ʿumrah*," replied the Apostle ﷺ. "The Quraysh are already wrecked by war. It they agree I will make peace with them for a specified period and they should grant my companions and me safe passage. If they want they may ally themselves with the group others have joined and this would give them a respite. But if nothing is acceptable to them except war, then by Him Who holds my life, I will fight them until I lose my head or Allāh makes His religion victorious."

Budayl ibn Warqā' passed on to Quraysh what he had heard from the Messenger of God ﷺ. ʿUrwah ibn Masʿūd al-Thaqafī who happened to be present on the occasion, advised the Quraysh that they ought to accept the terms proposed by the Apostle ﷺ for they were absolutely reasonable. He also suggested that he would himself meet the Prophet ﷺ to which the Quraysh agreed. ʿUrwah went to the Prophet ﷺ to discuss the matter with him but he also kept his eyes open to watch the behaviour of the Companions towards the Apostle ﷺ. He noticed that if the Apostle ﷺ spat, his Companions ran to get it on their hands and rubbed it on their faces. If he asked for anything, they vied to comply with his order. If he performed ablution, they struggled to get the water he had used and if he spoke, everybody listened with rapt attention. None dared even to look straight into his eyes. When ʿUrwah went back to the Quraysh, he said, "I have been to the courts of the kings and have seen the splendour of Caesar and Chosroes and the Negus, but never have I seen any king so revered as Muḥammad by his Companions."[2] He gave the details of his discussion with the Apostle ﷺ and again advised the Quraysh to accept the terms offered to them.

THE TREATY OF PEACE

In the meantime another man of Banū Kinānah, Mikraz ibn Ḥafṣ, arrived in Makkah. He confirmed what the earlier emissaries had told the Quraysh and so they decided to send Suhayl ibn ʿAmr to negotiate the terms of treaty. As soon

1 Qur'ān 48:18.
2 *Zād al-Maʿād*, vol. I, p. 382.

as the Apostle ﷺ saw him coming, he said, "Given that they have sent this man, it seems they want peace." The Apostle ﷺ also asked to prepare a draft of the agreement.[1]

EXEMPLARY MODERATION AND PRUDENCE

The Apostle ﷺ summoned ʿAlī and told him to write: "In the name of Allāh, the Beneficent (*ar-Raḥmān*), the Merciful (*ar-Raḥīm*)." Suhayl protested, "I do not recognise *al-Raḥmān,* but write as the custom goes." The Prophet ﷺ then told ʿAlī, "Write: In Thy name, O Allāh." Certain Muslims demurred, "No, We must write: In the name of Allāh, the Beneficent, the Merciful." But the Prophet said again, "Let it be: In Thy name, O Allāh."

Then the Apostle ﷺ asked ʿAlī to write: "This is what Muḥammad the Messenger of God has decided." Suhayl again objected, "I swear by God, if we had witnessed that you were God's messenger we would not have turned you away from the House of God nor fought with you. You should write: Muḥammad ibn ʿAbdillāh."

"I am God's Messenger even if you disbelieve me," replied the Prophet ﷺ, but asked ʿAlī to rub out what he had written earlier. "By God, I cannot do it," replied ʿAlī.

The Apostle ﷺ, however, asked ʿAlī to point out the place to be rubbed out. ʿAlī pointed it out to the Apostle ﷺ who erased it.[2]

TREATY OR TRIAL

The Apostle ﷺ started dictating the clause: "The agreement is made that the Quraysh shall not hinder the passage of Muslims to the House of God and shall allow them to circumambulate it." Suhayl again raised an objection: "I fear the Arabs would say that we have been pliant to you in making this agreement. You can circumambulate the Kaʿbah next year." The Prophet ﷺ agreed to include the clause in the treaty.

Suhayl now made bold to say, "If one of us goes over to you, he shall be returned to us even if he professes your religion." The Muslims jumped up saying, "What! How can we return one who seeks our shelter as Muslim?"

The contentious argument was still going on when Abū Jandal, Suhayl's son, appeared in chains. He had escaped from Makkah and had come to the

---

1 *Ibn Hishām,* vol. II, p. 316; *Bukhārī.*

2 Muslim: Kitāb al-jihād wa 's-siyar.

Apostle ﷺ straggling in fetters by a rugged, rocky track between the passes. Suhayl lost no time to assert, "Muḥammad, this is the first man I demand from you under the Treaty." The Apostle ﷺ replied, "But the treaty is still being written and has not become final." Suhayl was upset. He huffed, "If this is so, then I am not prepared to make any treaty with you." The Apostle ﷺ said again, "Let him go for my sake," but Suhayl refused. He said, "I will not allow him to go even for your sake." Now, the Apostle ﷺ replied, "Then do as you please." Suhayl was still foaming at the mouth. He retorted, "I have nothing to do."

Grieved to hear it, Abū Jandal said plaintively, "I have come as a Muslim to you and I am being returned to the polytheists. Do you not see what they are doing to me?" Abū Jandal had been put to severe torture for the sake of his faith.[1] The Apostle ﷺ returned Abū Jandal as demanded by his father.

The Treaty concluded between the Muslims and the Quraysh provided that both the parties would observe a ten-year truce so that men might live in peace and that no party would lift its hand against the other during the period. Another condition of the treaty was that if anyone from the Quraysh came over to the Apostle ﷺ without the permission of his guardian he would be returned to them, but if any one of those with the Apostle ﷺ escaped to Quraysh, they would not be bound to return him. Yet another provision stipulated that anyone who wished to enter into a bond and security with the Apostle ﷺ would be permitted to do so and, likewise, that anybody could come to a similar agreement with Quraysh.[2]

FAITH PUT TO TRIAL

The terms of agreement and the obligation to return without performing *ʿumrah* plunged the Muslims into profound gloom. It seemed incredible to them how the Messenger of God ﷺ had agreed to those seemingly ignominious terms. So dismayed were they that ʿUmar went as far as to speak his mind. He stepped up to Abū Bakr and asked him, "Did the Apostle ﷺ not tell us that we would repair to the house of God and go round it?" "Yes", replied Abū Bakr looking calmly at the distressed face of his friend, "but did he tell you that you would go to the House of God and go round it this very year?"[3]

Having concluded the treaty, the Apostle ﷺ sacrificed the animals and had his head shaved. The Muslims sat with long faces for they felt beaten and crushed

1 *Zād al-Maʿād*, vol. I, p. 383; Bukhārī: Bāb ash-shurūṭ fi 'l-jihād.

2 *Ibn Hishām*, vol. II, pp. 317–18.

3 Bukhārī, Bab al-shurūṭ fi 'l-jihād wa 'l-maṣāliḥ

at being prevented from visiting Makkah and circumambulating the Kaʿbah, but when they saw the Prophet ﷺ performing the rites, they rushed to follow him in sacrificing the animals and shaving their heads.

IGNOMINIOUS PEACE OR SIGNAL VICTORY

The Apostle ﷺ then broke camp to return to Madīnah. He was still on his way when God confirmed that the truce of al-Ḥudaybiyyah was not a setback but a signal victory.

> Lo! We have given you (Muḥammad) a signal victory. That Allāh may forgive you of your sin, that which is past and that which is to come, and may perfect His favour unto you, and may guide you on a right path. And that Allāh may help you with strong help."[1]

ʿUmar ؓ asked the Prophet ﷺ, "Is it a victory, O Apostle of God?" The Apostle ﷺ replied, "Yes."[2]

FAILURE OR SUCCESS

Not long after the Apostle ﷺ had arrived in Madīnah, Abū Baṣīr ʿUtbah ibn Usayd ؓ broke away from the Quraysh and escaped to him. He was followed by two emissaries of the Quraysh who sought to bring him back. They reminded the Apostle ﷺ of the pledge given by him and he promptly handed over Abū Baṣīr ؓ to them. However, on his way back to Makkah, Abū Baṣīr ؓ got clear of his guards and fled to the coast. Later on, Abū Jandal ؓ and some seventy Muslims ؓ persecuted by the Makkans also made good their escape and joined Abū Baṣīr ؓ at the sea shore where they established themselves on the road taken by Quraysh for their commerce with Syria. Abū Baṣīr's ؓ band now sought out the Qurayshi caravans, robbed their property and spread fear by killing any Qurayshite that came into their power. Once again the trade of Makkah was endangered. Things got so bad that the Quraysh wrote to the Apostle ﷺ, begging him by the ties of their kinship to him, to recall these highwaymen to Madīnah and pledged to demand no more of those who escaped to him in future.[3]

1 Qur'ān 48:1–3.

2 *Muslim*: *Kitāb al-Jihād*, section on the Treaty of Ḥudaybiyyah.

3 *Zād al-Maʿād*, vol. I, p. 384.

THE TREATY TURNS TO VICTORY

The event that followed established the truce of Ḥudaybiyyah as a decisive step in gaining victory after victory for Islam. The trader-statesmen of Makkah had gloated over their success in extracting undue concessions from the Apostle ﷺ, while the Muslims, on their part, had been led to accept the seemingly inglorious terms of the treaty simply because of their strong faith in the Apostle ﷺ. Both parties soon found Islam making rapid strides in the Arabian Peninsula. It opened the door to the occupation of Makkah and, before long it became possible to send deputations to invite Caesar, Chosroes and the Negus to accept Islam. The revelation of God had come to pass:

> Though it is hateful unto you; but it may happen that you hate a thing which is good for you, and it may happen that you love a thing which is bad for you. Allāh knows, you know not.[1]

One of the advantages issuing from the truce was that the Muslims were no longer reckoned as exiles and outlaws, but regarded as a community worthy of the attention of the Quraysh with whom they had made a treaty as equals. The alliance conceded the rightful place to the Muslims they deserved in the Arabian body politic, and perhaps even more important was the atmosphere of peace and tranquillity. The unending war of attrition so long carried on by the Muslims for their existence had been dissipating their vigour and strength; peace could now be availed of to take the message of Islam to the non-hostile or rather ambivalent tribes of the desert. The truce provided an opportunity for the Muslims to meet and indulge in conversation and discussion with the tribes thus far hostile and antagonistic to them, and this allowed the latter to appreciate the beauties and virtues of Islam. They now began to discover how people who ate the same food, wore the same clothes and spoke the same language, and were born and brought up in Makkah like them, had, in a few years been transformed into a new class of people disdaining the corruption of polytheism and idol worship, hating tribal pride, vengeance and lust for blood and pillage and had begun to take the path of virtue and justice. They could now clearly see that this change of heart had been brought about by the teachings of Islam and the guidance of the Apostle of God ﷺ.

Thus, within a year of the truce, and even before Makkah had been captured by the Muslims, as many Arabs embraced the faith of the Prophet ﷺ as had not entered Islam during the last fifteen years.

"There was never a victory in Islam," says Ibn Shihāb az-Zuhrī, "greater than this. When the armistice came and war laid down its burdens, people began to

1 Qur'ān 2:216.

meet in safety and converse together. And there was no intelligent man apprised of Islam who did not enter it. Within two years of the truce as many as those that had entered it before embraced Islam, or even more.[1]

Ibn Hishām says, "Az-Zuhrī's assertion is demonstrated by the fact that the Apostle ﷺ went to Ḥudaybiyyah with 1,400 men according to Jābir ibn ʿAbdillāh ؓ but two years later the Apostle ﷺ marched with 10,000 men for the conquest of Makkah."[2]

Those Muslims who had been left behind in Makkah for one reason or the other were harassed and persecuted by the Quraysh, but now they succeeded, after the conclusion of the treaty, to convert a considerable number of young men to their faith until the Quraysh began to consider them as a new menace. These young men joined the band of Abū Baṣīr ؓ which proved itself to be a new sword-arm of Islam, even more dangerous to the Quraysh than the open warfare with Madīnah. Finally, the Quraysh were forced to beg the Apostle ﷺ to call these men to Madīnah. To this the Apostle ﷺ agreed, and thus ended the distress of these poor men. All this came to happen as a result of the treaty of Ḥudaybiyyah.[3]

The attitude of peace and amity displayed by the Apostle ﷺ on this occasion, which also demonstrated his exemplary patience and moderation, did not fail to impress the tribes that joined their faith to Islam. They were led to hold a high opinion of Islam and to love and revere it, which, by itself, created a healthy atmosphere for its rapid expansion without any conscious effort on the part of the Prophet or the Muslims.

KHĀLID IBN AL-WALĪD AND ʿAMR IBN AL-ʿĀṢ

The treaty of Ḥudaybiyyah also won the hearts. Khālid ibn al-Walīd ؓ was the promising general of the Quraysh army who handled sword and lance with the same dexterity as he did the troops. Soon after the truce had been signed at Ḥudaybiyyah he accepted Islam and was conferred the title of the "Sword of Allāh" by the Apostle ﷺ. Khālid ؓ proved himself worthy of the title as the conqueror of Syria.

ʿAmr ibn al-ʿĀṣ ؓ was another striking commander who subsequently became the celebrated conqueror of Egypt. He, too, accepted Islam along with Khālid ibn Walīd when both of them called upon the Apostle ﷺ at Madīnah shortly after the treaty of Ḥudaybiyyah.[4]

---

1 *Ibn Hishām,* vol. II, p. 322.

2 Ibid.

3 *Zād al-Maʿād,* vol. I, pp. 38–89.

4 *Ibn Hishām,* vol. II, pp. 277–78.

15
Letter to the Monarchs

THE PEACEFUL CONDITIONS following the treaty, naturally, gave a spur to the missionary activities that kept on advancing day-by-day: Islam grew like an avalanche and showed the signs of assuming vast proportions. The Apostle ﷺ then sent several letters to the sovereigns outside Arabia and the tribal chiefs within the country inviting them to accept Islam.[1] The Apostle's ﷺ letters were not only judiciously phrased, he also took care to select the envoys to different kings keeping in view the station and dignity of the different potentates. The envoys were conversant with the languages spoken as well as with political conditions of the countries to which they were sent.[2]

When the Apostle ﷺ expressed the desire to send letters to the king of the

1 The letters were lent, as Wāqidī says, in the month of Dhū 'l-Ḥijjah, 6. AH, which coincides with 627 AD. One of these letters was sent to Chosroes Pervez, the Emperor of Iran, who was killed in March 628 AD. The letter to Heraclius would have also been sent in 627 AD but he set out on tour to Armenia during 628 AD. Heraclius should have, thus, received the letter on his return from Armenia when he went forth to the pilgrimage of Palestine. (See Alfred J. Butler, *The Arab Conquest of Egypt,* p. 140).

2 According to Ibn Saʿd (*Ṭabaqāt,* vol. II, p. 23) and Suyūṭī (*Al-Khaṣā'iṣ al-kubrā,* vol. II, p. 11), the Apostle's ﷺ ambassadors received the miraculous gift of languages and were able to speak in the language of the country to which they were sent. While a miracle similar to that conferred on the disciples of Jesus on the Day of Pentecost cannot be ruled out, for, the Prophet of Islam ﷺ worked many a wondrous miracle mentioned by his earliest biographers, it appears more reasonable to expect that the Prophet ﷺ had selected envoys who could speak those languages. The envoys were sent only to four foreign countries-Byzantium, Egypt, Iran and Abyssinia which had very close trade relation with Arabia. The Arabs fitted out caravans to these lands and we also find the nationals of these countries visited Arabia or even settled down there. It was, therefore, not at all difficult for the Prophet to select such men who could already speak the languages of these countries. The embassies to Arab chiefs should, however, have presented no difficulty since all of them spoke Arabic.

Arabs and non-Arabs, the companions advised him to affix his seal on the letters for the unsealed letters were not recognised by the kings. The Apostle ﷺ accordingly had a silver seal made on which was engraved: Muḥammad the Messenger of Allāh.[1]

LETTERS OF THE PROPHET

Of the many letters sent by the Apostle ﷺ, those written to Heraclius, the Emperor of Byzantium, Chosroes II, the Emperor of Iran, Negus, the king of Abyssinia and Muqawqis, the ruler of Egypt, are remarkably significant.

Diḥyah ibn Khalīfah al-Kalbī ﷺ, who was assigned to take the letter to Heraclius, had it forwarded to the Emperor through the ruler of Buṣrā. The Apostle wrote in this letter:[2]

> In the name of Allāh, the Beneficent the Merciful.
>
> This letter is from Muḥammad, the slave and Messenger of God, to Heraclius, the great King of Rome. Blessed are those who follow guidance. To commence, verily I call you to Islam. Embrace Islam so that you may find peace, and God will give you a twofold reward. If you refuse, then on you shall rest the sin of your subjects and followers.[3] O People of the Book, come to that which is common between us and you; that we serve none but Allāh, nor associate aught with him, nor take others for lords besides God. But if you turn away, then say: Bear witness that we are Muslims.[4]

The letter sent to the Chosroes II read:

> In the name of Allāh, the Beneficent, the Merciful.
>
> From Muḥammad, the Messenger of God, to Kisrā, the great King of Persia. Peace be upon him who follows guidance, believes in Allāh and His Apostle, bears witness that there is no god but Allāh and that I am the Apostle of Allāh to all mankind so that every man alive is warned of the awe of God. Embrace Islam that you may find peace; otherwise on you shall rest the sin of the Magians.[5]

---

1 *Bukhārī*: *Kitāb al-jihād* and *Shamā'il at-Tirmidhī*

2 The original letter of the Prophet to Heraclius was in Spain for many centuries and it has reappeared now (Muḥammad Ḥamīdullah, *Muḥammad Rasūlullah*, p. 211).

3 The Arabic word used by the Prophet ﷺ was *Yarīsiyyin* or *arissen* variously translated by latter biographer, which has been discussed later on in this Chapter.

4 *Bukhārī*, "How the Revelation to the Prophet Began."

5 *Al-Ṭabarī*, vol. III, p. 90.

In the letter[1] addressed to Negus, the Prophet had written that:

> In the name of Allāh, the Beneficent, the Merciful.
>
> From Muḥammad, the Messenger of Allāh, to Negus, the great King of Abyssinia. Peace be upon him who follows the guidance. To commence, Glory be to Allāh besides whom there is no God, the Sovereign, the Holy, the Peace, the Faithful, the Protector. I bear witness that Jesus, the son of Mary, is the Spirit of God, and His Word which He cast unto Mary, the Virgin, the good, the pure, so that she conceived Jesus. God created him from His Spirit and His breath as He Created Ādam by His hand and His breath. I call you to God, the Unique, without any associate, and to His obedience and to follow me and to believe in that which came to me, for I am the Messenger of God. I invite you and your men to the Great Lord. I have accomplished my task and my admonitions, so receive my advice. Peace be upon him who follows the guidance.[2]

The letter[3] sent to Muqawqis, the Chief of the Copts of Egypt, read:

> In the name of Allāh, the Beneficent, the Merciful. From Muḥammad, the Messenger of Allāh, to Muqawqis, the Chief of the Copts.
>
> Peace be upon him who follows the guidance. To commence, I call you to Islam that you may find peace, and God will give you a twofold reward. If you reject, then on you shall be the sin of your countrymen. O People of the Book! Come to that which is common between us and you; that we will serve none but Allāh, nor associate aught with Him, nor take others for lords besides God. But if you turn away, then say: Bear witness that we are Muslims.[4]

WHO WERE THESE KINGS?

To appreciate the gravity and significance of the steps taken by the Apostle ﷺ it is necessary to know Heraclius, Chosroes, Negus and Muqawqis, the extent of their realms, and their prestige and splendour and might in the world of the seventh century. Any one not well acquainted with the political history of the time might take them as local suzerains, since many of them are found in every country.

---

1 The original letter exists at Damascus (Muḥammad Ḥamīdullāh, *Muḥammad Rasūlullāh,* p. 216).

2 *Ṭabaqāt Ibn Saʿd,* vol. III, p.15.

3 The original letter of the Prophet ﷺ to Muqawqis is exhibited in the Topkapi Museum at Istanbul (Muḥammad Ḥamīdullāh. *Muḥammad Rasūlullah,* p.216.

4 *Mawāhib Ladunniyah,* vol. III, pp. 247–48.

But, someone mindful of the political map of the world in the seventh century and the power and splendour of the ambitious monarchs who had divided the world among themselves, would arrive at but one conclusion that only a man sent by God on a mission would dare to summon the imperious autocrats to put their trust in his apostleship. Such a man had to have not the least doubt in the success of his sacred task, nor a speck of fear in his heart. He had to possess such a glowing conviction in the glory and majesty of God that the proudest sovereign was to him not a whit more than an illusory puppet going through the motions of grandeur. For all these reasons, it would be worthwhile to give a brief sketch of the monarchs to whom the Prophet had sent his epistles.

Heraclius (610–611). The Byzantine Empire then calling itself "New Rome", had along with its Iranian counterpart kept a tight hand over the civilised world for several hundred years. Its emperors ruled in direct succession to the Roman Emperors over vast and populous lands in Europe, Asia and Africa.[1] The Empire was enormously rich while its phenomenally efficient armies and navies had compiled a successful military record.

Coming of a Greek family, Heraclius was born in Cappadocia but was brought up in Carthage where his father was the Exarch of Africa. In his early years he never made any allusion to his fire of genius, avarice for power or qualities of leadership. When Phocus killed the tyrant Emperor Maurice in 602 AD, and usurped the throne, the Chosroes of Persia declared himself the avenger of his former benefactor. The Byzantine Empire absorbed heavy losses as the Iranians reduced Antioch, Damascus, and Jerusalem and took away the True Cross in triumph. Soon afterwards they entered Alexandria, and Egypt too was gone. It seemed to be the end of the great Roman Empire in the East.[2]

It was then that the secret emissaries of the Senate prevailed upon the Burch of Africa to send his son from Carthage to Constantinople. Heraclius was crowned in 610 AD, when the Empire, afflicted by famine and pestilence, was incapable of resistance and without hope of relief against the enemy siege of the capital. Heraclius spent the first few years of his reign beseeching the clemency of the Persians and suing for peace, but in 621 AD he was suddenly awakened from his sloth. This was the year in which the prediction of Roman Victory—something most "distant in its accomplishment"[3]—was made in the Qur'ān.

---

1 The extent of its boundaries have been given in chapter I under the subtitle "The Eastern Roman Empire."

2 E. Gibbon, *The Decline and Fall of the Roman Empire*, London, 1908, vol. V, pp. 70–72 and *Īrān Ba ʿAhd Sasāniyān*.

3 E. Gibbon, *The Decline and Fall of the Roman Empire,* vol. V, p. 74. Also see the Chapter "Romans in the Qur'ān" and the author's article: "Prediction of the Victory of Romans in the Qur'ān."

Suddenly, displaying the courage of a hero, Heraclius exchanged his purple for the simple garb of a penitent and a warrior and decided to become the deliverer of Christendom and restorer of the greatness of the Eastern Empire. He began a great counter offensive and defeating the Persians on their own territory, carried his victorious arms to the capital of the Iranian Empire. Amidst the glories of his successful campaigns, Heraclius avenged the honour of Byzantium, crushed the arms as well as the glory of Iranian Empire until it seemed to be nearing its end. Heraclius returned to Constantinople in 625 AD and then, in 629 AD, marched in triumph to Jerusalem to restore the True Cross to the Holy Sepulchre. The people went forth to meet the victor, with tears and thunderous applause, spreading carpets and spraying aromatic herbs on his path.[1] The glorious event was celebrated with a great tumult of public joy. While the Emperor triumphed at Jerusalem, he was given the letter of the Apostle of God ﷺ inviting him to embrace Islam.[2] By that time, Heraclius seems to have exhausted himself. He became the "slave of sloth, of pleasure, or of superstition, the careless and impotent spectator of the public calamities"[3] as he had been in the beginning until the new movement of Islam exploded out of Arabia and took away the very provinces Heraclius had recaptured from the Persians. The boundaries of the Byzantine Empire again shrank to Asia Minor and the coastal regions of the Mediterranean Sea in Europe. The work of Heraclius was undone, but he was decidedly one of the most extraordinary and inconsistent Emperors who assumed charge of the Byzantine Empire. Great were his exploits and adventurous campaigns and he ruled the greatest empire of the day. In the vastness of his dominions, wealth and military powers he could be compared only with Chosroes II, the Emperor of Persia. Heraclius died at Constantinople in 641 AD and was buried there.

Chosroes II. Known as Khusro Parvez to the Arabs, was the fourth son of Hormouz and the grandson of Chosroes I, Anushirvan the Just. The murder of Hormouz in 590 AD was succeeded by enthronement of Chosroes II, but after suffering a defeat at the hands of a rebel chief, Bahrām, he had to solicit the protection of Maurice, the Byzantine Emperor. The fugitive prince was helped by Maurice with a powerful army which restored his kingdom after two fierce battles on the banks of Zab and the confines of Madā'in. While the majesty of the Persian Emperor was revived, his adopted father, Maurice, was killed by Phocas,

1 *Fatḥ al-Bārī*, vol. I, p. 21.

2 The Apostle's ﷺ letter was sent to the ruler of Buṣrā to be forwarded to Heraclius, but as the latter was pre-occupied with the affairs of the State on return from War and Constantinople was far away, the letter could not be sent to him earlier. Heraclius was also away from his capital to subdue an insurrection in Armenia. Thus the letter reached him in Jerusalem in 629 AD.

3 E. Gibbon, *The Decline and Fall of the Roman Empire*, vol. V, p. 76.

who promoted himself to the vacant post. Chosroes II decided to avenge the death of Maurice and invaded the Byzantine dominions in 604 AD. Chosroes II continued to press his triumphant march to Constantinople, even after the death of Phocas, rolling in the dust of all the Byzantine provinces, Syria, Egypt and Asia Minor, in the rapid tide of his success. By 616 AD, Chosroes II had reached the summit of his victorious campaign for he seemed to announce the approaching dissolution of the Byzantine Empire. But his insolent demands at last animated the dormant valour of Heraclius who put the Iranians to rout and penetrated into the heart of Persia. Chosroes II had ultimately to leave his country and seek refuge in some far off place and thus the quarrel between the two Empires came to an end in 628 AD.

Chosroes II was, according to the unanimous verdict of historians, the greatest Emperor of Iran. In the East, his writ ran up to the north-western parts of India.[1] During his rule the glory and magnificence of the royal court had surpassed the limits of fancy. Iran was during this period, more than a match to any country of the world in its ostentatious living, the luxury of its nobles and the splendid workmanship of its artisans. Writing about the attainments of Chosroes II, the noted Arab historian Ṭabarī says:

> Made of a sterner stuff, he was the most prudent and far-sighted Emperor of Persia. Deeds of valour, exploits of victory, abundance of wealth, the stroke of luck and favourable circumstances had so amassed during his reign as never before. It was for these reasons that he came to be known as Abrawīz (Parvez) which meant victorious in Arabic.[2]

In the arts of civilisation and innovations in the preparations of edibles and drinks Iran was without any parallel.[3] In the manufacture of perfumes it had attained perfection. The people had developed a taste for savoury preparation, luscious liquors and the finest perfumes. Love of music had grown into a craze which had stimulated its development in the reign of Chosroes II. He was so fond of amassing wealth and artefacts that when his treasure was transferred from an old building to a new one at Ctesiphon in 607–8 AD, it consisted of 460 million *mithqāls* of gold. Which was worth 370 million gold sovereigns. In the thirteenth year of his reign Chosroes II had 880 million *mithqāls* of gold in his exchequer.

The reign of Chosroes II lasted thirty seven years. His son Sherveh ascended the throne after him.

1 *Īrān fi 'Ahd Sasāniyān*, p. 602.
2 *Tarīkh Ṭabarī*, vol. II, (Egypt), p. 137.
3 Ibid., p. 995.

Muqawqis: He was the Prefect as well as Patriarch of Alexandria acting as the Governor of Egypt on behalf of the Byzantine Emperor. The Arab historians normally mention him by his title "Muqawqis" but his personal identity is hotly disputed. Abū Ṣāliḥ who wrote in the sixth century after *hijrah* (12th century AD), gives his name as Jurayj ibn Mīnā al-Muqawqis (which is a corruption of George, son of Mīnā). Ibn Khaldūn says that the then Muqawqis was a Copt while al-Maqrīzī asserts that he was a Roman. When the Persians conquered Egypt in 616 AD, the Byzantine Prefect and Patriarch was John the Almoner who fled from Egypt to Cyprus and died there. George was appointed in his place as the Archbishop of the Merkite church who remained in office from 621 AD till his death in 630 AD. He is known to the Arab historians as Jurayj; they give the year of his appointment as 621 AD. Alfred J. Butler is of the opinion that practically all the Arab historians speak of a person by the title of Muqawqis, appointed by the Byzantine Emperor Heraclius after the recovery of Egypt from the Persians who was both the Patriarch and Governor of Egypt. They have, therefore, identified George as Muqawqis. But he also says that Muqawqis was only a title of the Patriarch since it was applied to the governor in the early Coptic manuscripts.[1] It is also possible that a Coptic Patriarch might have assumed the ecclesiastical and political powers after the Persian conquest of Egypt. However, as the treaty of peace between the Romans and the Persians was executed in the year 628 AD, it is more probably that the letter of the Prophet ﷺ would have been received by the Patriarch of Egypt when he was more or less independent. This is why, it appears, the Apostle ﷺ addressed him as the Chief of the Copts.

Egypt was the most fertile dominion of the Byzantine Empire, far exceeding other provinces in population as well as resources. It was also the granary of the Byzantine capital. When ʿAmr ibn al-ʿĀṣ ﷺ entered Egypt at the head of the conquering Arab forces, fourteen years after the Apostle ﷺ had sent his letter to Muqawqis, he wrote to Caliph ʿUmar ibn al-Khaṭṭāb ﷺ describing it thus: "The country is exceedingly fertile and green. Its length covers a journey of one month and its breadth is of about ten days."[2] A census of Egypt taken by ʿAmr ibn al-ʿĀṣ ﷺ in 20 AH/640 AD to find out the number of persons on whom *jizyah* could be levied showed that the population exceeded six million[3] of whom one hundred thousand were Romans. ʿAmr ibn al-ʿĀṣ ﷺ also wrote to the Caliph:

1 A. J. Butler: *The Arab Conquest of Egypt*, Appendix C, pp. 508–26.

2 *An-Nujūm az-Zāhirah* by Ibn Taghrī Bardī, vol. I, p. 32.

3 See Art. "Egypt" in Muḥammad Farīd Wajdī's *Dā'irat al-Maʿārif al-Qarn al-ʿIshrīn*. The author, however, is doubtful about the population mentioned in view of the present population of Egypt and its growth rate for it is not more than forty million at present.

"I have taken a city of which I can but say that it contains 4,000 palaces, 4,000 baths, 40,000 Jews and 400 theatres for the entertainment of the nobles."[1]

Negus: Ethiopia is an ancient country in the eastern part of the Africa lying on the coast of the Red Sea. It has been known as Abyssinia since the distant past. Its boundaries, as they existed in the seventh century, are not easy to define now.

The kingdom of Abyssinia was also one of the oldest in the world. Jewish sources suggest that the queen of Sheba was Abyssinian and her progeny by Solomon ﷺ had ruled the country ever since. Jews started migrating to the country from the sixth century BC after the destruction of Solomon's Temple, but by the fourth century Christianity had become the dominant faith of the people. When the Jewish monarch of Yemen persecuted the Christians of his land, Emperor Justin I wrote to the Negus of Abyssinia to help the Christians.[2] The Negus of Abyssinia is said to have complied by sending an army which captured Yemen in 525 AD, and retained the hold of Abyssinia over it for about fifty years. Abrahah was the viceroy of the Abyssinian King in Yemen who led an army to destroy the House of God in Makkah whence came off the memorable event of *ʿĀm al-fīl* or the year of the Elephant.

The capital of Abyssinia was at Axum. Being a sovereign state, it was neither dependent nor a tributary to any alien power. Of course, as a Christian country, it had friendly relations with Byzantium which was then regarded as the "protector" of Christendom. The Byzantine Emperor respected the independence of Abyssinia for Justinian had sent his ambassador, Julian by name, to the court of Axum.[3]

De Lacy O'Leary writes in *Arabia before Mohammad* that "from 522 to the rise of Islam the Abyssinians controlled the southern end of the Red Sea and the trade with Africa, perhaps that with India as well."[4]

The official title of the King of Abyssinia was *Nagusa Nagashi* or King of Kings of Ethiopia,[5] but the name of the King to whom the Apostle ﷺ sent his letter inviting him to embrace Islam has been variously mentioned in different sources. However, we have before us two kings of Abyssinia; one of these is the king during whose reign the Muslims migrated from Makkah to Abyssinia under the leadership of Jaʿfar ibn Abī Ṭālib ؓ, in the fifth year of the apostleship of Muḥammad ﷺ; but it is highly improbable that the Apostle ﷺ wrote any letter to the Negus at that time. The circumstances in which the Prophet ﷺ was in

---

1 *Ḥusn al-Muḥāḍarah* by Suyūṭī.

2 De Lacy O 'Leary, *Arabia before Mohammad,* London, 1927, p. 119.

3 A. H. M. Jones and Elizabeth Monroe, *A History of Abyssinia,* Oxford, 1935, p. 32.

4 Ibid., p. 120.

5 Ibid., p. 63.

at Makkah were unfavourable for addressing such a letter to any potentate, and, in any case, it was neither an appropriate time for inviting any noble or king of a foreign land to accept Islam, nor had he sent any such letter to any foreign dignitary, according to the Ḥadith. All that the Ḥadīth suggest is that the Apostle ﷺ had requested the then Negus to afford protection to the Muslims in his country for they were being severely persecuted by the Quraysh. Similarly, the writings of Ibn Hishām and others imply that the Negus had admitted the truth of divine revelation and accepted that Jesus ﷺ son of Mary was a Prophet and word of God cast by Him into Mary.

In so far as the Negus to whom the Apostle ﷺ had sent his letter is concerned, according to Ibn Kathīr he was the king who succeeded the Negus who had given asylum to Jaʿfar ibn Abī Ṭālib ﷺ. Ibn Kathīr holds that the letter inviting him along with other monarchs to accept Islam was written to the Negus before the conquest of Makkah. Ibn Kathīr's view seems preferable for this second Negus ﷺ accepted Islam, and of whose death the Prophet ﷺ informed the Muslims and for whom he prayed for salvation. Wāqidī and some other biographers of the Prophet ﷺ have stated that the Prophet ﷺ had prayed for the Negus ﷺ on return from Tabūk in Rajab 9 AH.[1] The circumstances of the event suggest that Wāqidī is correct in holding this view and in its dating.

REACTION OF THE MONARCHS

Heraclius, the Negus and Muqawqis received the letters from the Apostle ﷺ with due respect and each gave a courteous reply. The Negus and Muqawqis showed the highest regard to the envoys and the latter even sent some gifts to the Apostle ﷺ. These included two slave-girls, one of whom was Māriyah who gave birth to the Apostle's ﷺ son Ibrāhīm ﷺ.

Chosroes II was indignant, he tore the letter into pieces, saying, "My slave dares to write me thus!" When his reply was conveyed to the Prophet ﷺ he said, "Even so shall God shatter his kingdom to pieces."[2]

Chosroes II wrote to Bādhān, who was his governor in Yemen, to have the Apostle ﷺ sent to him in Ctesiphon. Bādhān deputed Bābwayh to tell the Apostle ﷺ what Chosroes II had written to him and that he had come to take him to the King. But when Bābwayh came to Madīnah, the Apostle ﷺ told him, "God has given Sherveh power over his father and he has killed Chosroes II."

The prophecy of the Apostle ﷺ came true exactly in the way foretold by him.

---

1 *Ṣaḥīḥ Muslim*, vol. V, p. 166.

2 *Ṭabarī*, vol. III, pp. 90–91.

Chosroes' son Qubādh had by then deposed his father and seized the throne under the title of Sherveh. Chosroes II was murdered in March 628 AD, and with him ended the glory of the four hundred year old house of the Sasanids. Sherveh enjoyed only six months of the fruits of his crime, and in the space of four years the regal title was transferred to ten sovereigns, in quick succession, until the exhausted monarchy was assumed by Yazdagird III. He was the last Persian Emperor for he was soon to flee for his life before the advancing arms of the Muslims. And thus was realised the Prophet's ﷺ prophecy within eight years of his pronouncement.[1] The Apostle ﷺ had also said, "No more Chosroes after Chosroes dies."[2] This portion of the prediction also came to pass with the fall of Yazdagird III.

In a few years the whole of Persia would lie at the feet of the Muslims. The bulk of the population were to adopt Islam and there would be born in Persia men with such a lambent flame of intellect that proved true, word by word, what the Apostle ﷺ had once remarked: "If knowledge were to be found in Pleiades, some of the sons of Persia would attain it."[3]

HERACLIUS AND ABŪ SUFYĀN

Heraclius decided to satisfy himself about the contents of the Apostle's ﷺ letter. He ordered the search for a man from Arabia who could tell him about the Prophet ﷺ. Abū Sufyān ؓ happened to be there on a business trip and so he was brought before him. The questions that Heraclius asked on this occasion show his deep insight into the scripture and the teachings of the prophets of yore and that he knew how and when God sends them and the way they are usually treated by their people. Abū Sufyān ؓ, too, acted like a true Arab for he considered it below his dignity to tell the Emperor anything but the truth.

The conversation between Heraclius and Abū Sufyān is significant enough to be quoted here in *Extenso.*

Heraclius: Tell me of his lineage.

Abū Sufyān: He comes of the best lineage.

Heraclius: Did anybody before him make the claim he does?

Abū Sufyān: No.

Heraclius; Has there been any king in his family.

Sufyān: No.

1 See "The last days of the Sasanid Empire" in *Īrān ba ʿAhd Sasāniyān.*

2 *Ibn Kathīr,* vol. III. p. 513 and *Muslim.*

3 *Musnad Imām Aḥmad,* vol. II, p. 399.

Heraclius: Who have followed him? Are they the poor and the weak or the nobles?

Abū Sufyān: They are all poor and weak.

Heraclius: Are his followers increasing or deserting him?

Abū Sufyān: Their numbers are growing.

Heraclius: Do those who enter his religion despise and leave him?

Abū Sufyān: No.

Heraclius: Did you find him telling lies before he made the claim?

Abū Sufyān: No.

Heraclius: Did he ever break the word given by him?

Abū Sufyān: Not as yet, but we have to see what he does in future.

Heraclius: Did you ever fight against him?

Abū Sufyān: Yes.

Heraclius: What was the result?

Abū Sufyān: The fortunes have varied, sometimes in our favour, sometimes in his.

Heraclius: What is it that he teaches?

Abū Sufyān: He asks us to worship One God, and not to associate aught with Him; to offer prayers; to be virtuous; to speak the truth; and to be kind to kinsmen.

Heraclius then asked the interpreter to tell Abū Sufyān: "I asked you about his lineage and you replied that it was the noblest among you. Prophets always come from the best lineage. I asked you if any man in his family had made a similar claim and your reply was "No" If anybody had made a claim to apostleship in his family, I would have thought that he was imitating him. Then I asked if there had been a king in his family, and you said "No." Had it been so, I would have surmised that he was trying to recover his lost kingdom. And I enquired if you knew him to be untruthful before making the claim, and you said "No." I know that it is not possible for a man to be truthful to the people but to mince the truth in regard to God. Then I asked you if his followers were drawn from the people of rank and distinction or if they were the poor and the weak, and you replied that they were humble and meek. Prophets are always followed by the humble and poor in the beginning. And I asked if his followers were increasing and you said that they were gaining in numbers. Faith is always like that for it goes on increasing until it is triumphant. Then I asked if anybody had turned away from him and rejected his faith and your reply was "No." Faith, once settled in the heart, never leaves it. And then I asked if he ever broke his word and you said "No." Prophets never break their promises. Then I asked about his teachings and you told me that he asked you to worship One God; to associate nought with Him; bade you to turn away from the idols and to speak the truth; and to be virtuous and to glorify the Lord. Now, if you have told me the truth about him he will conquer the ground that is beneath my feet. I knew that a prophet was about to be born but I had never thought that he would come from Arabia. If it had been possible I would have called upon him, and if I had been with him, I would have washed his feet."

Heraclius summoned his chiefs and courtiers and got the doors of his chamber closed upon them. Then, turning to them he said, "You Chiefs of Rome! If you desire safety and guidance so that your kingdom shall be firmly established, then follow the Arabian Prophet." Whereupon they all started off but found the doors closed. When Heraclius saw them getting sore, he despaired of their conversion; so he ordered them to be brought back. He said, "What I said before was to test your constancy and faith and I am now satisfied of your firmness and devotion." The courtiers lowered their heads and were pleased to hear him speaking thus.

Heraclius lost the golden opportunity: he preferred his kingdom over the eternal truth. And, in consequence, he lost even his kingdom after a few years during the time of Caliph ʿUmar ﷺ.

WHO WERE THE ARĪSIYYĪN?

Arīsiyyīn or *Yarīsyyīn* was the word the Apostle used in his letter to Heraclius. No other letter written to any other Arab or non-Arab king and potentate contains the word whose significance is disputed by the scholars of ḥadīth and lexicographers. According to one version it is the plural of *Arīsī* which means the servants and the peasants.[1]

Ibn Manẓūr makes it out as a synonym for cultivators in the *Lisān al-ʿArab* and cites Thaʿlab as the authority for this view. He also quotes Ibn al-ʿArabī in his support but, at the same time, he adduces a quotation from Abū ʿUbaydah to show that the word also means the chief or the elder who is obeyed or whose orders are carried out.[2]

Now the question arises that if *Arīsiyyīn* means peasants, it should have been employed to denote the subjects of Chosroes rather than the population of Byzantine Empire. The class of cultivators was by far more numerous under the Persian Empire and formed the chief source of its revenues. Ibn Manẓūr has cited Azharī who says, "The people of Iraq who followed the religion of Chosroes were peasants and countrymen. The Romans were artisans and craftsmen and,

1 See Nawawī's Commentary on *Muslim*, and *Majmaʿ Biḥār al-Anwār* by Muḥammad Patnī.

2 *Lisān al-ʿArab*, see "Arīs."

therefore, they nicknamed the Magians the *arisīn* which meant that they were peasants. Arabs also used to call the Persians *fallāḥīn* or the peasants."[1]

Arisīn has also been interpreted as denoting Arians or the followers of Arius (280–336) who was the founder of a well-known Christian sect. The doctrine of Arius hovered for a long time between acceptance and rejection as the official creed of the Byzantine Empire, it upheld the Unity of God and denied the consubstantiality of the Son with the Father. In other words Arianism maintained a complete distinction between the Creator and the creature, and subordiancy of the latter. In short, Arius held that the characteristics of the One and Only God are solitude and eternity and He puts forth nothing on the earth from His own substance. God brought into being an independent substance as the instrument by which all things were created. This being is termed according to Arius, Wisdom, Son, Image, Word, etc. in the scripture. The Son is not truly God, but is only the so-called Word and Wisdom. Like all rational beings, the Son is endowed with free will. He is not absolute but only a relative, he is Knowledge of the Father.[2]

James Mackinon writes in his book *From Christ to Constantine*:

> Arius insisted that God alone is primeval, eternal and infinite; naught is consubstantial with Him. He it is who brought the Son into existence and, therefore, the Son is not eternal. God was not Father always; a time was there when the Son did not exist at all. The Son has an independent substance not shared by God for the Son is susceptible to change and contingencies. He cannot, therefore, be called God although he has perfection in his being. At any rate, He is a perfect being.[3]

The Church of Alexandria had, by the fourth century, come round to hold the view that the Father and Son were identical in nature, and that the Son was equal to, independent of, and contemporaneous with the Father. Arius, the presbyter of the district of Baucalis, disputed this view and was condemned by a local synod which met at Alexandria in 321 AD. Arius left Alexandria but the controversy between him and Bishop Alexander continued to be fought out not only among churchmen and thinkers but in the barbershops and among the longshoremen. After trying hard to stay out of the quarrel, and urging the bishops to stop discussing it, Constantine realised that it needed to be settled, but he did not succeed in his effort. In 325 AD he summoned the first council of the whole of the church—a council called ecumenical, at Nicaea, across the straits from Constantinople, which was attended by 2,030 bishops. Constantine was disposed

1 *Lisān al-ʿArab*, see Ars.
2 *Encyclopedia of Religion and Ethics*, vol. I, Art. "Arianism" p. 777.
3 James Mackinon, *From Jesus to Constantine*. London, 1936, (rendered from the Urdu translation).

to the divinity of Christ, as God the Son, and he gave his decision in its favour although a large majority of the bishops favoured the doctrine of Arius. Only 326 bishops are reported to have cast their votes in favour of the view held by the King. Arius was banished to Illyricum, his writings were burnt and their possession was declared a crime. But the decree of Nicaea did not dispose of Arianism.

At last Constantine himself wavered; the ban placed on Arianism was lifted. Athanasius succeeded Alexander, the bitterest opponent of Arius, but he was exiled and Arius returned to Alexandria. He was recalled by Constantine who ordered him to be restored; in fact, Constantine was about to accept Arianism as the official creed or the realm but Arius died suddenly.[1]

In his *History of Conflict between Religion and Science* John William Draper says that in the fourth century alone there were thirteen councils averse to Arius, fifteen in his favour, and seventeen for the semi-Arians: in all forty-five.[2]

The formulation of One God in three persons was, in point of fact, not solidly established in Christian life and its profession of faith prior to the end of the fourth century. The mystery of Trinitarianism was truly unravelled by the second half of the nineteenth century when Biblical theologians came round to acknowledge that when "one does speak of an unqualified Trinitarianism, one has moved from the period of Christian origins to, say, the last quarter of the fourth century. It was only then that what might be called the definitive Trinitarian dogma: 'One God in three persons,' became thoroughly assimilated into Christian life and thought."[3]

The Nicene dogma of the Trinity violated the plain and simple teachings of Christ. Both competed, for a long time, to possess the minds of the people. A large number of Christians, especially in the eastern parts of the Byzantine Empire, continued to deem the Arian doctrine as the trustworthy dogma of faith until Theaosodius the Great (346–395) summoned yet another council of the bishops at Constantinople which finally set its seal on the divinity of Christ or unity in the Trinity of Godhead. Arianism was thereafter made a capital offence and suppressed ruthlessly. Arians went underground but traces of Arianism remained in Christendom for a couple of centuries after the Council of Nicaea.

The word *arisīyyīn* used in the Apostle's letter to Heraclius can, therefore, be reasonably deemed to stand for Arians since Heraclius was himself faithful to the dogma of Arius which approached nearest to the Unity of God among the Christians.

1 *Encyclopedia of Religion and Ethics*, art. "Arianism."

2 J. W. Draper, *History of Conflict between Religion and Science*, London (1910), p. 205.

3 The *New Catholic Encyclopedia* (1967), art. "The Holy Trinity", vol. 14, p. 295.

Strange to say, but some of the learned scholars of the earliest times have also favoured this interpretation of the word in question, as, for example, Imām Ṭaḥāwī (d. 321 AH) writes in *Mushkil al-Āthār:*

> Some of the knowledgeable scholars say that a sect among the courtiers of Heraclius, known as arisin, believed in monotheism and the created nature of Christ. They did not accept what the Christians say about the divinity of Christ. They relied upon the Gospels and acted on its commandments, but the Christians disputed their faith. If that be so, the sect could be called arasiyin or arisin, as known to the scholars of Traditions."[1]

Nawawī (d. 676 AH), the commentator of the *Ṣaḥīḥ Muslim,* has also expressed a similar opinion in this regard. He says:

Others say that they were the Jews and Christians who followed ʿAbdullāh ibn Arīs.[2]

LETTERS TO THE ARAB POTENTATE

The Prophet ﷺ also sent letters to Mundhir ibn Sāwā, ruler of Baḥrayn;[3] Jayfar ibn al-Julandā, and ʿAbd ibn al-Julandā[4] Azdī, rulers of Oman; Hawdhah ibn ʿAlī, the ruler of al-Yamāmah[5] and Ḥārith ibn Shammār al-Ghassānī, Mundhir ibn Sāwā and the two sons of al-Julandā, Jayfar and ʿAbd ﷺ embraced Islam. Hawdhah ibn ʿAlī wrote back to say that he would accept Islam provided he was allowed to share the dominion with the Muslims. The Apostle ﷺ turned down his request and he died soon thereafter.

1 *Mushkil al-Āthār*, vol. II, p. 399.

2 Nawawī appears to be mistaken in holding ʿAbdullāh ibn Arīs as the founder of the sect, but he wrote at a time when Arians had been completely suppressed and hardly any reliable information about them was available. In any case, Arius was not an Arab and could not have had an Arabic Name. (Nawawī, *Sharḥ Muslim,* vol. II, p. 98).

3 Baḥrayn forms part of Najd and is now known as al-Aḥsāʾ. The party sent under Abū ʿUbaydah to raid the coast was dispatched to this region where it found a whale from the sea. The traditions refer to this region as al-Baḥrayn. The name is now applied to another region, a Sheikhdom on the coast of Persian Gulf. The tribes inhabiting the region belonged to Banū ʿAbd al-Qays, Bakr ibn Wāʾil and Banū Tamīm. When the letter was written the ruler of the area was Mundhir ibn Sāwā, the Chief of Banū Tamīm.

4 Al-Julandā was not the name of any person but a title meaning Chief or the religious leader in the dialect of Oman. Jayfar, being the eldest brother, was then the Chief of Oman.

5 Hawdhah ibn ʿAlī al-Ḥanafī was the King of Yamāmah, who professed Christianity. Salīṭ ibn ʿAmr was commissioned to deliver the Prophet's letter to him. Yamāmah was then a vast region between Baḥrayn, to the east, and Ḥijāz, to the west. Banū Ḥanīfah were settled in this region. Musaylamah belonged to this tribe, who was nicknamed Kadhdhāb or the liar after he made a claim to apostleship.

16
The Expedition to Khaybar

The Divine Reward

ALLĀH HAD PROMISED a great reward to all those who had sworn allegiance to the Apostle ﷺ at Ḥudaybiyyah which was known as *Bayʿat Riḍwān* or the oath of paradise. For they had submitted to the will of God and His Apostle ﷺ in that hour of crisis, Allāh foretold them of the coming victory as well as the booty they were to win shortly.

Allāh was well pleased with the believers when they swore allegiance unto you beneath the tree; and He knew what was in their hearts, and He sent down peace of reassurance on them, and has rewarded them with a near victory. And much booty that they will capture. Allāh is ever Mighty, Wise.[1]

The conquest of Khaybar was to serve as a prelude to the subsequent victories that followed in its train. Khaybar was a Jewish colony[2] comprising several citadels, some of which were built on the tops of hills and were virtually impregnable. It was thus the last but most formidable Jewish stronghold in Arabia. Anxious to punish the Muslims for what had happened to their brothers in Madīnah, the Jews of Khaybar were ever willing to spend their wealth for stirring up the neighbouring Arab tribes to wage war against the Prophet ﷺ.

At the time when the expedition to Khaybar was undertaken, the Jews of

1 Qur'ān 48:18–19.

2 The forts of Nāʿim, Qamūṣ and Ash-Shiqq were some of the famous forts of Khaybar. Yāqūbī says that Khaybar then had 25,000 able-bodied warriors. (vol. 2, p. 56. cited from Mujīb Ullāh Nadwī, *Ṣaḥābah wa Tābiʿīn,* Azamgarh).

that locality were in league with the tribe of Ghaṭafān with whom they were hatching up a plot against the Muslims.[1] The Prophet ﷺ had thus a reason to act against the Jews of Khaybar. He decided that the time had come to get rid of their intrigues once for all so that he might be able to divert his attention to other pressing affairs. Khaybar was situated at a distance of 70 miles to the north-east of Madīnah.

THE APOSTLE ﷺ LEADS THE ARMY

After his return from Ḥudaybiyyah the Apostle ﷺ stayed in Madīnah during Dhū'l-Ḥijjah and a part of the month of Muḥarram. Thereafter he marched off to Khaybar, it was the seventh year of the Hijrī calendar.

One of the companions of the Prophet ﷺ, ʿĀmir ibn al-Akwaʿ ﷺ by name, accompanied the Apostle on this expedition. He recited the verses given here while he rode with the army.

We'd have not been guided, but for Allāh,
    Nor given alms, nor chanted Gloria,
We are the people, when attacked
    Or treated unjustly, we resist.
Send down *Sakīnah* upon us,
    Against the enemy make us firm.[2]

The combatants who marched against Khaybar numbered 1,400 including 200 cavalry; all those who had lagged behind on the occasion of Ḥudaybiyyah were refused permission to go on this expedition. Twenty women also went along with the force so as to look after the sick and the wounded as well as to prepare food for the men.

The Apostle ﷺ halted at ar-Rajīʿ, a wadi between Khaybar and the Ghaṭafān so as to cut the communications between the two allies. The Jews had other confederate tribes as well but the Prophet's ﷺ halt at ar-Rajīʿ forced all of them to remain in their homes instead of trying to reinforce them. The road to Khaybar was thus left open to the Apostle ﷺ.

---

1 With the Jews straining every nerve to bring about the destruction of Muslims, as Montgomery Watt says in his Book, *Muḥammad: Prophet and Statesman* (p. 189), the action against Khaybar could not have been postponed any longer. Montgomery writes: "The Jews of Khaybar, especially the leaders of the clan of an-Naḍīr exiled form Madīnah, were still incensed at Muḥammad. They made lavish, though no doubt judicious, use of their wealth to induce the neighbouring tribes to take up arms against the Muslims. This was a straightforward reason for attacking Khaybar."

2 Ibn Kathīr, vol. III, pp. 344–45, Muslim: Gazwah Khaybar.

The Apostle ﷺ ordered that food for the army be found but nothing except parched corn was available.[1] When the Apostle ﷺ approached Khaybar, he raised his hands to pray to God for the conquest of the colony and sought the Lord's refuge from the evil of its people. The Apostle ﷺ would never launch offensive attacks during night but would delay them till the crack of dawn and if the call for prayer was given, he would first perform the prayer. Here, too, he passed the night and gave orders to march ahead before the call for prayer was given. The Muslims met the workers of Khaybar coming out with spades and baskets. As soon as they saw the Apostle ﷺ and the army, they turned on their heels shouting,

"Muḥammad and his force." The Apostle ﷺ said, "God is Great. Khaybar is destroyed. When we fall upon a people the morning is bad for those who have already been warned."[2]

THE VICTORIOUS COMMANDER

The Apostle ﷺ came at the forts and started overpowering them one by one. Marḥab, the well-known Jewish warlord, held one of these citadels. It was a fortified stronghold at which the initial drives did not meet with success while ʿAlī ﵁ was suffering from ophthalmia. After a few unsuccessful charges, the Apostle ﷺ said, "Tomorrow I will give the standard to a man who loves Allāh and His Apostle and he will conquer the fort." Every companion waited in suspense, hoping to get the standard. The Apostle ﷺ summoned ʿAlī ﵁, applied his spittle to ʿAlī's eyes and prayed for his success. ʿAlī's eyes were cured in no time; he was then given the standard[3] and told to fight the Jews until he prevailed over them. The Prophet ﷺ said to ʿAlī ﵁, "Go ahead and surround them. First invite them to accept Islam and explain the obligations they owe to God. I swear to God that if even one man is guided to the right path through you, this would be better for you than the red camels (which were considered of great value)."[4]

ʿALĪ FACES THE JEWISH WARRIOR

When ʿAlī ﵁ came near the fort, Marḥab the Jew came out on his horse protected by armour and shield, reciting a poem about his valour. ʿAlī ﵁ dashed out against Marḥab and both fell upon each other swinging their scimitars. ʿAlī's sword was first to plunge into Marḥab, running through his helmet and head

1 Ibn Kathīr, vol. III, pp. 345–46, Bukhārī: Gazwah Khaybar.
2 *Ibn Hishām*, vol. III, pp. 229–30.
3 Bukhārī and Muslim: Gazwah Khaybar.
4 Bukhārī: Gazwah Khaybar; Muslim and Nasā'ī.

until his face was divided into two equal parts. ʿAlī was at last successful in bringing down the fort.[1]

Muḥammad ibn Maslamah fought bravely at Khaybar and killed a number of well-known Jewish warriors.

AN EASY REWARD

The slave of a Jew of Khaybar had been hired to watch over the flocks of his master. When he saw the Jews taking up arms to give fight to the Muslims, he asked. "Why do you go?" The Jews replied that they were going to fight the man who had laid a claim to Prophethood. The slave's curiosity brought him to the Prophet ﷺ whom he asked about the faith that he preached. The Apostle ﷺ replied, "I call you to Islam, that is, you bear witness that there is no deity save God and that I am the Apostle of God, and you serve none other than God."

"If I bear witness as you say," asked the slave, "and have faith in God, what shall I get in return?"

The Apostle ﷺ replied, "If you die with faith, you will enter Paradise."

The slave accepted Islam and then asked the Apostle ﷺ, "What should I do with this flock? I hold it in trust."

The Apostle ﷺ told him to abandon the goats in the field near the fort and God would cause them to reach their owner. The man did as he had been told and the goats did find their way back to their master. The Jew also came to know that his slave has gone over to the Muslims.

Before the encounter started between the Muslims and the Jews, the Prophet ﷺ urged his men to fight for the sake of God. The slave also advanced with the Muslims and was killed in the battlefield. When his dead body was brought back by the Muslims the Apostle ﷺ cast a glance at him and turning to his companions, said, "Allāh blessed this man and brought him to Khaybar. I saw two houris standing by his side although he never prostrated to God."[2]

I DID NOT COME TO YOU FOR IT

A Bedouin came to the Apostle ﷺ and after accepting Islam expressed his wish to accompany him in the expedition. The Apostle ﷺ asked some of his Companions to take care of him and see to his needs. When the Muslims captured

1 The encounter between ʿAlī and Marhab has been reported by different authorities. Ibn Hishām relates that Marhab was in fact killed by Muḥammad ibn Salamah (vol.II, pp.333–334). However, the majority opinion is that he was killed by ʿAlī (see *Ṭabarī*, p.1579 and *Muslim*, ḥadīth number 1807).

2 *Zād al-Maʿād*, vol. I, p. 393.

one of the forts and won a large booty, the man had taken out a herd of cattle for grazing. The spoil was distributed among the combatants, and the share of the Bedouin was also apportioned. When he was given his share, he took it to the Apostle ﷺ and asked, "What is it?" The Apostle ﷺ explained that it was his share of the booty of war, but he said, "I didn't come to you for it." Then pointing to his throat he continued, "I followed you in the hope that I would be hit by an arrow here and would go to paradise." The Apostle replied, "If you desire it so, God will do likewise."

Then, in a subsequent battle at Khaybar the dead body of the Bedouin was found among those killed in the encounter. The Apostle ﷺ asked, "Is it the same man?" When the Companions ﷺ replied in the affirmative, the Apostle ﷺ remarked, "He was true to God and God made his wish come true." The Apostle ﷺ shrouded his corpse ﷺ with his own mantle and recited the funeral service for him. Thereafter, he said, "O Allāh, Your servant had come to emigrate in Your way and was killed for Your sake. I bear witness to it."[1]

The people of Khaybar were besieged in their forts which began to fall one by one. The Jews, unable to stand the siege any longer, asked for the terms of peace. The Apostle ﷺ wanted to banish them from Khaybar, but they requested to be allowed to live in their homes and to cultivate the fields. They pleaded that they were better farmers and knew more about it than others. The Apostle ﷺ did not want his Companions to till the soil since it would have required them to settle there and become occupied with farming the fields. He, therefore, allowed the Jews to retain their farms and houses on the condition that the Muslims would get half of the produce of their fields and groves. Another condition imposed was that the Apostle ﷺ could abrogate the agreement unilaterally.[2]

The Apostle ﷺ would send ʿAbdullāh ibn Rawāḥah ﷺ who would divide the produce into two equal parts, and then ask the Jews to choose one of them. The Jews often remarked on his even-handed justice: "This is that on which the heavens and the earth stand.[3]

RELIGIOUS TOLERANCE

The booty carried off by the Muslims in the battle of Khaybar included various copies of the Jewish scripture. The Jews requested the Prophet ﷺ for them and he ordered that they be returned to them.[4]

1 *Zād al-Maʿād*, vol. I, p. 394.

2 *Zād al-Maʿād*, vol. I, pp. 394–95. For details see *Sunan Abū Dāwūd*.

3 Balādharī: *Futūḥ al-Buldān*, Leiden, 1886, p. 34.

4 *Tarīkh al-Khamīs*, vol. II, p. 60.

…ish scholar, Dr. Israel Welphenson, reviewing the conquest of Khaybar, …o the magnanimous treatment of the Jews by the Apostle ﷺ in these …s:

> The event shows what a high regard the Prophet had for their scriptures. His tolerant and considerate behaviour impressed the Jews who could never forget that the Prophet did nothing which trifled with their sacred scriptures. The Jews knew the conduct of the Romans when they captured Jerusalem in 70 BC, they had burnt their scriptures and trampled them underfoot. The fanatic Christians persecuting the Jews of Spain had likewise consigned their scriptures to fire. This is the great difference we find between these conquerors and the Prophet of Islam.[1]

ARRIVAL OF JAʿFAR IBN ABĪ ṬĀLIB

Jaʿfar ibn Abī Ṭālib ؓ, the cousin of the Apostle ﷺ and other emigrants ؓ returned from Abyssinia while the Prophet ﷺ was still at Khaybar. The Apostle ﷺ was so pleased to see him that he kissed Jaʿfar ؓ on the forehead and said, "By God, I don't know which gives me the greater pleasure—the conquest of Khaybar or the arrival of Jaʿfar!"[2]

ANOTHER CONSPIRACY

It was during the Khaybar expedition that an attempt was made to poison the Apostle ﷺ. Zaynab bint al-Ḥārith, a jewess and the wife of Sallām ibn Mishkam presented a roast lamb to the Apostle ﷺ, having first enquired which joint he preferred. On coming to know that the Apostle ﷺ relished the shoulder she concentrated the poison on it and brought it to the Apostle ﷺ. The Prophet ﷺ tasted a morsel and quickly spat it out for he immediately came to know that it was poisoned.

The Apostle ﷺ summoned the Jews and enquired from them, "Will you be truthful, if I ask something of you?" They said, "Yes." The Apostle ﷺ again asked them. "Did you poison the lamb?" When they again replied in the affirmative, the Apostle ﷺ enquired what had made them to do that. They replied, "We thought that if you were a pretender, we would get rid of you but if you were really a prophet, the poison would be ineffective." Zaynab bint al-Ḥārith was then brought before the Apostle ﷺ. She confessed her guilt, saying, "I wanted to kill you." The Prophet ﷺ replied. "God would not allow you to gain power over

---

1 *Tārīkh al-Yahūd fī Bilād al-'Arab fī 'l-Jāhiliyyah wa Ṣadr al-Islām* p. 170.

2 *Zād al-Maʿād*, vol. I, p. 397.

me." Some of the Companions ﷺ asked for permission to punish the woman for her crime, but the Apostle ﷺ forbade them. Zaynab was set free but when Bishr ibn al-Barā' ﷺ who had eaten from the roast lamb with the Apostle ﷺ died a painful death Zaynab was slain.[1]

EFFECT OF THE CONQUEST OF KHAYBAR

The glorious victory won by the Muslims at Khaybar was of far-reaching importance, especially for the tribes that had still not accepted Islam. They were aware of the wealth and prowess of the Jews of Khaybar, their impregnable strongholds and valour of the well-known warriors like Marḥab and Ḥārith Abū Zaynab. They deemed its capture to be virtually impossible but their estimate of the nascent power of Madīnah had proved all in the wrong. They now knew that the Muslim arms were overwhelming.

Discussing the effect of the victory gained at Khaybar on the subsequent history of Islam. Dr. Israel Welphenson says:

> There is not the least doubt that the conquest of Khaybar occupies an important place in the history of the subsequent conquests of Islam. All the Arab tribes were anxiously watching for the outcome of the sabre rattling between the Anṣār and the Jews. The enemies of the Prophet spread over many cities and the Bedouins had pinned their hopes upon this battle.[2]

THE SPOILS OF KHAYBAR

Having finished with Khaybar, the Prophet ﷺ directed his attention to Fadak[3] which was the principal town, fertile and populous, with strong fortifications in the northern part of Ḥijāz.[4] The Jews of Fadak sent an offer of peace to the Apostle ﷺ, on the condition that they should be allowed to keep half of their produce. The terms were acceptable to the Apostle ﷺ who would spend the income from Fadak on the welfare of the Muslims.[5]

The Apostle ﷺ then moved on with the army to the Wādī al-Qurā,[6] a col-

---

1 *Zād al-Ma'ād*, vol. I, p.398, also related by *Bukhārī*.

2 *Tārīkh al-Yahūd fī Bilād al-'Arab fī 'l-Jāhiliyyah wa Ṣadr al-Islām*, p. 162.

3 The population of Fadak consisted of Jews belonging to Banū Murrah and Banū Sa'd ibn Bakr (*Nihāyat al-'Arab*, vol. XVII. p. 209).

4 *Ibn Hishām*, vol. II, p. 368.

5 Ibid.

6 Wādī 'l-Qurā was a valley with a large number of villages and towns, populated by Arab and Jewish tribes. It had fertile land with numerous wells and springs.

ony founded by Jews during the pre-Islamic period that lay midway between Khaybar and Taymā'. It had become a flourishing town with the settlement of a number of Arab tribes also. The Apostle ﷺ invited the Arabs of Wādī 'l-Qurā to accept Islam. He told them that if they acceded to Islam, their life and property would be safe and they would have a goodly return from the Lord.

The Jews decided to fight but a heroic assault led by az-Zubayr ibn al-ʿAwwām ‎ brought them to surrender the very next day. A great deal of property fell into the hands of the Muslims. The Prophet ﷺ distributed the spoils among his troops but left the groves of date-palms to the Jews.

When the Jews of Taymā'[1] learned of the fall of Khaybar, Fadak and Wādī al-Qurā and the terms on which they had made peace with the Apostle ﷺ, and they hastened to send him an offer of peace. The Prophet ﷺ accepted their proposal and allowed them to retain possession of their land and property. Thereafter the Apostle ﷺ returned to Madīnah.[2]

MAGNANIMITY OF THE MŪHĀJIRĪN

The Anṣār of Madīnah had shared their possessions with the emigrants when they had come from Makkah. Now, well provided with the spoils of Khaybar, the Mūhājirīn returned the property that their Anṣār brethren had earlier shared with them. Umm Sulaym, the mother of Anas ibn Mālik, had presented a few date palm trees to the Apostle ﷺ, who had given out these to his freed slave-woman Umm Ayman. After the Apostle ﷺ got the groves of Fadak, he returned the date-palm trees of Umm Sulaym to her and compensated Umm Ayman with ten trees of Fadak for every date-palm given earlier to her.[3]

The Apostle ﷺ sent forth a number of raiding parties under eminent Companions against some of the contumacious desert tribes. Some of these detachments had to fight them while others returned without any contest.[4]

THE MISSED PILGRIMAGE

The following year, in 7 AH, the Apostle ﷺ and his followers took the road to Makkah to perform the lesser pilgrimage missed by them earlier. Quraysh thought it best to lock their houses and retire to the heights of Jabl Quʿayqiʿān overlooking

1 Taymā' is further away from Wādī al-Qurā, in the north near the confines of Syria. The noted Jewish poet, Samaw'al ibn ʿĀdiyā' lived here in a castle called *al-Ablaq al-Fard*.

2 *Zād al-Maʿād*, vol. I, p. 405.

3 Ibid., p. 406.

4 *Zād al-Maʿād*, vol. I, pp. 409–410.

the valley.[1] The Apostle ﷺ stayed for three days in the holy city and made the circuit of the holy house. Referring to the joyous event, the Qur'ān says:

> Allāh hath fulfilled the vision[2] for his Messenger, in truth. You shall indeed enter the Inviolable Place of Worship, if Allāh will, secure, [your hair] shaven and cut, unfearing. But He knows that which you know not, and has given you a near victory beforehand.[3]

RIGHTS OF WOMEN RESTORED

Islam had changed the hearts and elevated the minds of the Arabs. The custom that prevailed in the pre-Islamic days of burying female infants alive, so as to save the honour of the family, was not only given up but the daughters came to be so dearly loved that the people vied with one another to lavish their affection on them. All Muslims, men and women, were equal, none possessing any privilege over another; only he was superior who was better in morals and piety. When the Apostle ﷺ left Makkah after performing the *ʿumrah,* the little daughter of Ḥamzah ﷺ, Umāmah by name, followed him calling "Uncle, Uncle." ʿAlī ﷺ took her and bade Fāṭimah ﷺ to look after her. Now Zayd and Jaʿfar ﷺ also claimed the guardianship of the child. ʿAlī ﷺ laid the claim for her since she was the daughter of his uncle. Jaʿfar ﷺ said that she was the daughter of his uncle and her maternal aunt was his wife. Zayd ﷺ, too, wanted to have the child for all the Muslims were brothers and he could very well look after the daughter of a deceased brother. The matter was brought to the notice of the Prophet ﷺ who decided that because the maternal aunt was in the position of the mother, the girl should be given to Jaʿfar ﷺ. To set ʿAlī ﷺ at ease, the Prophet said, "You are mine and I am yours" He reassured Jaʿfar ﷺ by saying, "You resemble me in your looks and conduct." Zayd ﷺ was also comforted with the words, "You are my brother and client."[4]

---

1 *Bukhārī*: ʿUmrat al-Qaḍā'.

2 The Prophet ﷺ had a vision that he was entering the Sanctuary at Makkah in peace and safety.

3 Qur'ān 48:27.

4 Bukhārī: Kitāb al-Maghāzī.

17
The Expedition to Mu'tah

The Apostle ﷺ had sent Ḥārith ibn ʿUmayr al-Azdī to deliver his letter to Shuraḥbīl ibn ʿAmr al-Ghassānī, a satrap of the Byzantine Emperor at Buṣrā.[1] Ḥārith was first tied up under the order of Shuraḥbīl and then beheaded.[2] It had never been the custom of kings to condemn envoys to death, however disagreeable the message they had conveyed. The crime dishonoured both the sender of the letter and the recipient, in addition to the harm it meant for the envoy, and could not go unpunished. The guilt of blood bayed to be avenged with firmness so that no tyrant dared repeat the crime in future.

FIRST EXPEDITION TO THE BYZANTINE TERRITORY

The Apostle ﷺ decided to send a detachment to Buṣrā in Jumādā 'l-Ūlā, 8 AH. A force 3,000 strong was drafted. It was the strongest force sent out so far and a number of leading companions had enlisted for active service, but the Apostle ﷺ gave its command to his freed slave Zayd ibn Ḥārithah . He also instructed that if Zayd were killed then Jaʿfar ibn Abū Ṭālib would take the command, and if he were also slain then the command would pass on to ʿAbdullāh ibn Rawāḥah . When the expedition got ready to depart, the people bade farewell

1 Mu'tah lies 12 km. to the south of Karak in Trans-Jordan. Thus Mu'tah is at a distance of about 1,100 km from Madīnah. The troops sent for this expedition had to cover the entire distance on horses and camels in an enemy country without any hope of assistance or provision being made available by the local population.

2 *Zād al-Maʿād*, vol. I, p. 414.

and saluted the commanders selected by the Apostle.[1] The force had to undertake a long and arduous journey and to face an enemy backed by the strongest empire of the time.

The force advanced to Maʿān in Syria where Zayd ﷺ came to know that Heraclius was present at Balqā' with a hundred thousand Roman troops joined by an equally strong force drawn from the Arab tribes of Lakhm and Judhām and Bulqīn and Bahrā' and Baliyy. The Muslims camped for two days at Maʿān, pondering over the situation. They decided at last to inform the Apostle about the strength of the enemy; if he sent reinforcements, well and good, otherwise they would face the enemy, if so ordered.[2]

DAUNTLESS WARRIORS

ʿAbdullāh ibn Rawāḥah ﷺ made an impassioned speech encouraging his comrades. He said: "Men, you dislike the thing, by God, for which you came out—martyrdom. We do not fight the enemy on the strength of our numbers, or our power; we fight them with the religion with which God has honoured us. So come forth, we shall be winners either way: we win or we court martyrdom." So the men got up and forged ahead to meet the enemy.

ACTION STARTS

When the Muslims reached near Balqā', they found the Byzantine forces stationed in a village called Mashārif. With the news of the arrival of Muslim forces, the enemy advanced towards them, and the Muslim troops took up their position in a village called Mu'tah where battle commenced.[3]

Zayd ibn Ḥārithah ﷺ, who held the Apostle's ﷺ standard, descended on the enemy and died fighting bravely. He received innumerable wounds with spears. Jaʿfar ﷺ now took the standard in hand and led the fight. When the battle closed in, he jumped off his charger and hamstrung its forelegs, and fought until he lost his right hand. He took the standard in his left hand but when it was also cut off, he caught hold of the standard with his teeth. He fell down dead in the battlefield after receiving ninety cuts from swords and spears on his chest and arms, but none on his back.[4] He was then 33 years of age.[5] Thus fought this young man

1 *Ibn Hishām*, vol. II, p. 373.

2 *Zād al-Maʿād*, vol. I, p. 415.

3 *Ibn Hishām*, vol. II, pp. 373–78.

4 *Ibn Kathīr*, vol. III, p. 474; and *Zād al-Maʿād*, vol. I, p. 415.

5 *Zād al-Maʿād* vol. I, p. 415.

with reckless courage in the face of great odds, defying the enemy's numbers and strength, until he was honoured by God with martyrdom.

The Apostle's ﷺ standard was then held aloft by ʿAbdullāh ibn Rawāḥah ؓ. He too dismounted from his horse and pressed onwards. One of ʿAbdullāh's cousins ؓ came up to him with a meat bone, saying, "Take it for you have not had anything for the last few days. It will give you strength to fight." ʿAbdullāh ؓ took it and ate a little. Then he threw it away and taking the sword in hand fought bravely until he was also killed.[1]

KHĀLID ASSUMES COMMAND

Now the Muslim troops rallied round Khālid ibn Walīd ؓ who took the standard in his hand. With his instinct as a general, Khālid ؓ made his way to the south while the enemy forces turned aside towards the north.[2] The day was done by this time and both the forces, tired by the day-long fight, thought it prudent to stop the fighting.

Khālid ؓ stationed a part of his force at a distance from his camp in the still of night. At the first flush of morning the detachment set apart by Khālid ؓ started shouting cries of war which gave an impression to the enemy that fresh reinforcements had arrived from Madīnah. The enemy had had the experience of fighting the small force of 3,000 Muslims the previous day. Now they dared not fight them again strengthened by additional troops. The Roman soldiery was disheartened and did not take the field. Muslims were thus spared the trouble of putting up a fight again.[3]

A GLIMPSE OF THE BATTLEFIELD

While the Muslims had been engaged in fighting the enemy at Mu'tah, the Apostle ﷺ was describing the conflict in Madīnah. Anas ibn Mālik ؓ relates that the Messenger of God ﷺ announced the death of Zayd, Jaʿfar and ʿAbdullāh ibn Rawāḥah ؓ before the report about them reached Madīnah. Anas ؓ reports that the Apostle ﷺ said: "Zayd took the standard and was smitten; then Jaʿfar took it and was smitten, then Ibn Rawāḥah took it and was smitten"; the tears meanwhile trickling down from his eyes. The Apostle ﷺ continued, according

1 *Zād al-Maʿād* vol. I, p. 415.

2 *Zād al-Maʿād* vol. I, p. 415; *Ibn Hishām,* vol. II, p. 379.

3 Al-Maghāzī li 'l-Wāqidī.

to Anas ﷺ, "Finally one of God's swords [meaning Khālid ibn Walīd] took the standard till God granted them success."[1]

JAᶜFAR AṬ-ṬAYYĀR

Another report about Jaᶜfar ﷺ says that the Apostle ﷺ said about him, "Allāh has given two wings to Jaᶜfar ﷺ in place of his arms. He flies in Paradise, wherever he likes."[2] Thereafter Jaᶜfar ﷺ came to be known as Jaᶜfar aṭ-Ṭayyār and Dhū 'l-Janāḥayn, meaning one possessed of two wings.

WORDS, KIND AND COMFORTING

The Apostle ﷺ went to the house of Jaᶜfar and asked his wife to bring her children ﷺ. When they were brought the Apostle breathed in their fragrance as tears run down from his eyes. Then he told them about the death of Jaᶜfar ﷺ. When news about Jaᶜfar ﷺ reached the Apostle ﷺ from the front, he sent word to his family, "Prepare food for the family of Jaᶜfar. They will be too shocked to cook their food." The Prophet's ﷺ face at the time reflected his grief.[3]

NOT DESERTERS BUT WARRIORS

When the army returning from Mu'tah drew close to Madīnah the Apostle ﷺ and the Muslims went out to receive them. The boys also came running while the Prophet ﷺ was on his camel. The Prophet ﷺ said, "Take the boys and give me Jaᶜfar's son." Jaᶜfar's son ᶜAbdullāh ﷺ was brought to the Apostle ﷺ who seated him before him.

This was the first time that a Muslim army had returned without winning a decisive victory. Some of the people started throwing dust on the men, saying the while, "You runaways you fled from the way of God." The Apostle ﷺ said, "They are not runaways but warriors, if God wills."[4]

SUBSEQUENT EXPEDITIONS

In between the two major expeditions to Mu'tah and Makkah, some smaller

---

1 Bukhārī: Ghazwah Mu'tah.

2 *Bukhārī: Ghazwah Mu'tah* and *Zād al-Maᶜād*, vol. I, p. 415. Bukhārī relates that ᶜUmar used to greet the son of Jaᶜfar thus: "Peace be on you. O son of the two-winged man."

3 *Ibn Hishām*, vol. II, pp. 380–81.

4 *Musnad Aḥmad ibn Ḥanbal.*

expeditions were also undertaken. One of them was the raid of Dhāt as-Salāsil in the country of Quḍāʿah near Wādī al-Qurā, in Jamād al-Ukhrā, 8 AH. The raiding party returned after they destroyed the enemy. Another raiding party consisting of 300 Anṣār and Mūhājirīn was sent under Abū ʿUbaydah ibn al-Jarrāh to Najd. The party was sent to chastise a clan of Juhaynah. The army was exhausted with hunger and had to live for a few days on the leaves of the trees until God brought them a whale named "ʿAnbar" from the sea. The men spent about fifteen days feasting on the flesh and fat of the whale and regained their strength. They brought back a portion of it, which the Apostle ﷺ took and said to the men, "God sent it for you."[1] This expedition goes by the names of Sīf al-Baḥr and Khabaṭ.

1 *Zād al-Maʿād*, vol. I, p. 417; Bukhārī: Ghazwah Sīf al-Baḥr.

18
The Conquest of Makkah

Background of the Conquest

ISLAM WAS NOW SET deeply into the heart of the Muslims who had, by now, not simply learnt the teachings of Islam but lived and breathed its divine commandments. Allāh had put them to severe trial in order to purify their motives and ascertain their level of piety. On the other hand, the Quraysh of Makkah had prosecuted, persecuted, exiled and battled with the Muslims; in short, they had been guilty of every sin of commission and omission against the Prophet ﷺ and his followers. The Will of Heaven now decreed that the Messenger of God ﷺ and his companions should enter the holy city as its conquerors and cleanse it of the defilement of idol worship, deceit, lies and wickedness. Providence determined that the sanctity of the sacred city should again be restored to it so that it might once more become the centre of divine guidance and blessings for mankind.

DERELICTION OF BANŪ BAKR AND QURAYSH

God created circumstances through the breach of faith by the Quraysh themselves who unwittingly provided a valid reason, or rather made it unavoidable for the Muslims to lay their hands on Makkah—Allāh's are the hosts of the heavens and the earth.[1]

The treaty of Ḥudaybiyyah gave an option to everyone to enter into an alli-

1 Qur'ān 48:7.

ance with the Apostle of God ﷺ or to come to a similar agreement with the Quraysh. Accordingly, Banū Bakr preferred to conclude a pact with the Quraysh while Banū Khuzāʿah entered into an alliance with the Messenger of God ﷺ.[1]

Banū Bakr and Banū Khuzāʿah had a long-standing feud from the pre-Islamic days. Now with one of the these tribes aligning itself with the Muslims and the other with the pagans, their mutual hostility was further intensified; in fact, both the tribes had made alliances with the two parties with no other consideration save to have their revenge upon the other. After the establishment of an armistice, Banū Bakr tried to take advantage of it against Khuzāʿah and, in league with certain persons, made a night attack on their enemy when it had taken up quarters at a spring. There was a fight between the two in which Banū Khuzāʿah lost a number of their men.

The Quraysh helped Banū Bakr with weapons while their chiefs, taking advantage of the night, fought Khuzāʿah along with Banū Bakr. Their combined charge drove Khuzāʿah into the sacred precinct where some of the Quraysh said to one another: "We are now in the sacred precinct. Mind your gods! Mind your gods!" But others replied imprudently: "We have no god today. Take your revenge, O sons of Bakr, for you may not get a chance again."[2]

COMPLAINT TO THE APOSTLE

ʿAmr ibn Sālim al-Khuzāʿī ﷺ went to the Apostle in Madīnah and recited verses describing how the Quraysh had violated their pledge. He asked the Apostle ﷺ to extend his help by virtue of the treaty of alliance between him and Khuzāʿah. He took the stand that the Quraysh had annulled the treaty with the Prophet ﷺ by attacking his allies when they were at their well and had not spared their lives even when they were performing prayers. After listening to his plaint, the Prophet ﷺ replied, "You will be helped, O ʿAmr ibn Sālim."

LAST BID TO SEEK JUSTICE

The Apostle ﷺ then sent a man to Makkah in order to get confirmation of the affair and also to allow the Quraysh to redress the wrong they had committed. The Apostle ﷺ ordered that three alternatives be placed before the Quraysh; they should either pay the blood money for the victims of Khuzāʿah or terminate their alliance with the aggressors belonging to Banū Nafāsah of Banū

1 *Ibn Hishām*, vol. II, p. 390.
2 *Zād al-Maʿād*, vol. I p. 419; *Ibn Hishām*, vol. II, p. 390.

Bakr—failing these they shall get in return what they had done. The terms were communicated to the Quraysh but in a fit of pride they replied, "Yes, we would prefer measure for measure." The Muslims were thus absolved of their undertaking with the Quraysh and it became incumbent on them to retaliate for the wrong done to their allies.[1]

EFFORTS TO RENEWAL THE TREATY

When the Apostle ﷺ was informed of the reply of the Quraysh, he predicted, "I see as if Abū Sufyān has come to you to strengthen the treaty and to ask for more time." The events took shape exactly as the Apostle ﷺ foretold. The Quraysh had become alarmed at the gravity of the situation and come to regret the indiscreet reply that the thoughtless among them had given. They charged Abū Sufyān to get the treaty ratified and extended again.[2]

PROPHET PREFERRED OVER PARENTS

When Abū Sufyān came to the Apostle ﷺ in Madīnah, he went in to his daughter Umm Ḥabībah ؓ, a wife of the Prophet ﷺ. He wanted to sit on the Apostle's ﷺ mat but she forbade him to do so. Abū Sufyān was puzzled. He said to Umm Ḥabībah ؓ, "Daughter I can't tell whether you think that the bed is too good for me, or whether I am too good for the bed!" Umm Ḥabībah ؓ replied, "The fact is that it is the Apostle's ﷺ bed and you are an unclean polytheist. I do not want you to sit on the Apostle's ﷺ bed." "By God," said Abū Sufyān, "You have gone to ruin since you left me."

ABŪ SUFYĀN BEWILDERED

Abū Sufyān went to the Apostle ﷺ, but he gave him no reply. Then he went to Abū Bakr ؓ and asked him to speak to the Apostle ﷺ for him, but Abū Bakr ؓ refused to do so. He tried to prevail upon ʿUmar, ʿAlī and Fāṭimah ؓ to intervene on his behalf but every one of them either excused themselves, or replied that the matter was too grave for them to straighten out. Abū Sufyān so lost his nerves that when he went in to see Fāṭimah he said pointing to Ḥasan ibn ʿAlī ؓ crawling before her, "O daughter of Muḥammad, will you let this

---

1 Az-Zurqānī relates in the *Sharḥ al-Mawāhib al-Ladunniyyah*, vol.II, p. 349 on the authority of Ibn ʿĀ'idh that the man sent by the Prophet ﷺ was Ḍamurah and Quraṭah ibn ʿAmr had given the reply on behalf of the Quraysh.

2 *Zād al-Maʿād*, vol. I, p. 420; *Ibn Hishām*, vol.,II, pp. 395–96.

child act as a peacemaker between the people so that he may be acknowledged as the lord of Arabia forever?" "My son is too young," replied Fāṭimah ﷺ, "to make peace between men. And nobody can persuade the Apostle ﷺ to reconcile against his will." ʿAlī ﷺ saw his perplexity and depression. At last, he said to Abū Sufyān, "I do not think that anything can help you now. You are the Chief of Banū Kinānah, so get up and try to smooth over and restore harmony and then go back to your home." Abū Sufyān felt uncertain. He enquired, "Do you think it would do any good?" "By God, I do not," replied ʿAlī ﷺ, "but there is nothing else you can do now." Abū Sufyān then went to the Prophet's ﷺ mosque and announced, "O Men, I have made peace between you." Thereafter he mounted his dromedary and rode off to Makkah.[1]

When Abū Sufyān told the Quraysh what had happened, they said, "You have brought us a report which is good for naught, neither to us nor to you."

AFFAIRS OF ḤĀṬIB IBN ABĪ BALTAʿAH

The Apostle ﷺ asked the Muslims to start making preparations for an expedition but also bade them to keep it a secret. Later on, the Apostle ﷺ informed the men that he intended to go to Makkah and ordered them to get ready for it. He also said, "O God, confound the spies and the informers of the Quraysh so that we may take them by surprise in their land."[2]

The Muslim society at Madīnah was, after all, a community composed of mortals and reflected, like any other social group, the passions and emotions, hopes and fears of human beings. Its members were virtuous in behaviour but they were also not immune to mistakes. Sometimes, one might deem right and proper that which others would not; he may be justified or not in holding a certain view; but it is always so with every open and free society sustained not by constraints but by mutual confidence among its members. The Apostle ﷺ would not tolerate any wrongful act on the part of his Companions but in such cases he either offered a plea to vindicate them or excused their mistakes. The Apostle ﷺ was large-hearted and readily pardoned the mistakes of others, and in doing so he never lost sight of the hardships that his Companions had undergone or the sacrifices and services they had rendered for the cause of Islam. That the compilers of Ḥadīth and biographers of the Prophet ﷺ and the historians of Islam have preserved a few instances of such indiscretion or lapses is in itself intrinsic evidence of the integrity and truthfulness of these writers.

1 *Ibn Hishām*, vol.,II, pp. 396–7.

2 *Zād al-Maʿād*, vol. I, p. 421; *Ibn Hishām*, vol. II, p. 397.

One such instance relates to Ḥāṭib ibn Abī Baltaʿah ﷺ. He was one of those Mūhājirīn who had migrated from Makkah and had taken part in the battle of Badr. It is related that when the Apostle ﷺ informed his Companions about his intention to attack Makkah and while they quietly started making preparations for it, Ḥāṭib ibn Abī Baltaʿah ﷺ wrote a letter to the Quraysh about the intended attack and gave it to a woman to deliver to the Quraysh. Ḥāṭib also promised to give some money to the woman who set off for Makkah after putting the letter on her head and plaiting her locks over it. A voice of Heaven informed the Apostle ﷺ about Ḥāṭib's actions. He immediately sent forth ʿAlī and Az-Zubayr ﷺ in pursuit of the woman, saying, "Go until you come to the meadow of Khākh,[1] where you will find a woman travelling on a camel who has a letter which you must take from her." The two went off racing on their horses until they came to the meadow, and there they found the woman going on her camel. They made her dismount and searched her baggage but found nothing. At last ʿAlī ﷺ said to her, "By God, the Messenger of Allāh is not mistaken nor are we. You must bring out the letter or we will search your person." When she saw that they were in earnest, she asked them to turn aside. Then she drew out the letter from her tresses and handed it over to them.

The letter, brought back to the Apostle ﷺ, had been written by Ḥāṭib ibn Abī Baltaʿah informing Quraysh about the departure of the Muslim army. When the Apostle ﷺ summoned him, Ḥāṭib ibn Abī Baltaʿah ﷺ said, "O Messenger of God, don't be hasty with me. I swear to God that I have faith in Allāh and His Apostle; neither have I abandoned nor changed my faith. I was once an ally of the Quraysh and was not one of them; I have my family there but no kinsmen who may protect them.[2] Other emigrants with you have their relations among the Quraysh who will take care of their families. I thought that as I did not have that advantage I should give them some help so that they might protect my relations." ʿUmar ﷺ sought permission of the Apostle ﷺ to behead Ḥāṭib, whom he charged with being a hypocrite, disloyal to God and His Messenger. But the Apostle ﷺ replied, "He was present at Badr. Do you know, ʿUmar, perhaps God has looked favourably on those who were present at Badr." To Ḥāṭib

1 A place between Makkah and Madīnah.

2 Ḥāṭib ibn Abī Baltaʿah belonged to the tribe of Lakhm settled in northern Ḥijāz and Syria. It is related by some that he was a confederate of Banū Asad ibn ʿAbd al-ʿUzzā in Makkah; others hold him to have been under the protection of Az-Zubayr; there are still others who say that he was a freedman of ʿAbdullāh ibn Ḥamīd al-Asadī (*Al-Iṣābah fii Tamyīz iṣ-Ṣaḥābah*, vol. I, p. 300). It is also related that he was deputed to convey the letter of the Apostle ﷺ to Muqawqis, the ruler of Egypt. Marzbāni lists him in the *Muʿjam ash-Shuʿarā'* among the noted poets and cavaliers of Quraysh. He died, according to Madā'inī, in 30 AH during the caliphate of ʿUthmān.

he said, "Do as you wish for I have forgiven you." ʿUmar dissolved into tears, saying, "Allāh and His Messenger know better."[1]

The Apostle ﷺ set out from Madīnah, during Ramaḍān, at the head of ten thousand Companions. The army made camp at Marr al-Ẓahrān. The Quraysh were, however, still uncertain, for God had kept them completely oblivious of the advance of the Muslim army.

THE WRIT OF AMNESTY

A cousin of the Apostle ﷺ whose name was Abū Sufyān ibn al-Ḥārith[2] happened to meet the Prophet ﷺ on the way. He tried to reach the Apostle ﷺ but was given the cold shoulder. Abū Sufyān had insulted as well as persecuted the Apostle in Makkah. Feeling distressed and disconsolate at the indifference of the Prophet ﷺ he approached ʿAlī to pour forth his lamentation. ʿAlī advised him to go to the Apostle ﷺ again and say what the brothers of Yūsuf[3] had said to him: "By Allāh, verily Allāh hath preferred you above us, and we were indeed sinful,"[4] for, said ʿAlī, the Apostle ﷺ does not like to have anybody surpass him in words that are kind and comforting. Abū Sufyān did as directed by ʿAlī and the Apostle ﷺ replied, "Have no fear this day! May Allāh forgive you, and He is the Most Merciful of those who show mercy."[5] Abū Sufyān accepted Islam and was thereafter know for his piety and strength of faith but he was ever ashamed of his past misdeeds. He always talked to the Prophet ﷺ with downcast eyes, out of respect and shame before him.

ABŪ SUFYĀN APPEARS BEFORE THE APOSTLE ﷺ

Campfires were now lit under the orders from the Apostle ﷺ. Abū Sufyān felt aghast as he saw them, and said, "I have never seen such fires and such an army before." He came out himself to explore secretly the camp and its people. ʿAbbās ibn ʿAbd al-Muṭṭalib had already left Makkah along with his family and joined the Apostle ﷺ. He recognised Abū Sufyān's voice and called him to say, "See the Apostle is here with his army. What a dreadful morning Quraysh are going to face!" ʿAbbās then thought that if any Muslim came to know of Abū Sufyān, he would surely be killed. He therefore asked Abū Sufyān to ride on the

1 *Zād al-Maʿād*, vol.1, p. 421. The *Ṣiḥāḥ* also relate the story.

2 Not to be confused with Abū Sufyān, the Quraysh chieftain, who was the son of Umayyah.

3 The prophet Joseph.

4 Qur'ān 12:91.

5 Qur'ān12:92.

back of his mule and brought him to the Apostle ﷺ. As soon as the Prophet ﷺ saw Abū Sufyān, he said, "Has the time not come, O Abū Sufyān, for you to acknowledge that there is but one God?"

"My father and mother be your ransom," replied Abū Sufyān. "How kind and gentle and noble you are; I think that if there had been another god besides Allāh, he would have been of help to me on this day." The Apostle ﷺ said again, "Woe to you Abū Sufyān, Is it not the time that you acknowledge me as God's Apostle?"

He answered, "My father and mother be your ransom. How kind and clement you are but I still have some doubt as to that."

ʿAbbās ﷺ now intervened to say, "Abū Sufyān, woe to you, submit and testify that there is no deity but Allāh and that Muḥammad ﷺ is the Apostle of God before you lose your head." Abū Sufyān ﷺ now recited the article of faith and thus he was converted to Islam.[1]

GENERAL AMNESTY

The merciful Messenger of God ﷺ now forgave the faults of all with the widest amnesty ever granted by any conqueror; only he could now lay himself open to danger who was bent upon renouncing peace. The Prophet ﷺ declared: "He who enters Abū Sufyān's ﷺ house will be safe, he who shuts his door upon himself will be safe and he who enters the sacred mosque will be safe."[2]

Before ordering the troops to enter Makkah the Apostle ﷺ instructed his men to raise their hands only against those who obstructed their advance or drew swords against them. He also directed them not to lay their hands on any moveable or immoveable property of the Makkans and not to destroy anything.[3]

ABŪ SUFYĀN WITNESSES THE ARMY

Before Abū Sufyān ﷺ returned, the Apostle ﷺ decided to demonstrate the power of Islam to him. He asked ʿAbbās ﷺ to take Abū Sufyān ﷺ to a place where he could review the marching squadrons.

The army on the move surged like an ocean. Different tribes passed by Abū Sufyān ﷺ with their tribal colours, and as each marched ahead he asked ʿAbbās ﷺ the name of the tribe. When he was told the name of the tribe he mumbled gloomily, "What have I to do with them?" Finally the Apostle ﷺ passed with his

1 *Ibn Hishām*, vol. II, p. 403; *Zād al-Maʿād*, vol. I, p. 422.

2 *Ibn Hishām*, vol. II, p. 409.

3 Ibid.

detachment; the troops clad in full armour and appearing greenish-black. It was the regiment of the Anṣār and the Mūhājirīn ﷺ whose eyes alone were visible because of their armour.

Abū Sufyān ﷺ sighed and asked ʿAbbās ﷺ, "Good heavens, ʿAbbās, who are these?" When ʿAbbās told him that they were the Anṣār and the Mūhājirīn accompanying the Apostle ﷺ, he said, "None of them enjoyed this magnificence before. By God, O Abū 'l-Faḍl, the empire of your nephew has assumed splendid proportions this morning!" ʿAbbās replied, "Abū Sufyān, it is the miracle of Prophethood." "Yes", said Abū Sufyān, "That's just it."[1]

Abū Sufyān hurried back to Makkah, assembled the Quraysh and announced to them: "O people of Quraysh, this is Muḥammad who has come to you with a force that you cannot resist. Now, he who enters Abū Sufyān's house will be safe." "God blast you!" cried some among the Quraysh, "How will your house suffice us?" He added, "And he who shuts his door upon himself will be safe and he who enters the sacred mosque will be safe." Thereupon the people dispersed to take shelter in their houses and the mosque.

TRIUMPHANT ENTRY INTO MAKKAH

The Apostle ﷺ entered Makkah with his head lowered in thanksgiving to Allāh, his head almost touching the saddle of his dromedary, and with *Sūrah al-Fatḥ*[2] on his lips,[3] to signify the honour and victory granted to him.

On the day the Apostle ﷺ victoriously entered Makkah, which was the religious and political centre or rather the heart of Arabia, he took care to exemplify the principle of justice and equality to man and humility and submission to God, not forgetting even one cardinal virtue upheld by Islam. He seated Usāmah ibn Zayd, the son of his freed slave ﷺ, with him on his camel although all the nobles of Quraysh and of his own family, Banū Hāshim, were present on the occasion. The Apostle ﷺ entered Makkah on Friday, the 21st of Ramaḍān, 8 AH.

The day Makkah fell to the Apostle of God ﷺ, he happened to talk to a man who began to tremble because of his awe. The Apostle ﷺ consoled him saying, "Be at ease and do not fear. I am not a king but merely the son of a Quraysh woman who used to take meat dried in the sun."[4]

---

1 *Ibn Hishām,* vol.,II, p. 404; *Zād al-Maʿād,* vol. I, p. 423.

2 48th chapter of the Qur'ān, entitled "Victory."

3 *Ibn Kathīr,* vol III, p. 554; *Bukhārī* relates on the authority of Muʿāwiyah ibn Qurrah that he saw the Prophet on the day of the conquest of Makkah when he was riding his camel and reciting aloud the *Sūrah al-Fatḥ.*

4 *Bukhārī: Kitāb al-Maghāzī,* "The Farewell Pilgrimage."

THE DAY OF MERCY AND FORGIVENESS

Saʿd ibn ʿUbādah passed by Abū Sufyān with a detachment of the Anṣār ﷺ. While marching ahead he shouted:

Today is a day of conflict,
  Sanctuary is no more!
Allāh has humbled the Quraysh.

In a short while, the Prophet's ﷺ column came near Abū Sufyān ﷺ. He complained to the Prophet ﷺ and repeated what Saʿd ﷺ had said. The Apostle ﷺ was displeased with Saʿd's bragging and replied.

Nay, today is the day of mercy and forgiveness,
  Today Allāh will honour Quraysh,
And raise glory of the Sanctuary.[1]

The Apostle ﷺ sent for Saʿd and taking the standard from him gave it to his son Qays ﷺ; thus this act was as if the standard had not been taken from him in the first place.[2]

Whatever the Prophet ﷺ said or did, he was in fact guided from on High. The transfer of the standard was merely symbolic but not superfluous. On the one hand, the Apostle ﷺ set Abū Sufyān ﷺ at ease after his feelings had been hurt and, on the other, he avoided humiliating Saʿd ibn ʿUbādah ﷺ whose services for the cause of Islam were of no mean order.

A FEW SKIRMISHES

Ṣafwān ibn Umayyah, ʿIkrimah ibn Abī Jahl and Suhayl ibn ʿAmr came up against Khālid ibn Walīd ﷺ and tried to obstruct the advance of the Muslim forces. There were a dozen casualties or so and then they gave in without any further bloodshed. The Apostle ﷺ had already forbidden his troops to measure swords with anyone except those who resisted them.[3]

---

1 Ibn Amwī relates this story in *Maghāzī*. See *Fatḥ al-Bārī*, vol. VIII, p. 7. *Bukhārī* has also related the incident, with a slight variation, in the form of a dialogue between Saʿd ibn ʿUbādah and the Apostle. The full name of Ibn Amwī is Yaḥyā ibn Saʿīd ibn Abān who is regarded as a reliable narrator and known as "the truthful." He died in 594 AH.

2 *Zād al Maʿād*, vol. I, p. 423.

3 *Zād al-Maʿād*, vol. I, pp. 407–8.

KAᶜBAH CLEARED OF IDOLS

Finally, when normality returned to Makkah and the populace settled down, God's Apostle ﷺ went to the sacred House of God. First he went seven times around the sanctuary. The sanctuary held, at that time, three hundred and sixty Idols: he prodded each with a bow in his hand, saying:

> Truth has come and falsehood has vanished. Falsehood is ever bound to vanish.[1]

And the idols collapsed, one after the other, falling on their faces.[2] There were also some images and figures inside the Kaᶜbah. These were destroyed under the orders of the Apostle ﷺ.[3]

PRINCELY GENEROSITY

Having gone round the sanctuary, the Apostle ﷺ sent for ᶜUthmān ibn Ṭalḥah, who had charge of the keys to the Kaᶜbah. He took the keys from ᶜUthmān and had the doors opened for him. Once, before his migration to Madīnah, the Apostle ﷺ had requested ᶜUthmān to give him the keys to the Kaᶜbah, but ᶜUthmān had not only refused his request but had also been impertinent to him. With exemplary forbearance the Apostle ﷺ had then said to him, "ᶜUthmān, the day will come when you will see this key in my hands. I will give it to whom I would like." ᶜUthmān had then retorted. "If the day comes, the Quraysh will be humiliated and crushed." "No," the Prophet ﷺ had said calmly, "it will be the day when they will be honoured and secured." It is related that the prediction had so haunted ᶜUthmān's mind that he had come to believe that it would happen exactly as foretold by the Apostle ﷺ.[4]

When the Apostle ﷺ came out of the sanctuary he had the keys in his hand. ᶜAlī رضي الله عنه stood up and said, "Allāh have mercy and peace on you. Grant us the right to guard the Kaᶜbah along with the watering of pilgrims." But the Apostle ﷺ ignored his request and enquired, "Where is ᶜUthmān ibn Ṭalḥah?" ᶜUthmān was summoned and then the Apostle ﷺ said, "ᶜUthmān, take the keys for these are yours. This is the day of good faith and benevolence. This key shall ever remain with you and none but a tyrant will take it from you."[5]

---

1 Qur'ān 17:81.

2 *Zād al-Maᶜād,* vol. I, p. 424; *Ibn Hishām,* vol.II, p. 424.

3 Ibid.; *Ibn Hishām,* vol.,II, p. 411.

4 *Zād al-Maᶜād,* vol. I, p. 425, also *Bukhārī.*

5 Ibid., and *Ibn Saᶜd.*

ISLAM, THE RELIGION OF MONOTHEISM

The Apostle ﷺ stood at the door of the Kaʿbah, holding its frame, while Quraysh arrayed themselves in front of him in the courtyard. The Apostle ﷺ then addressed them, saying:

> There is no God but Allāh alone. He has no associate. He has made good His promise and helped His servant. He has alone overthrown all the confederates. Lo! All the privileges and claims to retaliation and bloodwit are beneath my feet except the custody of the Kaʿbah and watering of the pilgrims. O people of Quraysh, God has abolished the haughtiness of paganism and the pride of lineage. Man springs from Ādam and Ādam sprang from dust.

Thereafter the Apostle ﷺ recited the Qur'ānic verses: "O mankind! We have created you male and female, and have made you nations and tribes that you may know one, another. The noblest of you, in the sight of Allāh, is the best in conduct. Allāh is the Knower, the Aware."[1]

THE PROPHET OF MERCY

The Apostle ﷺ then asked the Quraysh. "O Quraysh, What do you think I am about to do with you?" "We hope for the best," they replied. "You are a noble brother, son of a noble brother." The Apostle ﷺ said in reply, "I say to you what Yūsuf[2] said to his brothers: Have no fear this day,[3] go your way for you are all free."[4]

Then the Apostle ﷺ ordered Bilāl ؓ to climb onto the roof of the Kaʿbah and give the call for prayer. This was the first time that the chiefs and nobles of the Quraysh heard the call to prayer resounding in the valley of Makkah.

Thereafter the Apostle ﷺ went to the house of Umm Hānī bint Abī Ṭālib ؓ, took a bath and offered eight *rakʿāts* of prayer in thanksgiving for the victory God had granted to him.[5]

EQUALITY BEFORE LAW

Fāṭimah ؓ, a woman of Banū Makhzūm, was in the meanwhile apprehended on the charge of theft. Her clansmen approached Usāmah ibn Zayd ؓ in the

1 Qur'ān 49:13; *Zād al-Maʿād*, vol. I, p. 424.

2 The prophet Joseph.

3 Qur'ān 12:92.

4 *Zād al-Maʿād,* vol. I, p. 424.

5 *Bukhārī*: "The Day of Victory"; *Zād al-Maʿād,* vol. I, p. 425.

hope that, the Prophet ﷺ being well disposed towards him, he might be able to intercede with him for the woman. When Usāmah ﷺ mentioned the matter to the Apostle ﷺ, he found his expression completely altered. The Apostle ﷺ said to Usāmah, "Do you speak to me about the bounds put by God?" Usāmah felt so ashamed that he beseeched the Apostle ﷺ. "O Messenger of Allāh, pray God to forgive me." In the evening, when the people had gathered, the Apostle ﷺ said after praising God:

> The people before you were destroyed because they would turn a blind eye when a highborn or a man of substance among them committed a theft but when the poor or the weak did the same they punished him as ordained by the law. I swear by Him who holds my life that if Fāṭimah bint Muḥammad had committed theft I would amputate her hand.

The Apostle ordered to cut off the right hand of the culprit. She is reported to have sincerely repented of her sin and led a normal life after marrying.[1]

KINDNESS TO ENEMIES

Now that the victory was complete, all the citizens of Makkah were granted amnesty. Only nine persons were condemned to death. Of these was one who had been guilty of apostasy after accepting Islam, another man had deceitfully killed a Muslim while a few others had been busy shouting down Islam and vilifying the Prophet ﷺ. ʿAbdullāh ibn Saʿd ibn Abī Sārah had abandoned Islam. ʿIkrimah ibn Abī Jahl so detested Islam that he fled to Yemen. His wife became a Muslim ﷺ and asked the Prophet ﷺ to grant him immunity. ʿIkrimah was the son of Abū Jahl, the greatest enemy of the Prophet, yet he was not only pardoned but when he came back to Makkah the Apostle ﷺ accorded him a warm welcome. The Prophet ﷺ rose to receive ʿIkrimah in such a haste that his robe fell from his shoulders.

The Prophet ﷺ was well pleased to admit ʿIkrimah ﷺ into the fold of Islam. Accorded a place of honour among the Muslims, ʿIkrimah ﷺ distinguished himself by his deeds of valour in the battles fought against the Apostates and the Byzantines.

One of these culprits was Waḥshī ﷺ, the slave of Jubayr ibn Muṭʿim, who had killed the Prophet's ﷺ uncle Ḥamzah ﷺ. The Apostle ﷺ had condemned him to death but when he came to witness the truth in God and His Apostle, the Prophet ﷺ accepted his allegiance.

1 Bukhārī and Muslim.

There was Habbār ibn al-Aswad ﷺ also who had attacked the Prophet's ﷺ daughter Zaynab ﷺ. She ﷺ had fallen from her litter and as a consequence miscarried. Habbār had also fled from Makkah but when he came back to accept Islam, he was also forgiven by the merciful Prophet ﷺ. Among those found guilty were two singing girls, Sārah and her friend, who used to sing satirical songs denigrating the Apostle ﷺ. When immunity was demanded for them, the Apostle ﷺ pardoned their guilt and they acknowledged Islam.[1]

HIND ACCEPTS ISLAM

A large crowd of the citizens of Makkah assembled to be received in Islam. The Apostle ﷺ came to Mount Ṣafā, where, one after another, the Makkans stepped up to take the oath of allegiance at the hands of the Prophet ﷺ.

After the men had pledged their faith the women came up to take the oath. Among them came the fury of Uḥud, Hind ibn ʿUtbah, who was the wife of Abū Sufyān ﷺ. She came veiled because of what she had done to Ḥamzah ﷺ.

The Apostle ﷺ said to her, "Take your oath that you will associate nothing with God." "By God", she replied, "You lay on us something that you have not laid on men." The Prophet ﷺ said again, "And you shall not steal." Hind acknowledged, "I used to take a little of Abū Sufyān's money but I do not know if it was lawful or not."

Abū Sufyān was present on the occasion. He intervened to say, "So far as the past is concerned, there is no blame on you. It was lawful." The Apostle ﷺ now recognised Hind ﷺ and said, "Ah! You are Hind bint ʿUtbah!" Hind said in reply, "Yes, I am. Forgive me what is past and God will forgive you." The Apostle ﷺ again said to her, "And, you shall not commit adultery." "Does a woman of noble birth commit adultery?" she enquired in reply.[2]

Ignoring her question, the Apostle ﷺ further said, "And you shall not kill your children." Hind answered back, "We brought them up when they were young and you killed them when they were grown up. Now you and they should know better." ʿUmar ibn al-Khattāb ﷺ began to laugh heartily at her reply.

The Apostle ﷺ continued, "And you shall not utter slander about anybody." "By God", replied Hind, "slander is vile and shameful. It is better sometimes to ignore it." Finally, the Apostle said to her, "And you shall not disobey me." "Yes", acknowledged Hind, but she added, "in matters virtuous."[3]

---

1 *Zād al-Maʿād*, vol. I, p. 425.

2 *Ibn Kathīr*, vol. III, p. 603.

3 *Ibn Kathīr*, vol. III, pp. 602–3.

INSEPARABLE COMPANIONS

Allāh had opened the gates of Makkah to the Prophet ﷺ. It was the city of his birth as well as his ancestral home. Some of the Anṣār said to one another that since God had given power to the Apostle ﷺ over his homeland and the city he might now remain there instead of going back to Madīnah.

After a short while, the Apostle ﷺ asked them what they were talking about. Now, no one else knew the content of their conversation; at first they were too embarrassed to tell him, but ultimately they expressed regret and told him what had been said. Thereupon the Apostle ﷺ said to them, "God forbid, I will live and die with you."[1]

SINNER TURNS INTO SAINT

Faḍālah ibn ʿUmayr wanted to kill the Apostle ﷺ. He made up his mind to attack the Apostle ﷺ when he was busy circumambulating the Kaʿbah. As he drew near, the Apostle ﷺ called out, "Faḍālah" to draw his attention. He replied, "Yes, O Apostle of God." The Apostle ﷺ then asked him, "What are you thinking?" "Nothing", replied Faḍālah, "I was recollecting God." The Apostle ﷺ smiled and said, "Seek forgiveness from God," and at the same time he put his hand on Faḍālah's chest. His heart was at once set at ease and, as Faḍālah related later on, "The Apostle ﷺ had not yet removed his hand from my chest than I found him dearer to my heart than every creature of God."

Faḍālah ﷺ further says, "Then I went back to my house and passed the woman with whom I used to converse. She asked me to sit down and talk with her, but I replied, "No, Allāh and Islam do not permit it now."[2]

ALL TRACES OF PAGANISM ERASED

The Apostle ﷺ sent a few parties to destroy the idols installed in the city of Makkah and in the valley around it. All of them, including those of al-Lāt and al-ʿUzzā and Manāt ath-Thālithah al-Ukhrā were broken to pieces. The Apostle ﷺ then sent a crier to announce that every man who had faith in God and the Hereafter should destroy his household idol. The Apostle ﷺ also sent some of his companions to different tribes in the vicinity of Makkah who destroyed the idols with them.

Jarīr ﷺ relates that a temple known as Dhū 'l-Khalaṣah existed during the

---

1 *Ibn Hishām,* vol. II, p. 416.

2 *Ibn Hishām,* vol. II, p. 417; *Zād al-Maʿād,* vol. I, p. 426.

time paganism prevailed in Arabia. Similarly, there were two more temples, one of these was al-Kaʿbah-al-Yamāniyyah and the other was al-Kaʿbah-ash-Shāmiyyah. The Apostle ﷺ said to Jarīr ؓ, "Why do you not relieve me of Dhū 'l-Khalaṣah?" Jarīr ؓ took a vow and went with a hundred and fifty resolute horsemen of Aḥmas[1] and broke up the temple as well as killing those who were present in it. When Jarīr ؓ returned and gave the report to the Prophet ﷺ, he prayed for Aḥmas.[2]

Thereafter the Apostle ﷺ assembled the Muslims and announced that God had made Makkah a sacred territory forever. He said: "It is not lawful for anyone who believes in Allāh and the Hereafter to shed blood in the city or to cut down a tree. It was not permitted to anyone before me, neither shall it be permitted to anyone after me." The Prophet ﷺ then returned to Madīnah.[3]

IMPACT OF MAKKAH'S CONQUEST

The conquest of Makkah had a tremendous impact on the Arabs. It was a great victory, for it vindicated the claim that Islam was the religion of God and paved the way for its reception across all of Arabia. Tribesmen from distant deserts started coming to Madīnah in bands or sent deputations to give faith to Islam. A number of tribes had treaty relations with the Quraysh which bound them to keep away from the Muslims, while others feared or respected the Quraysh as the guardians of the holy sanctuary. With the submission of the Quraysh to Allāh and his Apostle, all these obstacles were removed. There were also tribes who believed—the fate of Abrahah being still fresh in their minds—that no tyrant could lay his hands upon Makkah and, therefore, they preferred to wait and see the result of the contention between the Muslims and the Quraysh. Some of them had actually decided to leave the Prophet ﷺ alone and to accept him as the Apostle of God ﷺ if he were successful in winning over his own tribe.[4]

When God allowed His Apostle ﷺ to gain the upper hand over Makkah, and the Quraysh yielded obedience to him, willingly or unwillingly, the whole of Arabia bowed its head to Islam in a way unheard of in a country given to disorder and unruliness throughout the ages. The Bedouins came thronging to Madīnah, from every clan and tribe, to pay their respect to the Apostle ﷺ and

---

1 Aḥmas (brave) is said to have been a term applied to Quraysh, Kinna, Jādila and Qays because of their horsemanship and bravery.

2 *Bukhārī*: Ghazwah Dhū 'l-Khalaṣah.

3 *Zād al-Maʿād*, vol. I, pp. 425–26.

4 *Bukhārī* on the Authority of ʿAmr ibn Salamah

accept Islam at his hands. It was then that the *Sūrah al-Naṣr*[1] was revealed by God which said:

> When Allāh's succour and the triumph comes and you see mankind entering the religion of Allāh in troops.[2]

THE YOUTHFUL ADMINISTRATOR

The Apostle ﷺ appointed ʿAttāb ibn ʿUsayd ؓ to look after the arrangements of the pilgrimage and other affairs of Makkah before leaving the city.[3] ʿAttāb ؓ was then only twenty years of age. There were several other older persons in Makkah, more experienced as well as more prominent than ʿAttāb ؓ, but his selection by the Apostle of God ﷺ showed that he entrusted responsibility to a person solely on the basis of his merit and capability. ʿAttāb continued to hold that office during the period of Abū Bakr's ؓ caliphate.[4]

1 Meaning "succour". See '*Raḥmatul LilʿĀlamīn*', by the renowned author Qādī Muhammad Sulaymān.

2 Qur'ān 110:1–2.

3 *Ibn Hishām*, vol. II, p. 440.

4 Al-Iṣābah and Usd ul-Ghābah.

19

The Battle of Ḥunayn

THE RESOUNDING VICTORY of the Muslims over the Quraysh and the ever increasing conversions to Islam frightened the enemies of Islam out of their senses. They made another attempt, as a last resort, to check the fast growing power and popularity of Islam but their effort was no more than lashing the waves in vain expectation.

ASSEMBLAGE OF HAWĀZIN

The Hawāzin were the old enemies of the Quraysh. They regarded themselves as their rivals in power and prestige. The submission of the Quraysh to the rising power of Islam had made them the undisputed champions of paganism. Now they began to harbour hopes of winning the laurels by bringing the Muslims to their knees. They saw a godsend opportunity to build up their fame on the declining prestige of the Quraysh.

The Hawāzin chief, Mālik ibn ʿAwf an-Naṣrī, declared war against the Muslims which was seconded by several other tribes like Thaqīf, Naṣr, Jusham and Saʿd ibn Bakr. Two clans of Hawāzin, the Kaʿb and Kilāb, kept away from Mālik ibn ʿAwf, but the rest of the confederacy marshalled its forces to descend on the Prophet ﷺ. They also took their cattle, women and children, staking everything on the battle, in order to ensure that everyone would fight to the last and that no one would think of taking to his heels.

An old veteran Durayd ibn aṣ-Ṣimmah, who was considered wise in the art of warfare, also accompanied the Hawāzin army which made camp at Awṭās.[1] Their camp resounded with the groaning of camels and the braying of asses and the bleating of the sheep and goats and the crying of children. Mālik instructed his men: "Break your scabbards as soon as the Muslims are in sight and then attack them as one man."[2]

The Apostle ﷺ had with him two thousand Makkans, some of whom were recent converts while others had yet to accept Islam, along with the ten thousand troops he had brought from Madīnah. This was thus the strongest force mobilised so far to defend the honour of Islam. The Muslims were, naturally, overconfident because of their great strength while some even exultantly boasted that they could not be defeated now for want of numbers.[3]

The Apostle ﷺ obtained on credit, on this occasion, some coats of mail and arms from Ṣafwān ibn Umayyah although he was still a polytheist.[4]

NOT A SIGN OF IDOLATRY

The people of Makkah who had joined the Apostle ﷺ in this battle were fresh from paganism. In the days of pagan past, some tribes of Arabia would venerate a great green tree known as Dhāt-Anwāṭ, under which they stayed for a day, suspended their weapon to its branches and offered sacrifices beneath it. When these men were going with the army they happened to pass by a big shady tree that reminded them of past fetishism. They immediately requested the Apostle ﷺ: "Make us a tree as they used to have Dhāt-Anwāṭ, O Messenger of Allāh." The Prophet ﷺ replied, "God is Great! By Him who holds my life in His hands, you say what the people of Moses said to him: Make for us a god even as they have gods. He (Moses) said: You are a people, who know not!"[5] The Apostle ﷺ then added, "Verily, you will follow every custom of the people before you."[6]

IN THE WADI OF ḤUNAYN

It was the 10th of Shawwal, 8 AH, when the Muslim army reached Ḥunayn, descending the wadi in morning twilight, the enemy had already taken its position in the glens and hollows and craters, of the valley. Hawāzin were celebrated

---

1 A wadi near Ṭā'if, in the territory of Hawāzin, where the battle of Ḥunayn was fought.

2 *Ibn Hishām*, vol. II. pp. 437–39.

3 *Tafsīr Ṭabarī*, vol. X, pp. 63–64.

4 *Ibn Hishām*, vol. II. p. 440.

5 Qur'ān 7:138.

6 *Ibn Hishām*, vol. II. p. 442.

archers. A volley of arrows was all that the Muslins saw of the enemy, and then suddenly the enemy followed up the attack with full force.[1]

The sudden onslaught forced the Muslim flanks to fall back and they fled in terror, none heeding the other. The battle had taken a dangerous turn: a complete rout of the Muslims was in sight without any possibility of an orderly retreat or rallying of their forces again. Like at Uḥud, when the rumour of the Apostle's ﷺ death had disheartened the Muslims, the troops were once more driven to despair in Ḥunayn by a similar misgiving.

RIFT WITHIN THE LUTE

Some of the rude fellows from Makkah who had joined the Muslim army but were still not strong in faith started talking in a way that showed their antipathy to Islam. One said, "Their flight will not stop before they get to the sea." Another man remarked, "The spell of their sorcery has ended today."[2]

VICTORY AND PEACE OF GOD

The Muslims had to suffer this defeat after the brilliant victory of Makkah as if by way of punishment for their reliance on numbers instead of the succour of God. Their faith needed to be strengthened by a misadventure for they had to learn the lesson that both victory and defeat came from God; neither should the one make man exultant nor the other despondent. The Muslims were all over with their trepidation when the peace of God appeared to be descending on them and the Apostle ﷺ. The Prophet ﷺ had all the while stood firm on his place, riding his white mule, without any fear or fidgets. Only a few of the Anṣār and Mūhājirīn or his relatives were then with him. ʿAbbās ibn ʿAbd al-Muṭṭalib ؓ was holding the bridle of his mule while God's Apostle was calling aloud:

> Verily, I am the Prophet without falsehood!
> I am son of ʿAbd al-Muṭṭalib![3]

In the meantime a detachment of the enemy advanced towards him. The Prophet ﷺ took a handful of dust and threw it into their eyes. When the Apostle saw his men in confusion, he said, "ʿAbbās call out, O Anṣār, O comrades of the acacia tree."[4] All those who heard the cry, responded, "Here are we." ʿAbbās had a loud

1 Ibid., pp. 442–43
2 *Ibn Hishām*, vol. II. pp. 442–44.
3 According to Bukhārī Abū Sufyān ibn Al-Ḥārith was holding the bridle.
4 A reference to the Companions who had taken the pledge of Riḍwān at Ḥudaybiyyah.

voice. Whoever heard him calling got off from his camel and came to the Apostle ﷺ. When a sufficient number of men had gathered, they bore down upon the enemy. A combat between the two parties started afresh. The Apostle ﷺ then took to a height along with some of his Companions. He saw the two sides clashing with one another. He said, "Now the battle has grown hot."[1] He threw a few pebbles on the enemy. ʿAbbās ﷺ relates that he saw the enemy becoming slack thereafter and losing the day to the Muslims.[2]

Both the armies fought bravely. However, before all those Muslims who had fled had come back, the enemy was discomfited and a party of bound persons was brought before the Apostle ﷺ.[3] Allāh helped the Apostle ﷺ with the hosts of heaven to win the day and brought Hawāzin to their knees.[4]

> Allāh has given you victory on many fields and on the day of Ḥunayn, when you exulted in your multitude but it availed you not, and the earth, vast as it is, was straitened for you; then you turned back in flight. Then Allāh sent His Peace of reassurance down upon His messenger and upon the believers, and sent down hosts you could not see, and punished those who disbelieved. Such is the reward of disbelievers.[5]

THE LAST ENCOUNTER

The bitterness and rancour borne by the pagans against Islam melted away after the battle of Ḥunayn. The last stronghold of paganism was toppled in this battle and no formidable opponent of Islam remained in Arabia. The remaining tribes streamed to Madīnah from every part of Arabia to put their trust in Allāh and His Apostle.

IN AWṬĀS

A group of the enemy put to rout fled to Ṭā'if and shut the gates of the city. The chief of Hawāzin, Mālik ibn ʿAwf, was also with them. A detachment sent by the Apostle ﷺ under Abū ʿĀmir al-Ashʿarī ﷺ overtook another party of the enemy encamped at Awṭās, engaged it in a fight and routed it completely.[6] When the

1 *Ibn Hishām,* vol. II. p. 445.
2 *Ṣaḥīḥ Muslim.*
3 *Ibn Hishām,* vol. II. p. 445.
4 *Ṣaḥiḥ Muslim*: Kitāb al-Jīhād, Ghazwah Ḥunayn.
5 Qur'ān 9:25–26.
6 *Ibn Kathīr,* vol. III. p. 460.

captives and spoils of Ḥunayn were brought to the Apostle ﷺ he ordered them to be taken to Jiʿirrānah[1] and kept in custody there.[2]

The captives of Ḥunayn numbered six thousand. The spoils included twenty-four thousand camels, forty thousand or more goats and four thousand *ūqiyyah* of silver. This was the largest spoil that had fallen so far into the hands of the Muslims.

The Apostle ﷺ had given orders to the troops, before the battle started, not to raise their hands against women, children, men hired for non-combatant purposes and the slaves. A woman was, however, killed in the battle. The Apostle expressed regret when the matter was brought to his notice.[3]

1 A stopover on the road leading north-east from Makkah to Ṭā'if. It is a distance of more than 20 kilometres, and is outside the Ḥaram.

2 *Ibn Hishām*, vol. II. p. 459.

3 *Ibn Kathīr*, vol. III. p. 638.

20

The Battle of Ṭā'if

Fugitives of Thaqīf

The warriors of Thaqīf escaping from Ḥunayn returned to Ṭā'if. They closed the gates of the city after storing stocks of food to suffice for a year. Thus, they prepared to battle the Muslims.

The Prophet ﷺ went at once to Ṭā'if (it was the month of Shawwāl, 8 AH). After pitching his camp outside the city, he set about besieging it. The siege dragged on for some time, but the Muslims were unable to enter Ṭā'if whose approaches had already been blocked up by the defenders. Thaqīf were good archers. The thick volley of arrows discharged by the enemy appeared like the swarms of locusts.

Siege of Ṭā'if

As the Muslims' camp was within the range of the arrows shot from the ramparts of Ṭā'if, the Apostle ﷺ moved his camp to another side of the city. The siege continued for some twenty-five to thirty nights during which the two sides fought tooth and nail to get the better of one another and exchanged volleys of arrows. The Prophet ﷺ used, for the first time, catapults in the siege of Ṭā'if whose entry and exit were completely blocked. The arrows shot by the enemy took its toll and several Muslims were slain.[1]

1 *Ibn Hishām,* vol. II. pp. 478–483.

KINDNESS IN THE BATTLEFIELD

When the siege did not have the desired effect, the Apostle ﷺ threatened to cut down the vineyards of Thaqīf. The enemy was extremely perturbed, for its economy depended on the fine quality of grapes grown in these vineyards. Thaqīf begged the Prophet ﷺ in the name of God and their relationship to him to spare their crops. Taking pity on the enemy, the Apostle ﷺ said, "Certainly, I leave it to God and kinship between us."

The Apostle ﷺ announced that if any slave of Thaqīf came to him from the city, he would be set free. Among the ten or more slaves who deserted Ṭā'if, one was Abū Bakrah ؓ. Later on he distinguished himself by his deep knowledge of Traditions. The Prophet freed all of them and asked the Muslims to take care of their needs. However, the people of Ṭā'if were sorely angered by the desertion of their slaves.[1]

THE SIEGE RAISED

Allāh had not willed the fall of Ṭā'if. The Apostle ﷺ asked ʿUmar ؓ to announce the raising of the siege and return of the army. Feeling disappointed, some of the people raised an outcry at the sudden order of retreat. They said, "Shall we go back without reducing Ṭā'if?" The Apostle ﷺ replied, "Alright, mount an attack." They bore down on the enemy but were repulsed with losses. Then the Apostle ﷺ said, "God willing, we shall return very soon." The people now felt relieved and started making preparations for breaking the camp. The Prophet ﷺ smiled when he saw them returning.[2]

THE SPOILS OF ḤUNAYN

On his way back from Ṭā'if, the Apostle ﷺ stayed over at Jiʿirrānah with his men. He intended to give an opportunity to the Hawāzin to make amends by calling upon him and accepting Islam. Thereafter, he distributed the spoils. The Apostle ﷺ gave out first to those whose hearts were yet to be won. Abū Sufyān and his two sons Yazīd and Muʿāwiyyah ؓ were doled out handsome gifts, as well as Ḥakīm ibn al-Ḥizām Naḍr ibn al-Ḥārith, ʿAlā' ibn al-Ḥārithah ؓ and others. The leaders of the Quraysh were treated generously and finally every man in the army was awarded his share of the spoils.[3]

---

1 *Zād al-Maʿād,* vol. I, p. 457 (on the authority of Ibn Isḥāq).

2 Ibid.

3 *Zād al-Maʿād,* vol. I, p. 448. See also *Bukhārī* and *Muslim*; *Ghazwah Ṭā'if*

LOVE FOR ANṢĀR AND THEIR SELFLESSNESS

The Prophet ﷺ gave out a large portion of the spoils to Quraysh who had to be conciliated to Islam while the Anṣār received a small share. Some of the youth among the Anṣār aired their grievance at the meagre gifts made over to them. The Apostle ﷺ ordered the Anṣār to assemble in an enclosure. Then he gave an extremely moving speech, which stirred the hearts of the Anṣār and brought them to the verge of tears.

The Apostle ﷺ said, "Did I not come to you when you were aberrant and God guided you through me; you were poor and God made you rich; you were divided and He softened your hearts to unite?" The Anṣār replied, "Yes, indeed, God and His Apostle are most kind and generous." But the Apostle ﷺ again asked them, "O Anṣār, why don't you answer me?" They said, "What answer can we give! O Messenger of God. Kindness and generosity belong to God and His Apostle." The Apostle ﷺ continued, "Had you wished, you could have said, and verily you would have spoken the truth and I would have acknowledged it. If you had replied, 'You came discredited and we believed you; you came deserted and we helped you; you were a fugitive and we gave you shelter; you were poor and we comforted you."

The Apostle ﷺ then turned to speak of the love he had for the Anṣār and, at the same time, explained the reason for differentiating between them in giving out the gifts. He said, "Do you have any misgivings about me, O Anṣār, because of what I have given to them for the short-lived bloom of this life by which they may become Muslims while I have entrusted you to Islam?" The Apostle ﷺ then posed a question that inflamed the Anṣār with the love of the Prophet ﷺ. He asked, "O Anṣār, are you not satisfied that these men should take away sheep and goats while you return with the Apostle of God? By Him who has the life of Muḥammad in His hand, what you take back with you is better than the things with which they would return.

"Had there been no migration I myself would have been one of the Anṣār. If all the people go one way in a wadi and the Anṣār take another, I would take the way of the Anṣār. The Anṣār are the undergarment and others are over-garments. O Allāh, have mercy on the Anṣār, their children and their children's children."

All the Anṣār wept until tears ran down their beards as they said, "We are satisfied and happy that the Apostle of Allāh ﷺ falls to our lot."[1]

---

1 The incident has been narrated in the two *Ṣaḥīḥ*s, but *Zād al-Maʿād* gives more details.

CAPTIVES RELEASED

A deputation of the Hawāzin consisting of fourteen persons called upon the Apostle ﷺ. They requested him to take pity on them and return their kinsmen and property. The Apostle ﷺ replied, "You see the people accompanying me. What I like best is that you come out with the truth. Now tell me, which of the two is dearer to you? Your children and your women, or your property?"

They replied with one voice, "We treasure nothing more than our children and women."

Now, the Apostle ﷺ advised them, "Tomorrow morning when I have finished the prayer you get up and say: We ask the Apostle's ﷺ intercession with the Muslims, and the Muslims' intercession with the Apostle ﷺ that our children and women be returned to us." When they did as told by the Apostle ﷺ he gave the reply, "Whatever was apportioned to me and the Banū ʿAbd al-Muṭṭalib is yours. To others I make a recommendation for you."

Thereupon the Mūhājirīn and the Anṣār said, "Whatever share has been given to us is passed on to the Apostle."

Three persons belonging to Banū Tamīm, Banū Fazārah and Banū Sulaym refused to part with their shares. The Prophet ﷺ said to them, "These fellows have come after accepting Islam. I awaited their arrival and gave them a choice but they preferred nothing over their women and children. Now, if anybody has serfs whom he wants to donate cheerfully, the way is open to him. But if anybody does not want to do so, he may refuse. He who holds a right to such captives shall be given six shares in lieu of each from the first booty Allāh grants us."

Everyone replied, "We give back our shares cheerfully for the Apostle's sake." The Prophet ﷺ, however, said, "I do not know who among you is contented and who is not. You go back now and your chiefs will tell me correctly about your affairs." All of them returned the captives, women and children, and not one of them decided to retain his share. The Prophet also gifted out a garment to every released captive.[1]

LOVING KINDNESS

Among the captives rounded up during the battle, the Muslims also held Shaymā' bint Ḥalīmah Saʿdiyyah ﷺ. The men who took her captive did not know her and although she told them that she was the foster-sister of the Apostle ﷺ, they paid her no heed and treated her roughly.

When Shaymā' was brought before the Apostle she said,

1 *Zād al-Maʿād*, vol. I, p. 449; and *Bukhārī*.

"O Prophet of God, I am your foster-sister." The Apostle ﷺ asked for proof and she replied. "The bite you gave me in my back when I carried you at my hip. The mark is still there." The Apostle ﷺ accepted the proof and stretched out his robe for her to sit on and treated her courteously. He gave her the choice of living with him in affection and honour or going back to her people with gifts. She chose to go back to her tribe. She accepted Islam and the Prophet ﷺ gave her three bondsmen, a slave girl and some goats.[1]

THE LESSER PILGRIMAGE

After distributing the spoils and captives at Jiʿirrānah, the Apostle ﷺ put on the *iḥrām* to perform the lesser pilgrimage for this was the place from where the people going for pilgrimage to Makkah from Ṭā'if changed into *iḥrām*. Having completed the lesser pilgrimage the Apostle ﷺ returned to Madīnah.[2]

The Apostle ﷺ came back to Madīnah in Dhū 'l-Qaʿdah, 8 AH.[3] While the forces were returning from Ṭā'if, the Apostle of God ﷺ asked the men to recite: "We are those who revert and repent and worship and glorify our Lord." Some of the people then asked the Prophet ﷺ to call down evil on Thaqīf. The Apostle ﷺ raised his hands to entreat; "O Allāh! Guide Thaqīf on the right path and bring them here."

ʿUrwah ibn Masʿūd al-Thaqafī ﷺ met the Apostle ﷺ while he was on his way back to Madīnah. He became a Muslim and returned to his people to invite them to Islam. He was very popular and enjoyed the esteem of his clansmen but when he broke the news that he had accepted Islam, the people turned against him. They shot arrows at him from all directions; one hit him and he died.

Thaqīf held out for a few months after killing ʿUrwah ﷺ but after taking counsel among themselves they reached the conclusion that it would be beyond their power to fight all those tribes which had already taken the oath of allegiance at the hands of the Apostle ﷺ. Ultimately, they decided to send a deputation to the Apostle ﷺ.

NO COMPLAISANCE TO IDOLATRY

When the deputation of Thaqīf came to Madīnah a tent was pitched for them in the Prophet's ﷺ mosque. They requested the Apostle ﷺ not to destroy their

1 *Zād al-Maʿād*, vol. I, p. 449.

2 *Ibn Hishām*, vol. II. p. 500.

3 Bukhārī.

chief deity, the idol of al-Lāt, for three years. The Apostle ﷺ refused; then they continued to reduce the period by one year, but the Apostle ﷺ remained firm in refusing their request until they finally asked for a period of one month after they had returned to their homes. The Apostle ﷺ again rejected their request and ordered Abū Sufyān and Mughīrah ibn Shuʿbah al-Thaqafī to destroy al-Lāt. Thereafter Thaqīf asked the Prophet ﷺ that they might be excused from offering prayers. To this the Apostle replied; "Nothing remains of a religion which has no prayer."

Abū Sufyān and Mughīrah ibn Shuʿbah accompanied the deputation of Thaqīf when they returned to Ṭā'if. Mughīrah smote al-Lāt with a pickaxe and broke it into pieces. Thereupon the people of Ṭā'if accepted Islam. Not one of them remained attached to paganism.[1]

KAʿB IBN ZUHAYR ACCEPTS ISLAM

Kaʿb ibn Zuhayr paid a visit to the Apostle ﷺ after the he returned to Madīnah from Ṭā'if. Kaʿb was a poet whose father had also been a versifier. He had composed many satirical poems ridiculing the Apostle ﷺ but when he fell on evil days, his brother Bujayr wrote to him that he should rather go to the Apostle ﷺ as a repentant sinner and accept Islam. Kaʿb's brother also warned him of the dire consequences of disregarding his advice. Kaʿb, at last, came to the Apostle ﷺ and composed the famous panegyric ode praising the Apostle beginning with *Bānat Suʿād*.[2]

When Kaʿb came to Madīnah he called upon the Apostle ﷺ just after he had finished the morning prayers and placed his hands in his. The Apostle ﷺ, however, did not know who he was. Kaʿb then said to the Prophet ﷺ, "O Messenger of Allāh, Kaʿb ibn Zuhayr has come as a repentant Muslim and asks for security from you. Will you accept his repentance?" One of the Anṣār leapt upon him saying, "O Apostle of God, let me deal with this enemy of God. I will cut off his head this instant." But the Apostle ﷺ asked him to let Kaʿb alone since he had come repentant of his past deeds. It was then that Kaʿb recited the well known ode beginning with the verses:

Suʿād is gone, and today my heart is lovelorn;
  Enthralled, in chains, no bloodwit coming to un rein.

Then, in another verse he praised the Prophet thus:

---

1 *Zād al-Maʿād,* vol. I, pp. 458–59.

2 Meaning Suʿād has departed.

Indeed the Messenger is a light whence illumination is sought;
A drawn, sharp-edged sword, the sword of Allāh.

The Apostle gave away his robe to Kaʿb ﷺ when he recited these verses.[1]

1 *Zād al-Maʿād,* vol. I, pp. 466–68. Qasṭalānī relates in the *Mawāhib,* on the authority of Abū Bakr ibn al-ʿAnbarī that when Kaʿb recited this verse, the Apostle gave his robe to him. Caliph MuʿĀwiyah offered 10,000 dīnārs for the Apostle's robe, but Kaʿb refused and said that he could not part with it for anything. MuʿĀwiyah obtained the robe, after the death of Kaʿb, for 20,000 dīnārs, from the heirs of Kaʿb. Qasṭalānī further says that the robe remained with the Caliphs for a long time (*Az-Zurqānī,* a commentary on *Al-Mawāhib,* vol. III, p. 70).

21
The Expedition to Tabūk

SOME OF THE tribes still suffered from the delusion that the rise of Islam was transient like a cloudburst, whose shower would be stemmed before long. It was necessary to warn or even threaten such people before they took an opportunity to clench their fist at the Muslims. The expedition of Tabūk[1] had the desired effect on such lukewarm tribes, in much the same way as the conquest of Makkah had gone a long way in clearing away the clouds of opposition. This expedition against the Byzantine Empire whose might and magnificence was well known to the Arabs, virtually meant that the Muslims were ready to fling down the gauntlet even to the greatest power of the day. The esteem in which the Arabs held the Byzantines, whom they called Romans, is well illustrated by Abū Sufyān's ﷺ remark after he had seen Heraclius rendering honour to the Apostle's ﷺ letter sent through Diḥyah ibn Khalīfah al-Kalbī ﷺ. He had heard Heraclius say that he, too, expected a prophet to be born. Abū Sufyān ﷺ had then got up, as he related later on, rubbing his hands and saying that the affair of Ibn Abī Kabshah[2] (i.e. the Prophet) had become so great that the king of the

1 Tabūk is half-way between Madīnah and Damascus lying to the south-east of Aylah, the biblical Elath or ʿAqabah. Yaqūt writes, quoting Abū Zayd, in the *Muʿjam al-Buldān* that Tabūk is the fourth stop on the road from Ḥijr to Syria. It is reported that the Prophet Shuʿayb was sent to the people living there. Tabūk is at a distance of six days journey from the Red sea and lies between two mountains known as Ḥismā and Sharawrā (*Dāʾirāt al-Maʿārif li ʾl-Bustānī*). It is now a military cantonment in the district of Madīnah at distance of 700 km. from it.

2 Abū Sufyān used the name sarcastically since a man of that name belonging to Khuzāʿah had given up idol worship, or perhaps, someone going by that name was among the forefathers of the Prophet ﷺ (*Majmaʿa Bihār al-Anwār*).

Romans dreaded him. Abū Sufyān ﷺ further said that he was then convinced that the Apostle ﷺ would ultimately emerge victorious and this was how Islam took root in his heart.[1]

The Arabs could not then dream of attacking the Byzantine Empire. Rather, they either feared a Byzantine invasion or did not consider themselves so significant as to be coveted by any great power. Whenever the Muslims of Madīnah were faced with a grave danger or felt their safety compromised, their minds went to the attack of Ghassān who were under East Syria and Caesar. What ʿUmar ﷺ said during the affair of Īlīyā', which took place in the beginning of 8 AH, throws sufficient light on the state of affairs in those days. He says that he had an Anṣārī friend with whom he had arranged that one of them should alternately remain in attendance upon the Prophet ﷺ and inform the other about the incidents happening in his absence. ʿUmar ﷺ further says that in those days they were alarmed by a rumour that the Ghassānid King intended to invade Madīnah and were thus constantly agitated by it. Once, when his Anṣārī friend ﷺ came to his house and knocked at his door asking him to open it, ʿUmar ﷺ enquired of his friend if the Ghassānids had attacked Madīnah.[2]

Byzantine was in the ascendant in those days. Its armies had, under Heraclius, dealt a death blow to the Persian forces and carried their arms to the Persian capital. The glorious victory was celebrated by the Emperor's stately march from Ḥimṣ[3] to Īlīyā'[4] in the seventh year of the *hijrah*. Heraclius himself carried, in the guise of a penitent pilgrim, the True Cross retrieved from the Persians while carpets were spread and rose water sprinkled beneath his feet all over the path by the people who went forth to meet their hero with tears and acclamations. Hardly two years had passed after this splendid victory of the Emperor of the Romans, when the Apostle ﷺ led an army to face him. The Apostle's ﷺ daring venture made such a deep impression on the minds of the Arabs that it would be no exaggeration to claim that the expedition of Tabūk served as a prelude to the conquest of Syria during the reign of Abū Bakr and ʿUmar ﷺ. The expedition of Tabūk really ignited the train of victories which eventually made the Muslims masters of Syria.

What was the starting point of this expedition? It is related that the Apostle ﷺ got reports of Byzantine forces converging on the northern frontiers of Arabia with the intention of mounting an attack on the Muslims. Ibn Saʿd and Wāqidī are on record that the Apostle ﷺ was informed by the Nabataeans that

1 Bukhārī.

2 Bukhārī and Muslim.

3 Emessa or Edessa.

4 Elath or ʿAqabah.

Heraclius, after stocking a year's provisions for his army and drafting the pro-Byzantine tribes of the Lakhm, Judhām, ʿĀmilah and Ghassān under his banner, intended to come upon him and that his advance columns had already reached Balqā'.

Even if we ignore this report, it can hardly be said that the purpose of the expedition was to strike terror into the neighbouring power which was a potential source of danger to the rising power of Islam. The Apostle ﷺ intended to warn the Byzantines that they should not consider the Muslims weak nor should they take any precipitate action to violate their territorial sovereignty. The expedition was thus a warning sign since one with insufficient strength would not shake his fist at a great power nor could one take the risk of descending on its borders. It is certain, at all events, that the true purpose of the expedition was what the revelation, (revealed during the expedition of Tabūk) in this connection has explained in these words:

> O you who believe! Fight those of the disbelievers who are near to you and let them find harshness in you, and know that Allāh is with those who keep their duty (unto Him).[1]

This objective was more than achieved as was subsequently borne out by the far-reaching consequences of the expedition. No retaliatory action was taken, nor were any Byzantine detachments moved to their borders to drive back the Muslim army. The Emperor, exhausted by his Persian campaigns, remained an impotent spectator to the raid on his confederate border tribes or perhaps he thought it fit to wait and see before taking up arms against the new power rising in the East.

The pro-Byzantine Christian tribes in northern Arabia were impressed by the first rattle of the new Arabian power. This was a great advantage accruing from the expedition of Tabūk for it made these tribes shift their allegiance from Constantinople to Madīnah which eventually led them to the acceptance of the religious aspect of the Islamic power. The expedition also went a long way to drive home the reality that the rise of Islam was not a momentary success, fated to burst like a bubble, as some of the Arabs had assumed, but that it was solid as a rock with a great future lying ahead of it. In fact, severance of the ties between these border tribes and Byzantium served as a precedent before they could pay attention to Islam, the new source of power and strength which was taking root and raising its head in their own homeland. The divine revelation too makes an allusion to this aspect of the expedition in a verse of *Surah at-Tawbah*:

---

1 Qur'ān 9:123.

> Nor step they any step that angers the disbelievers, nor gain they from the enemy a gain, but a good deed is recorded for them therefore.[1]

The battle of Mu'tah was still fresh in the minds of the Byzantines who had failed to humble the Muslim army in spite of their vastly superior numbers. The Muslims, on the other hand, having once measured swords with the Byzantines, had overcome their traditional terror of the impregnable Roman legions.

In short, the expedition of Tabūk was a landmark in the life of the Prophet ﷺ as well as in the onward march of the Islamic mission for it had a far-reaching effect on the future course of events leading to the glorious conquests of Islam that were yet to come.

THE TIME OF EXPEDITION

The Tabūk campaign was undertaken in the month of Rajab, 9 AH.[2] It was the time when the date crop had ripened and the shade of the trees was pleasant. The Apostle ﷺ undertook a long journey for the Tabūk expedition and traversed deserts and arid plains to face an enemy vastly superior in numbers. As the Muslims were then passing through a period of drought, the Apostle told the Companions beforehand, unlike on previous occasions that he intended to attack the Byzantines so that they might make suitable preparations.[3]

The hypocrites fell out on different pretexts. They either disliked strenuous war against the powerful enemy or disliked to go out in the oppressive heat. They even doubted the truth and had little interest in fighting for the sake of God, so they refrained from accompanying the Apostle ﷺ on this occasion. Such disaffected persons were admonished by God:

> Those who were left behind rejoiced at sitting still behind the messenger of Allāh,

1 Qur'ān 9:120.

2 It is difficult to determine the dates of the Tabūk campaign according to the solar calendar. Some of the Prophet's ﷺ biographers have computed that Rajab, 9 AH coincided with November as computed by Ḥabīb ar-Raḥmān Khān in his *Miftāḥ al-Taqwīn*. ʿAllāmah-Shiblī also holds this view. But the internal evidence furnished by reliable ḥadīth included in the *Ṣaḥīḥayn* and other trustworthy books of ḥadīth shows that the expedition was undertaken in the summer season. Kaʿb ibn Mālik says: "God's Messenger undertook it in extreme heat, facing a long journey, desert country and a teeming enemy." Mūsā ibn ʿUqbah describes the journey to have been undertaking during "autumn nights in severe heat when people take shelter under the date-palm trees. . ." Also, the pleas of the hypocrites and its contradiction in *Surah at-Tawbah*: "And they said: Go not forth in the heat! Say: The heat of the hell is more intense of heat, if they but understood," leaves no doubt that the journey was undertaken during the summer season. Be that as it may, the internal evidence is so strong and irrefutable that it cannot be brushed aside, as certain historians have done, to hold the view that the expedition was undertaken in November instead of July-August, merely for the reason that it is now difficult to compute the dates given by the earlier biographers with the Gregorian calendar.

3 *Ṣaḥīḥayn,* on the authority of Kaʿb ibn Mālik.

> and were averse to striving with their wealth and their lives in Allāh's way. And they said: Go not forth in the heat! Say: The heat of hell is more intense of heat, if they but understood.[1]

ENTHUSIASM OF THE MUSLIMS

The Apostle ﷺ took particular care to make preparations for the expedition. He urged the affluent Companions ﷺ to donate handsomely to the campaign with the result that many a well-to-do Companion made lavish contributions to it. ʿUthmān ﷺ spent one thousand dīnārs on the force known as the brigade of distress or *Jaysh al-ʿUsr* and the Apostle ﷺ invoked God's blessings for him. A number of Companions who were unable to raise money for their mounts asked the Apostle ﷺ to help them. As, however, their requests could not be met for want of funds, the Apostle ﷺ expressed his inability to fulfil their requests and they returned disconsolate and disheartened. Some of them were so sorrow-stricken and depressed that God sent down the revelation exempting them from the duty of joining the expedition:

> Nor on those (is any blame) whom, when they came to you (asking) that you should mount them, you did say: I cannot find whereon to mount you. They turned back with eyes flowing with tears, for sorrow that they could not find the means to spend.[2]

There were still others who could not make up their mind to participate in the campaign although their indecision was not because of any doubt or misgivings.

THE ARMY'S DEPARTURE FOR TABŪK

The Apostle ﷺ set out from Madīnah for Tabūk with an army 30,000 strong. In no other expedition to Tabūk had such a large number of men shouldered arms. Before the departure, the Apostle ﷺ ordered the men to pitch their camp at Thaniyāt al-Wadāʿ. He put Muḥammad ibn Maslamah al-Anṣāri ﷺ in charge of Madīnah and left behind ʿAlī ﷺ to look after his family. When ʿAlī ﷺ complained to the Apostle ﷺ that the hypocrites were going about spreading false rumours about him, he replied, "Are you not content ʿAlī that you are to me as Harūn[3] was to Mūsā,[4] except that there will be no prophet after me?"[5]

1 Qur'ān 9:81.

2 Qur'ān 9:92.

3 Aaron.

4 Moses.

5 Bukhārī: Gazwah Tabūk.

When the Apostle ﷺ made camp in al-Ḥijr, the land of Thamūd, he told the Companions that it was the country of those who were being tortured for their sins. He said, "If you enter the houses of those who did wrong to themselves, enter tearfully with the fear that you might also meet the same fate that befell them."[1] He also instructed his men, "Do not drink any of its water nor use it for ablutions. If you have used any for dough, then feed it to the camels and eat none of it."

The journey was extremely arduous; the scarcity of water added to the misery of the army. When the men complained to the Apostle ﷺ about their distress, he prayed to God and a cloud sent down torrents until every man had quenched his thirst and stored enough water to meet his needs.[2]

DEMORALISED HYPOCRITES

Some of the hypocrites kept company with the Apostle ﷺ. While the Muslim army was on its way to Tabūk, one of them said to another, alluding to the Apostle ﷺ, "Do you think that the executioners of the Romans will deal with you in the same way as the Arabs do? By God, we seem to see you bound with ropes tomorrow.[3]

TREATY OF PEACE WITH AYLAH'S RULER

Yuḥannah ibn Ru'bah, the governor of Aylah called upon the Apostle ﷺ at Tabūk. Yūḥannah made a treaty of peace and also paid the poll-tax (*jizyah*). Similarly the people of Jarbā' and Adhraḥ paid the tax, and in return they were all granted peace as well as a guarantee for the safety of their territory and their ships and caravans by land and sea. The treaties were signed by the Apostle ﷺ and delivered to the parties. The Apostle ﷺ received Yūḥannah cordially showing him due respect.[4]

BACK TO MADĪNAH

Byzantium did not stir. When the Apostle ﷺ saw that there was no movement of troops by the enemy who seemed to have abandoned the border towns, he gave orders for the return march. The objective of the expedition having been

1 *Zād al-Maʿād,* vol. II, pp. 3–4; *Ibn Hishām,* vol. II p. 522.
2 *Ibn Hishām,* vol. II p. 522.
3 *Ibid.* p. 522.
4 *Ibid.* pp. 525–26.

achieved, the Prophet ﷺ did not consider it necessary to advance further into enemy territory to carry on hostilities. Only one Christian chieftain, Ukaydir ibn ʿAbd al-Malik, who was the ruler of Dūmat al-Jandal[1] and enjoyed the patronage of the Byzantines, was reported to be harbouring hostile designs. The Apostle sent Khālid ؓ with five hundred troops who captured Ukaydir and brought him to the Apostle. The Prophet, however, spared his life on the condition that he surrendered unconditionally and agreed to pay the poll-tax.[2]

After staying for a few nights in Tabūk, the Apostle returned to Madīnah.[3]

FUNERAL OF A POOR MUSLIM

ʿAbdullāh Dhū 'l-Bijādayn ؓ died at Tabūk. He had been very eager to accept Islam but his tribesmen had prevented him from converting. At last they turned him out with only one coarse sheet of cloth in which he repaired to call upon the Apostle ﷺ. By the time he came to the Apostle ﷺ the sheet of cloth had been torn into two pieces, one of which was used by him as a loincloth and the other he had wrapped over him. He was known as Dhū 'l-Bijādayn ؓ from the day he appeared before the Apostle ﷺ in that condition.

When he died at Tabūk the Apostle ﷺ took part in his burial along with Abū Bakr and ʿUmar ؓ. By the light of a torch that someone held aloft, a grave was dug for him and the Apostle ﷺ himself went down into it to lay him at rest. While Abū Bakr and ʿUmar let down the corpse of ʿAbdullāh Dhū 'l-Bijādayn ؓ, the Apostle ﷺ said to them, "Bring your brother nearer to me." After the Apostle ﷺ had arranged ʿAbdullāh ؓ in his niche, he said, "O God, I am pleased with him; be Thou pleased with him!" ʿAbdullāh ibn Masʿūd ؓ used to say thereafter, "Would that I had been the man in that grave."[4]

TRIAL OF KAʿB IBN MĀLIK

Among those Muslims who had stayed behind in the expedition of Tabūk, not because of any doubt or disaffection, were Kaʿb ibn Mālik, Murārah ibn ar-Rabīʿ and Hilāl ibn Umayyah ؓ. All of them had accepted Islam in the earlier stage

---

1 Dūmat al-Jandal was a populous town near Tabūk where the Arabs used to go to transact business in olden times. Dūma had been forsaken and was deserted when Ukaydir again developed the town and started olive plantations. The town thus regained its past importance. The place enclosed by a surrounding wall had a strong fort, which made it an important outpost at the northern border. The town was populated chiefly by the tribe of Kalb and Ukaydir was known as the king of the town. He professed Christianity.

2 *Ibn Hishām*, vol. II, p. 526.

3 Ibid. p. 527.

4 *Ibn Hishām*, vol. II, pp. 527–8.

of the Prophet's ﷺ mission and undergone hardships for the sake of their faith. Murārah ibn ar-Rabīʿ and Hilāl ibn Umayyah ﷺ had also taken part in the battle of Badr. In fact, none of them had ever been remiss in accompanying the Apostle ﷺ in the previous battles, and, therefore, their failure to do so in the expedition of Tabūk could have been brought about only by the Will of Providence which perhaps wanted to set another example of severe trial to test the strength of their faith for the benefit and example for the coming generations. They had been held back on this occasion partly on account of indolence and indecision and partly, because of their placing reliance on worldly means and objects, or, perhaps, they had not given thought to the urgency of the matter as it deserved. These are common human failings which have very often let down those who have been second to none in the sincerity of their faith in God and the love of His Apostle ﷺ. In fact, this is the moral so pointedly illustrated by these words of Kaʿb ibn Mālik ﷺ:

> Every day I would go out to get ready for the journey so that I might leave with them, but I would come back having done nothing. I would say to myself, 'I can do that whenever I want to', but continued procrastinating until the time for departure came and the Apostle of God ﷺ left with the Muslims. And I had still not made necessary preparations. I thought that I could go after a day or two and then catch up with them. I went to make the preparations after they had left but again returned without having done what was necessary. Day after day passed, until I became sluggish while the army had gone far ahead at full speed. I still thought of leaving Madīnah to overtake them and I wish that I had done so, but I did not.[1]

All the three Companions were called upon to prove, in a way unknown in the annals of any religion, the sincerity of their faith in God and their love for the Apostle ﷺ. It was undoubtedly, an excruciating trial of their loyalty to Islam, of their perseverance and tenacity, in times of ease as well as in difficulty, in cheer as well as in despondency.

There is also not the least doubt that all these true-spirited Companions spoke the truth when the hypocrites had offered excuses for justifying their absence from the expedition.

The incident as related in the traditions, on the authority of Kaʿb ibn Mālik ﷺ, continues with a narrative bespeaking his sincerity:

> Those who had stayed behind came and began to make excuses with oaths. There were about eighty of them and the Apostle ﷺ accepted their pleas, administered oaths to them and asked divine forgiveness for them, leaving what they had con-

1 Bukhārī: Kitāb al-Maghāzī.

cealed in their hearts to God. Then I came and saluted him and he smiled as one who is angry. He said, "Come nearer." I went and sat before him. Then he asked, "What had kept you back? Did you not purchase a mount?" I replied, "By God, it was exactly so. O Apostle of God, were I sitting with anyone else in the world I would have thought of offering some excuse for saving myself from his anger for I know how to argue and justify myself but, true to God, I know that if I were to satisfy you by telling a lie, God will soon make you angry with me. And if I displease you now by telling the truth, I have hopes that God will pardon me in the end. Honest to God, I have no excuse at all and I was never stronger and richer than when I stayed behind.

The hour of trial came at last. The Apostle ﷺ forbade everyone to speak to the three who had made a clean breast. Such were those Muslims, who knew nothing but to listen and obey the Apostle, that not even the members of their own families would address a word to these men. All the three felt forsaken and abandoned, as if they were alone in an alien country. They endured it for fifty nights. Murārah ibn ar-Rabīʿ and Hilāl ibn Umayyah shut themselves up in their houses, lamenting and shedding tears all the while. Kaʿb ibn Mālik was, however, young and sturdy. He would go out and join the prayers with others, roam about in the market, but nobody seemed willing to keep company or talk to him.

But the aloofness did not cause to increase the distance between them and the Apostle of God ﷺ. Nor was there any diminution in the loving regard that the Apostle ﷺ had for them. The admonition by the Apostle ﷺ rather gave rise to a still more acute longing in them to regain the affection of the Prophet ﷺ. The narration of Kaʿb ibn Mālik, which bears the savour of the plain truth, goes on to say:

And I would go to the Apostle ﷺ and salute him when he sat with others after the prayer, thinking whether his lips had moved in returning my salutation or not. Then I would pray near him and see him with half an eye. I marked that he fastened his eyes on me when I was busy in prayers but he turned away from me as soon as I tried to take a look at him.

The wide world seemed to have closed in on these men. Kaʿb ibn Mālik relates about the behaviour of one whom he considered to be his inseparable friend.

When the harshness of the people became unbearable, I scaled the wall of Abū Qatādah's orchard and went to him. He was my cousin and held dearest by me. I greeted him but, by God, he did not even return my salutation. I said: "O Abū

Qatādah, I adjure you by God, do you not know that I love God and His Apostle?" But he still kept quiet, so I repeated my question again. He remained silent for a while and then said: "God and His Apostle know best!" At that my eyes gave way to tears and I jumped back over the wall.[1]

The ordeal, however, did not come to a close at that. The ban was extended to their wives and the three were ordered to separate themselves from their wives, though without divorcing them. All of them obediently yielded to the command.

The faith and loyalty and firmness of Kaʿb ibn Mālik ﷺ was brought to a yet more delicate and crucial test when the king of Ghassān tried to angle him with a silver hook. He was the ruler of a kingdom that had exercised a deep influence upon the Arabs. The Arab nobles and chieftains vied with one another to enter the circle of his entourage, or even to be invited to attend his court, and eminent poets composed splendid eulogies in the honour of Ghassānid kings.[2] A Nabataean courier of the king contacted Kaʿb ibn Mālik ﷺ when the Apostle's ﷺ aloofness and the coolness of the people to him had become agonising enough to drive him mad. The courier delivered him a letter from the king in which he had written: "We have learnt that your master has treated you badly. God has not destined you to be humiliated and wasted, so come to us and we shall deal kindly with you."

Kaʿb ﷺ took the letter as a challenge to his integrity. His conscience smote him to the point of provoking his love for God and His Apostle ﷺ, and so he took the letter to an oven and burnt it.

Their test was over at last. None of the three was found wanting. Then came the revelation from God that illustrated their personal example to make it a general lesson, good for all times to come. They had demonstrated by their action that solace and refuge could not be found by fleeing from God, but rather only in coming back to Him. The spacious earth of God had become straitened for them; in their own souls they had a feeling of constraint, but they did not sway from the right path. Then it was that God forgave them and took them back into His grace. But a noteworthy feature of the verses revealed on this occasion was that the Most Gracious God did not make a mention of the repentance of these three persons lest they might feel singled out and humiliated. Their penitence was spoken of after mentioning the contrition of the Apostle ﷺ and other Mūhājirīn and Anṣār who had been ready and willing to take part in the expedition. The revelation goes to show that whatever sufferings and hardships they had endured had raised their degree in the spiritual world.

1 Bukhārī.

2 Ḥassān ibn Thābit and other poets have immortalized the Ghassānid kings through their glowing eulogies.

Allāh has turned in mercy to the Prophet, and to the Mūhājirīn and the Anṣār who followed him in the hour of hardship. After the hearts of a party of them had almost swerved aside, then turned He unto them in mercy. Lo! He is full of pity, merciful toward them. And to the three also (did He turn in mercy) who were left behind, when the earth, vast as it is, was straitened for them, and their own souls were straitened for them till they bethought them that there is no refuge from Allāh save toward Him. Then turned He unto them in mercy that they (too) might turn (repentant unto Him). Lo! Allāh! He is the Relenting, the Merciful.[1]

THE EXPEDITIONS AT A GLANCE

The expedition of Tabūk, which took place in the month of Rajab, 9 AH, was the last campaign during the lifetime of the Apostle ﷺ. The number of his battles was twenty-seven while he is reported to have sent out sixty forays and expeditions[2] although no fighting had taken place in many of them.

Never in the history of human conflict had any conqueror shed so little blood and been crowned with such a remarkable success. In all these battles only 1,018 persons,[3] Muslims as well as non-Muslims lost their lives. But it would be to attempt the impossible to hazard any guess as to how much blood of the ferocious Arabs was saved from being spilled or how many souls escaped degradation and debasement because of this minimal loss of human life. Such was the public tranquillity and orderliness resulting from the Apostle's ﷺ campaigns that a female pilgrim would go from Hīrah to Makkah and return after circumambulating the Kaʿbah without any fear in her heart, save the fear of God.[4] Another report says that the women from Qadissiyya "Went alone on their dromedaries for pilgrimage to Makkah without the least anxiety or fear."[5] This was the country in which, from the time immemorial, fights and forays, battles between nomadic tribes and raids on one another's flocks and property had been accepted unquestionably as a part of the desert life. Even the caravans of neighbouring powerful kingdoms dared not cross the country in pre-Islamic days without powerful escorts and guides.

The campaigns of the Apostle ﷺ were warranted by two universal truths enunciated in the Qur'ān. One of these says that "Persecution is worse than

1 Qur'ān 9: 117–18.

2 Estimate by Ibn al-Qayyim (*Zād al-Maʿād*).

3 Qādī Muḥammad Sulaymān Mansūrpūrī gives this figure after a detailed study in *Raḥmat li 'l-ʿĀlamīn*).

4 Bukhārī: ʿAlāmāt an-nubuwwah.

5 *Ibn Hishām*, vol. II, p. 581.

slaughter"[1] and the other declares that "There is life for you in retaliation, O men of understanding."[2] These twin principles, which refused to acquiesce in wrongdoing and urged to strive for the defence of honour and justice, soon established peace and order at the cost of little labour and time on the part of Muslims. This was achieved under the benevolent and altruistic guidance of the Apostle who was ever vigilant to secure the well-being and enlightenment of the enemy, instead of allowing the satisfaction of vindictive feelings to become the objective of his campaigns. Whenever the Apostle sent out any detachment on forays or brought battle to the enemy he invariably issued strict instructions to his men to be God-fearing and kind to the friends as well as foes. The directions he once gave to his troops were:

> I ask you to fear God and to be considerate to the Muslims with you. Fight in the Name of God and slay those in his Name who have disbelieved Him. Neither should you break your promise, nor pilfer the spoils, nor kill any child or woman or a man infirm and old or a priest who has withdrawn to seclusion. Never lay your hands on a date palm, nor chop down a tree, nor yet pull down any building.[3]

The success of these campaigns of the Apostle ﷺ can be judged from the fact that within a brief period of ten years more than a million square miles was won for Islam: the Islamic state expanded at an average rate of some 274 square miles daily at the cost of one martyr a month.[4] This respect for human life is unequalled in the annals of man. The truth of this assertion is amply borne out if the losses of these campaigns are placed by the side of casualties in the last two world wars, the first of which was fought from 1914 to 1918 and the second from 1939 to 1945. According to the *Encyclopedia Britannica* 6,400,000 persons lost their lives[5] in the first war and the number of casualties in the second ranged between 35 and 60 million.[6]

Yet, neither of these two blood stained wars can claim to have done any good to humanity nor did they solve any of the world's problems.

The ecclesiastical tribunal known as the Inquisition established by the Roman Catholic Church in the Middle Ages for the trial and punishment of heretics is reported to have taken a toll of 12 million lives.[7]

---

1 Qur'ān 2: 119.

2 Qur'ān 2: 179.

3 Wāqidī, on the authority Zayd ibn Arqam in connection with the expedition of Mu'tah.

4 Brig. Gulzār Aḥmad, *The Battles of the Prophet of Allāh,* Karachi, (1975), p. 28.

5 *Encyclopedia Britannica* (1974) vol. 19, p. 966.

6 Ibid, p. 1013.

7 John Devenport: Apology for Mohammad and the Qur'an.

THE FIRST HAJJ

The pilgrimage was enjoined in the year 9 AH.[1] The Apostle ﷺ sent Abū Bakr ﷺ in command of the pilgrims. The polytheists were, during the year, at their pilgrimage stations.[2] Abū Bakr ﷺ led a party of three hundred Muslim pilgrims from Mādinah.

The opening verses of *Sūrah at-Tawbah*[3] were revealed after the pilgrims had left for Makkah. The Apostle ﷺ sent for ʿAlī ﷺ and charged him to proclaim the verses at Minā when all the pilgrims had assembled there after performing the sacrifice. It signified the end of idolatry in Arabia for no idolater was allowed to perform the *ḥajj* or to go round the Kaʿbah in a nude state after that year. The divine revelation also laid down that if the Apostle ﷺ was obliged to fulfil any obligation under a treaty with the polytheists it would be discharged up to a stipulated period after which the compact would be considered dissolved.

ʿAlī ﷺ went forth on the Apostle's ﷺ camel and overtook Abū Bakr ﷺ en route, who asked ʿAlī if he had come to give orders to him or convey them. ʿAlī ﷺ replied that he had only been charged to convey orders to him. Thereafter both went on to Makkah where Abū Bakr ﷺ managed the arrangements for *ḥajj*. When the day of sacrifice came, ʿAlī ﷺ proclaimed what the Apostle ﷺ had ordered.[4]

1 There are some scholars who hold the view that the command of *ḥajj* was received in the 6 AH. Shaykh Muḥammad al-Khuḍarī takes this view in the *Tarīkh at-Tashrīʿ al-Islāmī* (p. 52).

2 *Ibn Hishām*, vol. II, p. 543.

3 Qur'ān 9 ff.

4 *Ibn Hishām*, vol. II, pp. 543–46.

22

The Year of Deputations

Arrival of Deputations in Madīnah

Allāh first caused the Apostle of God ﷺ to prevail over Makkah, thereafter he returned from the expedition of Tabūk with flying colours. Prior to that, he had sent letters to the rulers within the country and to the kings and emperors of neighbouring lands, inviting them to accept Islam; these were received by some with the greatest of honour, who sent back courteous replies; others were astounded or indifferent and yet others were irreverent and insolent. Before long, God requited the arrogant suzerains by taking their lives or kingdoms, or both, and all these happenings were spoken of all over Arabia.

Makkah had been the spiritual and religious centre of Arabia. The submission of the Quraysh nobles to Islam was of the greatest importance for the whole of Arabia. The airy dreams of those who had counted on the Quraysh to bring Islam to its knees had fizzled out while those who were in two minds, marking time to see the result of the struggle between the Muslims and the Quraysh, found the obstacle to their acceptance of Islam removed. The noted Indian scholar of traditions, Muḥammad Ṭāhir Patnī (d. 986/1578) writes in the *Majmaʿ Bihār al-Anwār*:

> This was the Year of Deputations. As the Quraysh were their religious leaders and guardians of the House of God, the Arab tribes had adopted a policy to watch and wait in regard to Islam. When the Quraysh bowed their heads to Islam, Makkah was captured and Thaqīf also accepted Islam, they, too, realised that it would not be possible for them to resist the power of Islam. Then deputations began to

arrive in Madīnah from all over Arabia and the people entered the faith of God in legions.[1]

It was only natural that the events, stated earlier, had a deep effect on the Arabs and prepared them to accept Islam. Representative parties of the Arab tribes came to the Apostle to accept Islam in such a succession like the beads of a broken rosary falling one by one.

These deputations returned to their homes charged with a new spirit of faith to call their brethren to Islam and to efface all traces of paganism in their tribes.

One such deputation came from the large tribe of Banū Tamīm with a number of its orators and poets and challenged the Muslims to a contest in oratory and poetry. The contest ended in establishing the superiority of Islam and its adherents. The chiefs and nobles of Banū Tamīm ﷺ acknowledged the superiority of the Muslim orators and poets, accepted Islam and left for their homes with valuable gifts that the Apostle ﷺ presented them with.[2]

The deputation of Banū ʿĀmir also came to Madīnah. Banū Saʿd ibn Bakr sent Ḍimām ibn Thaʿlabah ﷺ as their representative to the Apostle ﷺ. He accepted Islam and went back to his tribe determined to invite them to his faith. When his tribesmen gathered round him, the first thing he said to them was, "Woe be to al-Lāt and al-Uzzā!" "Heavens forbid! Ḍimām", they said. "Beware of leprosy, elephantiasis and madness!" Ḍimām replied, "Confound you! By God, they can neither hurt nor heal. God has sent an Apostle ﷺ and given a Book to him, and delivered you thereby from your present state. I bear witness that there is no god but one God who is without any associate and that Muḥammad is His slave and Apostle. I have brought you what he has commanded you to do and what he has forbidden you." And by the time the evening was over there was not a man or woman in his tribe who had not entered the fold of Islam.[3]

The deputation of Banū Ḥanīfah came to the Apostle ﷺ. With it came Musaylamah, the arch-liar. He accepted Islam but later turned apostate and made a claim to apostleship. He was killed fighting with the Muslims.

The reputation of Banū Ṭayy also came to Madīnah bringing with them their chief and gallant cavalier, Zayd al-Khayl. The Apostle of God ﷺ changed his name to Zayd al-Khayr ﷺ[4] and he proved himself to be a staunch Muslim strong in faith.

1 *Majmaʿ Bihār al-Anwār*, vol. V, p. 272.

2 *Ibn Hishām,* vol. II, pp. 560–68.

3 *Ibn Hishām*, vol. II, p. 526.

4 Zayd al-Khayl means Zayd of the horses and Zayd al-Khayr, Zayd of goodness. The Apostle preferred good and meaningful names.

ʿAdī, the son of Ḥātim, whose name has long been known for generosity, called upon the Apostle ﷺ. Impressed by the courteous bearing and considerateness of the Apostle ﷺ, ʿAdī ﷺ accepted Islam and said, "By God, this is not the way kings behave."

The delegation of Banū Zubayd also came to the Apostle ﷺ. It was led by ʿAmr ibn Maʿdīkarib, the noted warrior of Arabia. Al-Ashʿath ibn Qays came with the deputation of another tribe, Kindah. Then came the deputation from Azd and the envoys of the king of Ḥimyār, who brought a letter to the Apostle ﷺ informing him of the acceptance of Islam of their tribes.

The Apostle ﷺ sent Muʿādh ibn Jabal and Abū Mūsā ﷺ to invite the people of Yemen to Islam. He also instructed them: "Make things easy and do not make them difficult. Cheer up (the people) and do not scare (them)."[1]

Farwah ibn ʿAmr al-Judhāmī ﷺ was the governor of Maʿān and surrounding lands in Syria on behalf of the Byzantines. He sent an envoy to the Apostle ﷺ informing him of his acceptance of Islam.

Banū al-Ḥārith ibn Kaʿb ﷺ living in the territory known as Najrān were converted to Islam by Khālid ibn al-Walīd ﷺ, who stayed with the tribe and instructed them in the teachings of Islam. Khālid ibn al-Walīd ﷺ came back to the Apostle ﷺ with the representatives of Banū al-Ḥārith. When these men returned to their tribe the Apostle ﷺ sent ʿAmr ibn Ḥazm ﷺ to instruct them in religion and to teach them the *Sunnah* and the rituals of Islam as well as to collect the poor-tax from them. Another deputation from Hamdān called upon the Apostle of God ﷺ.[2]

The Apostle ﷺ sent Mughīrah ibn Shuʿbah ﷺ to break the idol al-Lāt. Mughīrah and his friends ﷺ broke the idol into pieces and then razed to the ground the boundary-wall enclosing it. They returned the same day after accomplishing the task assigned to them and the Apostle ﷺ praised them for it.[3]

The Apostle ﷺ welcomed the deputation of ʿAbd al-Qays when it came to him but he also forbade them the glazed jars used for brewing intoxicants. He took this precaution since ʿAbd al-Qays were given to drinking liquors.[4]

Ashʿariyyīn and the people of Yemen came to Madīnah singing verses which expressed their eagerness to meet the Apostle ﷺ.

Tomorrow we shall meet our soul mates,
  Muḥammad and his comrades.

---

1 Bukhārī: Kitāb al-Maghāzī.

2 *Ibn Hishām*, vol. II, pp. 575–96.

3 *Ibn Kathīr*, vol. IV, pp. 62–63.

4 *Zād al-Maʿād* vol. II p. 28; *Bukhārī* and *Muslim*, on the authority of ʿAbbās.

When the Apostle ﷺ saw them he remarked: "The people of Yemen have come to you. They have the tenderest minds and the gentlest hearts. Faith belongs to Yemen and wisdom belongs to Yemen."[1]

The Apostle ﷺ had sent Khālid ibn al-Walīd ؓ with a party to invite the people of Yemen to Islam. He stayed there for six months, preaching the faith to them, but none accepted his summons. Thereafter ʿAlī ؓ who was assigned the task went there and read out the Apostle's ﷺ letter to the people of Hamdān. The entire tribe entered the fold of Islam and ʿAlī ؓ communicated the news to the Apostle ﷺ. He prostrated before God in thanksgiving and then raising his head from the dust, said, "Peace be upon Hamdān. Peace be upon Hamdān."[2]

A delegation of 400 men paid a visit to the Apostle ﷺ from the tribe of Muzaynah. Another deputation from the Christians of Najrān called upon the Apostle ﷺ. There came 60 people riding the mules, 24 of whom were chiefs and ecclesiastics including Abū Ḥārithah, the great scholar of their religion. The kings of Byzantium honoured him because of his extensive knowledge, gave him stipends and built churches for him. A number of Qur'ānic verses concerning these people were sent down by God on this occasion.[3]

The delegation from Najrān had come to see the Apostle ﷺ after he had sent a letter inviting them to Islam. They asked the Apostle ﷺ a number of questions and God answered them in the verses included in *Sūrah Āl ʿImrān*.[4] The Apostle of God ﷺ proposed a *mubāhalah*[5] that is, a solemn meeting in which both sides were to summon not only their men, but also their women, and children, and to earnestly pray to God invoking His curse on the party that belied His revelations. The Christians, being afraid to accept the challenge of the Apostle ﷺ, declined. They presented themselves to the Apostle ﷺ on the following day and asked that the protection of the Islamic State be granted to them in return for a tribute. The Apostle ﷺ gave them a document specifying the tribute and sent Abū ʿUbaydah ibn al-Jarrāḥ ؓ with them. The Apostle ﷺ also said, "He is the trustee of these people."[6]

The Apostle of God ﷺ felt happy on the arrival of a deputation from Tujīb. They asked questions about a number of things and the Apostle ﷺ had the answers to their questions written down for them. Then they asked to be told

---

1 *Bukhārī*—in another version "and understanding of faith" also occurs after the word "wisdom."

2 *Zād al-Maʿād* vol. II, p. 33.

3 Ibid, pp. 35–36.

4 Verses 1–34 in the 3rd chapter of the Qur'ān.

5 *See* verse 3:61 of the Qur'ān and its commentaries.

6 *Ibn Kathīr*, vol. IV, p. 100; see also *Bukhārī*.

more about the Qur'ān and the *Sunnah* which caused the Apostle ﷺ to have a liking for them. He instructed Bilāl ؓ to entertain them well. However, they stayed but for a few days with the Apostle ﷺ and expressed the desire to return to their homes. When asked why they wanted to depart so soon, they replied, "We want to go back to tell our people how we met the Messenger of God ﷺ, what talks we have had with him and what replies he gave to our questions." Thereafter they returned and again called upon the Apostle ﷺ during the pilgrimage in 10 A. H. when the Prophet ﷺ was at Minā.[1]

Deputations also called upon the Apostle ﷺ from Banū Fazāra, Banū Asad, Bahrā' and ʿUdhrah, and all of them ؓ accepted Islam. The Apostle ﷺ promised them the capture of Syria. However he forbade them to have recourse to oracles for divination of the future and commanded them to cease offering the sacrifices they had been doing hitherto. He also told them that only the sacrifice on the occasion of ʿĪd al-Aḍḥā was lawful for them. When the delegations of Balī, Dhī Murrah and Khawlān called upon the Apostle ﷺ, he asked them about the idol of Khawlān[2] to which they had been paying divine honours. They said, "God bless you! God has replaced it by what has been brought by you. There are however a few elderly persons and senile women who are devoted to it but we will break it when we return."[3] Deputations also came to the Apostle ﷺ from Muḥarib, Ghassān, Ghāmid and Nakhaʿ.[4] The envoys of Arab tribes coming to Madīnah learnt about Islam and its institutions, watched the graceful and genial behaviour of the Apostle ﷺ and benefited from the company of Apostle's ﷺ Companions. Tents were often pitched for them in the courtyard of the Prophet's ﷺ mosque where they saw the Muslims offering prayers and reciting the Qur'ān. They spoke plainly and frankly, asked whatever they wanted while the Apostle ﷺ answered their questions in all soberness, explained the wisdom of Islam and quoted the scripture to them which imparted in them certitude and peace of heart.

THE APOSTLE'S CONVERSATION WITH A PAGAN

Perhaps the most remarkable feature of the Arab character was their lack of inhibition, a frankness to the point of being blunt and rugged. The conversation a pagan chief Kinānah ibn ʿAbd Yālīl ؓ had with the Apostle of God ﷺ illus-

1 *Zād al-Maʿād*. vol. II, p. 43.
2 Ibid., pp. 44–47.
3 Ibid., p. 47.
4 Ibid. pp. 47–55.

trates the brusqueness of the sons of the desert. Kinānah said, "As for adultery, we mostly remain bachelors or cannot get married[1] so we have to indulge in it."

The Apostle ﷺ replied, "That is unlawful for you. God has commanded: And come not near unto adultery. Lo! It is an abomination and an evil way.[2]

Kinānah said again, "What you say about usury means that our entire property is nothing but usury."

"You have a right," replied the Apostle ﷺ, "to get back the original sum that you lent for God has ordered: O you who believe! Observe your duty to Allāh, and give up what remains (due to you) from usury, if you are (truly) believers."[3]

"As regards wine," Kinānah said further, "it is the juice of our lands and a must for us."

"Allāh has forbidden it," replied the Apostle ﷺ and then recited the verse, "O you who believe! Strong drink, games of chance, idols and divining arrows are only an infamy of Satan's handiwork. Leave it aside in order that you may succeed."[4]

Kinānah again asked, "And what do you say about the idol Rabbah?"

"Break it," answered the Apostle ﷺ.

Kinānah and his companions were taken aback. They protested, "If Rabbah were to know that you want to break her, she would finish off all her priests!"

ʿUmar ﷺ now intervened to say, "O ʿAbd Yālīl, woe to you! How ignorant are you? What else is Rabbah except a stone?"

Kinānah and his friends replied angrily, "Ibn al-Khaṭṭāb, we have not come to ask you." Then turning to the Apostle ﷺ he said, "You may break it, but we cannot."

The Apostle ﷺ then said to them, "I will send someone with you who will do it for you."

The deputation then took its leave of the Apostle ﷺ who bade them farewell. Before leaving for their homes they asked the Prophet ﷺ to appoint a leader for them. The Apostle ﷺ selected ʿUthmān ibn Abī 'l-ʿĀṣ ﷺ to act as their leader. He was the youngest among them but the Apostle ﷺ had noticed his keen interest in religion and he had also learnt some of the Qur'ān before leaving Madīnah.[5]

Thus the year of deputations was a year in which idolatry was once and for all purged from the Arabian Peninsula.

---

1 Kinānah perhaps meant that they could not get married as they were mostly out with commercial caravans.

2 Qur'ān 17:32.

3 Qur'ān 2:278.

4 Qur'ān 5:90.

5 *Zād al-Maʿād*, vol. II, p. 25.

COMMANDMENT FOR ZAKĀT AND CHARITY

The divine commandment making it incumbent upon the Muslims to pay *zakāt* i.e. a tax at a fixed rate in proportion to the worth of the property, was revealed in the ninth year of the *Hijrah.*[1] The Apostle ﷺ sent the order for collection of *zakāt* to all the functionaries appointed in the areas where the people had accepted Islam.

---

1 *Tarīkh aṭ-Ṭabarī,* vol. IV, p. 724.

23

The Farewell Pilgrimage

Everything had come about as willed by Heaven. The faith in One God had cleansed and illuminated the souls. The devil within had been cast away along with the vileness of the pagan past, and the false deities had been turned out of the House of God. Once again the believers were smitten with the love of God and their hearts were set on going round the holy sanctuary for it was long since they had been there. The mission of the Apostle of God ﷺ was also nearing completion. He was soon to bid farewell to his loving Companions. And so Allāh permitted His Messenger ﷺ to take them on pilgrimage. It was the first *ḥajj* of the Prophet ﷺ in Islam.

EDUCATIVE APOSTLE OF THE PILGRIMAGE

There were several reasons for the Apostle's ﷺ setting out from Madīnah for the pilgrimage: he had to meet the Muslims coming from far and near; to teach them the observances of faith and the rituals of *ḥajj;* to bear witness to the truth and thus finally redeem his pledge to God; to advise them as well as to give them final instructions; to charge them with an oath to follow his teachings, and to trample under his feet the last vestiges of the pagan past. His pilgrimage was, in truth and reality, better than a thousand sermons and lessons. It was an itinerant school, a mosque on the move, or a peripatetic training centre which imparted knowledge to the unenlightened, animated the slothful and indolent souls and invested the weak in spirit with the power of faith. All this was achieved under the benevolent and affectionate care of the greatest teacher, the Apostle of God ﷺ.

UNIQUE RECORD OF THE FAREWELL PILGRIMAGE

The minute details of the Prophet's ﷺ journey have been preserved by the most trustworthy narrators, the Companions of the Prophet ﷺ. It is a record so authentic and detailed, and there has never existed a historical document of comparable genuineness, either of an Emperor's itinerary or of the memoirs of any saint or scholar.[1]

A SYNOPSIS OF THE FAREWELL PILGRIMAGE

We provide here a brief outline of this journey undertaken by the Apostle ﷺ which is variously known as *Ḥajjat al-Wadāʿ*,[2] *Hajjat al-Balāgh*[3] and *Hajjat al-Tamām*,[4] but actually it was all of these and much more than to give it a single name. More than a hundred thousand Companions went along with the Apostle of God ﷺ to perform the pilgrimage.[5]

HOW THE PILGRIMAGE WAS PERFORMED

When the Apostle ﷺ decided to go on pilgrimage he had a public announcement made and the people started making preparations for the journey.

Large numbers came to Madīnah as the news spread, and even larger throngs joined the Apostle ﷺ on the way, until there were more people than one could tell. The teeming crowd of the faithful around the Apostle ﷺ extended as far as the eye could see in every direction. The Apostle ﷺ set out from Madīnah on Saturday, the 25th of Dhū 'l-Qaʿdah, after performing the four *rakʿāt*[6] of *ẓuhr*[7] prayer followed by a sermon in which he explained the essentials of putting on the *iḥrām*.[8]

The Messenger of God ﷺ then went ahead raising his voice in praise of God:

---

1 For details see *Ḥajjat al-Wadāʿ wa ʿUmrāt an-Nabī* by Sheikh al-Ḥadīth Mawlānā Muḥammad Zakariyyah and the introduction to the book by the writer.

2 Lit. farewell pilgrimage.

3 Lit. instructive pilgrimage.

4 Lit. completive or perfected pilgrimage.

5 It is variously reported as being one hundred and fourteen thousand and one hundred and thirty thousand. We will be relying on the abridged version of *Zād al-Maʿād*, by Ibn Qayyim al-Jawzīyyah (d. 751 AH) to relate the happenings of the farewell pilgrimage.

6 A section of the Islamic prayer consisting of recitation of the Qur'ān in the standing position, to bow and two prostrations. A prayer may consist of two or more *rakʿāt* (plural).

7 The time for the prayer performed when the sun has begun to decline from its zenith.

8 Lit. "prohibiting." The pilgrim's dress consisting of two white cotton sheets, one of which is thrown over the back, exposing the arm and the shoulder, while the other is wrapped round the loins from the waist to the knee and tucked in at the middle.

"At Your service, O God, at Your service. You have no partner. At Your service. Praise and Grace are Yours and the Dominion. You have no partner." The entire crowd chanted the *talbiyyah*[1] along with the Apostle ﷺ; some curtailed a few words while others supplemented it with a few more in a tremor of excitement; but the Apostle ﷺ did not admonish them. He kept on repeating the praise of God until he reached ʿAraj where he encamped. Abū Bakr ؓ and the Apostle ﷺ rode on the same dromedary.

The stages in the journey ahead were at al-Abwāʾ, the wādī of ʿAsfān, Sarif and then Dhī Ṭuwā where he stayed during the Saturday night. It was now the 4th of Dhū 'l-Ḥijjah. The Apostle ﷺ performed the morning prayer at this place and also took a bath. The caravan now bent its way towards Makkah and entered the valley from its heights. It was an hour or so before noon when his glance fell on the Kaʿbah. He exclaimed: "O God, increase the honour and estimation and deference and awe for Your House." And then lifting up his hands he raised his voice to say: "God is Great." Then he said: "O God, You are the source of all Peace, Peace is from You. Cause us to live in peace, O Lord."

The first thing he did on entering the sanctuary was to go straight to the Kaʿbah. He kissed the sacred Black Stone set in the south-east corner, and then moved on to circumambulate the Kaʿbah seven times, commencing to the right and with the Kaʿbah to his left. He made seven circuits, three at a quick step and then four at a slow pace.[2]

The Apostle ﷺ was walking at a quicker step but the paces were not long. The seamless garment in which he had wrapped himself was thrown loosely over one shoulder, the other being left bare. Each time he passed the Black Stone he touched it with a stick in his hand and kissed it. Thereafter he took to the Station of Ibrāhīm and recited the Qur'ānic verses: "Take as your place of worship the place where Ibrāhīm stood (to pray),[3] and performed two *rakʿāt* of prayer. Going to the Black Stone after the prayer, he kissed it again and then he went to Aṣ-Ṣafā from the opposite door. On reaching near Aṣ-Ṣafā the Apostle ﷺ said: "Lo! Aṣ-Ṣafā and al-Marwah are among the signs of Allāh.[4] I begin with what Allāh began with." So he mounted it until he could see the House of God, declared God's Oneness and proclaimed His greatness facing the *qiblah*. He said: "There is no god but God alone who has no partner. To Him belongs the dominion. To

1 Lit. "waiting or standing for orders." It stands for the words, given here, recited during the pilgrimage to Makkah, declaring one's readiness to be present for the service of God.

2 The act of circumambulating the Kaʿbah is known as *tawāf*, the first three quick steps are known as *ramal*.

3 Qur'ān 2:125.

4 Qur'ān 2:158.

Him praise is due. He is omnipotent. There is no god but God, Who alone has fulfilled His promise, helped His servant and alone routed the confederates."

The Apostle ﷺ remained in Makkah from Saturday to Wednesday. On Thursday morning he went to Minā along with the Muslims, performed the *ẓuhr* and *ʿaṣr*[1] prayers and stayed there for the night. It was the night before Friday. After the sun had risen he made for ʿArafāt where he saw the tent set up for him at Namirah. God's Messenger ﷺ rested in the tent and when the sun had passed the meridian he ordered Qaṣwāʾ to be brought. When it was saddled for him he went down into the valley and addressed the people wherein he explained to them the fundamental principles of Islam and struck at the roots of polytheism and ignorance. He commanded the people to treat as inviolable and sacrosanct the life, honour and property of every man as warranted by all the religions—and declared that all the usages and customs of the pagan past were trampled under his feet. The Apostle ﷺ abolished the usury of the pre-Islamic days, although he allowed recovery of the original sums lent to the debtors. The Apostle ﷺ dwelt in his sermon on the rights of women, threw light on the mutual obligations of the husband and wife and bade the people to deal kindly and provide food and clothing to their spouses in a fitting manner. Thereafter, referring to the Book of God, he told his Companions that if they held fast to it they would never fall into error. Finally, he told them that on the Day of Judgment God would ask them about him, so what answer would they give on that Day. The entire congregation replied, as one man, that they would testify that he had conveyed the message and fulfilled his mission.

Then, raising his finger towards the sky the Apostle ﷺ said, "O God, be a witness," repeating it thrice. He also asked those present to inform all those who were absent about it.

The sermon ended, and the Apostle ﷺ asked Bilāl ﷺ to give the call to prayer. After the call was over, he performed the noon and afternoon prayers, performing only two *rakʿāt* for each. The day he delivered this sermon was Friday.

The Apostle then mounted his camel and came to Mawqif,[2] the place of standing, where he remained on the back of his camel till sunset, lamenting and beseeching and glorifying the Lord. He appeared to be tormented and disconsolate, repeatedly raising his hands in prayer to his chest, like a man bereaved and indigent, crying for his livelihood. He was heard saying:

> O God, You hear what I say and see where I am and know what I conceal or reveal. Nothing can remain hidden from You. I am discontented, exhausted and distressed, seeking refuge with You as one sorrow-stricken and horrified. I acknowl-

---

1 The time for the prayer performed midway between noon and sunset.

2 A place in ʿArafāt still known by that name.

> edge my sins and confess my faults. I call as a beggar upon You and cry as an abased sinner unto You! I beseech You as one who is troubled and humbled, falling prone before You, shedding tears as one who has thrown himself at Your feet and bitten the dust. O God, cause me not to be misfortunate in my supplication to You. Be Kind and Merciful unto me. Lo! Thou art the Best of all those who are implored and the Most Generous of all who bestow.[1]

It was then that God sent down the revelation: "This day have I perfected your religion for you and completed My favour unto you, and have chosen for you Islam as your religion."[2] When the disc of the sun had disappeared, the Apostle ﷺ took Usāmah ibn Zayd ﵁ up behind him and wended ahead slowly, holding the halter of his camel in a way that his head, lowered in submission to God, almost touched the saddle. The Apostle ﷺ was repeating the *talbiyyah*: "At Thy Service, O God, at Thy Service." And asking the people to proceed slowly and gently he kept raising his voice in *talbiyyah* until he came to Muzdalifah. There he ordered Bilāl ﵁ to give the call to prayer and performed the sunset prayer before the camels were knelt down and unloaded. He recited the night prayer after the camels were unburdened and then went to take rest and slept till dawn.

Having performed the dawn prayer early in the morning, the Apostle ﷺ mounted Qaṣwā' and came to Mashʿar al-Ḥarām, the sacred site in Muzdalifah, where he faced the *qiblah,* supplicated to God and declared His Greatness until the morning light was clear. Thus he glorified God before the sun had risen. Then he left Muzdalifah with Faḍl ibn ʿAbbās ﵁ up behind him on the back of his camel, chanting the *talbiyyah* all the way. He asked Ibn ʿAbbās ﵁ to pick up seven small pebbles for *ramī jimār.*[3] When he came to the middle of the valley of Muḥassar, he urged his camel to go fast and passed the plain quickly for it was the place where punishment was inflicted upon the army, of Abrahah. The Apostle ﷺ came to Minā and from there to the *jamrat al-ʿAqabah*[4] There he cast the pebbles after the sun had well risen and ended it with the recitation of *talbiyyah.*

Returning to Minā the Apostle ﷺ delivered a glowing address in which he dwelt upon the sacredness of *yawm an-Naḥr*[5] and the significance God has assigned to the day. He elucidated the honour and distinction that God had conferred on Makkah over all the cities of the world and called upon the people to follow whoever guided them in accordance with the Book of God. Then,

---

1 *Kanz al-ʿUmmāl,* on the authority of Ibn ʿAbbās

2 Qurʿan 5:3.

3 Throwing of the pebbles at the pillars or *jamrah* in Minā, which mark the spots where the Devil appeared to Ibrāhīm and Ismāʿīl.

4 There are three pillars, *Ūlā,* the first, *Wusṭā* the middle and *ʿAqabah* the last.

5 The Day of Sacrifice, the tenth day of Dhū 'l-Ḥijjah.

asking the people present there to learn the rites of pilgrimage from him, the Apostle ﷺ urged them not to revert to the ways of the infidels, spilling blood and tribal warfare after him. He asked those present to convey everything he had told them to those who were absent. Then, he said:

> Worship your Lord, offer prayers five times a day, observe fast for a month (in Ramaḍān), obey those of you who are in authority and you shall enter the paradise of your Lord.

The Apostle ﷺ also said something to his Companions on this occasion which alluded to his farewell and hence the pilgrimage came to be known as the *Ḥajjat al-Wadāʿ*.

The Apostle ﷺ then went to the place of sacrifice in Minā and sacrificed sixty-three camels with his own hand—the number of sacrificial camels being the same as the years he remained alive. He ordered ʿAlī ؓ to sacrifice the remainder to make up a total of one hundred camels sacrificed on his behalf. The sacrifice having been completed, he sent for the barber, had his head shaved and distributed his shaved hair among the people. Then returned to Makkah on his mount and went round the Kaʿbah again. After that he came near the well of Zamzam and drank its water without sitting down, and returned to Minā on the same day. He spent the night at Minā where he stayed until the sun had passed the meridian. Then he went to stone the *jamrah* and starting from the first one he went on to throw pebbles on the middle *jamrah* and finally on the last one. The Apostle ﷺ delivered two sermons at Minā, one on the Day of Sacrifice which has been mentioned earlier and the next one the day after.

The Apostle ﷺ remained at the place to perform the stoning at the *jamrah* on the three days after the Day of Sacrifice, known as *Ayyām tashrīq*.[1] Then he left for Makkah. First he circumambulated the House of God at dawn and then after taking farewell of the House asked his Companions to get ready to depart. Thereafter he set forth for Madīnah.[2]

Having arrived at Ghadīr Khum,[3] the Apostle addressed the people again and said:

> Whoever loves me should love ʿAlī also. O God, hold him dear who is attached to ʿAlī and be hostile to him who bears ill-will to ʿAlī.[4]

---

1 *Ayyām tashrīq* comprise five days, i.e. from the 9th to the 13th of Dhū 'l-Ḥijjah.

2 The account of Farewell Pilgrimage given here has been summarised from the detailed description given in the *Zād al-Maʿād* (vol. I, pp. 180–249). The matter pertaining to the legal aspect of the pilgrimage has been left out however.

3 A place midway between Makkah and Madīnah, about three km from Juḥfa.

4 On the authority of Aḥmad and Nasā'ī. The reason for what the Apostle ﷺ said on this occasion

The Apostle ﷺ stopped for the night at Dhū 'l-Ḥulayfah. When the outskirt of Madīnah came in sight he raised his voice to say, "God is Great", three times and then said, "There is no god but God. He is One, without any partner. To Him belongs the dominion and the praise and He has power over all things. We are the returning and the repenting and the submitting and the worshipping. God has fulfilled His promise and helped His bondman and alone routed the confederates."[1]

The Apostle ﷺ entered Madīnah in broad daylight.

THE ADDRESSES OF THE APOSTLE

The sermons delivered by the Apostle ﷺ on the Day of Sacrifice and on the second day of *Tashrīq* are given here, as both are fitting and eloquent as well as being vitally instructive.

> Your blood and your property are inviolable like the sacredness of this day in this month in this city of yours. Lo! Everything pertaining to the days of paganism is unlawful, and claims of blood-vengeance belonging to the pre-Islamic period have been abolished. The first claim on blood I remit is that of Ibn Rabīʿah ibn al-Ḥārith who was suckled among the Banū Saʿd and killed by Hudhayl.
>
> The usury of the days of ignorance is abolished, and the first of our usury I abolish is that of my own uncle, ʿAbbās ibn ʿAbd al-Muṭṭalib, for it is all abolished.
>
> Fear Allāh concerning women. Verily, you have taken them under God's security and have made their persons lawful unto you by God's word. It is incumbent upon them that they must not bring into your houses anyone whom you dislike, but if they do that then you have authority to chastise them, yet not severely. You are responsible for providing them with their food and clothing in a fitting manner.
>
> I have left among you something, by which, if you hold to it, you will never go astray. What is that? It is the Book of God!
>
> And you will be asked by God about me so what will you say?

The Companions replied with one voice, "We testify that you have conveyed the message and fulfilled your mission." The Apostle ﷺ then raised his forefinger towards the sky and said thrice, "O God, be a witness."[2]

The text of the other sermon, delivered by the Apostle ﷺ, on the second

---

was that certain persons who were displeased with ʿAlī had made a complaint against him to the Prophet ﷺ. These persons had been with ʿAlī in Yemen and suspected him of being unjust in some his decisions although their complaint was unfounded and based on a misunderstanding (*Ibn Kathīr,* vol. 4, pp. 415–16)

1 *Zād al-Maʿād* vol. p. 249.

2 *Muslim, Abū Dāwūd* and other books of traditions, on the authority of Jābir ibn ʿAbdullāh.

day of *Tashriq,* is as follows: O people, do you know in which city you are, what month and what day this is?" The Apostle ﷺ asked his audience. They replied, "This is the sacred month, the day has a great sanctity and the city is the holy city." Resuming his address the Apostle ﷺ said:

> Like this day, this month and this city, your lives and your property and your honour shall remain sacred to the Day of Resurrection. Behold! Take it from me so that you may live and be prosperous. Beware! Do no wrong. Beware! Do no wrong. Beware! Do no wrong. It is not lawful for you to take anything from the property of a Muslim save by his consent. Every claim of blood vengeance and blood money that was due in the days of ignorance is now abolished till the Day of Judgment. And the first claim of blood-vengeance that I remit is that of Rabīʿah ibn al-Ḥārith ibn ʿAbd al-Muṭṭalib who was suckled among Ibn Layth and killed by Hudhayl. The usury of the pagan past is abolished and God has commanded that the first one to be abolished is that of ʿAbbās ibn ʿAbd al-Muṭṭalib
>
> Time has completed the cycle to reach the same point when God created the heavens and the earth.

Thereafter he recited the Qur'ānic verse:

> Lo! The number of months with Allāh is twelve months, by Allāh's ordinance in the day that He created the heavens and the earth. Four of them are sacred—that is the true religion. So wrong not yourselves in them.[1]
>
> Behold! Do not become infidels after me, beheading one another. The Devil has despaired of ever being worshipped by those who pray, but he will create dissension among you. Fear Allāh concerning women. You have claims on your womenfolk and they on you. They are saddled with the obligation not to bring in anyone whom you dislike, but if you suspect that they are disobedient, instruct and withdraw from them and chastise them but lightly. You are obliged to provide them with food and clothing in a befitting manner for they are your spouses under God's security, and have a right to their person by God's word.
>
> Behold! Whoever holds anything in trust should return it to the person who trusted him with it.

The Apostle ﷺ then asked. "Have I delivered the message? Have I delivered the message? Thereafter he said, "Let him who is present convey it to him who is absent, for many a one to whom a message is conveyed can better commit it to his memory."[2]

1 Qur'ān 9:36
2 *Aḥmad* on the authority of Abū Ḥurrah ar-Raqāshī.

24
The Eternal Rest

Completion of the Apostle's ﷺ Mission

After the religion brought by the Apostle ﷺ had been made perfect and complete, God sent down the revelation: "This day have I perfected your religion for you and completed My favour unto you, and have chosen for you Islam as your religion."[1]

The Apostle of God ﷺ had delivered the message truthfully. He had spared no pains nor was he shaken by any hardship or sacrifice. He had brought up people who could be trusted to live up to the spiritual heritage of the prophets of God, who could shoulder the grave responsibility of the prophets without being invested with the mantle of apostleship. These were the people who were charged with the responsibility of carrying the banner of Faith and Truth and to guard the message of God against every interpolation and distortion. That they were capable of the obligation laid on them had even been vouched by God.

> You are the best community that has been raised up for mankind. You enjoin right conduct and forbid indecency, and you believe in Allāh.[2]

The Qur'ān contained God's pure and holy truth—the source of inspiration and conviction to these people which enjoyed the assurance of God from being eclipsed or from undergoing any corruption in its text.

---

1 Qur'ān 5:3.
2 Qur'ān 3:110.

> Lo! We, even We, reveal the Reminder, and Lo! Verily We are its Guardian.[1]

On the other hand, God's help and victory came to enliven the Prophet ﷺ who saw the people entering the religion of God in large numbers; deputations from Arab tribes followed one after another in rapid succession to pledge their allegiance to him. The lightning speed with which Islam gained converts promised its victory over all religions of the world. An allusion to the rapid success of Islam was made by God in *Sūrah an-Naṣr*.[2]

> When Allāh's help and the triumph comes and you see mankind enter the religion of Allāh in multitudes. Then praise your Lord, and seek forgiveness of Him. Verily He is forgiving![3]

RECITATION OF THE QUR'ĀN AND DEVOTIONAL EXERCISES

The Apostle ﷺ would withdraw into his mosque for private devotions during the last ten days of Ramaḍān, but during the last Ramaḍān of his life he retired for twenty days.[4]

The Prophet ﷺ would read the Qur'ān with Jibraʿīl[5] once annually, but this was done twice in the year in which he died. The Apostle ﷺ told his Companions that he inferred from it that the time of his departure from the world was drawing near.[6]

No man has ever desired to meet his Lord as intensely as the Apostle ﷺ, nor was the Lord Himself less eager to have him in His presence, He now gave him leave to quit the fleeting world.

The Companions of the Apostle ﷺ held him dear like the apple of one's eye. His death was thus a shock more terrible than what they could have been expected to endure. But God had in His infinite Wisdom prepared them for that unprecedented heartache. The rumour about the Apostle's ﷺ death had been bandied about in the battle of Uḥud, but later on it came out that the report was a whisper of the devil. They had soon learnt that God had still not deprived them of the blessed companionship of His Apostle ﷺ, yet none of them had regarded the Apostle ﷺ as immortal for they knew that he would have to leave

1 Qur'ān 15:9.
2 The 110th sūrah of the Qur'ān
3 Qur'ān 110:1–3.
4 Bukhārī: Kitāb al-iʿtikāf.
5 Gabriel.
6 Bukhārī: Kitāb al-manāqib.

this world sooner or later. It was on that occasion that the revelation was sent down by God to forewarn the Muslims:

> Muḥammad is but a messenger: messengers have passed away before him. Will it be that, when he dies or is slain, you will turn back on your heels? He who turns back does no harm to Allāh, and Allāh will reward the thankful.[1]

The earliest Muslims had been guided and trained and set right by the Apostle ﷺ. Their hearts were put in tune with God. They were all bound to the great task of spreading the message of Islam to the farthest corners of the world, and they never had any doubt that the Apostle ﷺ would one day be summoned by the Lord in order to be recompensed for the greatest service rendered by him to humanity. The verse "When Allāh's help and the triumph comes," had convinced the Companions that it was but the first announcement of the Prophet's ﷺ approaching departure from their midst. They were fully conscious of the fact that reference to the help and victory coming from God signified completion of the Apostle's ﷺ mission.[2]

Then, when the revelation came, "This day have I perfected your religion. . ."[3] a number of eminent Companions of the Apostle ﷺ were led to believe that the time for his final summons was drawing near.[4]

ARDENT DESIRE FOR NEARNESS TO GOD

After his return from the Farewell Pilgrimage a number of things that the Apostle ﷺ did indicated that he was approaching the journey's end[5] and was making preparations for meeting the Highest Companion. Eight years after the battle of Uḥud the Apostle ﷺ prayed over those who were slain there like one who was bidding farewell to the living and the dead. He then mounted the pulpit and said, "I am one who goes before you and I shall be a witness to you. Your appointed place is at the *Hawḍ al-Kawthar*[6] where I find myself standing. I have

---

1 Qur'ān 3:144.

2 Ibn ʿAbbās says that so far as he knew it alluded to death of the Prophet ﷺ. Imām Aḥmad who has handed down this tradition from Ibn ʿAbbās writes: "On receiving the revelation, 'When Allāh's help and the triumph comes. . .' the Messenger of God ﷺ said that he had been informed of his approaching death." (See *Tafsīr Ibn Kathīr*)

3 Qur'ān 5:3.

4 *Ibn Kathīr*, vol. IV, p. 427.

5 A tradition relates that while throwing pebbles at the *Jamrat al-ʿAqabah* the Messenger of God stopped and said to them, "Learn your rites, for I do not know whether I am likely to perform the pilgrimage after this occasion."

6 Lit. The Pool of Abundance, which is in Paradise.

been given the keys of the treasures of the earth. I do not fear for you that you would become polytheists after I am gone, but I fear you should long for worldly things and perish like your predecessors."[1]

BEGINNING OF THE ILLNESS

The sickness of the Apostle ﷺ began shortly before the end of Ṣafār.[2] Late one night the Apostle ﷺ went to the cemetery of Madīnah, known as *Jannat al-Baqīᶜ*, where he prayed for the dead and returned to his house. The next morning his ailment began.[3]

ᶜĀ'ishah relates that when the Apostle ﷺ returned from the *Jannat al-Baqīᶜ* he was suffering from a headache and said, "O my head." The Prophet ﷺ said, "Nay, O my head! ᶜĀ'ishah, O my head!"[4] His pain increased. Then, in the house of Maymūnah the Apostle ﷺ called his wives and asked their permission to be nursed in the house of ᶜĀ'ishah. All of them agreed and the Apostle ﷺ came out walking supported by Faḍl ibn ᶜAbbās and ᶜAlī. He had a cloth bound on his head and his feet were dragging as he came to the house of ᶜĀ'ishah.[5]

ᶜĀ'ishah tells that during the illness from which the Apostle ﷺ never recovered, he told her, "ᶜĀ'ishah, I still feel pain from the food I took at Khaybar; now I feel my aorta being cut because of that poison."[6]

THE LAST ARMY

The Apostle ﷺ summoned Usāmah ibn Zayd and asked him to lead an army to Syria. He ordered him to take his cavalry into the borders of Balqā' and Dārūn in the land of Palestine.[7]

The leading Mūhājirīn and the Anṣār and notable Companions amongst whom the most eminent was ᶜUmar, were enlisted in the Army. The Prophet ﷺ asked ᶜUmar to join the army under Usāmah which was encamped at Juruf, although his illness had taken a serious turn.[8] Abū Bakr sent the army forward under Usāmah after the death of the Apostle ﷺ in order to effect to his Master's last wishes.

1 This tradition has been accepted as authentic by all the scholars of Ḥadīth.
2 It was perhaps on a Monday, as most of the traditions have reported.
3 *Ibn Hishām,* vol. II, p. 642: *Ibn Kathīr,* vol. IV, p. 443.
4 *Ibn Hishām,* vol. II, p. 633.
5 Bukhārī, Chap. Marḍ an-Nabī.
6 *Ibn Kathīr,* vol. IV, p. 449.
7 *Ibn Hishām,* vol. II, p. 642.
8 *Ibn Kathīr,* vol. IV, p. 441.

KEEN INTEREST IN THE DETACHMENT OF USĀMAH

The Apostle ﷺ felt that the people were a bit sluggish in joining the Usāmah's ﷺ army. Certain people had even expressed their disapproval of putting a youth in command of a detachment comprising the best of the Mūhājirīn and Anṣār ﷺ around. The Prophet ﷺ came out in spite of his severe headache, ascended the pulpit and, after glorifying God as becomes His dignity, said, "O People! Send out the army of Usāmah ﷺ. You criticise his appointment but you have done the same before about his father's appointment. He is indeed worthy of the office of commander as was his father before him."[1] The Apostle ﷺ descended the pulpit terminating his address, and the people quickly started making preparations for undertaking the journey. The Apostle's ﷺ illness increased day by day while Usāmah ﷺ took his detachment out of Madīnah and took up quarters at Juruf about 5 km from the city so that others desirous of enlisting in the army might join him before his departure. In the meantime the Prophet's ﷺ condition grew worse while Usāmah and his comrades ﷺ anxiously awaited the news about him.

It was then that the Apostle ﷺ gave out his last two orders. They were: "Dispatch the troops just as you have been sending out the detachments earlier. Allow not two religions to remain in the Arabian Peninsula and chase out all the idolaters from the country.[2]

SOLICITUDE FOR THE WELFARE OF MUSLIMS

Some of the Apostle's ﷺ Companions came to see him in the house of ʿĀ'ishah ﷺ during his illness. He welcomed them and prayed for their guidance on the right path and invoked the help and blessings of God for them. Thereafter he said, "I enjoin you to fear God and assign you to His care after me. I am a warner unto you from God. Behold! Never give yourselves to arrogance and vainglory in the habitations of Allāh's servants for God has told you and me: "As for the Abode of the Hereafter We assign it unto those who seek not oppression in the earth, nor corruption. The outcome is for those who ward off (evil)."[3] Then he recited another verse: "Is not the home of the scorners in hell?"[4]

---

1 *Ibn Hishām*, vol. II, p. 650. *Bukhārī*: *Kitāb al-Maghāzī*. It has been stated in another tradition included in the section Gazwah Zayd ibn Ḥārithah that the Prophet ﷺ also said, "By God, he deserved to be appointed a commander; Surely, he (Zayd) was among the most beloved of all people to me, and this (Usāmah) is among the most beloved after him."

2 Bukhārī: Marḍ an-Nabī.

3 Qur'ān 28:83.

4 Qur'ān 39:60; Bayhaqī, *As-Sīrat an-Nabawiyyah*; Ibn Kathīr, vol. IV, p 502.

INDIFFERENCE TO THE WORLD AND WEALTH

ʿĀ'ishah relates that during his illness the Messenger of God asked her, "ʿĀ'ishah, what has happened to those pieces of gold?" When she brought five or seven or nine, he took them in his hand and said. "How shall I face God with these in my possession? Give these away in charity."[1]

ANXIETY FOR THE PRAYER

While the Apostle ﷺ lay in the grip of illness, he enquired. "Has everybody offered prayers?" Those attending him replied, "No, O Apostle of God, they are waiting for you." He asked to bring water in a pan. When it was brought he took a bath and tried to get up, but fell unconscious. On regaining consciousness after a short while he again asked. "Has everybody offered prayers?" They replied, "No, O Apostle of God. They are waiting for you." All the people were then sitting silently in the Prophet's ﷺ Mosque for the night prayer. He sent word to them asking Abū Bakr to lead the prayer. Now Abū Bakr was tender-hearted, so he asked ʿUmar to lead the prayer. ʿUmar however, declined saying that he (Abū Bakr) was more qualified. Thus, Abū Bakr led the prayer during the period of the Prophet's illness.

When the Apostle ﷺ felt a little better he came out with help of ʿAbbās and ʿAlī for the noon prayer. As soon as Abū Bakr came to know of the Apostle's ﷺ arrival, he tried to step back, but the Apostle ﷺ motioned him not to leave his place and asked the two who were supporting him to let him take the seat by the side of Abū Bakr. Thus, the Apostle ﷺ performed the prayer sitting while Abū Bakr remained standing in the prayer.

Umm al-Faḍl bint al-Ḥārith says that she had heard God's messenger ﷺ reciting *Sūrah al-Mursalāt*[2] at the sunset prayer. Thereafter he did not lead any prayer until God summoned him to His presence.[3]

THE FAREWELL SPEECH

Of the few occasions when the Apostle ﷺ made for the pulpit during his illness, he once said, while a cloth was tied round his head, "Behold, God gave one of His bondsmen the choice between this world and that which is with Him, so he chose that which is with God." Abū Bakr realised the significance of the Prophet's words, for he knew that it was the Prophet ﷺ himself who had been

1 *Musnad Aḥmad* vol. VI, p. 49.

2 Chapter 77 of the Qur'ān.

3 Bukhārī: Marḍ an-Nabī.

given that choice. He broke into tears and exclaimed, "No, our lives and our children be your ransom."

The Apostle ﷺ then replied, "Abū Bakr, have patience and don't be hasty. Indeed, of all the people, the most generous toward me in regard to his life and property was Abū Bakr. And were I to choose anyone to be my dearest friend indeed I would choose Abū Bakr, but the love and concern for Islam takes precedence over all others." The Apostle ﷺ also said on this occasion, "No door to the mosque shall be left open save Abū Bakr's door.[1]

DIRECTIONS FOR KINDLINESS TOWARD THE ANṢĀR

Once, during the illness of the Prophet ﷺ, Abū Bakr and ʿAbbās ﵄ happened to pass by a group of Anṣār. They saw them weeping and asked, "What makes you weep?" They answered, "We have been recalling our meetings with the Apostle of God ﷺ." When the Prophet ﷺ was informed of the incident, he came out, the end of his mantle wound round his head, and mounted the pulpit[2]—he did not mount the pulpit again after that day—and praised God and extolled Him. Then he said, "I commend the Anṣār to you, for, behold, they are my intimates and bosom friends. They have fulfilled their duty, and now whatever claims they have on others remain to be requited. Therefore, you shall welcome whatever is done by the good among them, and forgive those that do wrong."[3]

LAST LOOK ON THE MUSLIMS IN PRAYER

Abū Bakr ﵁ continued to lead the prayer. On Monday morning when the people were performing the dawn prayer, the Apostle of God ﷺ lifted the curtain of his door and kept his gaze fixed on the worshippers for some time to see how they paid divine honour to the Lord. He perhaps wanted to see the result of his life-long endeavour and struggle, training and guidance. Or, perhaps, having ever been so fond of prayers, he wanted to know how his followers lifted up their hearts to the Lord and whether they were enthralled and lost in prayers in his absence as they had always been in his presence. What the Apostle ﷺ saw was extremely satisfying, for, never had the mission of any prophet been carried to completion in that manner. It reassured him that the attachment to Allāh

---

1 Bukhārī: Kitāb aṣ-Ṣalāt.

2 The Prophet's ﷺ sermon on this occasion is generally accepted as his last sermon. It was delivered on Thursday after the midday prayer. Anas ibn Mālik who has handed it down says, "He mounted the pulpit on that day but he did not ascend it again. Thereafter He praised the Lord as is his due."

3 Bukhārī: Faḍā'il al-Aṣḥāb.

of the community that he had brought up and His religion was durable and unfading, not fleeting and set to wear away after his death. God knows better how delighted he was, but, as his Companions say, his face was beaming with joy. They relate:

> Standing in ʿĀ'ishah 's door the Messenger of God ﷺ lifted the curtain and kept his eyes fixed upon us. It seemed as if his face was an open book. He smiled and then laughed. We thought that we might be drawn from our prayers and get carried away because of our joy. We also thought that perhaps he was coming out for prayers but he told us to complete our prayers and pulled down the curtain. And that was the day on which he died.[1]

INTERDICTION OF PRAYERS AT SEPULCHRES

The words uttered last by the Apostle ﷺ were: "May God ruin the Jews and Christians, they have turned the sepulchres of their prophets into places of worship. Let no two religions be left in the Arabian Peninsula."[2]

ʿĀ'ishah and Ibn ʿAbbās ﷺ relate that when the time for the Apostle's ﷺ eternal rest drew nigh he had a black striped sheet over him. Often, he pulled it over his face and then feeling restless he removed it. It was in this condition that he said: "May the curse of God be upon the Jews and Christians; they have turned the sepulchres of their prophets into places of worship." He was warning the Muslims against such practices.

THE LAST DIRECTIONS

When he was about to breathe his last, he said repeatedly "Lo! Be careful of prayer and those whom you possess or have under your charge." He continued to repeat these words until they became inaudible but it appeared that he was trying to utter them.[3]

ʿAlī ﷺ says that he heard the Apostle ﷺ commending Muslims to be careful of prayer and poor-due, and to be generous to their slaves and subordinates.[4]

ʿĀ'ishah ﷺ relates that, while she started reciting the last two *Sūrah*s of the Qur'ān in order to blow upon the Apostle ﷺ, he lifted up his eyes and said, "With the Exalted Companion! With the Exalted Companion!" Just at that moment ʿAbd ar-Raḥmān ibn Abū Bakr ﷺ entered the room with a fresh *miswāk* in his

1 Bukhārī: Maraḍ an-Nabī.

2 *Muwaṭṭa' Imām Mālik*; Ibn Kathīr, vol. IV, p. 471.

3 Bayhaqī and Aḥmad; Ibn Kathīr, vol. IV, p. 473.

4 *Ibn Kathīr*, vol. IV, p. 473 from the *Muwaṭṭa'* of *Imām Aḥmad*.

hand. The Apostle ﷺ looked at it in a way that she thought he wanted it. She chewed it a little to make it soft and pliable, and then gave it to him. He rubbed his teeth with it as he used to and tried to hand it over to her, but it fell from his hand.[1]

She further says that a cup of water was kept near him. He dipped his hand in it and wiped his face with it, saying, "There is no god but God. Verily, death has its pangs." Then he lifted up his forefinger and said, "With the Exalted Companion! With the Exalted Companion!" until his soul took flight to the regions sublime and his hand dropped on one side into the water.

ᶜĀ'ishah says that when the Apostle ﷺ was about to leave us, he had his head on my thigh. He fainted for a split second and then regaining consciousness, looked up towards, the ceiling, saying the while, "Verily, with the Exalted Companion!" And with these words on his lips, the Apostle of God ﷺ yielded his last breath.

HOW THE APOSTLE ﷺ LEFT THIS WORLD

When the Apostle ﷺ quitted this world he had all of Arabia well in his hand. The sovereigns and rulers feared his rising power while his Companions were ever willing to undergo any sacrifice, to lay down their own lives and to give up their wealth, property and children for his sake. Yet he left this world without a single dīnār or dirham or a slave or a bondmaid in his possession. All that he owned at the time was one white mule, some weapons and a piece of land which had already been given away in charity.[2]

The Prophet's ﷺ coat of mail had been pawned with a Jew for thirty *ṣāᶜs* of barley[3] when he died and nothing was left by him to have it returned.[4]

The Apostle ﷺ restored freedom to forty slaves during his illness; only six or seven dīnārs were left with ᶜĀ'ishah, but he asked her to give away even those in charity.[5]

ᶜĀ'ishah relates that the day the Apostle of God ﷺ died there was nothing in her house which could be taken by a living being excepting a little barley left in a cupboard. It lasted for a few days until she weighed it and that very day it was all used up.

The Prophet ﷺ died on Monday, the 12th day of Rabīᶜ al-Awwal in the heat of

1 Ibn Kathīr, vol. IV, p. 474; Bukhārī: Maraḍ al-Nabī.

2 Bukhārī: Maraḍ an-Nabī.

3 Ibid.

4 Bayhaqī, p. 562.

5 *As-Sīrat al-Ḥalabiyyah,* vol. III, p. 381.

the noon after the sun had passed the meridian. He was then sixty-three years of age. This was the darkest hour for the Muslims, a day as gloomy and lamentable for all mankind as his birth had signalled hope and cheerfulness for the whole world. Anas and Abū Saʿīd al-Khudrī ﵄ say that when the Messenger of God ﷺ came to Madīnah, everything looked better and brighter but no day was worse or more dark than the day he died. Some of the people saw Umm Ayman ﵂ weeping when the Apostle ﷺ was bedridden and when they asked what made her weep, she replied, "Of course I know that the Prophet of God ﷺ will quit this world but I am weeping because the revelation from heaven has come to an end."[1]

BEWILDERMENT OF THE COMPANIONS

The news of the Prophet's ﷺ death fell like a thunderbolt on his Companions. All were stunned because of the ardent love and esteem they had for him. Such was their reliance on his loving care as the children are assured of the protection of their parents. Their agonising distress was not at all unusual for God has himself spoken of the Apostle's ﷺ concern for his followers.

> There has come to you a Messenger from among you, grievous is your suffering to him, full of concern is he for you, kind to the believers—merciful.[2]

The Prophet ﷺ was so gracious and considerate that every Companion believed himself to be the closest to him and never had any misgivings about his love and confidence. It was a reliance born of absolute trust mingled with devotion which had made it difficult for some to imagine a day when the Prophet ﷺ would depart from this world leaving them alone. One of these was ʿUmar ﵁, who had been closest to the Apostle ﷺ, and when he was told that the Messenger of God ﷺ was no longer alive, he protested violently. He went so far as to address the people in the Prophet's ﷺ mosque and told them that God's Apostle ﷺ would not quit this world until God had destroyed the hypocrites.[3]

THE BRAVE WORDS OF ABŪ BAKR

A man of determination and courage was needed at this difficult hour. And this man was Abū Bakr ﵁, the senior-most of the Prophet's ﷺ Companions who

1 *Ibn Kathīr,* vol. IV, pp. 544–46.

2 Qur'ān 9:128.

3 *Ibn Kathīr,* vol. IV, pp. 544–46.

had been picked out by God to take over the inheritance of the Prophet ﷺ with a firm hand. When the news reached him, he hurried back from his house. For a moment he stopped at the door of the Mosque where ʿUmar ؓ was excitedly speaking to the people. Without paying any attention to anybody he made for ʿĀ'ishah's ؓ room where the body of the Prophet ﷺ lay covered with a mantle. He uncovered the Apostle's ﷺ face and kissed him, saying, "My father and mother be your ransom. You have tasted the death God had decreed for you, a second death will never overtake you." Replacing the mantle on the Apostle's ﷺ face, he went out to the Mosque. ʿUmar ؓ was still haranguing the people, so he said gently, "Umar, be quiet." But ʿUmar was too excited to listen. Now, Abū Bakr realised that ʿUmar ؓ was in no mood to terminate his speech, so he stepped forward and called out to the people, whereupon they gathered round him leaving ʿUmar ؓ. Abū Bakr ؓ praised God and then said:

> O men, if anyone worships Muḥammad, let him know that Muḥammad is dead. But if anyone worships God, then God is alive and He dies not.

Then continuing his speech he recited the Qur'ānic verse: "Muḥammad is but a messenger: messengers have passed away before him. Will it be that, when he dies or is slain, you will turn back on your heels? He who turns back does no harm to Allāh, and Allāh will reward the thankful."

All those persons who were present on the occasion later stated on oath that when Abū Bakr ؓ recited that verse, it seemed as if it had just been revealed. ʿUmar ؓ said: "When I heard Abū Bakr reciting the verse, I was taken aback and fell down as if I did not have a leg to stand on. I felt as if I had then come to know of the Prophet's death."[1]

OATH OF FEALTY TO ABŪ BAKR

All the Muslims then swore fealty to Abū Bakr ؓ, in the Hall of Banū Sāʿidah[2] as the successor of God's Messenger. The reason for making haste was to avoid old rivalries flaring up suddenly through machinations of the devil and selfishness of the faint-hearted hypocrites. Those who were sincere and well-meaning wanted to ensure that the Muslims remained united and strong under a leader, who could look after their affairs and give Messenger of God a burial as his successor and head of the Muslim community.

1 *Ibn Hishām*, vol. II, pp. 655–56; for details see Bukhārī: Maraḍ an-Nabī.

2 Known as Thaqīfah Banū Sāʿīdah, it was a thatched platform where the people of Madīnah usually met to discuss public affairs of the city.

BURIAL OF THE APOSTLE

Normality then returned. The initial shock and grief gave place to tranquillity and confidence, and the Muslims again turned to the great task for which the Apostle of God ﷺ had trained and prepared them for. The Apostle's ﷺ family members washed and shrouded him, and the bier was placed in his house. On this occasion Abū Bakr ؓ told the people that he had heard the Apostle ﷺ saying that every prophet was buried on the spot where he died. The Apostle's ﷺ bedding was accordingly removed from the place and a grave was dug for him at the same spot by Abū Ṭalḥah Anṣārī ؓ.

Then the people came to pay their last respect to the Apostle ﷺ and to say the funeral prayer in groups, one after another. Women came in after the men and after them came the children, all of whom prayed over him. Nobody acted as *Imām*[1] in the prayers over the Apostle ﷺ.[2] The day this came to pass was a Tuesday.[3]

It was a sad day for Madīnah. When Bilāl ؓ gave the call for the morning prayer he could not help recalling the Apostle ﷺ in the mirror of his mind, he broke down in tears and sobs. His laments lacerated the hearts of all others who, until now, had heard the call when the Apostle ﷺ was alive. But, it was quite different now: everything seemed to be bleak, gloomy.

Umm Salamah ؓ says, "What a tormenting affliction it was! When we recall the distress we were in, every other trouble appears to be lighter and easier to endure."[4]

The Apostle ﷺ had once said to the believers, "O people! If anyone of you comes to grief, he ought to console himself in his bereavement by calling to his mind the anguish that will rend his heart on my death. For no sorrow will be greater for my followers than the agony caused to them by my death."[5]

After the people had completed the burial of the Apostle ﷺ, Fāṭimah ؓ asked Anas ؓ, "Anas, have your people found it easy to scatter the dust over God's Messenger[6] In spite of their longing for him they did not lament loudly over him.

1 One who leads the prayer.
2 *Ibn Hishām*, vol. II, p. 663.
3 Ṭabaqāt Ibn Saʿd; Ibn Kathīr, vol. IV, p. 517.
4 *Ibn Kathīr*, vol. IV, pp. 538–39.
5 *Ibn Kathīr*, vol. IV, p. 549.
6 Bukhārī: Maraḍ an-Nabī.

25

Wives and Children of the Apostle

THE FIRST AMONG the wives of the Apostle ﷺ was Khadījah bint Khuwaylid. The Prophet's ﷺ marriage with Khadījah took place before the beginning of revelation when he was twenty-five and she forty years old. Being deeply devoted to the Apostle of God ﷺ, she supported him during the most difficult period of his life, shared his adversities and troubles with good grace and helped him with her wealth and kind words. She had died three years before the Apostle ﷺ migrated to Madīnah. She had borne the Apostle ﷺ all his children except Ibrāhīm. The Apostle ﷺ always held her in high esteem and very often praised her. There was never an occasion that he would kill a sheep and cut it into pieces and not send them to Khadījah's friends.[1]

After the death of Khadījah, the Apostle ﷺ married Sawdah bint Zamaʿah. He was then united in wedlock with ʿĀ'ishah, whom he adored and loved dearly. There has been no woman like her in the whole history of Islam who so deeply understood the teachings of Islam and convincingly explained the issues of jurisprudence; even the most eminent and learned Companions of the Prophet ﷺ consulted her on intricate legal issues. Ḥafṣah, the daughter of ʿUmar, was the next to join the nuptial tie with the holy Prophet ﷺ. Thereafter, he married Zaynab bint Khuzaymah who died two months after her marriage to the Apostle ﷺ. Umm Salamah was then wedded by the Apostle ﷺ and she was the last of his wives to leave this fleeting world. After her, the Apostle ﷺ contracted matrimony with Zaynab bint Jaḥash, the daughter of his aunt

1 *Bukhārī*: ʿĀ'ishah relates that she was jealous of Khadījah although she had never seen her.

Umaymah ﷺ. Thereafter, the Apostle ﷺ took as wives Juwayriyah bint al-Ḥārith ﷺ, belonging to the tribe of al-Muṣṭaliq and Umm Ḥabībah bint Abū Sufyān ﷺ in succession. His next wife was Ṣafiyyah ﷺ, the daughter of the chief of Banū 'n-Naḍīr. Her father, Ḥuyayy ibn Akhtab ﷺ, traced his descent to Ḥārūn[1] ibn ʿImrān ﷺ, the brother of Prophet Mūsā ﷺ.[2] The honour of being the last spouse of the Apostle ﷺ went to Maymūnah bint al-Ḥārith ﷺ of the tribe of Hilāl.

There is no difference of opinion that nine of the Prophet's ﷺ wives survived him. Khadījah and Zaynab bint Khuzaymah ﷺ had died during his life time. All of them, except ʿĀ'ishah ﷺ, were widows.[3]

The Apostle of God had also two bondswomen who were alive when he died. One of these was Māriyah ﷺ the Copt, daughter of Shamʿūn, who had been presented to him by Muqawqis, the ruler of Egypt. She bore a son, Ibrāhīm ﷺ, to the Apostle ﷺ. The other was Rayḥānah bint Zayd ﷺ who belonged to the tribe of an-Naḍīr.[4] She was let free on her profession of Islam and thereafter the Apostle ﷺ took her in marriage.

All the wives of the Prophet ﷺ being *Umm al-Mu'minīn*[5] (mothers of the faithful) to the Muslims, they were forbidden to remarry anyone after the death of the Apostle ﷺ. This was in keeping with the honour and respect due to the Prophet ﷺ as well as the loving regard every Muslim had for the Messenger of God ﷺ. The writ of God for the Muslims was:

> And it is not for you to cause annoyance to the messenger of Allāh, nor that you should ever marry his wives after him. Lo! that in Allāh's sight would be an enormity."[6]

THE PROPHET'S ﷺ MARRIAGES

Up to his twenty-fifth year the Apostle ﷺ lived alone, enjoying single blessedness. In the flower of his youth, he possessed all the qualities of the life's morning march: he was good-natured, sound of mind and body and a specimen of Arab manliness. His well-moulded, strongly built frame, courage, generosity, skill in horsemanship and unpretentiousness—the qualities esteemed by the Arabs—came of the wild, barren desert where he had spent his childhood. All these physical and mental gifts are, according to psychologists and scholars of ethics, no less important in moulding the character of a man.

1 Aaron.

2 Moses.

3 *Zād al-Maʿād*, vol. I. pp. 26–29.

4 According to some, she belonged to Banū Qurayẓah.

5 *Ibn Kathīr,* vol. IV. pp. 604–5.

6 Qur'ān 33:53

The youthful days of the Apostle ﷺ, before the beginning of revelation, were free from every blemish; neither his worst enemies during his lifetime nor the mud-slinging critics of later times have ever been able to find the slightest fault with this critical period of his life. His veracity, chastity, innocence and pureness of heart were proverbial for he never indulged in anything unbecoming of a true-souled youth like him.

He married Khadījah at the age of twenty-five. She was a widow who had been twice married, and had also children from her earlier husbands. As most of the authorities agree, she was fifteen years older than the Apostle of God ﷺ. His next marriage was contracted with Sawdah bint Zamaʿah when he had already crossed his fiftieth year. She had migrated to Abyssinia with her husband who had died there. The Prophet ﷺ never married any virgin save ʿĀ'ishah —all his marriages were dictated by considerations of kindliness, cementing the bonds of friendship with the alien tribes, setting some example of virtuous behaviour for the Muslims, achieving some public good or forestalling some danger to the nascent community of Islam.

In the tribal society of Arabia, family and matrimonial relationships had a special significance unknown in any other part of the world. Ties of blood lent security, importance and dignity in the tribal society of Arabia. The marriages of the Apostle ﷺ were, thus, invariably conducive to the dissemination of the message of Islam among pagan tribes and thus they were a means of strengthening the idealistic society of Madīnah to the extent the ties of blood created through these marriages were helpful in putting a check to unnecessary bloodshed—the perpetual sport of the Bedouin- and both of these were absolutely necessary for the survival of the Muslim community. Also, neither the Prophet ﷺ nor his wives ever led a life of ease and luxury—as one is apt to think of polygamous marriages. His was a life of exemplary restraint and frugality, self-denial and temperance, a life so uniquely pure and chaste that not even the greatest puritan of any time or clime can be compared with him. We shall cite some examples of his simple and frugal living while describing the Apostle's ﷺ character and manners, but the testimony of God should be sufficient to convince every honest man about the absence of ease and comfort in the married life of the holy Prophet ﷺ.

> O Prophet! say unto your wives: If you desire the world's life and its adornment, come! I will content you and will release you with a fair release. But if you desire Allāh and His messenger and the abode of the Hereafter, then lo! Allāh hath prepared for the good among you an immense reward.[1]

The great objective which the Apostle of God ﷺ had set before his wives as

1 Qur'ān 33:28–29.

well as their own immaculate and upright disposition had guided all of them to give but one answer to the question posed by God. None of them had the least hesitation in making her choice in favour of God and His Messenger ﷺ and the ultimate salvation. The Apostle ﷺ recited the verses above before ʿĀ'ishah ﷺ and said, "Lo! Do not make haste in giving your reply and consult your parents." She replied, "What is there to consult my parents about? I want God and His Apostle ﷺ and the abode of the Hereafter."[1] She relates that all the wives of the Prophet ﷺ gave a similar reply.[2]

The Prophet's ﷺ polygamous bonds of matrimony and the multifarious demands they entailed never caused him to neglect, even for the shortest period of time, either the great responsibility of his mission or the affairs of the Muslims or even his own exacting religious and spiritual practice. They rather helped him to devote himself to his mission with a renewed vigour and enthusiasm. The wives of the Apostle ﷺ always lent him a helping hand in the dissemination of his message and expounding the teachings of Islam to his followers. They accompanied him in his expeditions and nursed the sick and the wounded. In fact, about one-third of the teachings of Islam in regard to social, marital and household responsibilities of the Muslims has come to be known through the Apostle's ﷺ wives who enlightened and guided the Muslims about the family life and behaviour of the Prophet ﷺ with the members of his household.[3]

The great service rendered to Islam by the wives of the Apostle ﷺ is best illustrated by ʿĀ'ishah ﷺ about whom adh-Dhahabī (d. 748/1347), one of the most eminent scholars of the science of ḥadīth writes in the *Tadhkirat al-Ḥuffāz*:

> Among the Companions of the Prophet ﷺ well-versed in jurisprudence she was the most prominent, for even the leading jurists referred to her for advice on intricate questions of law. Qabīṣah ibn Dhuwayb says that ʿĀ'ishah ﷺ knew more about law than most of the Companions who would ask her questions. Abū Mūsā ﷺ says that if any Companion of the Prophet ﷺ amongst us had any difficulty in finding out the real purport of any tradition, he would enquire about it from ʿĀ'ishah ﷺ, for she invariably knew about it. Ḥassān ﷺ says that he found nobody more deeply versed than ʿĀ'ishah ﷺ in the Qur'ān, injunctions about the things permitted and forbidden or mandatory and obligatory, poetry, Arabian history and genealogy.[4]

1 *Bukhārī*, on the authority of ʿĀ'ishah.

2 *Bukhārī*, on the authority of Ibn Abī Ḥātim.

3 The significance and indispensibility of polygamous marriages have been expounded by Qādhī Sulaimān Mansūrpūri in vol. II of *Raḥmat li 'l-ʿĀlamīn* (pp. 141–144) and an Egyptian scholar ʿAbbās Maḥmūd al-ʿAqqād throws light on subject in the *ʿAbqariyyah Muḥammad*.

4 *Tadhkirat al-Ḥuffāz*. vol I, p. 28.

The moral virtues of the Apostle's ﷺ wives are beyond words; their clemency and benignity, grace and compassion, generosity and nobility, and open-hearted magnanimity are demonstrated by the incident handed down by Hishām ﷺ on the authority of his father. He relates that "Once the Caliph Muʿāwiyah ﷺ sent one hundred thousand dirhams to ʿĀ'ishah ﷺ and, by God, the month was not over when she had given it all away to the poor and the needy." Thereupon a bondmaid said to her, "It would have been better if you had bought meat for a dirham." ʿĀ'ishah ﷺ replied, "Why didn't you tell me earlier?"[1] It is also related that ʿĀ'ishah ﷺ was then fasting.[2]

The question of polygamous marriage allowed by Islam has long troubled the minds of orientalists and Western writers. Their vexation springs from their desire to hem in the matrimonial laws of Islam and the time-honoured practice of the Arab countries, within their own Western concepts and customs. They are too often anxious to transpose their own standards—the product of peculiar circumstances in a particular type of society, lacking the sanction of divine authority—into a system growing out of the innate disposition and circumstances of Arabian society that carries not only social and moral benefits but also rests on the law of God. Truly speaking, it is a failing of the Western way of thought and its protagonists that they present the Western concepts of morality as the standard of human behaviour and then ruthlessly proceed to set a value on everything that goes contrary to it. What they actually do is to raise a whimsical issue and then go ahead to find an answer to the problem. This is all due to their self-conceitedness and chauvinistic approbation of everything originating in the West.

A Western biographer of the Apostle ﷺ has been bold enough to pin-point this common weakness of the Occidentals who try to bring in a verdict on the marriages of the Prophet ﷺ.

> Mohammad's married life must not be looked at from an Occidental point of view or from that set by Christian conventions. These men and women were not Occidentals and they were not Christians. They were living at a period and in a country where the only known ethical standards were theirs. Even so, there is no reason why the codes of America and Europe should be considered superior to those of the Arabs. The people of the West have many things to give to the people of the East. They have much to glean, too, and until they can prove that their way of living is on a higher moral standard than anybody else's, they should reserve judgement on other creeds and castes and countries.[3]

1 Ibid.

2 Ibid., on the authority, of Umm Dharah.

3 R. V. C. Bodley, *The Messenger: The Life of Mohammad* (London, 1946) pp.202–203.

The West condemns polygamy as an unmitigated evil and refuses, unwittingly, to attach any value to it. But, the so-called evil is neither unnatural nor abnormal, nor is its condemnation based on any universally accepted principle that it would continue to be rejected by the coming generations. The system envisages the role of men and women according to their nature while its rejection resting merely upon imaginary and fanciful scruples, derives support from powerful mass media that the West possesses. With the fast changing social, economic and moral pattern of the modern society the world will, in all probability, ultimately reject the Western values of monogamous marriages.

In one of the most challenging and appalling studies of the modern time, Alwin Toffer analysed the symptoms of terrifying changes emerging in the Western super-industrial society as a result of its present dehumanising values. He has even predicted that as sexual attitudes of the West loosen up, as property rights become less important because of rising affluence, the social repression of polygamy may come to be regarded as irrational.[1]

THE PROPHET'S CHILDREN

Khadījah ﵂, the first wife of the Apostle ﷺ, gave birth to his son al-Qāsim, after whose name the Prophet ﷺ was given the honorific Abū 'l-Qāsim, that is, father of Qāsim. He died in infancy. Thereafter she bore the Apostle ﷺ four daughters, Zaynab, Ruqayyah, Umm Kulthūm and Fāṭimah ﵅. One more son named ʿAbdullāh was also born to her. ʿAbdullāh was given the cognomens Ṭayyab and Ṭāhir according to Ibn al-Qayyim, but there are others who regard the three as separate sons of the Prophet ﷺ. All these sons and daughters of the Apostle ﷺ were born to Khadījah ﵂.[2]

Fāṭimah ﵂ was held dearest by the Prophet ﷺ amongst his children. The Apostle of God ﷺ once said about her: "She will be the leader of women in Paradise."[3] and "Fāṭimah ﵂ is a part of me, and whoso offends her offends me."[4] After the Prophet's ﷺ death, she was the first amongst his family members to bid farewell to this world.

Māriyah ﵂ the Copt was the mother of Ibrāhīm ﵁, another son of the Prophet ﷺ. He also died in infancy. In his deep sorrow over the child's death God's Apostle

1 Alwin Toffler, *Future* and Schock, (London 1975) pp. 227–232.

2 *Zād al-Maʿād*, vol. I, pp. 25–26.

3 *Tirmidhī*, vol. II, p. 421.

4 *Bukhārī* and other authentic collections.

ﷺ said, "The eyes weep and the heart grieves, but we say nothing that displeases our Lord, and we are grieved over being separated from you, Ibrāhīm."[1]

There was a solar eclipse on the day Ibrāhīm ﵁ died. Some of the Companions attributed the eclipse to Ibrāhīm's ﵁ death, but the Apostle corrected them in a speech wherein he said, "The sun and the moon are two of the signs of God; they are not eclipsed on account of anyone's death."[2]

Zaynab was married to Abū 'l-ʿĀs ibn Rabīʿ ﵁, a nephew of Khadījah ﵂, and had two children, a son named ʿAlī and a daughter whose name was Umāmah ﵂. Ruqayyah, another daughter of the Apostle ﷺ, was betrothed to ʿUthmān to whom she bore a son named ʿAbdullāh ﵁. Ruqayyah died while the Apostle ﷺ was at Badr and ʿUthmān was left behind to look after her. Umm Kulthūm, sister of Ruqayyah, was then united in marriage with ʿUthmān ﵁ whence he came to be known as *Dhu 'n-Nūrayn,* "the possessor of two lights."

Fāṭimah was joined in wedlock with ʿAlī ﵁ the son of Abū Ṭālib and a cousin of the Apostle ﷺ. Their elder son was Ḥasan ﵁, by whose name ʿAlī acquired the title of Abū 'l-Ḥasan and the younger one was Ḥusayn ﵁. Both of them were dearest to the Prophet's ﷺ heart and were praised by him in these words; "The two are my sweet-smelling blossoms in the world."[3] On another occasion he said about them, "These two will be the leaders of youths in Paradise."[4]

God blessed Ḥasan and Ḥusayn ﵄ with a progeny numerous as stars in the firmament and caused them to serve Islam and its followers. Great leaders and scholars and heavenly-minded saints were born amongst them who raised the banner of revolt against every corruption and iniquity and restored the health of the soul to the Muslims.[5] ʿAlī and Fāṭimah had two more daughters, Zaynab and Umm Kulthūm ﵄. The first was married to her cousin, ʿAbdullāh ibn Jaʿfar, who was regarded as one of the most generous persons in Arabia. Zaynab bore two sons, ʿAlī and ʿAwn to ʿAbdullāh ﵁. Umm Kulthūm was given in marriage to ʿUmar ibn al-Khaṭṭāb to whom she bore a son named Zayd ﵁.[6]

All the sons and daughters of the Apostle of God ﷺ except Fāṭimah ﵂, died during his lifetime. Fāṭimah ﵂ yielded her breath six months after the demise of the Prophet ﷺ.[7]

---

1 *Muslim,* on the authority of Asmā' bint Yazīd ibn as-Sakan.
2 Muslim: Kitāb al-Kusūf.
3 *Al-Anwār,* Ibn Ad-Dībaʿ p.67.
4 Bukhārī: Kitāb al-Manāqib.
5 *Tirmidhī,* vol. II, p. 221.
6 *Ibn Hishām,* vol. IV, pp. 581–82.
7 *Zād al-Maʿād,* vol. I, p. 26.

26
Character and Features

A COMPREHENSIVE AND graceful account of the noble qualities, merciful disposition and distinctive traits of the Prophet's character has been left by Hind ibn Abī Hālah ﷺ.[1] He says:

Being care-laden with the anxiety of after-life, the Prophet ﷺ would remain engrossed in the thought of the Hereafter continually for long spells, and seemed to be endlessly perturbed by it. He would often remain silent and never spoke without need. When he spoke, he pronounced each syllable distinctly,[2] and thus he would also end his speech. Whatever he said, it was always explicit and in plain terms. His speech was neither long-winded nor unnecessarily concise. He was kind-hearted and soft-spoken, never harsh or cool in his behaviour. He neither humiliated anyone nor did he himself like to be treated with disrespect.[3] The Prophet ﷺ set much by every provision; even if it was small in quantity he never deprecated it. As for the edibles he never disapproved nor praised; nor did he show anger about anything of the world or what it stands for. However, whenever one failed to meet one's obligation to God, nothing could cool down his indignation until he had paid back in full measure. But, for the wrongs done to his own person, he would never become angry.

---

1 The son of Khadījah by her former husband and the maternal uncle of Ḥasan.

2 That is, neither rapidly nor running his words into one another as conceited and careless persons are wont to do.

3 The Arabic word used in the tradition can be construed both for disrespectful treatment to him as well as giving offence to any one. In the former case, it would mean that the Apostle ﷺ was neither harsh nor weak but had a self-respecting mien which cannot stand any indignity.

> When he pointed something out, he did so with his whole hand; and when he was astonished he turned his hand over. In speaking with another man, he would strike the palm of the left on the thumb of his right hand. Angry, he would avert his face; joyful, he would look downwards. His laughter was but a smile, and when he laughed, his teeth used to appear white as hailstones.

ʿAlī ﵁ was one of those nearest to the Apostle ﷺ, a member of his family who had the opportunity to know him intimately; and he was also a keen observer of the manner and morals of men. In addition, ʿAlī ﵁ also had the power of description, capturing the essence of a subject with vividness and intensity. He says about the holy Prophet ﷺ:

> He was predisposed to refrain from unseemly language, curses and vilification and shameful deeds. In no ways did he say or do anything improper. He never raised his voice in a market place, nor returned evil with evil. Rather, he was given to forgive and forget. Never in his life did he lay his hands on anyone, save in a fight for the sake of God, nor did he ever strike anybody with his hand, neither a servant nor a woman. I never saw him exacting retribution for any offence or excess excepting when the honour of God was concerned or the limit set by Him was transgressed, in which case the Prophet ﷺ would be more enraged than anyone else. If he had the choice between two courses, he would choose the easier one. When he came to his house, he behaved like a common man, cleaned his garments, milked the sheep and performed the household chores.
>
> The Messenger of God ﷺ was not given to idle talk; he spoke only when he was concerned and comforted the people instead of frightening them through his speech. If a man of rank or nobility from another tribe called upon him, he showed him due honour and appointed him to some respectable post. He was always as cautious in his dealings with the people as he was prudent in forming an estimate of them, although he never denied anyone his courtesy and sweet temper. He kept his Companions appraised of the events and happenings and would ask them about their affairs.
>
> He commended what was good and deprecated what was bad or vile; strengthened the one and weakened the other; was always moderate and steadfast without going back and forth; never allowed anything to escape his attention lest others should become negligent or be distracted; he took care to possess the means for meeting every contingency and was never found wanting in doing what was right and proper but in no ways did he ever exceed the limits. Those who kept his company were all virtuous and of the elect; those best in his estimation were the most benign and courteous to all; and those most esteemed in his eyes were those who excelled others in benevolence and kindliness and helpfulness to oth-

ers. The Prophet ﷺ would stand up with the name of God on his lips and when he sat down. Wherever he went, he sat down in the rear and instructed others to do the same. He paid such attention to everyone attending his meetings that each considered that none attracted his notice like himself. If anybody asked him to sit down or spoke of his affair, the Apostle ﷺ listened to him patiently and gave heed to him until he had finished his talk and departed. If anybody asked for something or wanted his help, he never allowed him to leave without disposing of his business or at least comforting him with words kind and sweet. Such was his grace and kindness to one and all that everybody took him as his father. In regard to what was right and proper he regarded all on the same plane. His were the gatherings of knowledge and edification, of seemliness and modesty, of earnestness and probity. Neither did anybody talk in a loud voice, or censure others, or cast a reflection on anybody, or found fault with others; all were equal on even ground, and only those enjoyed a privilege who were more pious and God-fearing. In his meetings, the elders were held in reverence, the youth were treated kindly, those in need were given preference by all and the wayfarers and strangers were afforded protection and looked after.

Further he says:

Of a cheerful disposition, the Apostle of God ﷺ was always bright and radiant; he was tenderhearted[1] and sweet tempered; not stern by nature, he never spoke harshly; nor was he accustomed to speaking loudly; nor to saying anything unseemly or lewd; nor yet did he find fault with others; he was not stingy or miserly; if he disliked the request made to him, he simply ignored it and instead of refusing it outright he gave no reply. From three things he always kept aloof; one was squabble, the other, arrogance, and the third, dabbling in a futile task. And the three things he spared others were that he never spoke ill of anyone, nor maligned anyone, nor pried into anyone's failings; He attended only to those things which were decent. When he spoke all those present listened to him attentively lowering their heads as if birds were perched on them.[2] Others spoke only when the Apostle ﷺ had finished his talk, nobody joined issue with others in his presence and when anybody said something others kept quiet until he had finished his talk. The Prophet of God ﷺ would smile at remarks which made others laugh and expressed surprise over things which astonished others. He always gave heed

1 It is related that the Apostle ﷺ was bighearted, benign and accommodative, and forgave the faults of others. He never engaged in a row with anybody while others report that he was always calm and composed.

2 The people listened with such rapt attention and without making a stir as if there were birds sitting on their heads that would flyaway if they made any movement.

> to the wayfarers and would put up patiently with the rudeness of strangers until his Companions diverted the attention of such persons. He used to say: Help those whom you find in need. He gave ear only to such tributes as were modestly worded and never interrupted nor cut in the talk of others. If anybody exceeded the limits, he either forbade him or got up to cut short such prattle.
>
> He was the most generous, large-hearted, truthful, clement, lenient and amiable. One who saw him for the first time was overawed, but when one kept his company and came to know him intimately, one became attached to him like an inseparable companion. Those who had seen him say that they never saw a man like him either before or after him—May God bestow peace and blessings on His Apostle ﷺ.[1]

God had endowed His Prophet ﷺ with an impressive personality. His features displayed a harmonious blending of lovely elegance and grace, sublime splendour and impressiveness. Says Hind ibn Abī Hālah ﷺ, "He was self-respecting, graceful and pleasing to the eyes set on him. His face had the brilliance of a full moon."[2]

Barā' ibn ʿĀzib ﷺ relates, "God's Messenger ﷺ was of medium height. I saw him once wearing a red robe and had never seen anyone more beautiful than him."[3] Abū Hūrayrah ﷺ says: "The Prophet ﷺ was of a moderate height, slightly taller than short, his complexion was very fair, his beard was black, the mouth was of moderate size and pretty, the eyelashes were long, the shoulders were broad—I have never seen a man like him, either before or after him."[4] Anas ﷺ reports, "I have not touched any brocade or silk softer than the palm of God's Messenger nor smelt anything sweeter than the Prophet's scent."[5]

LOVE OF GOD

The holy Prophet ﷺ was the Messenger of God, the chosen and the exalted, all of whose sins,[6] past and yet to come, had been forgiven by the Lord, yet he was the most painstaking, eager and earnest in paying homage to God.

Al-Mughīra ibn Shuʿbah ﷺ reported that the Prophet ﷺ once got up at night and stood praying for such a long time that his feet became swollen. When he was asked why he did this since all of his past and future sins had been forgiven, he replied, "Should I then not be a grateful servant (of God)?"[7]

---

1 *Shamā'il at-Tirmidhī.*

2 *Shamā'il al-Tirmidhī,* on the authority of Hind ibn Abī Hālah.

3 An accepted tradition of the *Ṣiḥāḥ Sittah.*

4 *Al-Adab al-mufrad li 'l-Bukhārī.*

5 Bukhārī.

6 The prophets of God are impeccable and protected even against committing minor mistakes.

7 Bukhārī has mentioned this tradition in his commentary on *Sūrah al-Fatḥ* while Tirmidhī and

ʿĀ'ishah ؓ relates that the Apostle of God ﷺ once stayed awake throughout the night and till morning reciting only one verse. Reporting on the same event Abū Dharr ؓ says that the Prophet ﷺ kept praying throughout the night reciting one verse until the dawn appeared. The verse he recited was:

> If You punish them, they are Your slaves, and if You forgive them, You, only You are the Mighty, the Wise.[1]

ʿĀ'ishah ؓ says, "The Apostle of God ﷺ would fast to such an extent that we thought he would never give it up, and when he would go without fasting we thought that perhaps he would never fast again."[2]

Anas ؓ reports that whoever wanted to see the Prophet ﷺ praying at night could do so[3] and similarly one could see him sleeping.

ʿAbdullāh ibn ash-Shikhkhīr ؓ says that once he went to see the Prophet ﷺ. He was then offering prayers and sobbing—the sound emitting from his chest was like that of a boiling pot.[4]

The Apostle ﷺ was never at ease except when he performed the prayers. It seemed that even after saying his prayers, he eagerly looked forward to the time when he would again be paying homage to God. The Apostle ﷺ often remarked: "The comfort of my eyes lies in prayers."[5]

The Companions of the Prophet ﷺ relate that whenever he had any trouble he would prostrate in supplication to God.[6]

"Whenever the wind blew at night," says Abū'd-Dardā' ؓ, "the Apostle of God ﷺ took shelter in the mosque until it became calm. And whenever there was a solar or lunar eclipse, the Prophet ﷺ got up in trepidation seeking refuge from God until it was over and the sky was clear."[7] The Apostle ﷺ always seemed solicitous to commune with God; uneasy and restless until he had again fallen prone before the Lord. Oftentimes he sent for Bilāl ؓ and said, "Bilāl, make arrangements for prayers and put me at ease."[8]

INDIFFERENCE TO THE WORLD

Not the most apt words, arranged in the best order, in any language can ade-

---

Nasā'ī narrate it in connection with the nightly vigils of the Prophet ﷺ.

1 Tirmidhī.

2 Nasā'ī and Ibn Mājah.

3 Bukhārī: Kitāb at-tahajjud.

4 *Shamā'il at-Tirmidhī*.

5 *Nasā'ī* (Chapter on the Ten Women and Love of Women).

6 Abū Dāwūd.

7 Ṭabarānī, *al-Kabīr*.

8 Abū Dāwūd, Kitāb al-Adab.

quately depict the way God's Messenger ﷺ looked at dirham and dīnār, wealth and property and the world and all that it stands for. Indeed, even the disciples who had served their time at the feet of the Apostle's ﷺ Companions or the disciples of such disciples regarded fortunes and treasure unfit even to fill a hole in the dust. Their pure and pious lives, their indifference to wealth and worldly possessions, the way they showered bounty on one and all and preferred others over their own selves, their contentedness with the barest minimum and their heroic selflessness and self-denial takes one's breath away.[1] One can only picture to oneself the nobleness of heart and open-handed generosity as well as self-abnegation and unearthly disposition of the great teacher who had enlarged the minds of all the later pious souls.

We shall, therefore, cite here only a few of those authentic reports which have been handed down by the most trustworthy narrators since the Prophet's ﷺ own words and actions can best illustrate his outlook and sentiments in this regard.

Two of the well known sayings of the Apostle of God ﷺ which sum up his attitude towards worldly life are: "O God, truly life is the life of the hereafter," and "What have I to do with the world! My only business with it, is like that of a rider who finds shade under a tree, then goes off and leaves it."[2]

ʿUmar ؓ once saw the Apostle ﷺ lying on a reed mat which had left its marks on his body. ʿUmar ؓ gave way to tears at the frugal living and privation of his mentor. The Prophet ﷺ asked, "What's the matter, ʿUmar?" He replied, "O Messenger of God, of all the creatures of God, you are the most venerated, but it is Caesar and Chosroes who are rolling in the lap of luxury." ʿUmar's reply made the Apostle's ﷺ blood boil in anger and his face became red. He said, ʿUmar have you any doubt about it?" Then he added, "These are the men who have been given all the pleasures of life in advance here in this world."[3]

God's Messenger rejected the life of ease not only for his own self but also for his dependents. He was heard praying, "O God, make the provision of Muḥammad's family sufficient only to sustain life."[4] ʿAbū Hurayrah ؓ says, "By Him in whose hands, is Abū Hurayrah's life, the Apostle of God ﷺ and his family never had wheat bread continuously for three days until he departed from this world."[5]

---

1 For a detailed study of the lives of these souls moved by God see *Al-Zuhd* by ʿAbdullāh ibn Mubārak: *Ṣifat aṣ-Ṣafwah* by Ibn al-Jawzī and the *Ḥilyat al-Awliyā'* by Abū Nuʿaym.

2 Abū Dāwūd.

3 See the two *Ṣaḥīḥ*s for the full report.

4 Bukhārī: Kitāb ar-Ruqaq; Muslim: Kitāb az-Zuhd

5 Bukhārī and Muslim.

ʿĀ'ishah ﷺ relates "We, the members of the Prophet's ﷺ household caught sight of one moon and then the next, but no fire was lighted in our hearth. We had to live only on dates and water."[1]

The Prophet's ﷺ coat of mail had been pawned with a Jew but he had not enough money to get it back from him. When the Messenger of God ﷺ departed from the world the coat of mail was still with the Jew.

The Prophet ﷺ proceeded to perform the Farewell Pilgrimage followed by a huge crowd which obscured the horizon at a time when the entire Arabian Peninsula had acknowledged his spiritual and temporal supremacy. Yet, the saddle of his dromedary was outworn covered by a sheet which was worth not more than four dirhams. The prayer he then sent up to God was, "O Allāh, make it a *ḥajj* devoid of all pretensions and show."[2]

Abū Dharr ﷺ reports the Apostle ﷺ telling him on an occasion, "I would hate to possess as much gold as Mount Uḥud and then to allow three days to pass with a single dīnār remaining with me except that which I may hold back for the cause of religion. Rather, I would give it away to God's servant this way and that, on my right and left and in the back."[3]

Jābir ibn ʿAbdullāh ﷺ says that it never happened that God's Messenger ﷺ was asked to give anything and he said "No" in reply. Ibn ʿAbbās ﷺ testifies that in generosity and munificence the Apostle of God ﷺ was swifter than the wings of the wind.[4] Anas ﷺ says that once when a man asked the Apostle ﷺ to give him something, he gave him a flock of sheep enough to fill the space between two hillocks. The man returned to his people and said to them, "O people, embrace Islam. Muḥammad gives so open-handedly as if he fears not poverty." Another time, ninety thousand dirhams were presented to the Prophet ﷺ. He asked to heap them up on a mat and then started giving it away. Nobody who asked for it was denied until the entire heap of money disappeared.

NATURAL DISPOSITION

The holy Prophet ﷺ had an excessive zeal for devotions to God, his uninterrupted communion with the Lord took the shape of extensive orisons and vigils, supplications and lamentations; and his indifference to the world surpassed the abstinence of hermits and ascetics but he was never wanting in sympathy and

1 Ibid.

2 Tirmidhī.

3 *Bukhārī* and *Muslim*. The version narrated in *Ṣaḥīḥ Bukhārī* reads, "I would disdain to possess as much gold as Uḥud. . . ."

4 See the full version in the two *Ṣaḥīḥ*s.

compassion, courtesy and mannerly behaviour to one and all; nor was he ever lax in restoring justice to one whom it was denied or in bidding welcome to everyone according to his status and position. Once he said to Anas, "If you know what I know, you would laugh little and weep a great deal."

The Apostle ﷺ came of the noblest stock, yet he was very modest, exceedingly large-hearted and most sweet tempered; he never kept aloof from his Companions; cherished a kind and tender disposition towards children and often took them in his lap; accepted the invitation to eat with the slaves and maidservants, the poor and the indigent; visited the sick even if he had to go to the farthest corner of the city and always accepted excuses offered for misdeeds.[1] He was never seen stretching his legs whilst sitting with his Companions lest anyone of them should feel inconvenienced.

Abdullah ibn al-Ḥārith reports that he had not seen anyone smiling so often and with a more cheerful disposition than the Apostle of God ﷺ.[2] Jābir ibn Samurah says that he had joined the sittings of the Apostle ﷺ and his Companions more than a hundred times. He saw the Companions listening and reciting poems, describing some incident of the pagan past while the Apostle of God ﷺ either sat silently or smiled with them at some amusing remark. Sharīd states that the Prophet ﷺ asked him to recite the verses of Umayyah ibn Abī 'ṣ-Ṣalt and he recited them.[3]

The Apostle ﷺ was extremely kindhearted and affectionate—the finest human sentiments and virtues were discernible in his character. Anas ibn Mālik heard God's Apostle ﷺ saying to Fāṭimah, "Bring my two sons."[4] In a moment they came running and the Prophet ﷺ kissed and embraced them.[5] Another time the Prophet ﷺ summoned his grandson, Ḥasan ibn ʿAlī. He came running falling into the Prophet's ﷺ lap and passing his finger through his beard. The Prophet ﷺ opened his mouth and put his mouth in his mouth.

Fāṭimah tells that when the Prophet's ﷺ freedman Zayd ibn Ḥārithah came to Madīnah, the Prophet ﷺ was in his house. Zayd knocked at the door. The Prophet ﷺ immediately got up to greet him although he was not properly dressed. His mantle hanging loosely on his shoulders, he went out to receive Zayd, shook hands with him and kissed him.[6]

---

1 Abū Nuʿaym: *Ḥilyat al-Awliyā'*.

2 *Shamā'il at-Tirmidhī*.

3 *Al-Adab al-Mufrad li 'l-Bukhārī*, p. 127. Umayyah ibn Abi 'ṣ-Ṣalt was a pre-Islamic poet whose verses are chiefly on religious topics. He was a monotheist contemporary of the Prophet ﷺ.

4 al-Ḥasan and al-Ḥusayn.

5 *Tirmidhī*: Merits of al-Ḥasan and al-Ḥusayn.

6 Tirmidhī.

Usāmah ibn Zayd ﵁ reports that one of the Prophet's ﷺ daughters sent him a message telling him that a son of hers was at the ebb of life, asking him to come to her. The Prophet ﷺ sent her greeting, saying at the same time, "What God has taken away belongs to Him and what He has given belongs to Him, and He has appointed a time for everyone; so let her be patient and seek her reward from God." She then sent for him adjuring him to come to her, and he got up to go accompanied by us. The boy who was at the last gasp was brought to the Prophet ﷺ who took him in his lap, his eyes overflowing with tears. Saʿd ﵁ asked, "What is this, O Messenger of God?" He replied, "This is compassion which God deposits in the hearts of His servants of whom He will. Verily, God shows compassion to those who are compassionate."[1]

When the prisoners taken in the battle of Badr including ʿAbbās ﵁ were tied, the Apostle ﷺ could not sleep because of the groaning of ʿAbbās. The Anṣār, on learning of the Prophet's ﷺ unease, untied him. The Prophet ﷺ was pleased with the Anṣār but when it was suggested to him that ʿAbbās should be set free on payment of an indemnity, he refused the request since he did not like to discriminate between ʿAbbās ﵁ and other prisoners.[2]

A Bedouin came to the Apostle ﷺ and said, "You kiss your children but we do not." The Apostle ﷺ replied, "What can I do if God has withdrawn compassion from your hearts."[3]

The Prophet ﷺ was extremely kind to the children and was always considerate and benevolent to them. Anas ﵁ says that God's Messenger ﷺ passed by some children who were playing. The Prophet ﷺ greeted them.[4] He also reports that the Prophet ﷺ used to mingle with us and ask my younger brother, "Abū ʿUmayr, what has happened to your bird?"[5]

He was very soft and merciful to Muslims, and was very tolerant, overlooking their occasional weariness and listlessness.

ʿAbdullāh ibn Masʿūd ﵁ says that the Prophet ﷺ would intersperse his exhortations and counsels to the people lest they should get tired with them. Although prayer was most pleasing to him, he would always cut it short if the cry of any child reached his ears. He said once, "When I stand up for prayers I intend to make it long, but when I hear any child crying I shorten it for fear that his mother might be distressed."[6]

---

1 Bukhārī.

2 *Fatḥ al-Bārī*, vol. VIII, p. 324.

3 *Bukhārī*, on the authority of ʿĀ'ishah

4 Bukhārī.

5 *Al-Adab al-Mufrad*, p. 40.

6 Bukhārī: Kitāb aṣ-Ṣalāt.

Ibn Masᶜūd ﷺ narrates that someone said to the Prophet ﷺ, "O Messenger of God, I swear by Allāh that I keep away from the morning prayer on account of so and so who makes it too long." Ibn Masᶜūd ﷺ further says that he never saw the Apostle ﷺ more angry than when he saw him while giving an exhortation after that incident. He said, "There are some among you who scare the people away; so whoever of you leads a prayer, let him be brief, for the weak and the aged and those who have a business to attend are present."[1]

It is also related that Anjashah ﷺ was a singer of camel-songs who had a beautiful voice and used to lead the dromedaries of women. Anjashah's melodious singing made the camels go quickly which disturbed the women. Hence the Prophet ﷺ said to him, "Gently Anjashah, do not break the glass vessels."[2]

God had made the Apostle's ﷺ heart as clear as a crystal, bearing no ill will against anybody. Once he said to his Companions, "None of you should denounce another before me, for I like to come out to you without any ill-feeling."[3]

God's Messenger ﷺ was benign and gracious to all the Muslims as if he were their father. He treated everyone of them like his family members, as if they were his own charge. Or, the affection he had for them was like that of a mother for her child, for he had never had an eye to their wealth and property or their prosperity but he always deemed it his duty to lighten their burdens and to clear their debts. He would say, "Whoever leaves some property as a legacy, it belongs to his heirs, but his unpaid debts are my responsibility."[4]

There is yet another report citing the Apostle ﷺ: "No Muslim has a patron closer unto him than I. Or, if you wish, recite the verse: 'The Prophet is closer to the believer than their selves'[5]; for the property left by anyone goes to his nearest kin, whoever they may be. But if one dies leaving a debt, he (the creditor) should come to me since I am the patron of the deceased and responsible for discharging his debts."[6]

MODERATION AND SEEMLINESS

The cardinal virtues of the Prophet ﷺ, the geniality and seemliness of his character, which would remain a shining example of decorous behaviour for the

---

1 Ibid.

2 *Al-Adab al-Mufrad*, p. 185, *Bukhārī* and *Muslim*. The Prophet ﷺ indicated, figuratively, the weakness and delicacy of women who were troubled by the faster pace of the camels.

3 *Kitāb ash-Shifā'*, p. 55.

4 Bukhārī: Kitāb al-Istiqrāḍ.

5 Qur'ān 33:6.

6 Bukhārī

coming generations, present as well as future, consisted in his innate moderation, refined taste and gracefulness, restraint and temperance and even-handedness which always kept him on the middle path. ʿĀ'ishah ﷺ relates that the God's Messenger ﷺ was never given his choice between two things but that he would take the easier course provided it involved no sin—for if it did, no one kept farther away from it than him.[1]

The Prophet ﷺ disliked pretension and airs no less than he detested asceticism, self-mortification and renouncement of what was the just claim of one's body and soul.

Abū Hurayrah ﷺ reported the Apostle ﷺ as saying, "The religion is ease, if anyone overdoes it, it will wear him down. So take to moderation and steer an even course, approximate, and give good tidings, and get strength through prayer in the morning, the evening, and some part of the night."

The Prophet ﷺ also advised: "Exert only as much as you have strength, for, by God, Allāh will never tire until you grow weary." Ibn ʿAbbās ﷺ relates that the Apostle of God ﷺ was asked about the religion most liked by God. He replied, "The religion of ease and sincerity."[2]

ʿAbdullāh ibn Masʿūd ﷺ reported God's Messenger ﷺ as saying, "They are doomed who overdo or deal sternly or are given to hair-splitting."[3]

The Companions sent by the Apostle ﷺ for the education of or exhortation to any tribe were commanded by him: "Make it easy, not hard—gladden the hearts, don't frighten them off."

ʿAbdullāh ibn ʿAmr ibn al-ʿĀṣ ﷺ tells that the Prophet ﷺ said: "God likes to see the marks of His bounty on His servant."[4]

THE PROPHET IN HIS HOUSE

The Apostle of God ﷺ kept busy at home like a common man. As ʿĀ'ishah ﷺ relates, he would clean his clothes, milk the sheep and do odd jobs. She also says that he would mend his clothes, repair his shoes and carry out similar other works. When asked how the Prophet ﷺ occupied himself at home, she replied, "He would keep himself busy with household chores and went out when the time for prayer came."[5]

1 Bukhārī: Kitāb al-Īmān.

2 *Al-Adab al-Mufrad*, p. 181.

3 Muslim.

4 *Tirmidhī*: *Abwāb al-Ādāb*. The Prophet ﷺ meant that if a man blessed with prosperity led a miserable and shabby existence like a beggar, he showed his ingratitude to God.

5 Bukhārī.

In another report related on her authority, she is reported to have said, "The Prophet of God ﷺ would repair his shoes, mend his clothes and occupied himself at home, just as any of you occupy yourself."[1]

ʿĀ'ishah relates, "God's Messenger ﷺ was very kindhearted, the kindliest of all, He laughed often and smiled much."[2] Anas says that he had not seen a man more clement to his household members than the Apostle of God ﷺ. It is related on the authority of ʿĀ'ishah that the Prophet ﷺ said, "The best of you is one who is kindest to his wife and children and I am the kindest among you."[3]

Abū Hurayrah said that the Prophet ﷺ never expressed disapproval of any food, if he desired he ate it, and if he disliked he left it alone.

SELFLESSNESS

It was a settled principle with the Prophet ﷺ that he always kept to the fore his own kith and kin and those who were near to him in facing a risk or hazard but allotted them the last place in distributing favours and rewards and spoils of war. When the three well-known swordsmen of Quraysh, ʿUtbah ibn Rabīʿah, Shaybah ibn Rabīʿah and Walīd ibn ʿUtbah challenged the Muslims to single combat at Badr, the Prophet ﷺ sent forward Ḥamzah, ʿAlī and ʿUbaydah although he knew about the valour of enemy combatants and also had a number of veterans among the Mūhājirīn and the Anṣār who could have successfully fought with the Quraysh warriors. All three, Ḥamzah, ʿAlī and ʿUbaydah, belonged to the Prophet's ﷺ own clan, Banū Hāshim, and were his nearest relatives. The Apostle ﷺ also held them dear and disliked to imperil others for the sake of keeping his kindred out of danger. God helped the three to emerge from the combat successful; Ḥamzah and ʿAlī came back safe and triumphant while ʿUbaydah was brought back mortally wounded.

Again, when the Prophet ﷺ disallowed usury and abolished the blood vengeance belonging to the pre-Islamic period on the occasion of the Farewell Pilgrimage he declared, "The usury of the pre-Islamic period is abolished, and the first of our usury I abolish is that of ʿAbbās ibn ʿAbd al-Muṭṭalib. Claims of blood vengeance belonging to the pagan past have been abolished and the first of those murdered among us whose blood vengeance I remit is that of the son of Rabīʿah ibn al-Ḥārith."[4]

Unlike the kings, rulers and political leaders, the Prophet of God ﷺ always

1 *Muṣannaf* by ʿAbd ar-Razzāq. vol. XI, p. 260.

2 Ibn ʿAsākir.

3 *Musnad Aḥmad* and *Muslim,* on the authority of Anas.

4 *Muslim*: *Kitāb al-Ḥajj*, on the authority of Jābir ibn ʿAbdullāh.

kept his kith and kin in the background, giving preference to others when handing out gifts and rewards. ʿAlī relates that Fāṭimah ﷺ had to work hard in grinding corn. So when she got the news that some slave girls had been brought to the Prophet ﷺ, she went to him and requested that one to be given to her. The Prophet ﷺ, however, did not accede to her request. Fāṭimah then mentioned the matter to ʿĀʾishah ﷺ, who talked to the Prophet ﷺ about Fāṭimah's trouble. Relating this incident ʿAlī ﷺ says: "The Apostle of God visited us when we had gone to bed. We were about to get up but he told us to stay where we were. He then sat down near me and I felt the coldness of his feet on my chest. He then said, 'Let me guide you to something better than what you have asked. When you go to bed, say *Subḥān Allāh* (Glory be to God) thirty-three times, *Al-ḥamdu li-Llāh* (Praise be to God) thirty-three times, and *Allāhu akbar* (God is most great) thirty-four times. This will be better for you than a servant.'"[1]

In another report of the same incident handed down through another source, the Prophet ﷺ is also reported to have said, "By God, I cannot give you anything at the time when the bellies of my Companions of Ṣuffah[2] have been hollowed by hunger. I have nothing to meet their expenses and I will sell these to provide for them."[3]

INSTINCTIVE MAGNIFICENCE

Great was the responsibility lying on the Apostle ﷺ; teaching of God's truth in its purity, inviting the people to take the path of truth and virtue; guarding and guiding the nascent Islamic community; and the cares and anxieties for the suffering humanity were the charges heavier than flesh and blood can bear.

In between all these worries, stresses and strains we find the most sublime instincts of grace and goodness reflecting his worthiness and excellence of heart. In spite of his dauntless spirit of resolution and singleness of purpose which have always been the distinguishing features of the Prophet ﷺ, the Apostle of God ﷺ could never forget those faithful friends and Companions who had accepted his mission in its initial stages and made the supreme sacrifice of laying down their lives in the battle of Uḥud ﷺ. He would talk about them often, invoking divine blessings upon them and would pay visits to them.

Such was this immortal love, with an element of the transcendent in it, that it had gone beyond the flesh and blood and penetrated the inanimate hills and

1 Bukhārī: Kitāb al-Jihād.

2 A raised platform at the mosque in Madīnah where poor Companions lived, desirous of remaining in attendance to the Prophet ﷺ.

3 *Fatḥ al-Bārī* vol. VII, pp. 23–24 (on the authority of Aḥmad).

stones and ravines where these brilliant spectacles of noble love and sacrifice had played out. His Companions relate that they heard him saying, "this is the hill that loves me and which I love."[1] Anas ibn Mālik says that when the Messenger of God ﷺ caught sight of Uḥud, he said, "This is the hill that loves me and which I love." Abī Ḥumayd reports that he accompanied the Apostle ﷺ while returning from Tabūk. When they came near Madīnah, the Prophet of God ﷺ said, "This is Ṭābah,[2] and this is the hill which loves me and which I love."[3]

ʿUqbah tells that God's Messenger ﷺ went to the Martyrs of Uḥud and prayed for their salvation.[4] Jābir ibn ʿAbdullāh relates that when the martyrs of Uḥud were once mentioned to the Prophet ﷺ he said, "I swear to God that I would have liked to be sleeping with these martyrs by the side of this hill." The Apostle ﷺ had borne with equanimity the shock of Ḥamzah's death, who had been his loving uncle as well as foster brother and had parted with his life fighting valiantly for the cause of Islam. He had also remained calm and composed about what had been done to Ḥamzah's dead body. But when he passed by the houses of Banū ʿAbd al-Ashhal while returning to Madīnah, he heard the lamentations over the dead. Overcome with the grief for the departed comrade, his eyes gave way to tears and he said, "But there are no women to mourn over Ḥamzah!"[5]

But however noble and sublime and overflowing with human kindness these instincts and emotions were, the Apostle of God ﷺ never allowed them to trammel his mission or to disrupt the divine injunctions. Historians and biographers of the Prophet ﷺ relate that when Saʿd ibn Muʿādh and Usayd ibn Ḥuḍayr came back to the settlement of Banū ʿAbd al-Ashhal, they ordered their women to gird themselves and go and weep for Ḥamzah. They did as they had been told and when the Apostle ﷺ came he found them weeping at the door of his mosque. But, he told then, "May God have mercy on you, go back. Your presence has been enough for my consolation." It has been narrated by another Companion that on seeing the women the Apostle ﷺ asked "What is it?" When he was told that the Anṣār had sent their women to weep over Ḥamzah, he invoked God's mercy for the Anṣār and paid compliments to them for their love to him but also added, "I did not mean that. I do not like lamentation over the dead." Thereafter the Apostle ﷺ forbade mourning for the dead.[6]

An occasion still more poignant was when Waḥshī, the slayer of Ḥamzah,

1 Bukhārī: Kitāb al-Maghāzī
2 Madīnah Ṭayyibah.
3 Bukhārī: Kitāb al-Maghāzī.
4 Ibid.
5 *Ibn Kathīr*, vol. III. p. 95. Aḥmad has narrated this report on the authority of Ibn ʿUmar.
6 *Ibn Kathīr*, vol. III. p. 96.

stood before the Apostle of God ﷺ. The enemies of Islam deemed the Muslim conquest of Makkah as the darkest hour of their lives. A number of them had no hesitation deciding that it would now be well-nigh impossible for them to remain at Makkah. They decided to flee to Syria, Yemen, or some other place for fear of their lives. Their friends, however, told them: "Woe to you, Muḥammad does not kill anyone who enters his religion." Almost all these former enemies returned and embraced Islam. None of them had the least speck of fear in his heart on appearing before the Apostle ﷺ after pledging allegiance to Islam, nor did the Apostle ﷺ say a word to cast any doubt on their sincerity or to terrify them. And so it happened with Waḥshī ؓ also. The Apostle of God ﷺ learnt from Waḥshī, after he had accepted Islam, how he had killed Ḥamzah ؓ. It was but natural that the Prophet ﷺ was grieved and harrowed to know about Waḥshī's ghastly crime, but he did not allow his pain to get the better of his responsibility as the Apostle of God ﷺ. He neither refused to admit Waḥshī ؓ to the fold of Islam nor had him slain for his crime. All he said to Waḥshī ؓ was, "O man, hide your face from me and never let me see you again." Waḥshī ؓ would avoid the Apostle of God ﷺ so that he should not see him, until the time arrived for the Apostle's departure.[1]

These nobler emotions or tender feelings reflecting the warm-heartedness of the Prophet ﷺ were laid bare when he visited an old, dilapidated grave. Then, those with him found him in turmoil, and he said, "This is the grave of Āminah." This was many years after the death of the Apostle's ﷺ mother.[2]

MILDNESS, COURTESY AND FORBEARANCE

In his good manners, gentleness cordiality, sympathy and forbearance the Messenger of God ﷺ has left a perpetual and living example of noble behaviour for all mankind. Truly, he stood on such an exalted plane of graceful and courteous deportment that God extolled him in the Qur'ān:

> And verily you are of a high and noble nature.[3]

The Apostle ﷺ once told the Companions. "God Himself has disciplined me, a discipline in the best manner."

Jābir ؓ reported the Apostle ﷺ as saying: "God has raised me to perfect moral virtues and seemly behaviour."[4]

---

1 Ibn Hishām, vol. II, p. 72, Bukhārī: Kitāb al-Maghāzī.

2 *Bayhaqī,* on the authority of Sufyān Thawrī; *Ibn Kathīr,* vol. I. p. 236.

3 Qur'ān 68:4.

4 *Sharḥ as-Sunnah* and *Mishkāt al-Maṣābīḥ* p. 514.

When ʿĀʾishah ﷺ was asked about the character of the Prophet ﷺ, she replied, "His character was the Qur'ān."[1]

Indeed, such was his tolerance and forbearance, sympathy, graciousness and magnanimity that even the painters of souls with the gift of speech would seldom find words adequate to catch his likeness. Had the accounts about him not been handed down with the greatest caution by the most trustworthy narrators, it would have been difficult for one to accept them. But all these accounts have been transmitted with the greatest care by many narrators, each testifying to the piety, veracity, acumen and intelligence of the other from whom he learnt of an event, and, then, the reports transmitted through different sources and channels so corroborate one another that in their genuineness and authenticity they form a class by themselves in the entire continuous and methodical records of public events. There is, thus, not the least doubt that every unbiased student of these records will come to the conclusion that never has there existed a historical document which was more firmly based on facts or better authenticated by external and internal evidence than the ḥadīth of the Prophet ﷺ which represent the high point of the science of history.

A few incidents given here illustrate the Prophet's ﷺ tenderness and mercy towards the people. The clemency of the merciful Apostle of God ﷺ made no distinction between a friend and a foe. ʿAbdullāh ibn Ubayy was the leader of hypocrites whose revengeful attitude had always created difficulties for the Prophet ﷺ. But when he died and had been placed in his grave, the Apostle of God ﷺ arrived and asked him to be taken out. He then placed him on his knees, blew some of his saliva over him, and clothed him with his shirt.[2]

Anas ﷺ reports: "Once when I was walking with the Prophet ﷺ who was wearing a Najrānī cloak with a coarse fringe, a nomadic Arab met him and gave his cloak a violent tug. I saw that the man's tug had left a mark on the neck of God's Apostle ﷺ. The nomad said, 'Command that I be given some of God's property that you have, Muḥammad.' The Apostle ﷺ turned round to him and laughed, and then ordered that he should be given something."[3]

Zayd ibn Saʿnah came to the Prophet ﷺ and demanded payment of the money that the Prophet ﷺ owed him. Then he violently pulled the Prophet's ﷺ cloak from his shoulder, caught hold of it and addressed him rudely, saying, "You son of ʿAbd al-Muṭṭalib are dilly-dallying." ʿUmar ﷺ rebuked and reproached him but the Prophet ﷺ kept smiling and said to ʿUmar ﷺ: "This

1 Muslim.

2 ʿAbdullāh ibn Ubayy died in 9 AH, after his return from Tabūk. *Az-Zurqānī*, vol. III, pp. 112–13; *Bukhārī*.

3 Bukhārī: Kitāb al-Jihād, Musnad Aḥmad,, vol. III, p. 153.

man was entitled to better treatment from you. You ought to have advised me to repay the loan promptly and asked him to make his demand politely." Then, turning to Zayd ؓ, the Prophet ﷺ said, "There are still three days to go till the appointed time for repayment." At the same time he asked ʿUmar ؓ to repay the loan and give Zayd twenty *ṣāʿs* more so as to compensate him for his threatening attitude towards Zayd ؓ. The gracious and obliging behaviour of God's Apostle ﷺ caused Zayd ؓ to embrace Islam.[1]

Anas ؓ relates that once a band of eighty armed men of Makkah suddenly appeared at Wādī at-Tanʿīm with the intention of making a sudden attack on the Apostle of God ﷺ. They were all captured but the Apostle ﷺ spared their lives.[2]

Relating an incident when Jābir ؓ went with the Apostle of God ﷺ on an expedition, he says: "At midday the time for a siesta came during the journey. The valley was full of thorny bushes. The Apostle of God ﷺ went to take rest under an acacia tree on which he hung his sword. We also dispersed to take a break under other trees. All of a sudden the Prophet ﷺ called us and we saw that a nomadic Arab was sitting by his side. When we went to him he said, 'I was sleeping when this man came and unsheathed my sword against me. When I awoke I saw him standing over my head with the drawn sword, and he was asking me: "Who can now protect you from me?" I replied, "Allāh", and he sheathed the sword. Then he sat down and now he is before you.'" It is related that God's Apostle ﷺ did not exact any vengeance on the nomad.[3]

Every Companion of the Prophet ﷺ was sufficiently forbearing to throw the most pious soul into shade but the long-suffering patience of God's Messenger ﷺ rose above the patience of all of them. He was their kindhearted teacher and mentor and guide from whom all drew inspiration. An incident related by Abū Hurayrah ؓ illustrates the breadth and greatness of the Apostle's ﷺ heart. Once, a Bedouin passed urine in the holy Mosque. The Companions jumped at him and grabbed him for the sacrilegious act, but the Apostle ﷺ commanded, "Let him alone. Pour a bucket or two of water over what he has passed, for you have been sent to make things easy and not to make things difficult."[4]

Another Companion, Muʿāwiyah ibn al-Ḥakam ؓ reports, "I sneezed while praying along with the Apostle of God ﷺ and said: 'God have mercy on you!' The people around stared down at me, so I said, 'Woe is me! What do you mean by looking askance at me?' They began to strike their bands on their thighs. Now I understood that they wanted me to be silent and I kept quiet. When the Apos-

---

1 *Aḥmad,* vol. III, p. 153.

2 Muslim: Kitāb al-Jihād.

3 Bukhārī: Kitāb al-Maghāzī.

4 Bukhārī: Kitāb al-Wuḍūʾ.

tle of God ﷺ, for whom I would give my father and mother as ransom as I have seen no teacher better than him before or after, finished his prayer, by God, he neither rebuked, nor beat, nor reviled me. He simply said to me, 'No talk is fitting during the prayer, for it consists only of the glorification of God, declaration of His greatness and recitation of the Qur'ān.'"[1]

Anas ؓ has also related many an instance of the Prophet's ﷺ leniency, sympathy and noble mindedness. He says that God's Apostle ﷺ was very generous and kind. If anybody in need approached him for anything, he gave it to him or at least made a promise for the same. Once, when the Apostle ﷺ had taken his place to lead the prayer, a desert Arab stepped forward and holding his cloak said, "I stand in need but I fear lest I should forget it." The Prophet ﷺ went with him and prayed after he had satisfied him.

Recounting the indulgent and long-suffering nature of the Apostle ﷺ Anas ؓ has cited certain instances of the time when he was a young lad. He says, "I served the Prophet of God for ten years but he never blamed me for doing anything or leaving anything undone."[2]

Suᶜād ibn ᶜUmar ؓ called upon the Prophet ﷺ when, as he says, her cloak bore some marks of a scent mixed with saffron. The Prophet ﷺ exclaimed, "Saffron! Saffron! Lay off! Lay off! and hit me with a stick on my stomach which caused me a little pain. Suᶜād said, "O Apostle of God, now I have a right to make requital." The Prophet ﷺ bared his belly at once and said, "Have your revenge."[3]

MODESTY

The Prophet ﷺ was absolutely unassuming and modest. He hated to put on airs or to make himself conspicuous on any occasion. He did not even like the people to stand up to showing him respect nor did he allow anybody to extol him in the way the followers of other religions had praised their prophets. He was the Messenger and servant of God ﷺ and he wanted himself to be known by others in a like manner, neither more, nor less. Anas ؓ said that no man was dearer to the Companions than God's Messenger ﷺ, but they never stood up on seeing him for they knew his dislike for that.[4]

Once the Prophet ﷺ was addressed as "Best of creation." He promptly replied, "That was the position that Ibrāhīm ؑ enjoyed."[5]

---

1 Muslim.

2 Muslim: Kitāb al-Faḍā'il.

3 Kitāb ash-Shifā'

4 Tirmidhī; Musnad Aḥmad, vol. III, p. 132.

5 Muslim: Kitāb al-Faḍā'il.

ʿUmar ﷺ reported the Prophet ﷺ saying. "Do not exalt me as the Christians have exalted Jesus, the son of Mary. I am but His servant, so call me God's servant and Messenger."[1]

ʿAbdullāh ibn Abī Awfā' ﷺ reports: "The Apostle of God never disdained to accompany a slave or a widow to accomplish their tasks."[2] Anas ﷺ says that any slave-girl or maidservant of Madīnah could take the Prophet ﷺ by his hand and say whatever she liked and take him wherever she liked.[3]

When ʿAdī ibn Ḥātim came to see the Apostle ﷺ, he called him inside his house. A maidservant brought a cushion to rest on but the Prophet ﷺ placed it between him and ʿAdī and sat down on the floor. ʿAdī later said that he realised immediately that the Prophet ﷺ was not a king.[4]

Anas ﷺ reported that the Apostle of God ﷺ would visit the sick, attend funerals, ride on donkeys and accept the invitations of slaves to a meal.[5]

Jābir ﷺ states that the Prophet ﷺ would slow down his pace for the sake of the weak and also prayed for them.[6]

Anas ﷺ said: The Prophet ﷺ accepted an invitation even if he was presented barley bread and soup whose taste had changed."[7] He also reports the Prophet ﷺ as saying, "I am God's servant. I eat like a servant and sit like a servant."[8]

ʿAbdullāh ibn ʿAmr ibn al-ʿĀṣ ﷺ said: "Once when the Messenger of God ﷺ came to my house, I gave him a cushion filled with bark, but he sat down on the floor placing the cushion between me and him."[9]

The Apostle ﷺ would tidy up his house, tether the camels, feed the animals, take food with his servants, and help them in kneading flour and bringing provisions from the market.[10]

COURAGE AND SHYNESS

Courage and shyness are often regarded as conflicting traits but the two were balanced in the Prophet's ﷺ nature in a like manner. Being extremely modest, he blushed like a maiden, as Abū Saʿīd Khudrī ﷺ described, if he came across anything shocking or outrageous. On such occasions his countenance would

---

1 Bukhārī: Kitāb al-Anbiyā'.

2 Bayhaqī.

3 *Musnad Aḥmad*, vol. III, pp. 189–215, *Jamʿa al-Fawā'id*: Kitāb al-Manāqib.

4 *Zād al-Maʿād* vol. I, p. 43.

5 *Shamā'il at-Tirmidhī.*

6 *Al-Targhīb wa 't-Tarhīb.*

7 *Shamā'il at-Tirmidhī; Musnad Aḥmad*, vol. III, pp. 211–289.

8 *Kitāb ash-Shifā'*, p. 101.

9 *Al-Adab al-Mufrad*, p. 172.

10 *Kitāb ash-Shifā'*, p. 101.

change showing his displeasure.[1] Such was his coyness that he was even diffident to express anything disagreeable to one's face and usually asked somebody else to do the job for him. Anas reports that the clothes of a man present in one of his sittings were hued in a yellowish colour. Since the Prophet ﷺ did not like to say anything displeasing to anyone, he said to others, when the man had got up to leave, "It would have been better if you had told him to give up using the colour yellow."[2]

ʿĀ'ishah relates that if the Prophet ﷺ came to know of a misdeed that someone had committed, he would never asked why he had done it. What he would say on such occasions was, "What has happened to the people that say or do such a thing?" He deprecated the wrong but never named the wrongdoer.[3]

As for the dauntless courage and valour of the Prophet of God ﷺ, the testimony of ʿAlī, the lion of God, suffices to illustrate the point. He says: "When the battle became fierce and the eyes seemed to be coming out of the sockets, we were wont to look for the Prophet ﷺ in order to find a refuge behind him. Then, we found none closing upon the enemy as the Prophet ﷺ. This was how it happened in Badr. We were taking shelter behind the Prophet ﷺ who was then going at the enemy more closely than any one of us."[4]

Anas said, "The Apostle of God ﷺ was extremely handsome, most generous and the bravest of men. One night when the people in Madīnah were in a panic and some went in the direction of the sound they had heard, they were met by the Prophet ﷺ who had gone in that direction ahead of them, and he was saying, 'don't fear, don't fear.' He was then on a bareback horse without a saddle belonging to Abū Ṭalḥah and had a sword slung on his neck. Praising the horse he said, 'I found it swift and rushing ahead like an ocean.'"[5]

In the battles of Uḥud and Ḥunayn when the Muslims had fallen back and the bravest among them were unable to stand the charge of the enemy, the Apostle of God ﷺ had stuck to his position, riding his mule, as if nothing had happened, and was calling out, "I am the Prophet without falsehood! I am the son of ʿAbd al-Muṭṭalib!"

MERCY AND COMPASSION

God's Messenger ﷺ was the kindliest of men just as he excelled all others in courage and valour. Being extremely kindhearted, his eyes brimmed with tears

1 Bukhārī: Kitāb al-Manāqib.

2 *Shamā'il at-Tirmidhī*: Khulq an-Nabī.

3 Abū Dāwūd.

4 *Kitāb ash-Shifā'*, p. 89.

5 Bukhārī: *Al-Adab al-Mufrad*, p. 46.

at the slightest sign of inhumanity. Shaddād ibn Aws ﷺ reports the Apostle ﷺ as saying: "Indeed Allah has prescribed excellence in all things. Thus, if you kill, kill well; and if you slaughter, slaughter well. Let each one of you sharpen his blade and let him spare suffering to the animal he slaughters."[1]

Ibn ʿAbbās ﷺ relates that a man threw a goat on its side and then started sharpening his knife. When the Prophet ﷺ saw him he said, "Do you want to kill it twice? Why did you not sharpen the knife before throwing it on the ground?"

The Apostle ﷺ forbade his Companions to keep animals hungry or thirsty, to disturb or to overburden them. He commended that kindliness and putting them at ease were meritorious acts tending to bring man nearer to God.

Abū Hurayrah ﷺ reports the Prophet ﷺ as saying: "A traveller who was thirsty saw a well on the way. He got inside the well and when he came out he saw a dog licking mud because of thirst. The man realised that the dog must be as thirsty as he was and so he got into the well again, filled his leather sack with water and carried it out holding it with his teeth. And thus he quenched the thirst of the dog. God was pleased with this act of kindness and pardoned his sins. The Companions asked, 'O Messenger of God, is there recompense in the matter of beasts and wild animals also?' The Prophet ﷺ replied, 'there is recompense in regard to every creature that has a living heart.'"[2]

ʿAbdullāh ibn ʿUmar ﷺ told that the Prophet ﷺ said, "A woman was cast away into the hell only because she had denied food and water to her cat and refused to set it free so that the cat might satisfy its hunger by taking worms and insects."[3]

Suhayl ibn ar-Rabīʿ ibn ʿAmr ﷺ states that the Apostle of God ﷺ came across a camel so famished that its belly had shrunk to its back. He said, "Fear God in the matter of these creatures. If you ride them, ride when they are healthy and if you eat them, eat them when they are in a good condition."[4]

ʿAbdullāh ibn Jaʿfar ﷺ narrated the incident that once the Prophet ﷺ entered the enclosure of one of the Anṣār where there was a camel which started groaning on seeing the Prophet ﷺ, tears running down its eyes. The Prophet ﷺ went near it, patted it on its hump and face which set it at ease. Then the Apostle ﷺ asked who its owner was. The Anṣārī youth came and said: "O Messenger of God, it belongs to me." The Prophet ﷺ said to him, "Do you not fear God in the matter of this beast although He has made you its owner? It complained to me that you bore hard upon it and always kept it at work."[5]

1 Muslim: Kitāb adh-Dhabḥ.

2 Bukhārī and Muslim.

3 *Nawawī* on the authority of *Muslim*.

4 Abū Dāwūd.

5 Abū Dāwūd.

Abū Hurayrah ؓ quoted the Apostle ﷺ as saying, "When you travel in a fertile country do not deny the camels their due from the ground, and when you travel in a land barren and dry, cover it with speed. When you encamp at night keep away from the roads, for they are where the beasts pass and are the resorts of the insects at night."[1]

Ibn Masʿūd ؓ reports, "While we were on a journey with God's Messenger ﷺ, he went a short distance from where we had encamped. There we saw a small bird with two of its young and caught them. The bird was fluttering when the Prophet ﷺ came back and so he asked, 'Who has distressed it by taking its chicks?' Then he asked us to return the chicks. There we also saw an ant hill and burned it out. When the Prophet ﷺ saw he asked, 'Who has burnt it?' When we informed him that we had done it, he said, 'Only the Lord of fire has the right to punish with fire.'"[2]

The Prophet ﷺ strongly enjoined the duty of kind and generous treatment of the slaves, servants and the labourers engaged for manual work. Jābir ؓ relates the Apostle of God ﷺ as saying, "Feed them with the food which you eat, clothe them with such clothing as you wear and do not cause trouble to God's creatures."[3] The Apostle ﷺ is further stated to have said, "Those whom God has made your dependents are your brothers, servants and helpmates. Anybody whose brother has been made subservient to him ought to feed him with the food he eats and clothe him with the clothes he wears, command him not to do that which he is unable to do and if it becomes necessary to do so then he should help him in doing the job."[4]

ʿAbdullāh ibn ʿUmar ؓ says that once an Arab nomad came and asked the Prophet ﷺ, "How many times should I pardon my servant in a day?" The Prophet ﷺ replied, "Seventy times."[5] He also quotes the Apostle ﷺ as saying: "Pay the wages of a labourer before his sweat has dried."[6]

A COMPREHENSIVE AND ETERNAL MODEL

The Messenger of God ﷺ was the last and the greatest of all the prophets sent to provide guidance to all classes, ranks and grades in every age, time and clime. The comprehensiveness of the Prophet's ﷺ character summed up vividly by

---

1 Muslim.
2 Abū Dāwūd: Kitāb al-Jihād.
3 *Al-Adab al-Mufrad*, p. 38.
4 Bukhārī and Abū Dāwūd.
5 Tirmidhī and Abū Dāwūd.
6 Ibn Mājah.

Syed Sulaymān Nadwī in *Muḥammad The Ideal Prophet,* would be a fitting epilogue to this section dealing with the character of the Prophet. Syed Sulaymān Nadwī writes:

> A model that can serve for every class of the people acting under different circumstances and states of human emotions will be found in the life of Muḥammad ﷺ. If you are rich, there is the example of the tradesman of Makkah and the master of Baḥrayn's treasure ﷺ; if you are poor, you can follow the internees of Shiʿb Abī Ṭālib and the émigré of Madīnah ﷺ. If you are a king, watch the actions of the Ruler of Arabia ﷺ. If you are a vassal, take a look at the man enduring hardships imposed by the Quraysh of Makkah ﷺ. If you are a conqueror, lay your eyes on the victor of Badr and Ḥunayn ﷺ. If you have suffered a defeat, take a lesson from the one discomfited at Uḥud ﷺ. If you are a teacher, learn from the holy mentor of the school of Suffah ﷺ. If you are a student, look at the learner who sat before Gabriel ﷺ. If you are one who gives sermons direct your eyes to the speaker delivering lectures in the mosque of Madīnah ﷺ. If you are charged to convey truth and mercy to your persecutors, observe the preacher explaining the message of God to the pagans of Makkah ﷺ. If you have brought your enemy to his knees, look at the conqueror of Makkah ﷺ. If you want to administer your lands and properties, discover how the lands and groves of Banū an-Naḍīr, Khaybar and Fadak were managed. If you are an orphan, do not forget the child of Āminah and ʿAbdullāh ﷺ left to the tender mercy of Ḥalīmah. If you are young, see the character of Makkah's shepherd ﷺ. If you have a travelling business, cast a glance at the leader of the caravan on the way to Busrā ﷺ. If you are a judge or arbiter, look at the umpire entering the holy sanctuary before the peep of dawn and installing the Black Stone in the Kaʿbah ﷺ, or the justice of peace in whose eyes the poor and the rich were alike. If you are a husband, study the behaviour of the husband of Khadījah and ʿĀ'ishah ﷺ. If you are a father, go through the biography of Fāṭimah's father and the grandfather of Ḥasan and Ḥusayn ﷺ. In short, whoever and whatever you may be, you will find a shining example in the life of the Prophet ﷺ to illuminate your behaviour. If you have the life of the Prophet ﷺ before you, you can find the examples of all the prophets, Noah and Abraham, John and Jonah and Moses and Jesus. If the life and character of each prophet of God were deemed to be a shop selling the wares of one commodity, that of Muḥammad ﷺ would verily be a variety store where goods of every description can be had to suit the tastes and needs of all."[1]

1 Muḥammad, the Ideal Prophet, pp. 89–90.

27

Mercy of the World

WE SENT YOU NOT SAVE AS A MERCY FOR THE PEOPLE.[1]

THE WORLD WAS passing through a state of trauma at the close of the sixth century of the Christian era. The entire human race had effectively taken a pledge to commit suicide. God has portrayed, in the Qur'ān, the condition then obtaining in the world so vividly that no artist can draw such a true to life picture of the situation.

> And remember Allāh's favour unto you; how you were enemies and He made friendship between your hearts so that you became as brothers by His grace; and you were upon the brink of an abyss of fire, and He did save you from it."[2]

If our historians and litterateurs have not been able to preserve the heart-rending account of the pagan past, they need not be blamed for it because the limitations of human language and forms of expression would not have allowed them to capture in words the dreadful situation of the world as it was then. The shape of things was so dreadful, so critical, that not even a skilful painter could have succeeded in its faithful depiction. How could any historian have drawn a picture of that horrible situation? Did the Age of Ignorance merely mean moral

1 Qur'ān 21:107.

2 Qur'ān 3:103. This chapter, summing up the great benefits flowing from the prophethood of Muḥammad ﷺ, which have changed the destiny of human race, has been taken from the concluding part of a speech delivered by the author on the occasion of birth anniversary of the holy Prophet ﷺ.

corruption of the Arab or a few other nations? Did it merely pose the problem of idolatry, depravity and decadence or else self-indulgence, inequity and exploitation of the poor, or the criminal behaviour of the then stronger nations? Was it simply the question of the burial of innocent newborn daughters by their heartless fathers? It was all this and much more. There are hardly words to describe the terrifying conditions through which the whole world was passing in those days. Only those can understand it who had themselves lived in that horrifying age.

It was thus not a problem confronting any single nation or country—the destiny of the whole human race was at stake. If any artist capable of converting a vision into eternity were to paint the portrait of a good-looking young and vigorous man, a soul shining through its crystal covering, and could somehow show him to be the vicegerent of God on earth who was bent on taking a leap in a lake of fire and brimstone, then he would perhaps succeed in portraying the situation thus depicted in the Qur'ān: "You were on the brink of an abyss of fire, He did save you from it."[1] The holy Prophet ﷺ has also illustrated this critical situation through a simile. He says, "the mission and guidance I have been vouchsafed to deliver to this world is like this: A man made a bonfire and when it illuminated the surroundings, insects began to jump into it. You also want to take a leap into the fire in a like manner, but I am holding you by your waists to save you from falling into the eternal fire."[2]

The whole problem was how to lead the caravan of humanity to its safe destination. All the social and developmental endeavours, educational and literary efforts were possible only after man had been brought back to a normal, sensible frame of mind. There is not the least doubt that the greatest good the prophets have done for humanity consists in saving it from the unknown, imminent dangers threatening to destroy it from time to time. No literature or philosophy, reformatory or constructive effort, not even the survival of man on this planet could have been possible without the merciful endeavours of the prophets of God. But, so ungrateful is man that he has announced with the flourish of trumpets, time and again, that the prophets of God have had their time, and that the world no longer needs them. Its seers and guides have repeatedly declared that the prophets had nothing new to offer, no benefits to confer on humanity. Man has in this way, really jettisoned over and over again his own right to exist in this world!

When any civilisation becomes overly sophisticated it closes its eyes to ethi-

1 Qur'ān 3:103
2 Mishkāt, Bukhārī.

cal precepts. Man forgets everything save the satisfaction of his desires and replaces his loving, merciful heart by a selfish and ferocious disposition. His covetous greed takes the shape of an aching void which can never be filled. This is the time when man hankers after the world and all that it stands for and, then, Providence moves to chasten him and to give him his deserts. A poet of the East has given expression to the same truth in one of his verses:

The fever of lunacy then overtakes the kings,
    Ferules of God are they all, Timur and Chinghiz.

One can replace the words 'king' and 'kingship' by civilisation for the insanity of civilisation is nowadays much more dangerous and wider in scope than the madness of the kings of old. A single lunatic can make a hell of the life of all the people around him, and, one can very well imagine what would happen if all the people were to lose their heads.

During the era we speak of as the Age of Ignorance the entire human race had become so depraved, so cruel that it took pleasure in the suffering of man. This is not poetic imagery but is supported by hard facts of history: man had turned into a demon who was most enthusiastic to witness the death and suffering of his own species. He prized the spectacle of the pangs of death suffered by human beings more than the pleasure he derived from merry-making, eating and drinking.

Gladiatorial sports involving combat between men and wild beasts under the Romans displayed the bottomless chasm to which human nature could sink more vividly than anything the crimes against humanity. But this was not a depravity that had captured the imagination of a few guilty consciences. Writing about the immense popularity of these performances, Lecky says in his *History of European Morals* that "the magnificent circus, the gorgeous dresses of the assembled Court, the contagion of a passionate enthusiasm thrilling almost visibly through the mighty throng, the breathless silence of expectation, the wild cheers bursting simultaneously from eighty thousand tongues, and echoing to the farthest outskirts of the city, the rapid alteration of the fray, the deeds of splendid courage that were manifested were all fitted to entrance the imagination."[1] The interest and enthusiasm that attended these games of inconceivable atrocity was so intense that special laws were found necessary, and, sometimes proved even insufficient, to check them.

Thus, the beast in man had taken hold of him during the Age of Ignorance. He had, by his deeds, furnished the proof that he had forfeited the right to live in

1 W.E.H. Lecky: *History of European Morals*, vol. I, p. 119.

this world, or, rather he had himself lost the very desire to remain in this world any more. Yet, his Lord and Master, the Most Compassionate and the Most Merciful had decided otherwise. He wanted to save the world and the progeny of Adam from death and destruction through a Messenger who was told that:

> And (O Muḥammad) we sent you not save as a mercy for the peoples.[1]

It is plain as day that the entire duration of the world's existence since the entrance of the holy Prophet of Islam ﷺ stems from his merciful deeds. First of all he removed the Damocles sword hanging over the head of humanity by giving it a new ideal to live for and a new zest and confidence to work towards. A new age of culture and civilisation, arts and learning, material and spiritual progress came into existence through his efforts.

First and foremost, the service that he rendered to humanity consisted of the faith in the Oneness of God. No other creed more revolutionary, more life giving and more profitable could have been vouchsafed to humanity. Man had been proud and presumptuous, boastful of his inventions like philosophy and poetry and the art of government. He took pride in enslaving other countries and nations; often arrogated himself even to the position of God; but he also demeaned himself by bowing his head before inanimate, lifeless objects, things of his own creation, and mountains, rivers, trees and animals, and harboured misplaced beliefs and irrational fear of the demons and devils. He spent his life in the fear of the unknown and the hope from non-existent powers which could not but foster mental confusion, cowardice, doubtfulness and indecision in him. The Prophet of Islam ﷺ made him self-reliant, courageous, rational and undoubting by removing the fear of everything else save that of his real Master and Lord. It was because of him that man came to recognise his Creator as the Supreme Power, the Enricher and the Destroyer. This new discovery meant a world of change for him as it enabled him to free himself from the shackles of superstitious beliefs, irrational fears, doubt and misgivings. He could now see the unity of cause in the manifold of phenomena, was reassured of his pivotal position in the scheme of creation, became aware of his worth and dignity, in short, his acceptance of the serfdom of the One and only God made him the master of every other created being and object. It was, thus for the first time that man became aware of the exalted position that God had allotted him.

The oneness of God came to be recognised, thanks to the last Prophet ﷺ, as the guiding principle for all the philosophies and creeds of the world. Even polytheistic religions were so powerfully influenced by it that their votaries began to

1 Qur'ān 21:107. The word used for "peoples" in the Qur'ān is *ʿĀlamīn*, that is, the worlds.

fight shy of their creeds and started putting up constructions to explain away their rites and observances demanding devotion to gods and demigods. The heathen belief in the worship of numerous deities began to suffer from a sense of inferiority from which it has still not recovered. This was the greatest gift bestowed on humanity by the holy Prophet ﷺ.

The second great favour that the Messenger of God ﷺ conferred to mankind was the concept of equality and brotherhood of mankind. The world before him was divided by manifold divisions of castes and creeds, tribes and nations, some claiming ranks of nobility for themselves and condemning others to the position of serfs and chattels. It was for the first time that the world heard the revolutionary message of human equality from the Prophet of Islam ﷺ:

> O Mankind, Your God is one and you have but one father. You are all progeny of Adam, and Adam was made of clay. Lo! the noblest among you, in the sight of God, is the best in conduct. No Arab has any preference over a non-Arab nor a non-Arab over an Arab save by his piety.[1]

The Prophet ﷺ made this declaration on the occasion of his last *hajj* before a huge congregation. His announcement put the seal on the principles of the unity of God and the unity of mankind. These are the two natural foundations for raising any edifice of peace and progress, friendship and co-operation between different peoples and nations. They create a twin relationship between human beings—that of one Lord and one common ancestor. Oneness of God is the spiritual principle of human equality just as a common lineage of the high and the low, placing the various races on the same plane of humanity. As God explains:

> O mankind! Be dutiful to your Lord, Who created you from a single person (Adam), and from him (Adam) He created his wife [Hawwa (Eve)], and from them both He created many men and women and fear Allah through Whom you demand your mutual (rights), and (do not cut the relations of) the wombs (kinship). Surely, Allah is Ever an All-Watcher over you.[2]

The world was not in a frame of mind to pay heed to the message of equality of human beings when the Prophet of Islam ﷺ first announced it. It was then a radical call, making a clean sweep of the then social relationships and economic and political orders. So striking and revolutionary was this call that it sent the world into jitters. Today we find the principle of human equality enshrined in the constitutions of different countries and being proclaimed from the forum of

---

1 *Kanz al-ʿAmmāl.*

2 Qur'ān 4:1.

the United Nations Organisation in the shape of the Charter of Human Rights but it was all due to the pioneering efforts of the followers of Muḥammad ﷺ, Muslim missionaries and reformers, who made indefatigable efforts to establish a truly egalitarian Muslim society. It was this model established through their toil and tears that later on came to be accepted as the standard for human existence in this world. There was a time when numerous clans and families claimed their descent from the sun or the moon. The Qur'ān quotes the belief then held by the Jews and the Christians in these words: "The Jews and the Christians say: We are the children of God and those whom He loves."[1] The Pharaohs of Egypt claimed themselves to be the incarnation of the Sun-god while India had several ruling families which arrogated themselves as the progeny of the sun or the moon. The Emperors of Iran called themselves *Kasra* or Chosroes which meant that Divine blood flowed in their veins. The last Iranian Emperor was known as Yazdagird owing, chiefly, to the Divine respects paid to him by his subjects.

The Chinese rulers deemed themselves to be the sons of Heaven. They believed that Heaven was their God, who, with his spouse, the goddess earth, had given birth to the human beings and *Pau Ku,* the Chinese Emperor, was the first-born son of Heaven enjoying supernatural powers.

The Arabs were so proud of their language that every other nation besides their own was an *ʿajamī* or dumb to them. Likewise, the Quraysh of Makkah being extremely conscious of maintaining their superiority, claimed a position of privilege even in the performance of *ḥajj.* This was the shape of things, all over the world, when the Qur'ān proclaimed that all human beings were equal.

> O mankind! Lo! We have created you male and female, and have made you nations and tribes that you may know one another. Lo! the noblest of you, in the sight of Allāh, is the most god-fearing. Lo! Allāh is Knower, Aware.[2]

The opening chapter of the Qur'ān declares:

> Praise be to Allāh, Lord of the Worlds.[3]

The third great gift and boon to humanity that the Prophet of Islam ﷺ bestowed is the Islamic concept of human dignity. During the Age of Darkness when Islam made its appearance none was so ignoble and humiliated as man. Without worth, he had no sense of human dignity. Oftentimes trees and animals regarded as sacred, owing to religious beliefs or traditions, enjoyed a more coveted place than man himself. Human sacrifices at the altar of deities were a com-

1 Qur'ān 5:18.

2 Qur'ān 49:13.

3 Qur'ān 1:1.

mon spectacle. It was solely due to Muḥammad, the Prophet ﷺ, that man came to appreciate the fact that human beings, the glorious creation of God, were entitled to a much more loving regard, respect and honour than any other creature. The rank that the holy Prophet ﷺ accorded to man was next only to God, for God had Himself heralded the purpose of man's creation in these words of lasting beauty:

> He it is Who created for you all that is in the earth.[1]

Man was declared as the best of creations, the ruler of the world and all that exists in it.

> Verily We have honoured the children of Adam. We carry them on the land and the sea, and have made provision of good things for them, and have preferred them above many of those whom We created with a marked preferment."[2]

Man had been accustomed to associate nobility with those who claimed themselves to be the progeny of gods and demigods. In order that the honour of the common man was not usurped again by the selected few, the Prophet announced:

> The whole of mankind is under the care of God, and he amongst His creation who is dearest to Him is he who is best to those under his protection.[3]

A celestial tradition of the Prophet ﷺ alludes to the deep concern of God for the welfare of human beings. It says: "God will ask (someone) on the Day of Judgment, 'I was ill but you did not pay a visit to Me!' The man will reply: 'How could have I visited You when You are the Lord of the worlds?' But God will say, 'Do you not recollect that one of my slaves was ill? Had you gone to see him, you would have found Me by his side!' Then God will again ask, O Son of Adam, I asked you to feed me, but you refused it to Me.' The man would submit, 'How could have I fed You when You are the Lord of the Worlds?' But God will reply, 'Do you not remember that one of My slaves had asked you for food? Didn't you know that if you had given him food, you would have found it with Me!' God will again ask, O Son of Adam, I asked you for water to drink but you refused it to Me! The man will say in reply, 'O Lord, How could have I given water to You when You are the Lord of the worlds?' But God will reply, 'Do you not recollect that one of my slaves asked you for water, but you refused! Did you not know that if you had given him water, you would have found it with Me?"[4]

1 Qur'ān 2:29.
2 Qur'ān 17:70.
3 Mishkāt.
4 Ṣaḥīḥ Muslim.

Islam teaches unalloyed and absolute unity of God and rejects every form of anthropomorphism. Still, it employs this similitude to drive home the rank and dignity of man in the eyes of God. Has any other religion or philosophical thought accorded a nobler place to human beings than that assigned by Islam?

The Prophet of Islam ﷺ taught that the surest way to attract blessings of God was to be kind and considerate to others.

> The Most Compassionate [God] is kind to those who are kind to others. If you would show kindness to those who live on the earth, He who lives in the Heaven, shall shower His blessings on you.[1]

You can very well imagine the pitiable condition of man in the days when this powerful voice of human dignity had not been raised in the world. A mere whim of a king or an emperor could then cost the lives of a thousand men. It was then not unusual for an ambitious adventurer to put to sword the entire population of a conquered land. Alexander turned every country from Greece to India into a vast battlefield. Caesars played with the lives of human beings as if they were wild beasts. The two World Wars fought only recently cost the lives of millions merely to secure markets for the industrial products of advanced nations or to establish the national or political ascendancy of certain nations over all others. Iqbal has correctly assessed the political ambitions of man in this verse.

> Man is still possessed by the imperialistic lust,
> What a pity! Man prowling after man as yet.

At the time when Prophet Muḥammad ﷺ was invested with the mantle of prophethood, a general sense of pessimism springing from the then prevalent notions of the worthlessness of human nature and lack of hope for Divine succour filled the air. The ancient religions of the East and the mutilated Christianity, especially in the West, had an equal share in producing that mental climate. The philosophy of reincarnation, preached by the religions of ancient India, which assigned no place to the will and decision of man, meant that the present life was but a form of retribution for one's actions during a previous life with which the Christian dogma of Original Sin and atonement had joined hands to shake the confidence of millions, all over the world, in the despondence and amenability of human actions. Mankind had lost faith in the mercy of God whose eternal and immutable decree seemed to have condemned man to a predetermined destiny without reference to his evil or virtuous behaviour. But Muḥammad ﷺ affirmed that man was born with a clean slate and perfect freedom of action.

---

1 Abū Dāwūd.

Man was, declared the Prophet ﷺ, the author of his actions, both good and evil, and deserved reward or punishment in accordance with his own decision to shape the course of his actions. Discarding the theory of vicarious atonement, the Qur'ān established once for all that every man was his own redeemer.

> And that for man shall be naught
> Save that for which he makes an effort,
> And that his endeavour shall be presently observed.[1]

This was a message of salvation to man, which gave him a new confidence in himself and in his ability to chart out his destiny. He applied himself with a renewed vigour, confidence and determination to shape up his own life and brighten the future of humanity.

The Prophet of Islam ﷺ also declared that sins were but temporary deviations from the right path, inherent in the nature of man, and were brought about by ignorance, mistakes and the promptings of the devil or man's own sensual desires. But the innate urge of man was to regret his mistakes and seek the pardon of God with a contrite heart. To be broken in spirit by a sense of the guilt and to seek the forgiveness of God showed the goodness of human nature and attracted mercy of the Lord. This gospel of hope and good tidings was a revolutionary message to despondent humanity condemned forever by the guilt of Original Sin and one's past misdoings. What a great change it meant in the prevailing atmosphere of gloom and depression of spirits is illustrated by the fact that the Prophet ﷺ came to be known as the "Apostle of Repentance." Repentance, he said, did not involve faint-heartedness, nor did it arise from fear of disapprobation, but was a bold and daring step of the first man, Adam, who had thus shown the nobility of his innate nature. The Prophet of Islam ﷺ imbued repentance with the sacredness attached to the acts of devotion to God. He preached the virtues of seeking pardon so forcefully that even the irredeemable sinners, who had lost all hope of forgiveness, resolved to turn away from the sinful ways and to begin a new life of virtue and uprightness, and many of them attained a sublimity of spirit that was envied by others.

Describing the clemency of God Who is ever willing to forgive the sinners, the Qur'ān employs a diction so alluringly charming that one wonders whether God loves them more who seek His forgiveness after deviating from the path of virtue. The Qur'ānic verse quoted here shows how forbearing, how long-suffering and how magnanimous God is to the man who cares to turn towards Him for exoneration of his sins. Says the Qur'ān:

1 Qur'ān 53:39–40.

> Say! O my bondmen who have committed extravagance against themselves, despair not of the mercy of Allāh; verily Allāh will forgive their sins altogether. Verily He, He is the forgiving, the Merciful.[1]

Some other verses of the Qur'ān exhorting the believers to acquire positive merits and to win their way to the everlasting bliss, address them in these words:

> And vie one with another for forgiveness from your Lord, and toward the Garden as wide as are the heavens and the earth, prepared for those who ward off [evil];
>
> And those who spend [of that which Allāh has given them] in ease and in adversity, those who control their wrath and are forgiving toward mankind; Allāh loves the good;
>
> And those who, when they do an evil thing or wrong themselves, remember Allāh and ask forgiveness for their sins.—Who forgives sins but Allāh alone?—and will not knowingly repeat [the wrong] they did;
>
> The reward of such will be forgiveness from their Lord, and Gardens underneath which rivers flow, wherein they will abide forever—a bountiful reward for those who strive![2]

Among the characteristics of the true believers, enumerated in another verse, repentance takes precedence of all others.

> They are those who repent, who worship, who praise, who fast constantly, who bow down, who prostrate themselves, who command the reputable and restrain from the disreputable and who keep the ordinances of Allāh. Bear you glad tidings to the believers.[3]

The place of honour accorded to those who repent of their sins is illustrated by the verses of the Qur'ān revealed on the occasion of the forgiveness of three Companions[4] of the holy Prophet ﷺ, who were shunned for their failure to accompany the Prophet ﷺ in the expedition of Tabūk. Before the verse alludes to the mistake of these Companions being pardoned by God, it mentions the Prophet ﷺ and the Anṣār and the Mūhājirīn in order that no stigma was attached to them after their mistakes had been forgiven. In this way, the Qur'ān teaches all believers who take the Companions of the Prophet ﷺ as models of virtue that no ignominy attaches to a man after a genuine change of heart. The way these verses explain the consequences of the blotting out of sins and the

1 Qur'ān 39:53.

2 Qur'ān 3:133–36.

3 Qur'ān 9:112.

4 The Companions were Kaʿb ibn Mālik, Hilāl ibn Umayyah and Murārah ibn Rabīʿ. See "The Expedition of Tabūk."

elation of the repentant sinners can hardly be found in the scriptures of other religions or treatises on ethics. These verses read:

> Allāh has turned in mercy to the Prophet and to the Mūhājirīn and the Anṣār who followed him in the hour of hardship. After the hearts of a party of them had almost swerved aside, He turned to them in mercy. He is Full of Pity, Merciful toward them. And to the three who were left behind, when the earth, vast as it is, was straitened for them, and their own souls were straitened for them till they bethought them that there is no refuge from Allāh save toward Him. He turned then to them in mercy that they [too] might turn [repentant unto Him]. Allāh! He is the Relenting, the Merciful.[1]

Remission of sin leads us to one of the chief attributes of the Divine Being, that is, His mercy and compassion. The bounty of God's mercy is the constant theme of the Qur'ān. Says God: "My mercy embraces all things,"[2] while a celestial tradition of the Prophet ﷺ tells us: "Verily, My mercy precedes My wrath." To be despaired of God's mercy was made a cardinal sin. Quoting Yaʿqūb[3] ﷺ and Ibrāhīm ﷺ, the two great Prophets of God, the Qur'ān announces: "Verily, none despairs of the comfort of Allāh except a people disbelieving,"[4] and "Who despairs of the mercy of his Lord save those who are astray?"[5]

The misery and suffering the human race endured in the world was, according to the Jewish and Christian doctrines, but a feeble image of the never-ending agony that awaited man in the Hereafter. The monastic orders of the Medieval Ages had taken up this doctrine, which, in itself, was sufficiently revolting, but they had developed it with an appalling vividness and minuteness. Humanity, frightened by these ghastly visions and glimpses of eternal suffering, was relieved by the Prophet's ﷺ emphasis on God's all-embracing mercy and the efficacy of repentance which could wipe the slate clean of even the most vicious among the castaways of society.

And now we come to yet another gift of the prophethood of Muḥammad ﷺ which is still more far-reaching and more beneficial to humanity at large. This was the concept of the unity of spirit and matter, the harmony of the sacred and the mundane. He taught that the distinction between the two was superficial and formal for every action of man, whether secular or religious, was guided by his motive or mental attitude, which, in the terminology of religion, was known

1 Qur'ān 9:117–18.
2 Qur'ān 7:156.
3 The prophet Jacob.
4 Qur'ān 12:87.
5 Qur'ān 15:56.

as *niyyah* or intention. For no religious belief is entirely divorced from the realities of human experience in its manifold practical aspects, the intention or purpose with which any act is done sets the test of its being good or bad. He did not recognise the division between the temporal and the ecclesiastical since man's desire to propitiate God and to follow His commands permeates into every fibre of human activity, no matter whether it is the art of government or war, availing oneself of one's earthly possessions, or satisfaction of one's natural desires, or earning one's living, or leading a married life. With a noble intention every mundane act is turned into a virtuous deed and a means to attaining propinquity to God. On the contrary, no merit whatsoever attaches to acts like devotion to God or fighting in the path of God if the sincere desire to attain the will and pleasure of God are absent.

The ancient world had divided life into two compartments, the religious and the secular and the result was that a wedge had been driven between those who selected one of these as the pursuit of their lives. Oftentimes, the two groups were at loggerheads with one another, for, the "world" and "religion" were to them incompatible spheres of human life. Every man had to choose one of the two since nobody could be expected to travel in two boats simultaneously. The prevalent view was that the path of salvation lay not through the rough and tumble of life, but away from the social, economic and political problem of worldly pursuits. No concept of religion which bars the gates to material progress and acquisition of power, riches and fame, could be of interest to intelligent, capable and ambitious persons: the result being that a great segment of humanity had delivered itself from the rigorous discipline of asceticism which had come to be associated with religion. By withdrawing themselves and their virtuous pursuits, these men had prevented the great importance of morals from appearing perceptibly in public affairs. The State had revolted against the Church and made itself free from all moral obligations. This hideous schizophrenia not only divested what was called the worldly from the gifts of spiritual beatitude, but also gave birth to the modern faithlessness and agnosticism of Europe which is now threatening to inundate the entire world, if only, because of its political and cultural supremacy. The present wave of crass materialism, loss of faith and moral debasement is but a direct consequence of the division between the spirit and matter invented by the old pagan civilisations.

The Prophet of Mercy ﷺ, who was sent to the humanity as a warner as well as a messenger of glad tidings, converted the entire life of man into devotion to God by denying the existence of any cleavage between the spiritual and temporal spheres of human affairs. He demolished the wedge between the men of religion and those of the world and commended all of them to unite their efforts for attaining the pleasure of God and service of humanity. It was because of him that the world could see the ascetics who wore crowns on their heads and the warriors who spent their nights in devotions and prayers.

It would be difficult to conceive a more complete transformation of life than the one brought about by the fusion of the secular and the sacred, which would require several volumes to be explained in detail. Iqbal has very succinctly versified the significance of this concept in one of his immortal poems:

On monastic order was laid the foundation of Church,
  How could mendacity contain royalty in its confines?
The conflict was deep, between hermitry and kingship,
  One was triumphant, the other subdued,
Politics got rid of religion,
  Helpless was the high priest.
When the world and religion parted ways,
  Avarice was the Ruler, King and Vizier,
Dualism was the doom of mind and matter,
  Dualism made civilisation blind.
This is the miracle of a dweller of the desert,
  Whose warnings reflected the tidings glad;
That the humanity's only refuge was this,
  That (the mystic) Junayd unites with Ardsher (the king)!

Yet another radical change brought about by the Prophet of Islam ﷺ in the life of man was to make him conscious of the ultimate end of his life. Unaware of his goal and objective, man had his eyes fixed on profane and paltry objects. He directed his whole intelligence and labour to the acquisition of wealth or land or fame or power. Goodness having been associated with the pleasurable things, the main object of the vast majority of people was to sublimate their conceptions of happiness and interest with the satisfaction of carnal desires, songs and colour, merrymaking, fun and amusements. The revelry of the rich and the powerful soon brought up a class of parasites whose whole business was to tickle the fancy of their patrons. But Prophet Muḥammad ﷺ told man that his great business was to exert himself and to strive to attain the perfect knowledge of God; to contemplate His nature and attributes and to lead his wandering soul to divine propinquity through realisation of the Unlimited; to search out the Unity of the Cause of all Causes in the amazing diverse phenomena of nature; and to seek His pleasure through being kind and just and virtuous. He told man that these were the objectives whose achievement conferred a rank on him envied by the angels of God.

Thus, the prophethood of Muḥammad ﷺ made a clean sweep of the existing order of things in the world. The longings and desires of man were now centred on a new objective. The love of God took possession of his being. The pleasure of God became the immortal thirst of human heart. Mercy and kindness to God's creatures was recognised as the greatest virtue which became the sole object of man's endeavour.

It was then, after the advent of Islam, that the leading feature of all the countries, Arabia and Iran, Syria and Egypt, Turkistan and Iraq, North Africa and Spain became the search for higher and tender virtues, in the pursuit of which we find thousands of lovelorn souls. During this period we see innumerable men of God preaching love of God, kindness and compassion to every sentient being, the merits of virtuous living, the acquisition of knowledge for attaining the pleasure of God, revulsion to cruelty and indecency, and the grace of humility and modesty. They taught the lesson of human dignity and brotherhood of man and made this earth a kingdom of God.

If you could peep into the souls of these elevated individuals, you would witness the unbelievable flight of their imagination, the purity of their innermost feelings and liveliness of their perceptions. You would see how they were ever willing to put their own life at stake for others, how they made their own children and family suffer for the good of all and sundry, the way they compelled the autocratic kings and potentates to do justice to the weak and the poor and how rightfully just they were even to their enemies. In fact, it would have been difficult for us to believe today what a fine specimen of humanity, what a sublime soul were these men of God if the historians and biographers had not preserved a truthful record of their lives and acts.

This striking change in the manners and morals of the people was, indeed, the greatest miracle worked by the holy Prophet of Islam ﷺ.

Verily, God says in truth:

> We sent you not save as a mercy for the people.

Notes

Notes

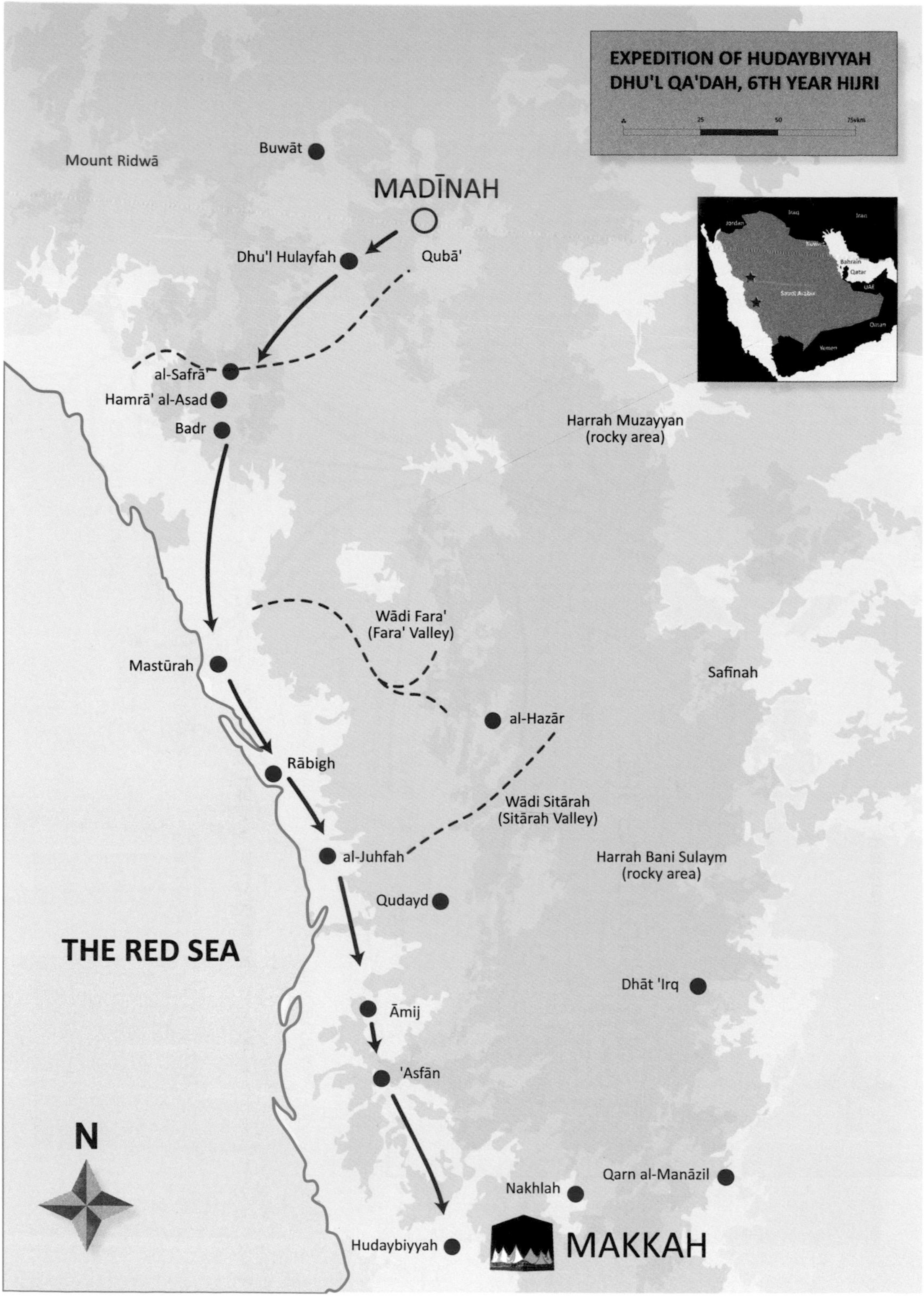
EXPEDITION OF HUDAYBIYYAH
DHU'L QA'DAH, 6TH YEAR HIJRI
25
50
Jordan
Iraq
Iran
Bahrain
Qatar
UAE
Oman
Yemen
Mount Ridwā
Buwāt
MADĪNAH
Dhu'l Hulayfah
Qubā'
al-Safrā'
Hamrā' al-Asad
Badr
Harrah Muzayyan
(rocky area)
Wādi Fara'
(Fara' Valley)
Mastūrah
Safinah
al-Hazār
Rābigh
Wādi Sitārah
(Sitārah Valley)
al-Juhfah
Harrah Bani Sulaym
(rocky area)
Qudayd
THE RED SEA
Dhāt 'Irq
Āmij
'Asfān
N
Qarn al-Manāzil
Nakhlah
Hudaybiyyah
MAKKAH

Notes

Index